RICH COUNTRY INTERESTS
AND THIRD WORLD DEVELOPMENT

Rich Country Interests and Third World Development

Edited by Robert Cassen, Richard Jolly,
John Sewell and Robert Wood

CROOM HELM London & Canberra

© 1982 Institute of Development Studies, Sussex
Croom Helm Ltd, Provident House, Burrell Row,
Beckenham, Kent BR3 1AT

British Library Cataloguing in Publication Data

Rich country interests and Third World development.
  1. Underdeveloped areas — Foreign economic
  relations   2. International economic relations
  I. Cassen, Robert
  337'.09172'4   HF1413

  ISBN 0-7099-1306-0

Limited paperback edition issued by Croom Helm Ltd
exclusively for the Overseas Development Council,
Washington, DC.

(ISBN 0-7099-1930-1)

Printed and bound in Great Britain
by Billing & Sons, Worcester

CONTENTS

PREFACE

A new subject emerged in the 1970s — what are the interests of the rich countries in Third World development, and how do these interests affect the policies and behaviour of the rich countries? Various authors attempted to show, and even to quantify, how individual countries might benefit or lose from pursuing given courses of action, particularly those under discussion and negotiation in the 'North-South dialogue'. The Brandt Commission argued forcefully that there are strong mutual interests between North and South, the developed and developing countries, in changing the international economic order in directions often considered beneficial mainly to the South.

Of course, once a band of scholarly enquirers looks into almost any subject in the social sciences, bold and simple truths tend to vanish into thickets of multidimensional reconsideration. We hope that readers will emerge from this book enlightened rather than confused. They will find here a good deal of straightforward information about different countries' attitudes and policies, and analysis of some of their underlying motives; but they will probably be left with more questions than answers.

Unlike earlier studies, this one tries to look broadly at individual countries and the historical, political and other factors which influence their relations with the Third World. The book is intended to stimulate discussion and provide a basis for raising new research topics; it does not claim to demonstrate a particular thesis about rich country interests. The Overview does, however, draw together the main threads of the country chapters, and also raises some issues which do not emerge fully in the context of discussion of individual countries.

The volume results from a project jointly organized by the Institute of Development Studies (University of Sussex), the Overseas Development Council (Washington, DC) and the Overseas Development Institute (London). The project was funded by a grant from the German Marshall Fund of the USA.

The individual country studies were written after two meetings of the authors with the project managers, Robert Cassen, Richard Jolly, John Sewell and Robert Wood, and advisers Dudley Seers and Hans Singer. The country studies and a first draft of the Overview by Ronald Dore were the subject of a conference at the Institute of Development

Studies in November 1979, following which the country studies were revised and the Overview further elaborated by the editors. The editors owe a considerable debt to Darrell Jackson (IDS) for administration of the project, and John Mathieson (ODC) for work on the Overview. The individual authors take responsibility for their chapters, and the editors for the Overview.

Robert Cassen, Richard Jolly,
John Sewell and Robert Wood

1 OVERVIEW

Robert Cassen, Richard Jolly, John Mathieson and John Sewell

Introduction

The North-South summit held in Mexico in October 1981 marked a new acknowledgement by the leaders of the developed world of their growing interests in the development of the developing countries. Both in the high level of its participation — heads of government and ministers of 22 nations, North and South, East and West — and in its final declarations, the summit signified what many had long struggled for: recognition of the increased level of interdependence within the world economy — particularly between developed and developing countries. The developing countries of the world are now accepted, not as objects of aid or charity, but as important participants in the international economic system.

The North-South summit concentrated its discussions on four areas of economic concern. Each area was one where developed countries of the North and developing countries of the South shared a mutual interest in co-ordinated action, especially at a time of persistent world recession and rising expenditures on armaments. These areas were: international trade, food production and food security, energy and finance.

The summit discussions demonstrated that the participants were far from agreed on the nature of or the solution to each of these problem areas, let alone on the specific actions which were needed to tackle them. The discussions and the final communiqué made clear that in each of these areas of concern, there was a substantial area of mutual interest between countries of the North and of the South in co-operation on a range of development issues and international economic problems. The agreement in principle to make a new start on global negotiations between developed and developing countries acknowledged, however tenuously, something of this belief. But the summit also pointed to differences among countries of the North about how far they would go to meet the desires and needs of the South; and also among countries of the South, especially over the character of global

1

negotiations, and whether they would accept limited gains on specific issues as opposed to comprehensive discussions in the UN. 'Interdependence' was accepted; but national views prevented further agreement.

Scope of this Study

The recognition that there are a broad set of mutual interests between developed and developing countries raises a number of serious questions which urgently need further analysis. Acknowledgement that there are significant areas of mutual interest does not mean that there are *common*, let alone identical, interests between all rich and poor countries. Indeed a serious analysis of 'interests' might well reveal that countries perceive their most important interests along lines other than North-South; for instance between grain exporting and grain importing countries. On some issues, recent recession has sharpened competition and the clash of interests between industrialized countries of the North. And interests differ considerably *within* countries where, for example, consumers may benefit from low cost imports while producers may suffer. Finally, there is the crucial question of how identification of interests may evolve over the 1980s either as a result of changes in the international economy or of changes within particular industrial countries. Were this volume being prepared in 1971, for example, Northern perceptions of their energy 'interests' would be quite different from what they are now.

This volume sets out to begin the process of delineating and comparing the various interests of the rich, industrialized nations in Third World development. The project originated in a desire to add a degree of concreteness to the assertion that the industrialized countries have such a set of positive interests, by analyzing the specific policies and actions taken by a variety of developed countries towards the Third World over the three decades since the Second World War. In other words, the interests of countries were to be judged not by what they say, or by what specific commentators judge their interests *ought* to be, but what their actions may have shown their interests to have been.

Global interdependence, though a term new to the late 1960s, is not of itself a new concept. Historians always recognized a two-way economic relationship underlying colonial and imperial systems, by which 'dependent territories' were not only prized as teritorial possessions but contributed to the economies of the imperial powers and in turn were profoundly affected by them. Hobson, and before him Marx and later Lenin, argued that this economic interaction was critical to the world economic system: the developing countries played a vital role in the development of the capitalist countries, contributing not only raw materials, but also the markets and investment opportunities which sustained demand and thus the level of economic activity in the developed countries themselves. More recently, since the Second World War, a whole school of development has arisen – the school of dependency analysis – influenced heavily by Latin American thinking and experience of development, taking this analysis into post-colonial times and emphasizing the negative effects on developing countries.

The nine case studies in this volume analyze the interests of eleven industrialized countries of the 'West'. They are: North America (United States and Canada); Europe (France, Germany, United Kingdom, The Netherlands and Scandinavian countries – Denmark, Norway and Sweden); and Asia and Australasia (Japan and Australia).

The assessment of interests through analysis of the specific actions of these countries proved a more formidable task than at first appeared, for layers of complexity in the formulation and pursuit of these interests soon emerged. The range of potentially relevant information to review was enormous – not surprisingly, given the number and diversity of the interactions involved between developed and developing countries. Even taking nine industrial countries and 120 developing countries gives over 1,000 potential *bilateral* interactions between countries alone, not counting the more bewildering set of combinations and permutations that take place in the real world.

To this was added the difficulty of assessing changing interests over a period marked by considerable economic and political change. The years under study cover the immediate post-war period of overwhelming US strength and economic dominance – with its Cold War concerns of containment to the much more diversified, and perhaps even disintegrating, world economy of the 1970s and 1980s, in which in important areas such as international finance and technological advance, effective economic power has slipped from the grasp of all governments, including that of the United States. Almost inevitably, one was drawn to studying broad areas and expressions of policy attitudes and perceptions, and the process of policy formulation towards developing countries, as a convenient distillation of a complexity of interactions.

These nine country case studies concentrate on the way relationships with the Third World have evolved, been perceived and been acted upon in recent years. While a common framework for the study was agreed, no author could follow it precisely, nor, in the amount of space allotted, could any study be other than selective. While 'interests' are at the heart of each study, authors have on the whole treated issues according to the importance they judge them to have received in practice, not as the authors think they should or might have received. As a result, each of their analyses of national interest brings out the fact that the overall goal of improved North-South relations is very often superseded by the more direct self-interest of the countries in question, even though each of the authors tends personally to be highly sympathetic to development objectives and improved North-South relations.

The case studies treat the 'Third World' simply as the 120-or-so countries conventionally classified as developing countries which join together in the 'Group of 77' for United Nations negotiations. 'Development' is taken simply as 'movement towards a better society', with 'better' in this context extending to whatever goals of economic and social change the developing countries themselves adopt. In practice, the central components of 'better' which the studies assume to be widely − though not universally − shared in developing countries is the growth of economic output and productive capacity, greater national control over their economies and widespread improvement in living standards. While these basic objectives of development may not seem all that controversial, the means of achieving them and the interplay of these development goals with other goals and interests bring out major differences of views and policies among the various countries of both South and North.

The North-South Setting

These analyses must be seen against the backdrop of the changing North-South environment. The immediate post-war period, from the viewpoint of the West, was preoccupied with European and Japanese reconstruction, Cold War confrontation and US economic supremacy, which set the framework for international economic management and stability and provided the power to back it up. But within this framework, positions were in fact changing rapidly. Japan and Germany were rebuilding their defeated war economies, largely free from costly armaments programmes or reparations, to lay the foundation for rising productivity and rapid growth, which accounted for their growing economic strength and success in the 1960s and 1970s. The British economy, in contrast, and in spite of a rate of economic growth as good or better than at any time in its previous history, was in fact slipping relatively behind, and only slowly adjusting its structure and strategic commitments to the realities of its diminishing position in the world economy. More significant but less clear at the time, the productivity and economic strength of the US economy was also shifting relative to other economies and was put under further strain by the heavy costs of its military establishment, especially but not only at the time of the Vietnam War. As mentioned earlier, economic structures and institutions within countries were also changing, together with shifts of political power and economic philosophy. With the Smithsonian agreement in 1971, the core of the Bretton Woods economic system of gold convertibility, fixed exchange rates and reasonably effective international monetary control was finally abandoned, perhaps an inevitable counterpart to the decade of the seventies characterized by economic instability, lower growth and eventually deep stagnation and recession.

At the same time the developing world has undergone very significant changes. Over the past three decades, a large number of developing countries became politically independent. Considerable efforts were made to accelerate economic growth and social progress. For all the continuing difficulties, a great deal has been accomplished. It is worth noting that the developing countries in the aggregate have grown more rapidly since 1950 than the now-rich countries did over any decade during their industrial revolution. Even during the troubled 1970s, the annual GNP growth rate of the developing countries was 5.7 per cent, compared with 3.4 per cent in the industrial countries. And progress in terms of human well-being was also impressive. Life expectancy in the Third World increased in two decades by as much as it increased in the industrialized nations in a century.

This progress has, however, been very uneven, both between and within countries. There now are at least four distinguishable groups of developing countries:

(1) the OPEC group whose control of oil and in some cases large financial surpluses gives them a considerable degree of influence within the international system;
(2) the dozen or so 'newly industrializing' countries whose growth performance has been spectacular and who are in a state of transition between the developing and industrial world;
(3) the seventy-odd 'middle income' countries that are expanding their exports of manufactures but who still depend mainly on primary products for export earnings; and
(4) the many 'low income' countries where *per capita* income remains below $350 and where economic conditions and prospects — especially for the poorest or 'least-developed' countries — have changed little over the decade.

Finally, one must emphasize that progress has been uneven *within* most developing countries. As a result there remain well over 800 million people living in absolute poverty with not even the barest essentials to support minimally decent human life.

Despite this undeniable, if mixed, record of progress, the Third World looks at the record rather differently — and with reason. Observers ask why progress cannot go faster and focus attention on relations between rich and poor countries. They believe that a major reason for their lack of development is the existing international economic system, dominated by the rich countries of the North and operating in the North's favour. In the view of some, the North even became rich at the expense of the South, and continues an exploitative relationship in the post-colonial era. But that radical view is not necessary to the most frequently expressed Third World position: that they do not want charity from the North, so much as better opportunities to develop in their own way and by their own efforts.

In the main, however, Northern governments do not easily concede that the international economy is so unfavourable to the Third World; nor that the economic difficuties of Third World countries are caused so much by the systems of international trade and finance, as by failings of economic management in the developing countries themselves. Even those governments that accept parts of the Third World's case about the inadequacies of the economic system have mostly not been prepared to move very far towards changing it, regarding the changes called for by the Third World as technically unsound or, if sound, too expensive — economically and politically.

In the late 1970s, a growing body of studies began to appear that pointed to the conclusion that both rich and poor countries faced a set of common political, economic and environmental challenges, and that changes in existing policies and institutions would be necessary in the interests of the North as well as the South.[1] These analyses (which are far from widely accepted) hold that there is more than a moral case for supporting development in the Third World and that a set of 'mutual interests' between developed and developing countries calls for reform of some aspects of the international economic system.

Perhaps the fullest expression of this viewpoint is found in the report of the Brandt Commission (The Independent Commission on International Development Issues). The Commission's report[2] puts the case for 'mutual interests' in greater co-operation between developed and developing countries in a very broad perspective. It analyzes the individual issues where a positive mutual interest in change could be found — most notably in trade, finance, energy, food and a reduction in military expenditures. But its overall viewpoint is even larger: it essentially sets out a reformed world order in which the development of the Third World is facilitated both because it is intrinsically important and because it is in the long-term interests of the developed world. In effect, changes in existing policies are necessary as a matter of 'survival' as well as of common humanity. If changes are not made, the costs to both developed and developing countries will be high. The report concludes: 'The South cannot grow adequately without the North. The North cannot prosper or improve its situation unless there is greater progress in the South.'

Differences in Interests: Nature and Causes

The country studies in this volume are virtually unanimous on one point: each of the industrial countries analyzed has a considerable range of economic, political and even ideological interests in the development of the Third World. There is no indication that any of the countries seriously puts forth the proposal that it has no interests in the developing countries. But the studies document the important and basic point that *degrees* of interest in both specific and general North-South issues vary enormously within and among the different Northern countries. There are several reasons for this. First, historical and cultural traditions differ widely between the various countries. The geography and colonial past of many countries still tend to colour their view of the world. Secondly, the economic structure and resource base of different developed countries, along with differences in current economic performance, create sharp variations in their stake in relations with developing countries. Finally, each Northern country is faced with a different set of domestic interest groups which make their presence felt in the political process.

A major question probed in the studies is the issue of how the interests of various sectional groups are balanced to form the *national interest*. Some authors confess to a certain bafflement as to how the outcome of a number of conflicting forces is derived, and whether indeed there is such a thing as 'national interest'. Is it realistic to think of or describe national policy-making as following a consistent and rational weighting of interests 'maximizing' national well-being, without the interjection of personalities, electoral consideration or passing expediencies highly specific to time or locality?

The papers do nevertheless consider how interests are aggregated, noting not only well-articulated group interests but also latent, under-articulated interests: not just those, for example, who lose their jobs from the import of low cost clothing but also the consumers who have to pay more if the clothing is not imported. The authors also examine the way sectional interests work through political processes, not assuming — as the economics of trade liberalization often does — that the arithmetical summations of overall national gains have a direct correspondence to political processes or perceptions of national interest.

The range of circumstances and preoccupations which the case studies reveal is so wide that one is almost surprised at the ability of the industrialized countries to arrive at *any* consensus on a 'common rich country interest' on any substantive issues in any forum. (Perhaps this is a clue to why the consensus positions are often so weak.) In North-South economic relations — the primary issue analyzed in these studies — the major distinctions between industrialized countries appear to be largely (but not completely) related to differences in economic structure and to the way those structural differences translate into varying needs and opportunities in international transactions. Clear differences in outlook and policy emerge between major exporters and importers of primary products; between the major exporters and importers of capital; between those who see themselves as having generally secure resource supplies and those who do not; between those who see themselves as playing a dominant role in the world economy and those who see themselves as 'price-takers'; and between those whose circumstances, especially rising productivity and competitive strength, lead them to look at the world with confidence that their past progress will continue and those for whom future developments look rather gloomy. Finally, some countries — most notably at this moment the United States — also see the Third World in terms of East-West relations and as an arena for competition and influence between the superpowers.

Commodities

The relative abundance of raw material resources in individual Northern countries varies significantly by commodity, and never coincides with any North-South division. In food products the US, Canada and Australia have become the world's major granaries, now responsible for almost all the world's net food grain exports. While this similarity of position may give them grounds for a common stand on many matters such as the negotiations for an international wheat agreement (at potential odds with the UK, Norway and Japan as major importing countries, along with many countries of the Third World), it also puts them into conflict with each other at the policy level due to competition in world markets — witness the discussion of Australia's attempts to counter the effect of US food aid on Australia's commercial markets in India, Pakistan and Malaysia.

The same three countries also show an ambivalent position as both major importers and major exporters of the commodities on which the Common Fund negotiations have focused. All have a greater interest as exporters in more commodities than all but a handful of 'Group of 77' nations. If commodity agreements are supposed to work primarily for the benefit of producers, as is so widely assumed, and if producer interests within countries are generally stronger than consumer interests, one would expect these Northern countries to support commodity pacts on economic grounds. Yet Australia's conversion to support of the Common Fund idea was a late development, an early Canadian initiative in that direction died a rapid death, and the United States has been basically opposed to such schemes on ideological and practical grounds. The three countries have also shown ambivalence towards producer cartels. The case-by-case approach to commodity agreements has been insisted on as the best means of reaching bargains on behalf of all interests within the country — producers' and consumers'.

The detailed account of the Canadian position makes a particular point of more general significance. The balance of importer-exporter interests in any particular country cannot be judged just from its import and export figures, since the ownership structure of the exporting firms adds a complicating factor. The fact that a substantial part of the exports of nickel, copper and iron ore from Canada is made by transnationals based in consumer countries is suggested as one reason for the 'confusion and inconsistency' in Canadian policy on metals. A similar situation exists in Australia with regard to bauxite and copper.

Two other examples illustrate the way policies on commodity issues cannot always be divined from where third-party observers might see 'objective' interest to lie. Despite their levels of energy reserves and positions as net oil exporters, Canada and the United Kingdom have shown little disposition to make common cause with OPEC, although they have followed OPEC's lead on prices. Similarly, there is nothing to distinguish the Scandinavian countries' position as net producers or consumers of commodities to explain why they, rather than other countries, should have supported UNCTAD's Common Fund proposals in 1976. The explanation for that position seems to lie partly in their long experience of interference in domestic-market mechanisms to ensure equitable and stable earnings for their farm producers (an experience which, however, they share with many other rich countries) and more important, perhaps, in their basic attitudes towards Third World countries — an 'ideology of equality and the concern for social justice'.

Overseas Investment

Interests in foreign investment divide Northern countries in various ways. First of all are differences in the level and share of investment. The United States must be distinguished from all other Northern countries since it owns nearly half the total stock of direct investment abroad of all the developed market economies. Less dramatic are variations between those whose total stock of overseas investment is substantial in relation, say, to Gross National Product — United Kingdom (17 per cent), United States (eight per cent), West Germany (four per cent) and Japan (three per cent), and those where it is less important. Some countries are steadily increasing their share in the total foreign investment of the developed countries (Japan three to seven per cent, West Germany five to eight per cent, 1971-7), whereas the share of others is declining (United Kingdom 15 per cent to 11 per cent, United States 52 per cent to 47 per cent, 1971-7).

Some countries also have in common a large share of their total overseas investment in developing countries (Japan 57 per cent, West Germany 22 per cent, United States 23 per cent in 1977), compared to others with relatively little invested in the Third World.

The form of investment is also instructive. For some Northern countries, a high proportion of developing country investment is in resource-extracting industries (United States, Japan, United Kingdom, the Netherlands), whereas for others, investment is mostly in manufacturing. One could also compare those whose manufacturing investment is predominantly a substitute for exports to the host country, a means of ducking under trade barriers (e.g. Sweden), and those with substantial export-platform type investment (United States, Japan).

Finally, it is useful to take note of the Northern countries' own experiences as hosts to foreign direct investment. Some are hosts to more foreign investment than they themselves are responsible for overseas (Australia, Canada, West Germany), whereas for most others the reverse is true.

It is, however, not altogether clear that these differences have much significance for policy, with one or two exceptions. In general, the higher a country's level of foreign investment, the more likely it is that a 'hands-off' attitude towards government policy will dominate. There is a suggestion that Japan's heavy involvement in export-platform type investment significantly colours Japanese attitudes towards industrial restructuring, since Japan has implicitly recognized the inevitability of international shifts in production patterns. In the United States, this type of investment is encouraged by tariff provisions but leads to direct complaints of the 'export of jobs' by United States companies and relatively more powerful labour unions.

The Canadian experience suggests that a position as net *importer* of capital and technology is likely to generate a considerable interest in an international code of conduct to control the practices of transnational corporations – though hardly to the degree of supporting some of the more interventionist measures suggested by some Third World countries. In addition, where the total volume of past investment, or its volume in relation to the national economy are high, as in the United States or United Kingdom, the protection of overseas investments can loom large in foreign policy preoccupations.

Trade

The pattern of involvement in trade in developing countries is diverse almost to the point of defying classification. As Table 1.1 shows, there are clear gradations in terms of the proportion of trade directed towards developing countries. Even excluding the special case of oil, the United States, Japan and France receive more than one-fifth of their imports from non-oil developing countries. The United Kingdom, West Germany, the Netherlands and Australia take between ten per cent and fifteen per cent, and the others between five per cent and ten per cent. For none, however, does this amount to a dependence on the developing countries for more than three per cent of GDP, except for the Netherlands (four per cent), with up to another three per cent (in the case of Japan) being additionally spent on oil. The export pattern is roughly similar, except that Japan's exports to non-oil developing countries were over four per cent of GDP in 1976. In terms of dependence on developing countries, however, and particularly of a *sense* of dependence, Japan stands out as the country with particularly heavy reliance on Third World resources, or rather on the resources of certain Third World countries. Japan's perspective is explained in part by the shortage of domestic energy resources and all but total dependence on imported oil, and in part by the implicit assumption that the other geographically distant rich countries might not be generous in pro-

Table 1.1: External Trade in Total and with LDCs in relation to GDP 1977

	Imports		Exports	
	% of GDP	LDC imports as % of total imports	% of GDP	exports to LDCs as % of total exports
USA	8^1	45	6	35
Japan	8^1	56	10^1	46
Germany	20	21	23	18
France	19	27	17	24
UK	26	21	24	25
Canada	20	13	21	8
Australia	9^1	22	13^1	24
Netherlands	43	24	41	11
Sweden	26	13	25	13
Denmark	29	12	22	13
Norway	36	10	24	14
EEC		22^2		19^2
OECD	15	29	14	23

Notes: 1. 1972; source, Annexe tables A and B.
2. Martin M. McLaughlin and the staff of the Overseas Development Council, *The United States and World Development: Agenda 1979* (Praeger for the ODC, 1979), Tables C-7 and C-8.

viding assistance during a crisis.

Perhaps the other major distinction between Northern countries with respect to Third World trade is that between those countries, notably Japan and West Germany, which have a predominant share of exports going to the expanding Third World markets of the newly-industrializing countries, and those like Canada, which carries out most of its trade in export lines with the slowest growth in world trade. (The United Kingdom would fit into this latter category but for some recent expansion of capital goods exports to the Middle East.)

The distinction is a reflection of differences in international competitiveness. The countries that take an optimistic view of the future — primarily Germany and Japan — are those which because of their own economic vitality can look forward with some confidence to capturing more than a proportionate share of the additional demand for imports which economic growth in the developing countries would generate. They are also the countries which can reasonably anticipate that as the exports of manufactured goods from developing countries increase, *their* industries will be the last to suffer significantly from the impact of competition in their domestic markets. The countries of declining international competitiveness, notably the United Kingdom, Canada and the Netherlands, by contrast, see *their* domestic industry as the most vulnerable and their prospects of capturing even a proportionate share of market expansion as limited at best.

It is not surprising that these different perceptions, rooted in the reality of recent trade trends, have led to marked differences in policy, for example on the matter of untying aid. More importantly, these two views of the world have led to distinctly dissimilar approaches towards the question of restructuring the manufacturing sector, to phase out those lines of production in which the developing countries have comparative advantage, and shift to the more technology-intensive, high-value-added activities.

One analysis of the European Economic Community (EEC) as a whole points to the EEC's growing deficits in trade with both Japan and the US between 1970 and 1975, and suggests that the EEC is likely to take an even tougher bargaining stance with other trade partners, notably the Third World.[3] The argument loses some of its force with the sharp fall in the EEC deficit with the US in the late 1970s, but remains strong as far as Japan is concerned. It raises the question, as the EEC takes an increasing role in trade negotiations in the 1980s, of how far its negotiating stance will reflect German optimism or British pessimism. One indication that the EEC is tending to follow the latter line is provided by the hard line the Community took in the renegotiation of the Multi-Fibre Arrangement.

Foreign Aid

The country analyses also demonstrate significant divergences in industrial-country attitudes towards economic assistance to the developing nations. The United States, initially spurred by the success of the Marshall Plan, gradually has become disillusioned with aid, especially over the last decade. Nevertheless, it remains the largest bilateral provider of aid in terms of amounts. The colonial powers of the United Kingdom, France and the Netherlands have retained a special relationship with their former colonies, based on a combination of ties that developed over the years, and strong commercial relations following independence. The Scandinavian and Dutch donors, over the last two decades, have shown strong interest first in raising, later in maintaining high levels of aid, in part on humanitarian grounds and pressed by strong socialist and labour coalitions. Aid has not been a major issue in Australia and Japan; each is a follower in that it has sought to meet internationally agreed pledges, but has not come up with new initiatives. In addition to regional interests, the Japanese have been very concerned with their international image, and to a large extent have viewed aid as a way to prove that they are responsible members of the OECD.

The United Nations in 1970 established an overall target for aid, defined in terms of official development assistance (ODA): most donor countries pledged that they would transfer 0.7 per cent of their total Gross National Product to the Third World in the form of ODA. In practice, as a percentage of GNP, aid levels from all OECD donors have actually fallen from about 0.5 per cent in the mid-1960s to around 0.35 per cent, a figure which has remained roughly constant throughout the 1970s. The aid performance of individual countries, however, has varied considerably, as shown in Table 1.2: from highs of over 0.9 per cent for the Netherlands and Sweden to barely 0.2 per cent for the United States, a country which has never formally accepted the UN target.

Aid has been justified to domestic constituencies on a variety of grounds ranging from security and self-interest, to humanitarian goals. Some authors note that in spite of large and growing commercial relations with developing countries, the general perception in most industrial nations is that aid is more important than all other links. As a result, the complex set of proposals under the NIEO have been viewed as little more than demands for more aid. This misperception, frequently encouraged by the press, particularly in the United States, has polarized positions and cemented stalemate in the North-South dialogue.

Aid is the area of North-South relations in which non-governmental organizations (NGOs) have tended to concentrate their activities and especially publicity in relation to fund raising. The NGO communities in the Scandinavian countries, the Netherlands and Germany have organized powerful lobbying coalitions, but have had less consistent success in the other donor countries. Churches, relief organizations and other liberal NGOs have continuously pressured their governments to help the developing countries as a moral imperative. Trade unions have at times lent support to these efforts, in part due to ideology, but also perhaps because aid is a substitute for employment-disrupting trade liberalization.

Geography, History and National Self-images

To economic differences which can be read out of statistical handbooks should be added other differences which can be read off the

Table 1.2: Net Official Development Assistance from DAC Countries to Developing Countries and Multilateral Agencies

Countries	Disbursements: $ million and per cent of GNP					
	1969-71 Average		1975		1979	
	$ m.	as % of GNP	$ m.	as % of GNP	$ m.	as % of GNP
Australia	205	0.59	552	0.65	620	0.52
Austria	12	0.08	79	0.21	127	0.19
Belgium	127	0.49	378	0.59	631	0.56
Canada	314	0.38	880	0.54	1,026	0.46
Denmark	63	0.40	205	0.58	448	0.75
Finland	11	0.10	48	0.18	86	0.21
France	1,001	0.67	2,093	0.62	3,370	0.59
Germany	638	0.34	1,689	0.40	3,350	0.44
Italy	153	0.17	182	0.11	273	0.08
Japan	468	0.24	1,148	0.23	2,637	0.26
Netherlands	185	0.57	608	0.75	1,404	0.93
New Zealand	14	0.22	66	0.52	61	0.30
Norway	36	0.32	184	0.66	429	0.93
Sweden	132	0.42	566	0.82	956	0.94
Switzerland	29	0.14	104	0.19	207	0.21
United Kingdom	528	0.42	897	0.39	2,067	0.52
Unted States	3,214	0.32	4,161	0.27	4,684	0.20
Total DAC countries	7,131	0.35	13,840	0.36	22,375	0.35

Source: Development Assistance Committee, *1980 Review*, OECD, November 1980, p. 179.

map. The Australians, for example, unlike the other countries studied, occupy 'a vast empty and well-endowed continent', physically much closer to poor, under-endowed Third World countries than to the rest of the rich world. Australians sometimes feel vulnerable as a result. Geographical position, too, greatly alters a rich country's perception of the archetypal Third World country. For Japan the Third World is pre-eminently represented by the dynamic industrializing countries of East Asia and resource-rich nations of Southeast Asia. France is more likely to see the economically-backward African countries as representative. The United States has tended to view Latin American countries as 'typical' Third World nations.

Such dissimilarities of interests do not, however, fully explain the policies and perceptions of interest of the industrial countries. It is notable, for instance, that the disputes which led to the collapse of negotiations over the International Wheat Agreement were not simply disagreements between importers and exporters of food grains. Instead, according to some observers, the main problem was conflicts between the US and the EEC over price — and hostility on the part of a number of developing country importers to the 'price fixing' activities of the 'Group of Six', which included not only the major exporters, US, Canada, Australia and Argentina, but also the EEC and Japan.[4] Canada's commodity policy appears 'especially confused and inconsistent' on items such as copper and iron-ore, where Canada's immediate material interests would seem to coincide with those of Third World producers. This inconsistency is attributed in part to a conflict between Canada's material self-interest and 'Canada's adherence to market principles and a broader Western interest'.

Belief in the existence of some concept of 'broader Western interest' is nevertheless undeniable. It lies behind the continuous (if often fruitless) efforts to arrive at common Northern positions and the growing attention paid to North-South issues at the annual summit meetings of industrial country leaders. It also explains much of the ambivalence of the primary producer rich nations towards UNCTAD's Common Fund. Many Western negotiators in these international gatherings see themselves as defending the forces of reason and 'sound' market economics against illogical, ill-conceived *dirigiste* and impractical demands from the world's poor countries. In the United States this has resulted in dramatic calls for 'going into opposition' against the unreasonable demands of the Third World in international organizations and 'educating them' about the realities of the world economic system. In such a view, as lines of solidarity become institutionalized in various negotiations, for a member of the 'Western' camp to support a Third World demand becomes almost a form of betrayal.

The papers on the United States and West Germany bring out the way in which East-West rivalries interact with North-South rivalries. The Soviet Union has been the dominant factor in US foreign policy, including US Third World policy, since the Second World War. For other countries, however, North-South issues are not so readily assimilated into an East-West framework. For reasons of culture and history, the Japanese cannot equate a 'rich country interest' with a 'Western interest' because they are very conscious of not belonging to the 'West'. France too preserves a distinctive position, which is manifested both in government policy and in the attitudes of the government's critics. Even among the remaining countries, which, if not all predominantly white, Anglo-Saxon and Protestant, at least share two of those three characteristics, there are also distinct differences. Some see the need for a common stance among the Northern countries that share a common culture and heritage. Others see their membership in world society as exercising some claims on their loyalty to balance the claims of 'the West', and consequently to show some sympathy with the aspirations of Third World countries.

General levels of sympathy count in the formation of a nation's character and outlook. The propensity to perceive mutual interests, to see a situation as offering room for a positive sum game, rather than a total conflict of interest, is not just a function of perspicacity and the ability to enter into the policy calculus — what game theorists call 'ease of generosity'. It is also a function of the *sentiment* of generosity, of the ability to stand in the other's shoes and see how the world looks from the other point of view, not only emotionally but also intellectually to realize that unless a contract also seems to operate to the other's advantage it will not stick.

The analyses offer interesting material on the factors which determine the 'general level of understanding and support' towards Third World aspirations in different Western countries. The religious past seems to be important in some countries, and the missionary experience is mentioned in several papers. Also noted is the sheer number of nationals resident in Third World countries, for which France provides some surprising figures. In the Netherlands and elsewhere, educational efforts in schools appear to have been important in raising the level of sympathetic support. The colonial heritage is obviously yet another factor which shapes attitudes towards developing countries. In all the ex-colonial powers it has served to provide a core of individuals with expertise and personal links to particular Third World countries. The extent to which it prompts a paternalist concern depends in part on whether the former colonial empire was seen as the object of a civilizing mission or not, and on how central the imperial mission was to the nation's self-image. Less important was the manner — rapid and with celebration, or slow and recriminatory — of withdrawal from empire.

Alliances among ex-colonies themselves vary, with the more egalitarian Commonwealth contrasting with the more France-centred French Association of States. The Canadian and Australian (and UK) papers mention initiatives by those countries to explore mutual interests in sympathy with Third World aspirations which were announced at Commonwealth meetings, though not always sustained thereafter. Likewise, membership in the OAS has on occasion prompted the US to initiatives it would not have taken *vis-à-vis* Third World states in general.

Great Power Status

Another factor of some importance in the development of Northern-country positions is the perceptions of individual countries as to their national standing. The more influential a country, the more it has to reckon with the possibility that the policies it advocates will actually be implemented. For example, the Netherlands might not appear quite so 'progressive' if its advocacy of liberal policies were likely to be heeded. Conversely, the more powerful and influential a country, the greater the possibility that it will assume a 'trusteeship stance', 'think for mankind' and on occasion sacrifice some specific short-term advantages for more general long-term ones. Such a country might assume the leadership exemplified by the United States in the 1950s and 1960s. The US experience in the 1970s suggests the qualification that the mantle will be worn as long as leadership is backed by convincing military and economic power, and is not ungratefully challenged by significant numbers of countries.

A quite contrary proposition may explain why there is more 'thinking for mankind' in Scandinavia (and Canada) than elsewhere. Precisely because Scandinavian countries are among the smaller and least influential of the rich countries, they have an interest in curbing the egotism of the great powers, and are more likely to have regard for a general world welfare transcending the interests of its citizens. These countries may be more likely to seek to build up the image, strength and authority of the United Nations. A rather different link between international status and approaches to the Third World is exemplified in the case of France. Here the Gaullist design might be seen as calling the Third World into being, to paraphrase Canning, to redress the balance of an American-dominated old one.

It is not only current international ranking which counts, but also changes in it. A country like Japan, whose international status is rising, but which still feels there is a discrepancy between its international prestige and its real economic power, may be more punctilious than others about conforming to the more idealistic standards of international conduct — such as moving towards aid targets. Likewise, a country which is declining in prestige but maintains the visions of glory derived from its former imperial power, may either seek to retain slipping status by magnanimous gestures – *or* decide to cut its losses and look after its own back garden. As illustrations of these last two possibilities, in both Japan and the United Kingdom, the respective papers record that it is the foreign offices among government agencies which are most keen to accommodate Third World viewpoints. However, the influence of all these factors is sometimes ambiguous and always hard to measure.

Ideology

The final general factor affecting perceptions of interests in Third World development is ideology. In many of the papers there are references to a belief in free-market principles as the factor determining, for example, attitudes towards commodity issues. There have always been and still are limits to the application of these principles. Genuine free-enterprise convictions lead to the belief that the market is sacred, that the distribution of income which it produces is thereby ordained by something more than the accidents of history, that the poor are properly destined to remain poor until they learn to help themselves or manage to find an oil well. The extent to which views of this kind seriously influence the business and official communities varies from country to country. There is a significant difference in this regard between the United States and West Germany on the one hand, and Scandinavia or the Netherlands on the other. Economic liberalism is seen as an essential ingredient in a development history which has made the United States feel it represents a 'moral and economic paradigm for the rest of the world', while West Germany's position as 'outspoken hardliner' is coloured by its experience of nationalization under national socialism. The papers do not make clear to what extent material 'interests' lie behind free-market philosophies. Perhaps they could not, since the philosophy is so often abandoned when expediency requires. In the more 'mixed' economies of Scandinavia, by contrast, state intervention, for example to secure more orderly international marketing arrangements for commodities, is less likely to be seen as 'contrary to prevailing domestic philosophy'.

The strength and character of left-wing traditions are obviously related and relevant ideological factors affecting different positions. Countries with a 'development lobby' which vocally concerns itself with aid and the reform of international institutions to promote Third World interests tend to be those with the kind of egalitarian, reformist, left-wing tradition which has produced the domestic mixed economy and the welfare state. Where the political parties espousing that tradition have organizationally embraced the labour unions — as in Scandinavia, the United Kingdom, the Netherlands and Canada, but not, for instance, in the United States with its business-union traditions — there are union leaders who are prepared to temper their protectionist instincts with a concern for promoting greater equality between nations or appreciating the benefits of expanding North-South trade. Where left-wing traditions derive more from the barricades than from reformist parliaments, as in France and Japan, the concern of the left has been more with support for liberation movements than with reform of international institutions which are seen to aid repressive Third World governments. In many countries, however, the left's concerns have shifted over the last decade from the reformist towards more revolutionary perspectives — partly in deference to the increasingly articulate rejections of paternalistic dependency and insistence on self-reliance on the part of Third World spokesmen, and partly out of frustration with the slow pace of reforms. The belief that transnational corporations are the villains of every problem is one on which many Third World, First World, and even Second World left intellectuals can unite. The other growing concern of Western counter-culture movements — that of the quality of life and 'new values' expressed in use of alternative technologies and new forms of social organization — is not necessarily complementary to the Third World's aspirations because it downplays the importance of international economic interchange.

These ideological trends have divided developmental lobbies and influenced some groups to divorce themselves from practical policy concerns. In addition, many interest groups, which espoused or tolerated liberal positions in more affluent periods, have during troubled domestic times turned their attention towards issues closer to home. As a result, the developmental groups do not now exert the influence they otherwise might on the day-to-day formulation of their country's policies. In Canada the left had criticized Canadian food aid, and been swayed in doing so by the fact that the farm lobbies are for it, but the same groups were silent on the very tough negotiating stance of the Canadian government on the International Wheat Agreement, where the detailed issues are so complex.

Finally, one should mention changes in public attitudes. A growth in 'conservatism' is detected in many countries and is achieving overwhelming strength in others. The recent French and Greek elections may be harbingers of a counter-swing, but it is too early to tell. During the late 1970s and early 1980s, recession encouraged protectionist views, and other factors have weakened internationalism, or at least eroded earlier, positive motivations. Very few trends are found indicating more responsive attitudes in the North towards North-South issues. The country studies were drafted in the main before the Brandt Commission's report was published. That report's reception in the media, if nowhere else, was quite favourable and pervasive in many countries in Europe, but in the United States its impact has been relatively modest. The Brandt report succeeded in raising the political visibility of the North-South dialogue, even if judged solely by the amount of prime-ministerial attention — previously negligible — which the report and its subsequent discussion evoked. The mere fact that the Mexico summit took place was a tribute to the persuasiveness of the Brandt report and the Commission members. But it was in late 1981 too early to say whether it will prove to have a lasting effect on public education or opinion.

Unanswered Questions

Several underlying questions remain which one would like to see explored much further in future studies:

(1)   Has the potential area of mutual interests been increased in the context of world recession or is it decreased? Keynesian analysis suggests that the existence of unemployed resources provides the potential for increased output from which all can gain. More conflictive analysis suggests that this very existence of recession exacerbates competition between countries, making co-operative action more difficult and the sacrifice of the weaker more likely.

(2)   Even if areas of mutual interest are identified, do governments today have either the will or the capacity to pursue them effectively? Many would argue that the level and effectiveness even of North-North economic co-ordination has been declining since the early post-war years, a reflection of the growing strength of transnational financial institutions and corporations and the decreasing effectiveness of national and international institutions of economic control. In this context, do governments have the capacity to implement effective economic initiatives in their relations towards developing countries?

(3)   The country case studies for the most part treat the Third World as a bloc. Would not a more differentiated approach reveal interests (or perhaps the lack of them in some cases) more clearly?

(4)   By assessing North-South issues from the separate viewpoint of

individual countries, do the case studies systematically underplay or even miss aspects of a more collective Northern interest, either of the North as a bloc or of major groups within the North such as the EEC?

Mutual Interests and Their Implications for the North-South Dialogue

Upon examination of the wide range of positions and approaches described in these papers, one might naturally conclude that it is impossible to distil a common set of rich country interests in Third World development. Looking at the interests of individual countries issue by issue, variations and differences within and between countries dominate over commonalities. In spite of this, can one identify any shared concerns among the industrialized countries that could build towards a common position regarding the developing countries in the years ahead?

The first is the immediate concern with economic stagnation and inflation and international measures to manage the world economy more effectively. Increasingly, the stability of the system depends on co-ordinated action among a number of developing as well as developed countries, whose participation in the management of the system, formally or informally, is a condition for achieving effective international action. At the moment, the basis for almost any international initiatives to tackle world recession are missing but this could change rapidly and when it does Third World participation would become vital.

Secondly, improvement in, even the maintenance of, levels of domestic living standards will over the longer term become significantly dependent on achieving further adjustment and structural changes in key sections of Northern economies, many of which directly involve adjustment with developing countries.

The rich countries are increasingly dependent on international transactions, in which a significant number of, though not all, Third World nations are playing a growing role. While these dependencies manifest themselves in different ways and degrees across the North, they add up to many specific interests in expanding Third World production and a steady longer-term adjustment in economic relations, which in turn is dependent on dynamism and order in the international economic system. Even when countries are competing with one another economically, like players in a board game, they can share many interests in having others remain in the game and follow generally accepted rules.

Thirdly, affluence itself and growing international awareness has generated widespread electoral support for maintaining programmes of aid towards developing countries. The evidence from opinion polls is not unmixed, but the case studies reveal steady support for continuing aid, though generally not for expanding it. Perhaps the critical issue for the future is whether with greater awareness of different forms of interdependence this will shift towards support for broader measures of international action or whether it will diminish. Much probably depends on how clearly and accurately political leadership and the media make the issues distinct.

Finally, the developed Western countries are, for all their variations in ideology and political approach, mixed economies, mostly party to NATO and anxious to maintain Third World countries politically non-aligned and economically open to the West. This strategic interest in avoiding shifts to Eastern alliances of developing countries either individually, or en bloc, is seen as an obvious interest of the North, though as with Eastern Europe, history may judge the long-term economic consequences of such moves as less significant than appears at the time.

Longer-term Prospects

The importance of growing North-South economic interdependence to the individual industrialized countries was spelled out in the *Interfutures* study carried out within the OECD. Designed as 'a study of the future development of advanced industrialized societies in harmony with that of the developing countries', *Interfutures* documented the growth of structural interdependence between the North and South and projected to the year 2000 a number of scenarios for future world growth based on different sets of assumptions. The results of two of these projections, shown in Table 1.3, provide a dramatic statement of the potential outcomes of greater co-operation versus a breakdown in North-South relations.

These two scenarios constitute the extremes of a number of projections made by the *Interfutures* team. The 'high growth' scenario assumes among other things successful collective management of the OECD zone by North America, Japan and the EEC in efforts to sustain high, stable growth; increased free trade; the progressive integration of the Third World countries into the world economy; and large aid flows. In this example, by the year 2000, total world product increases by a

Table 1.3: The Year 2000: Two Scenarios

	1975 GDP per capita (1970 $)	2000 High-growth scenario GDP per capita (1970 $)	2000 High-growth scenario Annual growth in GDP per capita (%)	2000 Breakdown in North-South Relations GDP per capita (1970 $)	2000 Breakdown in North-South Relations Annual growth in GDP per capita (%)
North America	5,080	9,775	2.7	7,780	1.7
Japan	2,870	10,280	6.0	3,590	1.7
European Economic Community	2,752	7,960	4.3	4,730	2.2
Other OECD	1,252	4,170	4.9	2,088	2.0
USSR, Eastern Europe	1,700	5,330	4.7	4,730	4.1
Developing countries, including China	256	860	5.0	656	3.8

Total world output, 1975: $3,800 billion.
Total world output, 2000:
High growth scenario: $12,970 billion; annual growth rate of 5.0 per cent.
Breakdown in North-South Relations: $8,980; annual growth rate of 3.4 per cent.

Source: *Facing the Future: Mastering the Probable and Managing the Unpredictable* (OECD, 1979).

factor of about three and a half and average *per capita* incomes are more than doubled. While the OECD's *share* of world output falls from 62 per cent in 1975 to about 53 per cent in 2000 (and the Third World's share rises from 21.6 per cent to more than 30 per cent), major gains are distributed throughout the world economy.

In contrast, the 'breakdown in North-South relations' scenario presents a strikingly different picture. This case assumes a deterioration in North-South relations in the early 1980s, resulting in the Third World breaking links which they feel have maintained their dependence on the North; greatly reduced aid flows; higher levels of protection; and slow or moderate growth in the OECD countries, depending on how individual nations are affected by the loss of markets in the South. In this scenario, the average annual growth of world product is reduced to 3.4 per cent, compared to 5.0 per cent in the high growth projection. Reductions in the *per capita* incomes of specific regions relative to the high growth scenario are dramatic, particularly in Japan but also in the EEC and other OECD countries, reflecting different levels of dependence. Due to their comparative self-sufficiency, the North

American region and the centrally-planned economies are not as adversely affected by a breakdown in North-South relations as are other regions in the OECD.

Projecting future outcomes is always a hazardous undertaking; but these figures, which are based on orthodox Western assumptions, illustrate the stake of the industrialized members of OECD, and particularly individual countries and regions within it, in maintaining and hopefully increasing levels of co-operation with the developing countries. (The point about orthodox Western assumptions is important. It is possible to take a sharply different view of the value of international economic integration, whereby reducing links would increase rather than decrease economic control and hence growth within the Third World and, even, it is sometimes argued, within parts of the North such as Europe or Britain. Although this viewpoint is often put forward in the South, it rarely is when protectionism in the North is under criticism. Similarly, or ironically, when new measures of protectionism are introduced in the North, they are invariably treated as unfortunate and temporary exceptions to a continuing general commitment to free trade – and orthodox economic analyses invariably establish some economic loss arising from the protectionist measures, both to the North and South.)

The *Interfutures* report stopped short of presenting a detailed set of recommendations designed to achieve a desired level of co-operation between industrialized and developing countries. Other groups have not, and most prominent among them was the Brandt Commission. Its basic task was to forge a comprehensive response to the various issues long debated in the so-called 'North-South dialogue'. This floating set of international conferences and negotiations has developed a history of its own, an essentially frustrating history to all participants. Given the subject of this volume, it is relevant to take some note of the Northern response to the dialogue.

Northern Participation in the 'Dialogue'

The OECD countries have always tended in North-South negotiations to react to proposals emanating from the South, rather than – except in isolated areas – putting forward measures of their own. It is a curious fact that the South discusses the possibility of a 'Third World Secretariat', one of whose main aims would be to assist them to formulate positions and negotiate them with the North, yet it is they, without such an organisation – rather than the North, which has one – who over the years have put forward a series of proposals for international change, including the agenda known collectively as the New International Economic Order (NIEO). In contrast, the North has never put forward a general position on what *it* would consider an adequate set of international measures to accelerate and sustain Third World development.

The 'North' in United Nations negotiations more or less excludes the communist countries, which so far have contributed only verbally to the dialogue. The Soviet Union in particular adopts the well-known (and to many developing countries, increasingly frustrating) view that underdevelopment is the product of colonialism, and its cure is the sole responsibility of the ex-colonial powers and the developing countries themselves. Neither do they seem interested in the debate on NIEO, which relates solely to relationships between capitalist industrial countries and the Third World. In contrast to this view, however, the terms and conditions of trade, technology transfer and many aspects of Eastern European countries' dealings with the Third World are sufficiently similar to those of Western industrialized countries that the Soviet Union and Eastern Europe are increasingly pressed to participate more fully in the NIEO debate and are included in 'the North' — especially by Third World observers.

The failure of the North to put forward an interrelated set of policies is one reason why the important interconnections between substantive issues are neglected. In fact, on many occasions the North has insisted that individual issues be discussed and negotiated separately, hence precluding even the possibility of 'linkages' between them. As a result, negotiations on the issues often take place in separate forums, so that arguments for accomplishing a number of objectives simultaneously may never be heard. An obvious case in point is that of investment in the production of minerals, which has dwindled in recent years. Reversing this trend should require comprehensive measures to ensure remunerative prices for mineral producers, to improve the operating conditions of private foreign investment for mineral development to the greater satisfaction of all parties, and to provide more international financial, technical and managerial assistance for mineral exploration. Yet to date there are no formal or informal means by which such considerations can be jointly brought to bear on international action.

There are many more examples of functional interconnections, such as that between trade and finance: several of the developing countries which borrowed most heavily from commercial banks in the 1970s depend on their manufactured exports for their capacity to repay their debts. In an environment of rising protectionist pressures or contracting markets in the rich countries, the stability of financial markets would be severely threatened.

In any negotiation, there are opportunities for bargaining which enable gains on one issue to be set against costs elsewhere in the pursuit of a mutually accepted package. The Brandt Commission proposed such a negotiation centred around four proposals dealing respectively with energy, finance, food and 'a start on some major reforms of the international economic system and institutions'. Together with trade, these formed the basis of discussion at the North-South summit in Mexico. Both the Brandt report and the North-South summit were initiated on the assumption that there had been something lacking in the official machinery, which has resulted in little substantive progress in the North-South dialogue. The last period of far-reaching international innovation, which set up the United Nations and Bretton Woods institutions and the GATT, came when one major world power — the United States — could provide leadership, and when the world had been shaken by the Second World War. The current problem is to find a more pluralistic substitute for that leadership in international co-operation — and, it must be hoped, a sense of urgency which anticipates, rather than emerges from, deepening world crisis.

The case studies of this volume discuss Northern interests in each of those areas. The following section attempts to identify the main lines of general Northern interest in these substantive areas and to show when greater co-operation or at least less confrontation is required if the 'general Northern interest' is to be served better than in the past.

Energy

All countries, oil-producers and non-oil producers alike, have a considerable area of common interest in ensuring steady rather than disruptive change in prices and supplies of petroleum and in measures to ease the transition towards a post-petroleum future, by greater energy conservation and research and development of alternative and especially renewable sources of energy. To sustain growth in the world's economies in the interim, oil supplies have to be increased through accelerated exploration and existing supplies have to be stretched through better conservation. Conservation has to be primarily an industrial country obligation given the current pattern of consumption. The ratio of total consumption between industrialized, middle-income and low-income developing countries, respectively, is 40:5:1.

In the area of exploration, co-operative action to assist developing countries in the capital- and technology-intensive business of developing new oil resources, is clearly a common interest at least to all net oil-importing countries in order to expand and diversify global reserves. So far this has been largely left to the oil majors. Intergovernmental cooperation has been inhibited by disagreements between various parties as to the role the majors and institutions such as the World Bank should play.

Conflicts between oil exporters and the deficit countries of both the industrial and the developing world have also emerged over price, production levels and control of the various stages of transport, refining, marketing and distribution which account for most of the value-added in a final gallon of oil or gasoline. But here, too, conflict has not and does not exclude the possibility of mutually beneficial arrangements. The OPEC countries have an interest in diversifying their excessive dependence on oil earnings, and in protecting the real value of their surpluses invested overseas; the North in avoiding unpredictable and large changes in price and supplies; the oil-importing South in assisting price increases which they can scarcely afford. A potential area for agreement between OPEC and the North lies in trading off security of supplies from OPEC – guaranteed production levels – against security of real prices paid for oil by the North, through some price/supply formula, perhaps involving indexation. Indexation might even in some way be extended to assets, though there the problems are more difficult. The interests of oil-importing developing countries could be incorporated by guarantees of supplies for the poorest countries, or by more comprehensive price arrangements as part of increased financial flows to developing countries, balanced by food exports or other commitments from the developing countries to OPEC.

This already makes clear that any international agreement which might resolve some of the problems posed by energy is unlikely to emerge over energy alone. In the North-South dialogue, the main oil exporters have consistently refused to discuss energy in isolation from other issues of concern to the Third World. Ultimately, other international political issues – most importantly the Palestinian question and Middle East instability – are linked to oil, which remains the strongest lever for change in the hands of the South, and hence increases the likelihood that the range of North-South issues can be resolved only if negotiated in the context of one another rather than individually in piecemeal fashion. At the same time, experience in this area already makes clear that the obstacles to agreement are not only due to differences between the groups concerned. Differences within OPEC, among countries of the North and among oil-importing countries of the South, can at times be seen to have precluded even discussion, let alone the reaching of agreement in this sensitive area.

Food Security

Table 1.4 indicates the extent to which, over the last 40 years, the world has moved towards greater regional imbalance in world food grain trade, with North America and Oceania now having a near monopoly of net exports of cereals. Food production in the developing countries has lagged behind demand, leading to major increases in imports, while output and exports from the United States, Canada and

Table 1.4: The Changing Pattern of World Cereal Trade (million tons)

Region	1934-8	1948-52	1961-5	1971-5	1976[a]
North America	+ 5	+22	+49	+79	+94
Australia and New Zealand[b]	+ 3	+ 3	+ 7	+10	+ 8
Western Europe	-23	-22	-26	-22	-17
Eastern Europe and USSR	+ 4	+ 2	- 4	-14	-27
Latin America	+ 9	+ 1	+ 2	- 1	- 3
Asia	+ 2	- 6	-22	-42	-47
Africa	+ 1	0	- 2	- 6	-10

Notes: Plus sign indicates net export; minus sign, net imports.
    a. Preliminary estimates of World Watch Institute, Washington.
    b. Including rest of Oceania.
Source: UN World Food Council, *Food Trade* (March 1977).

Australia have sharply increased. The resulting imbalance has increased instability in the market. The experience of 1973-4, when a three per cent variation in world supplies of food grains triggered a 300 per cent increase in prices has intensified the search for more orderly marketing arrangements. But little concrete progress has been achieved. Disagreements remain on price ranges and on the location and control of stocks, but the need for some new arrangements to achieve a greater degree of international food security is increasingly recognized, even in the exporting nations.

Beyond measures to stabilize trade in the event of emergencies, there are also common interests in concerted efforts to shift the pattern of world production over time. By 1990, the demand for food grains in developing countries will increase by some 350 million tons (over 1970), while supply in these countries is likely to increase by only some 200 million tons. Without major additional increases in Third World production, these developments will add greatly to demand for North American exports. This in turn will exert strong inflationary pressures on prices, which are already projected to increase because of rising costs of key inputs like fertilizer, and because of the already measurable levelling-off of yields. The interest of the industrial countries lies in avoiding instability and inflationary price trends, by increasing agricultural production in developing countries, where marginal returns to fertilizer and other energy-intensive inputs are often four to five times higher than in the industrial countries. Diversification of output across a greater range of ecological environments would also diminish the vulnerability of the world food system to variations in supplies from the North American continent.

Once again, differences of interest within and between countries of the North appear to be a significant obstacle in moving towards international agreement. Agricultural producer interests in the exporting countries have an interest in seeing prices kept high and, in the EEC at least, these groups dominate agricultural policies (especially in maintaining the Common Agricultural Policy). In contrast, consumers in the exporting countries largely benefit from lower prices. The balance of benefit and cost to the rich countries depends, as already noted, on the weighting given to these and other interests, including calculations of the investment needs for raising agricultural output in developing countries, and the alternative uses of such investment resources. The balance of interests in global food questions also has political dimensions. World food deficits, with a small number of surplus countries, unevenly distributed purchasing power and possibly inadequate stocks, could lead to explosive situations. Acute food shortages within countries have at times been politically destabilizing. The country case studies make clear the considerable electoral support for measures to deal effectively with hunger and food shortages.

There is thus a constellation of interests for international measures for stimulating greater food production and abolishing hunger in developing countries, and concerted action to create a system of international food security could well commend itself to the concrete interests of the rich countries. While the most important conflicts of interests over food are likely to remain between different Northern countries, the resolution of these conflicts is not necessary before at least a number of important measures towards greater international food security can be agreed upon.

Commodities

Many of the problems and opportunities arising over oil and food grains are duplicated for other commodities, with non-renewable minerals (whose production rates are also depletion rates) posing some of the more complex problems. The major interest of importing countries in both the industrial and the developing world is in secure supplies and stable low prices. Producers seek secure markets and stable high prices. At least they should find areas for common agreement on security and stability and perhaps reach a compromise on price levels.

International agreements to secure these ends can indeed bring benefits to both producers and consumers. For the producing countries, stabilization offers an end to damaging fluctuations in foreign exchange earnings, which can make domestic economic management extremely difficult. Price fluctuations have often led to wasteful investment cycles and ruinous distress sales on falling markets, aggravating or aggravated by debt problems, albeit offset occasionally by years of high prices. For the importing countries stabilization both eases the decision-making of individual economic units which could rely on given prices for long periods, and conveys macro-economic benefits.

Assessments differ as to whether various stabilization proposals would lead to substantial price increases. Price increases would of course favour the net exporters of commodities, which include most of the countries of the South and a few of the North. Perhaps the main current issue to be settled is the establishment of a floor below which export prices of developing countries' commodities will not be permitted to fall. There is no reason why this should necessarily be disadvantageous to the North; on the contrary, the North has an interest in secure supplies of raw materials, and as such cannot logically at one and the same time lament the lack of investment in raw material production and oppose measures which will ensure remunerative prices for producers.

Calculations have been made of the costs arising from instability in commodity prices to the rich countries. One effect is that of counter-inflationary measures required to offset commodity price increases, which due to structural rigidities push up domestic prices elsewhere with no counterpart declines in domestic prices in times of commodity price falls. Thus commodity price instability has been said to add to inflation with a measurable loss of production and output in the rich countries via the macro-economic mechanism of restraint. The actual calculation of this loss of output involves some heroic assumptions, especially in having to assume as stable certain relationships (e.g. the Phillips curve relationship between inflation and unemployment) which may in fact change over time. But where such calculations have been made – as in the American study quoted in the US paper – they show substantial advantage to importing as well as to exporting nations from commodity agreements.

Trade, Growth, Finance and the Location of Production

The discussion of mutual interests between the industrial and the developing countries in the trade field centres on two main topics: (i) the international transmission of economic activity and especially the Third World as a potential source of economic growth for the North; and (ii) the advantages to be gained from continuing industrial adjustment and eschewing protectionism. Both issues have important linkages with financial questions and trends in the international allocation of production facilities.

A strong case can be made in the longer term that the South (or parts of it) could serve as a major engine of world growth. The developing countries on average have been growing faster than the North in recent years, and in the case of the 'newly industrializing countries' (NICs), which weigh heavily in that average, very much faster. The investment opportunities both for manufacturing and for resource development have given credence to the belief that Third World countries offer a new frontier for economic growth in contrast with the more rigid Northern economies, in which both the possibility and desirability of maintaining rapid growth is questioned. Their demonstrated willingness to tolerate higher rates of inflation has also freed some of the more dynamic Southern countries from the deliberate demand-reducing measures common in the North in the 1970s and early 1980s. In this context, measures to stimulate greater transfers to the South, whether public or private financial flows, can add to *investment* in the Third World in areas helpful to the North, such as energy, food and minerals. This is an argument for long-term development to stimulate continuing growth and adjustment in the Northern economies as well as in the Third World.

The recycling of oil-surpluses which took place during the early 1970s through commercial bank lending achieved much of this, with marked benefits for the developed countries themselves. The continuation of this in the early 1980s seems less certain. For a variety of reasons there are now apprehensions that the banks might not continue the same volume of lending to developing countries, especially when trade conditions are threatening the borrowers' foreign exchange earning capacity and hence their ability to repay. The contribution to Northern growth of the South's commercial borrowing in the early 1970s was estimated to be equivalent to that of a significant reflation of the West German economy.[5] Any faltering of the recycling process would not only add unnecessarily to recession; it could also in the worst case occasion default or its equivalent by a bank or a country, or even a broader crisis in the international credit system.

The OECD countries have a vital interest in avoiding any such outcomes. Government and banking opinion still differs over the degree of danger, and of what is needed to reduce or remove it. The International Monetary Fund is already playing an increased part in the recycling process; but major differences continue between North and South on the extent and nature of international financial reform which is required. While both North and South recognize the need for action, the United States, Germany and Britain even if acknowledging in specific areas some of the case for IMF reform, will not contemplate major change in IMF procedures and management at so crucial a time. For many countries of the South, severe economic difficulties domestically, and often a different view of world economic crisis, make IMF reform appear all the more necessary.

In the longer run, growing Third World markets obviously present greater opportunities for the North. International trade has always played a large part in world economic expansion. But the South cannot buy from the North unless it can afford to do so, which requires not only adequate access to financial resources but, more fundamentally, greater opportunities for sales of its manufactures and strengthened commodity earnings. The real test for international co-operation aimed at achieving a faster-growing world economy is whether such a trading environment can be created, in which the North 'restructures out of recession', opening up its markets to the South and promoting production and sales where the South is more competitive, while the North itself moves out of uncompetitive and into more profitable economic activities.

There is a widespread perception that developing country exports of manufactures are a 'threat' to Northern manufactures, due to the concentration of Third World imports in particular industries. In fact, the current imbalance in trade in manufactures between the Third World and the industrial countries remains heavily in favour of the North. The developing countries' share in any rich country's consumption or imports of manufactures, is still relatively small, though the gains to consumers from freer trade are far from negligible. The US paper cites a recent American study which found that the retail prices of imported goods from developing countries were on average 16 per cent below the prices of domestically produced US counterparts of the same quality.

Clearly the currently slow pace of Northern growth and high levels of unemployment make it all the more necessary to find efficient and equitable adjustment measures which enable the rich countries to realize those gains from cheaper imports, and at the same time to compensate more equitably those who lose from the process in ways more dramatic and devastating than the gains which accrue to the larger number of beneficiaries.

Successful structural adjustment will depend on identifying means of compensation, to overcome the resistance from groups who lose. Between countries, the pattern of gains and losses from freer trade differ considerably between a dynamic Japan or West Germany, and a more vulnerable UK or Scandinavia or Australia. Differential 'indulgences' to impose trade barriers are the only equalizing measures so far envisaged by such policies as the Multi-Fibre Arrangement. Something more is needed. The creation of an international adjustment fund (where, for example, quotas would be replaced by tariffs, the proceeds of which would be used for compensation) is one possible solution. Some resurrection of the Keynesian proposal for a redistributive tax on excessive balance of payments surpluses could play a part of any proposals for securing better stability in the world monetary system.

Protectionism in the North does not stem from Third World competition alone and indeed, the most acute problems at the beginning of the 1980s are being caused by North-North competition: US textiles in several European countries, or Japanese and European cars in the UK and the US. Effective measures to deal with adjustment to the Third World will probably need to grow out of measures to achieve continuing adjustments between the industrial countries.

Nevertheless, trade with the Third World is still perceived more as a threat than an opportunity. There is little lobbying by those companies or organizations of workers employed in industries selling to the Third World, although they are numerous in the North. For the opportunities to be grasped, a greater degree of forward planning is needed both by corporations and governments. Of the countries studied here, Japan seems to have gone furthest in attempting active co-operation between the two.

In fact, while many sectors in the industrial countries view developing countries as a 'threat' to them economically, a strong case can be made that the economic activities of the poorer countries are largely complementary to industrial country activities, and that the real threat lies in intra-OECD competition for industrial base and market share. In the world economy, the greatest levels of competition seem likely to occur in the sectors producing capital goods, high-technology manufactures and services, and not in the sectors producing labour-intensive consumer goods. The trade wars of the past among industrial countries are giving way to sophisticated wars for value-added, and the wars may be fought with neomercantilist industrial policies. In such a world, groups of developed countries may increasingly adopt polices to limit competition among themselves and seek natural allies in developing countries and regions, which in the longer run might develop into integrated North-South economic units.

The Resurgence of Security Concerns

Over the last ten years there has been a pronounced increase in military spending in the major Western countries, along with rising military and armaments expenditures in the Soviet Union and Eastern Europe as well as in the Third World. Perhaps not surprisingly there has been growing concern over national security in the military or strategic sense of the term. As seen from the West, this rising concern has been prompted by a mixture of international circumstances: the long-term build-up of Soviet military capabilities, tensions in Poland, the Soviet invasion of Afghanistan, Soviet and Cuban involvement in Africa, political upheaval in Central America, and so forth. These factors have affected different Northern countries' perceptions in different ways, though in the major Western countries the principal threat to security is still seen to be the Soviet Union or its close allies. The election of conservative governments in a number of Northern countries, notwithstanding the recent French election, has reinforced this trend, since conservative politicians, at least in recent years, have publicly favoured a harder line than their opponents towards the Soviet Union. The mere fact that the current American administration has undertaken to respond forcefully to the perceived increased Soviet threat (at least in terms of US military expenditures) and to make East-West relations the primary focus of its foreign policy, has made other OECD nations respond to US initiatives, at least rhetorically.

One important effect of this trend on North-South relations has been a shift away from economic issues and towards more purely political and strategic considerations. In a sense, one could say that rather short-term security interests have overtaken longer-term security interests, since nearly all of the case studies indicate that in the final analysis, security is a direct function of sound economic, social and political relations. Whether or not current trends persist to the detriment of long-run North-South security is a question to be answered by future events.

Meanwhile other conflicts arise. The military build-up is already proving very costly, forcing additional sacrifices in other areas of public expenditure, which already had been cut as part of the widespread monetarist approach to current economic problems. A critical analysis would argue that rising military expenditures have considerably exacerbated the unemployment effects of current economic strategies and undermined domestic monetary and inflationary goals. Internationally, it is possible to argue that the return to an East-West military build-up involves a misreading of the lessons of the last three decades. Almost all of the more than 130 military interventions of the post-war years have taken place in Third World countries and responsive Western economic and political policy has in almost all cases been more important than military force in determining whether this outcome is pro- or anti-Western. As Robert McNamara put it, reflecting on his experience as Secretary of Defence: 'We still tend to conceive of national security almost solely as a state of armed readiness: a vast awesome arsenal of weaponry.' In contrast: 'if one ponders the problem more deeply it is clear that force alone does not guarantee security and that a nation can reach a point at which it does not buy more security for itself simply by buying more military hardware. Expenditures beyond a certain point are not only wasted on defense but will erode the funds available for other essential sectors. And by denying that dollar to other essential investment, the process may in the end diminish security rather than bolster it.'

Epilogue

What can be concluded from the studies for the future? It would be dishonest to pretend that a clear and simple set of conclusions emerges. Interests there are and strong they may be — but there is a complexity in the way they arise from the differing concerns of different groups within and across the developed countries which makes it difficult to compile a simple summary.

This is hardly surprising. Clear and strong interdependence exists between companies and unions within any of the countries of the North, or between, say, the economies of the European Economic Community. But the mere existence of this interdependence does not permit a simple summary of mutual interests, let alone a logical economic deduction that all forms of progress of one group or country necessarily will benefit all the others. Mutual progress can be mutually beneficial and co-operation to pursue this may be in the strong economic interests of all parties: but the terms and conditions of the progress and their implication for the distribution of the growing benefits are critical to determining the mutuality of the outcome and the interests of the various parties in pursuing it. If all this is true within and among the developed countries, why should it not also be true of the interdependence between the developed and developing countries?

Thus the critical question is not 'does interdependence between the North and South exist?' but 'on what terms is it in the interests of the North and South to pursue and fashion interdependence between them in the 1980s?' The acceptance of interdependence then becomes less a deduction from economic facts than a declaration of economic and political will. The essence of the Marshall Plan was not an econometric calculation of multipliers and linkages but the statesman-like vision that a reasonable post-war world required a reconstructed Europe and Japan and that it was in the broad interests of the United States to provide major economic support for its achievement. The terms on which interdependence was reconstructed included financial transfers, five year plans and the OEEC, an organization for co-ordinating economic advance and interaction.

The starting point with the Third World today is quite different. Parts of the Third World are growing rapidly and strongly, while many of the poorer parts are stagnating. The world economy is stagnating — if not in recession and crisis. The question posed is: does anyone have the vision for a purposeful reconstruction of a more dynamic world system — and how do the different groups of Third World countries fit into such a system? The answers to this are even more difficult than to earlier questions. Some will probably say that such a question is totally incongruous at the present time, politically and philosophically, because of widespread disillusion with the commitments to and capacity of international institutions and organizations. Such commentators may be 'realistic' in their disillusionment. The vision may be beyond our grasp.

But what the country-studies depict is the absence of any striving for a reconstruction of a new interdependence, a widespread failure to grasp the importance of what is at stake. In country after country of the North, economic interactions within the North are treated as serious *economic* issues, economic interactions with the South are treated as *political diplomacy*. Yet as the studies also show, the economic facts are otherwise: the Third World matters economically; the structural adjustments already facing the North in energy, food production, trade and finance, give it even greater incentives to establish new economic relationships with the South; and finally, in the context of continuing recession, there is a special area of mutual interest in any measures which would stimulate a greater level of economic activity through the growth of world trade.

While all the countries of the North have a variety of ties of interdependence with the large number of middle-income countries of the South, it is hard to see from the case studies what they have to gain economically from the prosperity, or even the continued existence, of the poorest among developing countries, even if security is considered as an important factor. A Nepal, a Bangladesh, a Lesotho, a Haiti, could go the way of Cambodia in more or less disappearing from the West's international community, with hardly a ripple of effect on the immediate well-being of the North's inhabitants, and even in the longest of long runs, with only a rather marginal loss of some opportunities for trade or the chance to import cheap immigrant labour at some distant time when the migration-potential of sources closer to hand is exhausted.

The satisfaction of humanitarian wishes that we should seek to aid the Nepalese and the Haitians can hardly, therefore, call arguments from self-interest in support. The case must rest mainly on support for measures of common humanity and poverty eradication, of shared membership in a 'world society' which have been mentioned throughout the case studies.

The papers discuss the factors which tend to strengthen support for this sort of action, in particular on the marginal incremental effects of binding arrangements involving partial renunciation of national autonomy for some collective interest. It is worth, finally, addressing one particular sort of international development – the entrenchment of 'class stratification' among the nations of the world. Most of the case studies examine the effects of 'class consciousness' in inhibiting the rich nations from 'defecting' into alliance with groups of Third World countries in confrontational situations. Similarly, there have been occasions, at the CIEC meetings, for example, when OPEC countries have seemed about to use their oil power quite consciously in the interests of the poor countries as a whole, and not just in their own national interest or in the interests of an Arab or Islamic grouping. To be sure, such solidarity remains weak in practice, and it is not clear that it will ever become a decisive force.

On the other hand, there are other possibilities. The effect of widening gaps in living standards is difficult to calculate. If the oil countries' industrialization and modernization plans turn sour and they remain the world's *nouveaux riches*, when will they feel they are entitled to be viewed as something better? Perhaps increased density of communications will have an effect: what Marx said the railways did for working-class consciousness in Germany, the jumbo jet and the international conference might do for Third World consciousness. If there were such a development, the effects would be uncertain just as the rise of class consciousness was for the Western democracies in the nineteenth century — on the one hand raising the level of dissension, on the other hand leading, eventually, to the 'incorporation' of the dissenters because the cost of the dissension to the ruling groups proved too great. That process of incorporation enabled the very poorest who had no bargaining power to have their claims to citizenship recognized by riding on the coat-tails of those whose bargaining power was stronger. This may be true of such countries as Nepal and Haiti. The Third World countries as a whole have a considerable role in determining the nature of the objective situation in which the rich countries find themselves and base their interest on.

While coalitions of specific interests could lead to progress on some limited issues, they do not seem adequate to forge a new order of a kind which would promise more solid opportunities of development for the Third World. For that, the question is whether the real interests in the areas of energy and economic security can bring the North to a greater understanding of the relevance to their own peace and prosperity of other economic and political issues in the Third World — or whether they feel they can do sufficiently well with the past strategy of maintaining the *status quo*, making a concession here and an advance there, and hoping they can get by without anything that seems to have major costs for themselves.

It is not the conclusion of this analysis that all issues have to be negotiated simultaneously. The negotiating process in the United Nations has suffered rather than gained from making attempts in that direction. But there evidently must be enough items on the agenda to make the potential outcome satisfactory for all parties. That there are mutual gains to be achieved seems clear; but they may only emerge in a situation where some bargaining of positive and negative elements is possible. It also seems clear from this analysis that progress in this endeavour is worth striving for, for the North's sake as well as the South's. The choice is between a world of growing poverty, instability, rapid population growth, resource depletion, conflict and insecurity – and a more manageable future. The idea that business can indefinitely continue as usual may prove to be an expensive illusion.

Notes

1. See, for example, William R. Cline (ed.), *Policy Alternatives for a New International Economic Order* (Praeger for the ODC, New York, 1979) and works cited both there and in the papers in this book.

2. The Independent Commission on International Development Issues (The Brandt Commission), *North-South: A Programme for Survival* (Pan Books, 1980).

3. C.Vaitsos, *From a Colonial Past to Assymmetrical Interdependencies: The Role of Europe in North-South Relations* (IDS, mimeo, 1978), p. 13.

4. Special Correspondent, 'Collapse of Grain Talks: The Reasons Why', *International Development Review*, no. 2 (1979), p. 21.

5. John A. Holsen and Jean L. Waelbroeck, 'The Less Developed Countries and the International Monetary Mechanism', *American Economic Review*, vol. 66, no. 2 (May 1976), p. 175.

2 THE UNITED STATES AND THE THIRD WORLD: TIES THAT BIND

John Sewell and John Mathieson

Introduction

At the beginning of the 1980s, America's relations with the developing countries seem to have come almost full circle since the 1950s. Over the past three decades, US policies towards the countries that comprise the Third World have gone through several phases. First there was a concern with alliances and aid designed to 'contain' the Soviet Union. In the 1960s the emphasis shifted towards 'nation-building' and winning the 'hearts and minds' of people in the Third World. The 1970s was a period of relative neglect as the United States focused on domestic problems, tempered only by a dawning awareness of dependence on certain developing countries — most notably for petroleum — and a sense that 'interdependence' was strengthening the links between developed and developing countries and at the same time making the conduct of American foreign policy more difficult. Most recently the primary concern seems to have swung back to the activities of the Soviet Union and its allies.

The Reagan Administration, which came to office committed to restoring America's relative economic and military power and pursuing America's national interests vigorously overseas, has been slow to define its policies towards the developing countries. Renewed worries over the strategic intentions and military capability of the Soviet Union is dominant along with growing anxiety about US resource dependence, most marked in the case of oil, but not negligible in the case of some other raw materials. Once again the developing countries are viewed largely as an arena for East-West competition reminiscent of the Cold War era, as a drain on scarce US budgetary resources, and as potentially unstable sources of key materials needed in the United States.

The preparation for participation in the Cancun summit provided the stimulus that helped the Reagan Administration develop its basic approach towards development issues and US-Third World relations. This approach, essentially a variant of the administration's domestic programmes, attaches great importance to the role of the private sector

41

as opposed to government and lays great stress on the need for developing countries to adopt a proper set of domestic policies, rather than to attempt to change the rules of the international economic game. Within this framework, efforts to inaugurate global negotiations on North-South economic issues are viewed with great scepticism by the Administration, as is the possibility of new governmental initiatives, whether bilateral or multilateral, to improve the economic prospects of the developing countries. By the end of 1981, however, the Reagan Administration's approach still lacked specifics and many issues remained to be decided.

Yet the world in which these 'new' concerns are being addressed is very different from the bipolar world of the 1950s and the 1960s, in which US economic and political pre-eminence as well as military power was unmatched. The position of the United States in the world's economy has changed considerably. The US now shares its formerly dominant position in the world economy not only with the other industrial countries, which have greatly increased their economic competitiveness in the post-Second World War period, but also with a number of developing countries that have emerged in recent years as major actors in international economic transactions. As a corollary development, the United States is no longer immune to external economic shocks. Floating exchange rates, import penetration, commodity shortages (with resulting inflationary pressures) and oil price rises have all signalled the end of the relative economic independence of the United States. These developments have in turn given rise to a growing unease among many Americans.

Moreover, most industrial nations are now beset with a combination of slow growth, high unemployment and high inflation, and only marginal improvements in economic performance can be anticipated. Most economists agree that a return to the historically spectacular growth rates experienced by much of the world in the 1950s and 1960s is unlikely at least for the first half of this decade. In this environment — and particularly in the absence of greater co-operation — the prospects are for dampened growth in trade (along with increasing pressures for restrictions), continued financial imbalances and instability and uncertainties in the supply and price of major commodities such as food and oil.

The international system has also become far more complex because of the greatly increased number of nations which are asserting considerable economic and political weight. The Bretton Woods system established in 1945 to govern international economic transactions was in effect designed by only two countries, the United States and the United Kingdom, and for several decades the system was managed almost exclusively by the United States. In contrast, the Law of the Sea negotiations include representatives of 154 independent countries. In 1959 there were only 92 independent countries; by the beginning of the 1980s, the number of independent countries had grown to 164, and all of the new entrants were developing countries. These numbers alone could complicate the management of any international problem, but in addition, the actions of the developing countries, in some cases individually and certainly collectively, now can affect the interests of the United States in significant ways.

The developing countries have for some time called for reforms in international economic and political systems, which are seen by the Third World nations to be providing inequitable representation and opportunity. Their proposals — referred to as the 'New International Economic Order' — call for comprehensive changes in existing rules and institutions, and are being advanced in practically every international meeting and forum. One of the remarkable features of the 1970s was the surprising unity of the developing countries in pressing for these changes despite their disparate levels of economic and social development.

The historic 'North-South' summit meeting of the leaders of the governments of 22 developed and developing countries who met at Cancun, Mexico in October 1981 underlines the new importance of relations between the rich and poor countries and sets the stage for a reassessment of American relations with the Third World. American policy-makers, and those concerned with US foreign policy, therefore need to identify US economic as well as political and strategic interests in the development of Third World nations and US relations with them, in light of the changes that have taken place over the last three decades both in the developing world and in the international environment in which those relations will be carried out. This paper is designed to contribute to that process.

America's Unique Position

This paper — initially prepared as a US contribution to an international symposium on the interests of the world's industrial countries in the development of the Third World — faces a particularly difficult challenge. The history and strategic position of the United States is unique among industrialized countries. Furthermore, due to the diversity of economic, political and ethnic groupings within the United States, there is no single, clear 'interest' in the developing countries, but rather a series of sometimes overlapping interests and objectives.

What makes the position and role of the United States different from those of other industrialized countries? First of all, until recently, the United States remained relatively insulated from international events and trends which have had significant, and in some cases overwhelming, impact on many other countries in both the developed and developing world. The United States is isolated geographically from its military adversaries, and for more than a century and a half has not had an enemy soldier within its borders. The raw material and agricultural abundance of the United States has historically limited its actual dependence and certainly its perception of dependence on external sources of supply. Even now trade remains a comparatively small percentage of US output. US goods and services exports in 1980 accounted for only 12 per cent of GNP, and the United States still remains one of the world's largest exporters of raw materials. In recent years, however, America's relative isolation from external factors has eroded rapidly.

Secondly, for many years after the Second World War, the United States enjoyed a position of overwhelming superiority in the international system. The design of the post-Second World War financial and political systems gave the US a dominant voice in many international institutions. The central importance of the dollar as the world's reserve and transaction currency provided the US with much more flexibility to pursue domestic objectives than any of the other industrial countries. Given its economic and military strength, the United States found itself charged with the responsibility of maintaining the security umbrella under which the strategic interests of the United States and its allies are protected. Today, the United States remains one of the few industrial countries that has troops permanently stationed outside its borders to protect its strategic concerns in various parts of the developed and developing world.

Thirdly, American political and economic traditions also distinguish its relations with Third World countries from those of many other industrial countries. The United States sees itself as a former colony that gained independence through revolutionary war, a fact which has governed its outlook on the Third World. The US did not have the same sort of colonial ties which are a predominant feature of the British, French and Dutch experiences. In addition, the evolution of the American economic system is rooted deeply in the historical abundance of resources and in the emphasis on individual entrepreneurship.

Fourthly, the American system of federal government, with power divided among the executive, legislative and judiciary branches, provides a decision-making process quite different from that of the parliamentary structures that characterize most other industrial countries. While the latter are designed to develop policy approaches by consensus, the US framework exhibits a strong degree of built-in conflict among the governing branches, which leads to difficulties in pursuing a consistent set of policies.

Both American attitudes and American policies towards the developing countries are currently in a state of flux. The 1980 election seems to have marked a considerable shift from ideas that dominated American foreign policies during the 1970s. American attitudes towards the developing world during the past decade were shaped by the Vietnam War and the Watergate scandals, which had the combined effect of tarnishing most Americans' self-esteem and the image of their country as the moral leader of the 'free world' and calling into question what the US government could and should attempt to accomplish overseas. This shift was supported by a growing feeling that the threat of the Soviet Union in the developing world had been overemphasized, to the detriment of American interests. Hence a new emphasis was placed on 'ground rules' to downplay US-Soviet competition in the Third World.

The perceived increase in US domestic problems – urban decay, racial tensions and poverty, as well as more recent concerns over domestic economic problems – in the late 1960s and 1970s also had an important impact on American views towards US relations with the outside world. For most policy-makers, poverty and race relations were invisible problems in the comfortable world of the 1950s. The upheavals of the 1960s, however, turned attention increasingly towards pressing domestic problems. The relative diminution of concern about foreign policy problems was a striking feature of the last decade – a seeming repetition of the cyclical pattern of isolationism following activism that has marked American history.

Over the same period, however, concern with global problems – environment, energy, food – led to a growing interest in issues of global interdependence and the 'management' of an interdependent world. The concept of the international system as 'spaceship earth' gained a currency in the United States among both political leaders and the public. In addition, several government reports – most notably the Global 2000 report, *Entering the 21st Century*, reported a number of common environmental problems facing both rich and poor countries. In this setting, the growing importance of the developing countries to the economic well-being of the United States began to be felt. American exporters came to view the developing countries as major markets, and bankers realized that some developing countries had become major profit centres for commercial lending. Relations with these countries came to be seen as a more important component of American foreign policy.

Currently, however, these perceptions are tilting in the other direction – with the developing countries seen mainly as arenas for competition with the Soviet Union and as sources of valuable raw materials. In addition, there is renewed concern about American power and how it can be used to further American interests. This concern is most marked in the willingness of voters to favour increased federal spending on defence.

This paper is designed to explore the richness and complexity of American relations with the developing countries. It begins with a description of the national ideology which has shaped American perceptions of the Third World. It then assesses US strategic and political interests and describes the political processes which govern the decisions about relationships with the Third World, as well as the impact of public opinion and policy in this area. Finally, the paper analyzes the different views of the 'national interest' in the developing countries that have arisen in response to a rapidly changing international environment.

The Impact of the American Political Tradition

American attitudes towards the developing countries and towards development stem not only from recent trends and events in those countries and of their importance to the United States, but also from attitudes and values deeply rooted in the American political system and its institutions. It is therefore necessary to identify those elements of America's political tradition that form the basis of views of development and the Third World. Their influence has been strong, even though they sometimes are inconsistent, contradicted by actual practice, or used to justify actions actually taken in a narrowly defined concept of national interest.

Abundance

The American political and economic traditions were initially shaped by settlers in a continent blessed with a rich endowment of natural resources, sparse population, and the absence of an entrenched social structure, the combination of which gave free rein to individual initiative. The amount and variety of land and the extensive deposits of minerals and other raw materials within the borders of the United States gave the country almost unlimited space and resources. There was little need to face the difficult choices necessary to divide existing assets. As a result, the economic and social development of the United States was not overly constrained by problems associated with redistribution, leading to a belief that any problem could be solved. When economic development and progress did not take place, it was not felt to be due to lack of resources or as a result of inequitable social structures, but rather the fault of individuals who did not take advantage of the opportunities available to them.

Individualism and Democracy

America is largely a nation of immigrants and their descendants who fled from economic calamities, oppressive governments and restrictive class structures. Due to the absence of rigid class divisions, Americans tend to see no inherent incompatibility between liberty and equality. As Alexis de Tocqueville wrote: 'The advantage of the Americans is, that they have arrived at a state of democracy without having to endure a democratic revolution; and that they are born equal, instead of becoming so.'[1] Several concepts flowing from this experience have become embedded in the American psyche. Mobility was accepted as an integral element of society whether in its social meaning or in its literal sense of relocating to seek new opportunities. The existence of the 'frontier' in both a literal and psychological sense had a profound impact on American society. In fact, it was not until the frontier was closed that Americans began to look beyond their own borders. In addition, equality in the American context took on a special meaning, referring not to political or economic levelling, as in a society striving to eliminate class barriers, but rather 'equality of opportunity' – the chance to improve one's own situation without barriers. Equality was not seen to be in conflict with liberty, but rather as complementary.

These beliefs place the individual as the cornerstone of the social and economic order and individual rights and participation as the foundation of political democracy. This view is reinforced by the perceived need to overcome what was considered to be arbitrary rule in

Europe, resulting in a series of checks and balances to restrain governmental power under the maxim of 'he who governs least, governs best'.

Revolution and Social Change

Americans like to think of their country as a former colony, a state created by revolution. Yet the American revolution had a rather special character. It was neither radical nor ideological, but 'practical', designed to relieve the former colonists of the burden of a distant government which seemed determined to exploit them. Unlike the French revolution, the American revolution was an effort not so much to build an improved society on the ruins of the old, but rather to build a new society in a new environment.

American experience with political development has led to certain ingrained and sometimes unconscious ways of looking at the developing countries. Robert Packenham has summarized these perspectives in four propositions.[2]

First, Americans have a tendency to assume that 'change and development are easy', given their national experience in a world of relative physical abundance with few social and political constraints, in which development was rapid and spectacularly successful. From this perspective, the problem in other countries seems primarily a lack of willingness on the part of individuals to undertake the necessary effort.

Secondly, Americans like to believe that 'all good things go together'; that the achievement of one desirable set of social goals aids in the achievement of others, and that economic development will promote social development, which in turn will promote political liberty and democracy. Again, this is based on a romanticized reading of the American experience, often erroneously projected as also feasible in countries with very different economic, social and political histories.

Thirdly, Americans tend to believe strongly that 'radicalism and revolution are bad', and that the costs of violent social upheaval are never worth the gains. It is only with greatest difficulty that Americans have been able to visualize a pattern of political development which takes a different path from their own, because the American experience indicates that moderate reformist solutions to political conflict have produced a wealthy society. The United States tends to see radical change as a disruptive and even counterproductive force, ignoring, of course, the fact that in many developing countries extremely scarce resources and the existence of a highly structured class system and well-entrenched elite makes moderate and gradual change at best extraordinarily difficult. In addition, abrupt change is now usually seen as opening opportunities for forces opposed to the United States, most often the Soviet Union and its allies.

Fourthly, Americans feel that diffusion of power is more important than concentration of power. While this belief may suit a situation of abundance or an open frontier, it may be less pertinent as limits begin to be encountered. The desire to decentralize political power led to a system of checks and balances being built into the American constitution, and a suspicion of central government that persists to this day. For many developing countries the problem may not be so much the evils of an omnipotent central authority as the need to mobilize national energies for economic and social development. American and developing-country views in this regard tend to be in conflict. On the other hand, concern with liberty and checking the arbitrary actions of the central government has led to the often admirable American interest in human/political rights and an emphasis on political participation in the development process.

Economic Liberalism and Attitudes Towards Poverty

The influence of classical liberal economic thought remains very strong in the United States. Americans generally believe that the market mechanism should be allowed free rein wherever possible, even if from time to time government intervention is necessary in the general public interest. Domestic regulation and planning are often opposed by considerable segments of the American public. Despite basic similarities among the economic systems of all industrial countries, the extent of governmental intervention is considerably less in the United States than in other OECD countries. This tendency is particularly marked in the current administration, but is not unique to it.

The influence of classical economic thought poses particular problems for Americans in discussions of the proposals of the developing countries for a New International Economic Order (NIEO), since in many cases these proposals seem to run counter to the US desire to maintain free markets, and also because they imply a larger role for governments in the economic sphere.

Two developments with respect to US policy towards the Third World do, however, fit naturally with traditional American beliefs. First is the concept of 'graduation' of such middle-income countries as Brazil, Korea and Taiwan into the ranks of the developed countries. These countries are viewed as the up-and-coming entrepreneurs emerging from the mass of poor developing countries. They are seen as following the capitalist path in some ways more successfully than the

United States itself, hence deserving the respect of the other industrial-ized countries and emulation by other developing countries.

Secondly, American perceptions of poverty also have an impact on the US position. The counterpart to the individualism mentioned above is a strong humanitarian spirit which pervades American attitudes towards poverty at home and abroad. For instance, private assistance given by individual Americans through non-governmental organiza-tions continues to run at a very high level. (In 1978 Americans provided $924 million in 'voluntary' foreign aid through private agencies — an amount equal to almost 50 per cent of the total US bilateral aid pro-gramme.) In addition, the United States has been a leader in accepting immigrants and refugees from developed and developing countries. From 1975 to 1980, the US accepted nearly 600,000 people for perm-anent resettlement, a commitment relative to population size exceeded only by Canada and Australia.

Until this century, however, the elimination of poverty was not seen to be a function of the government, but rather of individual efforts. Poverty was to be dealt with through charity rather than government programmes aimed at achieving greater equity. When the government has intervened to help poor people (as it has increasingly done in the twentieth century), its aim has not been to remove or ameliorate inequalities of income, but rather to raise individuals above a certain 'threshold' of absolute poverty. In other words, the provision of 'basic needs' should give individuals the ability to compete equally. This emphasis has been central to most of the social reform movements of the last hundred years. In each case — the Progressive Movement, the New Deal, or the Great Society — the propensity has been to provide basic goods and services to those who lack them, and jobs for those who can work. Equality of opportunity, the catchword for this atti-tude, is considered sufficient to overcome inequities. The Reagan Administration's approach towards poverty is illustrative of this outlook in seeking to generate more economic opportunities in the private sector, to reduce the dependence of the poor on government programmes, and to provide a 'safety net' of basic services for those clearly unable to support their own needs.

Robert Lampman has written that 'Americans do not seek any particular degree of income equality, but rather seek a system of sharing that recognizes human needs, restrains certain arbitrary or capricious inequalities, and serves social purposes.'[3] Roger Hansen adds that 'To the extent that Americans have in the past concerned them-selves with the issue of domestic income distribution, it would appear that their vague, and for the most part inarticulated, objectives have focused on a general broadening of equality of opportunity and on eliminating absolute poverty.'[4]

The same pattern revealed in the domestic economy emerges in America's international policies. To facilitate equality of opportunity is a praiseworthy objective, but to attempt to level incomes is a fruitless and needless task. One must strive to abolish absolute poverty but need not tackle relative income inequalities either within or between countries. The American support for programmes aimed at meeting basic human needs in the developing countries and opposition to proposals for a new international economic order is in line with this deep-seated national belief.

Political and Strategic Interests

Perceptions of American political and strategic interests in the developing countries have undergone major swings in the past and now again are in a state of transition. In the 1970s the defeat in Vietnam led to a great deal of rethinking about American interests in the Third World, leading to a decline in US activism. This reassessment was, however, largely overtaken by the emergence of OPEC, the continuing world economic crisis, and gathering concern about Soviet power and strategic intentions that is more marked than at any time since the 1950s and early 1960s. Recent events have had a far-reaching impact upon American attitudes towards the Third World: these include the fall of the Shah of Iran with the resulting shift in the strategic balance in the Persian Gulf, the taking of American hostages in Iran, the Russian invasion of Afghanistan – the first time Soviet troops have moved into a country outside Eastern Europe – Soviet and Cuban presence in Ethiopia and Southern Africa and continuing instability in Central America following the downfall of Somoza in Nicaragua and civil war in El Salvador.

American Strategic and Political Objectives

There is, of course, no such thing as a single, objective 'national interest' with respect to US relations with the developing countries. Rather, there are only the subjective and normative preferences of individuals and groups as they calculate their interests with respect to particular issues.

With this caveat in mind, there is consensus, among Americans of all political persuasions, on the specific set of very broad strategic and political goals the United States should seek globally. American interests in the developing countries are essentially a reflection of US global interests. Clear differences emerge on the means by which objectives are most effectively pursued, and on the relative priority warranted for individual objectives, but not on the desired ends themselves. Briefly stated, these goals include the following:

(1)   Maintain world peace, in the sense of avoiding a repetition of the world wars experienced in this century and particularly the outbreak of nuclear war which would threaten human existence itself. This includes the management and maintenance of the international system to the extent that it provides for peaceful outcome of conflicts.

(2)   Protect the American borders from potential military incursion and the rights and safety of American citizens and corporations abroad.

(3)   Maintain — and increase — international economic stability and access to foreign markets and sources of critical supplies. This objective includes assuring that lines of communication for goods, services and information remain open.

(4)   Contain the influence of those nations or groups seen as fundamentally opposed to the American system of values and indeed threatening the very existence of the United States. This goal directly implies the need to maintain or strengthen the economic and political stability of American allies.

(5)   Encourage the adoption of certain principles, such as self-determination, the participation of individuals in decisions that affect them and basic political and social rights, which serve as the foundation of the American political system.

Although these basic objectives are shared by the overwhelming majority of the American people, differences of opinion are rampant with respect to their relative priority and the proper US policies for achieving them. For example, is world peace best served by increased efforts to arrive at détente with the Soviet Union, or by an aggressive build up of US military capabilities? Cogent arguments can be made for both strategies, since the answer largely rests with the accurate interpretation of Soviet intention and likely Soviet reactions, about which there is a great deal of controversy.

Differences of opinion are also considerable on the subject of actual or apparent trade-offs between different tactics to achieve desired ends. Is the goal of maintaining stability in a country which is considered an ally best served by arming its military establishment or by assisting in its economic development? The answer frequently is not clear cut, as the case of Iran illustrates all too conspicuously. Another set of divergent views exists on the degree to which American values – human rights, for example – should be pressed in the developing nations, given the frequent interpretation of such pressure as undermining the stability and even sovereignty of the government in power.

Strong differences also abound as to the appropriate degree of forcefulness with which American interests should be pursued. There are occasions when active intervention can be effective, and other times when 'quiet diplomacy' offers a better chance of achieving the desirable ends. The same holds true for the use of various instruments of foreign policy; for example, the relative efficacy of economic incentives and sanctions versus other forms of political and military responses varies enormously by issue and over time.

The above observations of course apply to US relations with any country. To what extent do US strategic interests in developing countries of the Third World *differ* from US strategic interests in and relations with either America's industrial-country allies or the Soviet Union?

While the broad interests themselves are very much the same, the pursuit of US strategic objectives in the Third World is complicated by several important factors. In general, US relations with the developing countries are far less stable and less predictable than those with either industrial-country allies or even the Soviet Union. In general, the OECD countries are not threatened by serious instability and have over the years forged a unified stance towards a common external threat. Similarly, nations of the East and West have lived with the adversarial situation for over 35 years, and hence have developed a reasonably predictable set of foreign policy moves and countermoves. This is not true of a number of developing nations which are subject to serious internal instability and vulnerability to outside forces. Finally, much more policy attention and analysis has been focused on Atlantic and East-West relations than on America's relations with developing countries. As a result there is less understanding and knowledge of countries in the Third World than of other areas.

To what extent are Third World nations really important to the various security interests of the United States? Proceeding down the list of goals outlined earlier, one can first of all observe that while individual developing nations may not be capable of engulfing the major nations in a world war on their own, they are entirely able to do so by involving the United States and the USSR.

> The most serious difficulties for leaders of the Atlantic Alliance have usually been not in Europe but in the gray areas of the Third World — Korea in 1950, Dienbienphu in 1954, Suez in 1956, the Cuban missile crisis of 1962, the Vietnam war and, more recently, Iran and Afghanistan. This is where the fighting has been and where the danger of conflict with the Soviet Union has been greatest.[5]

Without diminishing the critical importance of Poland, one can conclude that rising East-West tensions have been for the most part the direct result of conflicts in the Middle East, Africa and Central America; each of these sets of conflicts carried strong implications for East-West relations.

Secondly, while no developing country threatens the sanctity of American borders in a military sense, the proximity of Mexico, Central America and certain Caribbean nations to the United States, and migration from those countries to the United States, has historically resulted in a great deal of attention being given to their security and stability. Expropriations of US firms, terrorism and the hostage crisis in Iran have confirmed that even relatively powerless nations can determine the security of Americans abroad.

The growing importance of developing countries to international economic stability and US economic performance — the third US 'strategic' interest identified earlier — will be discussed in the following section. In addition, Third World nations hold critical positions geographically, since many of the important sea lanes and other transportation routes (such as pipelines) proceed through developing countries or are contiguous with their borders.

The fourth, broad US objective — that of containing the influence of adversaries — has long been played out in nations of the Third World. The record of the Soviet Union in achieving influence in the developing world is at best mixed with current 'successes' in Ethiopia or Indochina balanced by notable 'failures' in Egypt, Somalia or Ghana. Nevertheless, it is clear that the rivalry between East and West has been and will continue to be played out on the soil of developing countries.

Finally, while the US goal of encouraging the adoption of certain principles of governance and basic rights may not be as directly related to American security interests as are the others, to the extent that this goal is pursued, it will be done so most vigorously in the developing countries. In general, other industrial countries of the West share these principles, and it is very unlikely that external pressure will lead to their embrace by most nations of the Soviet bloc. Hence, the greatest potential for US influence will be in the Third World countries which are still in the process of nation-building.

This brief review confirms that the developing countries are intricately involved in the entire range of US strategic and political interests, even while these interests remain focused on America's relations with the Soviet Union, which are perceived to present the greatest threat of nuclear war. Yet the present (and projected) configuration of national as well as global issues and interests suggests that the Third World role in enhancing or diminishing the security of the United States will be even more significant than in the past.

The Evolution of US Involvement in the Third World

Historically, American actions (like those of any other country) have not always been congruent with the self-image many Americans have of their role and behaviour in the world, particularly the image of a nation created by revolution and supportive of self-government and freedom elsewhere. In reality, since the late nineteenth century, the United States has seen itself as a global power and has acted accordingly, including intervention in the affairs of other countries. The cause of the US shift away from relative isolation undoubtedly lay partly in a desire to emulate the European powers, who in the late nineteenth century were engaged in a scramble for colonies in Africa and Asia. But domestic factors were also very important. America has been transformed since the Civil War from an agricultural to a manufacturing economy, and the limits of the domestic frontier have finally been reached.

There were other determinants of American expansionism. The rise in America of Social Darwinism, with its supposedly biological evidence of Anglo-Saxon supremacy, linked naturally with ideas of those who saw the United States as a revolutionary exemplar of the rest of the world. In addition, there was a growing sentiment that the United States had become a major power, and that sea power was one of the keys to world power. The belief that the United States should have a large and modern navy was stimulated by writings of Captain Alfred Thayer Mahan, whose book *The Influence of Sea Power Upon History, 1660-1783* was influential both in the United States and throughout Europe.

The last decade of the nineteenth century and the early years of the twentieth century were marked by a growing outward thrust, first in Alaska, Hawaii and Samoa, and then, as a result of the Spanish-American War, into Cuba, Puerto Rico and the Philippines. Successive American governments asserted an active claim to hegemony in Latin America (thereby extending the Monroe Doctrine), particularly in the Caribbean, where US intervention in Haiti, Nicaragua, Panama and the Dominican Republic became commonplace. In the Pacific, the United States saw a vital economic and political interest in maintaining access to China to avoid being closed out by the great powers, and in regulating relations with Japan. In comparison, very little attention was paid to Africa, South Asia and Southeast Asia, all of which were then under colonial rule.

Growing involvement in Asian and Latin American countries marked US foreign policy until the Second World War, flowing from a number of motivations.

> The forces influencing American policy were too complex to be explained as merely the machinations of capitalist imperialism. A determination to forestall any possible foreign intervention in the vicinity of the Panama Canal, a continued devotion to the ideals of the open door and independence of China, a sense of mission to promote democracy and progress played roles fully as significant as the desire to provide profitable opportunities for American trade and investments.[6]

Americans were not wholly supportive of the US expansionist thrust. Certain groups continuously opposed the existence of US colonies, on the basis of both moral grounds and fears that foreign commitments were dangerous. Traditional American isolationism was ultimately shattered by the Second World War, and a more active US stance continued throughout the late 1940s and early 1950s, due to concerns that the Soviet Union was bent on expanding its domain by any means, not only in Western Europe but also in the newly independent countries of the Third World. The Cold War goal of 'containing' the Soviet Union and later China led to the expansion of American military power throughout the developing world. Worries over the threat of communist expansion strongly influenced US-Third World relations across all functional lines such as trade and economic, technical and military assistance. Even now, US defence alliances and treaties are in effect with 26 different Third World countries, mainly in Asia and Latin America. The United States maintains bases in the Pacific (South Korea, Japan, the Philippines, and Guam), in the Indian Ocean (Diego Garcia) and in the Caribbean (Guantanamo in Cuba, and in Panama). In addition, the US is now negotiating to establish bases in the Middle East and has created a 'rapid deployment' military force meant to respond to contingencies in the Third World.

Recent Developments in US Involvement

American strategic thinking about the developing countries began to change in the late 1960s, influenced strongly by the long and fruitless American involvement in Vietnam. The emphasis shifted from the direct use of American forces to an increased reliance on friendly governments and local forces. This new policy – the so-called Nixon Doctrine – had a corollary: the US would continue to supply the arms, equipment and other forms of support necessary to help developing-country allies counter external aggression or internal subversion, both presumably led or inspired by Russia or China. One of the direct results of this shift in strategy was that the United States became one of the largest suppliers of arms to the world, with total arms transfers growing from $3.5 billion in 1969 to $6.7 billion in 1978. Much of these arms transfers went to the developing countries (about 80 per cent of the total over the 1969-78 period), primarily in Asia and the Middle East.

During much of the post-war period there was a basic consensus concerning the thrust of American economic, security and political interests in the Third World. American policy was designed to contain the Soviet Union and China and deny them political or ideological influence in the newly independent states, stimulate the economic development of the poor countries and encourage liberal economic and democratic systems to take root in the Third World. This consensus evaporated in the late 1960s and early 1970s under the impact of domestic and international events. By the early 1970s, many Americans felt there was little reason for deeper involvement in the Third World. At one point the US Senate even temporarily voted to end the US foreign assistance programme.

The tendency towards reduced US intervention was reinforced by the development of the policy of détente with the Soviet Union in the early 1970s. For a period it seemed as though an accommodation had been reached with the Soviets that would lead to a reduction in tensions and a broadening of economic and cultural relations. The impact of détente on American views of the developing countries was considerable from the American perspective, one of the implied ground rules of détente was an acceptance of the *status quo* of the Third

World. In the popular view, the 'threat' from the Soviet Union in the Third World diminished to a considerable degree.

Strategic interest in the developing countries, however, has been rekindled by several factors. The shift originated with the combination of the food crisis and the embargo and price actions of the Organization of Arab Petroleum Exporting Countries in the mid-1970s. For the first time many Americans began to realize that events in the developing countries could directly and immediately affect their well-being. The sense that at least some developing countries now had growing leverage has been joined by an understanding that the developing countries as a group are of growing economic importance to the United States, either as suppliers of raw materials and low-cost manufactured goods, or as rapidly expanding markets. In addition, the political and strategic influence of the Third World, previously discounted as relatively insignificant, began to be acknowledged, particularly in international forums. Finally, a number of Americans have become increasingly concerned about a series of global environmental problems — pollution, population, oceans — that transcend the normal definition of foreign policy issues and that extend beyond the capabilities of individual nation states to resolve either unilaterally or among the traditional industrial world powers.

Most immediately, however, American worries about the role and intentions of the Soviet Union have risen drastically in the past few years. Détente itself is now a subject of considerable controversy within the United States. Many have questioned its ultimate value to the United States, while others maintain that the policy was sound but engendered expectations in the United States that were bound to be disappointed. This shift was stimulated initially by growing concern over the activities of the Soviet Union in Ethiopia and South Yemen and its support for the Cuban presence in Angola and Mozambique. The 'discovery' of a Soviet Brigade in Cuba, the Vietnamese invasion of Cambodia, the ouster of Somoza in Nicaragua and the civil war in El Salvador strengthened this concern. It was, however, the invasion of Afghanistan that catalyzed a shift in view, suggesting that the Soviet Union, after a fairly lengthy period of consolidation, was once again aggressively seeking to extend its influence.

Whether or not the Soviet 'threat' has increased significantly is the subject of considerable controversy. (The various arguments will be discussed under 'The Political Process', as will their implications for US-Third World relations.) Clearly, what happens in the developing countries will be a key determinant of the intentions and actions of superpower adversaries. Hopefully, however, the security issue will not deflect attention from a new factor in US foreign policy – the increasing importance of the Third World to US economic interests.

Economic Interests

American economic involvement in the developing countries as a whole did not reach a significant level until the twentieth century. Prior to 1900, the international transactions of the United States were very similar to those of a developing country (which the US in fact was). America in large part traded crude materials and food to Europe in return for manufactured products. In most years before the turn of the century, the US balance of payments showed current account deficits being offset by net capital inflows, the latter of which played no small part in financing American development. Not until after the First World War did the US record net investment outflows.

As its economy matured, America's business activity in developing countries became more pronounced, particularly in Latin America. In 1929, almost half of the total US foreign direct investment was located in Latin America, almost three times as much as investment in Western Europe. In that same year, nearly one-fifth of total US exports were sold to and a quarter of total US imports were purchased from Latin America. Following the Great Depression of the 1930s, US economic relations with other developing countries, especially in the Middle East and Far East, grew in intensity. However, rapidly growing trade and investment transactions with Western Europe and Japan in the post-Second World War period reduced the attention given to economic relations with the Third World – until the 1970s.

The establishment of coherent US policies on specific functional areas of US-Third World economic relations is hampered by several factors. First, knowledge of the growing extent of US interests in economic relations with developing countries is limited due to the historical insulation of the US economy and primary emphasis placed on intra-OECD concerns. Secondly, misconceptions of the levels and forms of transactions with the Third World, as well as their impact on US interests, have led to the perception of developing countries being threats rather than economic partners capable of contributing positively to American well-being. Finally, and perhaps most importantly, real conflicts do emerge between different domestic economic sectors on individual policy issues, resulting in the greater likelihood that difficult decisions will be postponed or compromised.

Trade

While the composition of US trade with individual developing countries varies enormously, trade between the US and the Third World as a whole follows a predictable pattern: the US exports machinery, transport equipment and other relatively sophisticated manufactures and agricultural products to the developing countries, which in turn sell oil, other primary goods and labour-intensive consumer goods to the US. In other words, trade has developed broadly as one would expect according to comparative advantage — relative abundance of land, capital and technology in the US, matched by relative abundance of natural resources and labour in developing countries. In fact, since trade among industrialized countries is concentrated in similar categories differentiated primarily by quality and taste, US trade with developing countries is probably more in the US interest than trade with other developed countries due to the major differences in comparative advantage. In theory, this is because greater gains from trade are achievable when differentials of factor endowments (and costs) are more pronounced between trading countries, since trade results in the more efficient (less expensive) production of goods. However, the belief that trade along these lines is in the overall American interest is not universally shared.

The Third World as a whole represents the largest market for US goods. Developing market economies purchased 37 per cent of total US exports in 1979, a share larger than that of US exports to all other countries other than Canada. This 37 per cent share is also significantly larger than the average 25 per cent share of industrial country exports purchased by developing economies.

In spite of the large volume of American exports to developing countries, the US is experiencing a significant merchandise trade deficit *vis-à-vis* the Third World, amounting to some $33.6 billion 1979 (in 1980 the figure was $36 billion), therefore raising complaints of 'exported jobs' by certain sectors in the United States. But the aggregate figure is deceiving. Of the total $97.7 billion in US imports from developing countries in 1979, over half, or $54.3 billion, was accounted for by oil and petroleum products. The United States continues to record large surpluses in manufactured goods trade with the Third World, the surplus amounting to some $19 billion in 1979. Some 40 per cent of total US exports of manufactures are sold to developing countries. Since it has been estimated that about one out of eight jobs in manufacturing is attributed to exports, this suggests that somewhere in the order of one out of every 20 US jobs in manufacturing is accounted for by exports to the Third World. In addition, the US sells large amounts of agricultural products to developing countries on commercial and concessional terms.

While the US trade balance with the developing countries is quite favourable (with the exception of oil), US imports of manufactured goods from the Third World are growing rapidly, at an average growth rate for US imports of manufactures from all sources. The share of developing-country manufactures exports to the US as a proportion of total US imports of manufactured goods has risen from 16 per cent in 1965 to 24 per cent in 1979. Although not large in a macro-economic sense, these imports are concentrated in 'sensitive' commodity categories (textiles, footwear, consumer electronics), i.e. those requiring labour-intensive production and competing with relatively stagnant sectors in the US economy. This type of trade leads directly to the classical case of increased efficiency in the economy as a whole and welfare gains to consumers, but losses of employment opportunities in declining industries. An analysis based on a survey of actual US retail sales found that imports from developing countries were as much as 16.3 per cent cheaper than their domestically produced counterparts of comparable quality. By comparison, imports from developed areas were only marginally less expensive (0.4 per cent) than comparable US goods. Overall, American consumers were estimated to save more than $2 billion per year as a direct result of purchasing less expensive imports. This is particularly important for low-income consumers, whom the study sees as saving as much as 13.1 per cent on the purchase of imported goods rather than domestic goods.[7]

In public debates over policies affecting US imports of Third World products, the interests of consumers are often viewed as contradictory to the interests of workers. The welfare gains to consumers are significant, but they are dispersed widely throughout the economy, whereas displacement of employment opportunities is concentrated in a relatively few industries (e.g. textiles and apparel, footwear, consumer electronics, etc.). Even though the macro-economic employment effects of these imports are negligible (affecting perhaps one-tenth of one per cent of employment per year), especially when compared to other job displacement factors such as automation and shifts in demand, the fact that they are highly visible and subject to national policy has led unions and firms to focus a large amount of attention on them.

In response to these conflicting interests, the US government has adopted a policy of keeping markets relatively open to imports of manufactures from developing countries, but at the same time placing controls on certain imports growing at above-normal rates in 'sensitive' sectors (e.g. textiles, footwear, television sets, etc.). A large number of these 'sensitive' products have also been excluded from the US generalized system of preferences extended to developing countries. Finally, the US has taken the lead among industrialized countries in urging the advanced developing countries (ADCs) such as Brazil, Mexico and Korea to 'graduate' in the sense of receiving less preferential treatment and opening up their markets to imports from developed and other developing countries This policy of maintaining modified access to Third World goods and applying pressure for ADC trade liberalization is not likely to be altered in the foreseeable future. The initial indications are that the Reagan Administration will put a higher priority on lowering trade barriers. The 'orderly marketing agreements' with Asian countries on shoe imports were abolished. Although the current Administration has voiced a strong preference for liberalized trade, its policies are not yet fully articulated.

Commodities

Because the US is both a large producer and a large consumer of raw materials, the US interest in commodity production and trade is more complex than that of other developed countries. The US is not as dependent on imports of raw materals as are the EEC or Japan, but does import significant amounts of commodities from developing countries. For example, in 1976, US net imports from developing market economies accounted for 88 per cent of domestic consumption of columbium, 82 per cent of tin, 56 per cent of aluminium and 50 per cent of manganese. Literally all US consumption of certain items such as rubber, coffee, cocoa, hard fibres, jute, etc., are accounted for by imports from the Third World. On the other hand, the US produces large quantities of minerals such as iron, lead, copper and phosphates, although most of these are consumed domestically rather than exported.

A recent debate has grown over the potential for 'resource wars', particularly concerning the security of supply of certain key industrial raw materials, the supply of which is dominated either by the states of Southern Africa, particularly South Africa, or by the USSR. For instance, 96 per cent of known deposits of chromium are in South Africa and Zimbabwe. Most analysts have concluded, however, that these fears are exaggerated. Producer governments will continue to sell resources because they need foreign exchange and a series of domestic measures in importing countries can buffer any possible short-term disruptions.

The direct US interest in world trade of commodities is access to supplies of needed materials at reasonable prices and expansion of market sales of commodities produced by the US, again at remunerative prices. Added to this are the broader interests of assuring that world demand is largely met (for humanitarian reasons as well as avoiding negative feedback effects of shortages), dampening major fluctuations in commodity prices and promoting sufficient investment in raw materials industries in order to satisfy growth in demand. A recently published analysis concludes that the largest measurable economic benefits from commodity price stabilization would be gains to the *industrial* countries, including the United States, from reduced inflationary pressures.[8]

The actual record of the US strategy and policy towards commodities does not uniformly coincide with the admittedly generalized notion of the US interest, for three basic reasons. First, following the strategy of buy cheap and sell dear, the US rejects an integrated approach for dealing with all major commodities at the same time, preferring instead a case-by-case approach where specific US producer and consumer interests can be identified and balanced. Secondly, in the wake of OPEC's success in unilaterally raising the price of petroleum, the US actively resists the growth and questions the efficacy of producer cartels. Finally, perhaps more than any other country, the United States has been deeply ambivalent in its attitude towards market interventions. On the one hand, the American people and government extol the virtues of market mechanisms and castigate the evils of administered prices. On the other hand, the United States has had a long history of market interventions in terms of subsidies, price floors (wages, agricultural products), price ceilings (oil) and regulation of economic activity.

American ambiguity towards commodity issues has been reflected in its policies. Historically, the United States has participated in commodity agreements on sugar and coffee. When UNCTAD put forth its proposal for an Integrated Programme for Commodities (IPC) in 1974, however, the United States initially opposed the initiative, probably based on fears of new cartels. In recent years the US Congress has completed action in implementing legislation for participation in the International Sugar Agreement and International Coffee Agreement. An International Natural Rubber Agreement has been reached and joined by the United States. The United States participated in the recently concluded negotiations on a new International Cocoa Agreement, but did not join the agreement. Initially a strong opponent of the proposal for a Common Fund to finance commodity agreements, the United States eventually agreed to its formation but has succeeded in limiting the amount of direct contributions to the fund and has declined thus far to contribute to the 'second window' (a mechanism within the Common Fund to finance Third World efforts at diversification, market promotion, research and development, etc.). On a separate but related issue, the United States participated in the negotiation of the Wheat Agreement, which reached a consensus among major producers and consumers but collapsed due to developing-country disagreement over stockpile release prices and maintenance costs.

In sum, the United States appears to have employed a gradualist approach towards commodity issues in its attempt to bargain strongly to satisfy current domestic producer and consumer interests, which may have the effect of sacrificing long-term objectives on behalf of short-term concerns.

The Food Issues

One commodity of particular importance to the United States is cereal grains, of which it is the world's largest exporter, accounting for sixty per cent of total world trade in 1980/1. The 40 per cent of these exports that go to the developing countries constitute nearly two-thirds of the latter's imports. If control of a vital resource is a mark of national strength, then food is surely one important element of US strength – especially *vis-à-vis* the Third World.

Besides meeting domestic consumption requirements, US food production brought in more than $40 billion gross and $20 billion net in export earnings in 1980, a significant contribution to the balance of payments. With a population of less than five per cent of the world total the United States produces 13 per cent of the world's wheat (the major food grain traded), 29 per cent of the world's coarse grains (mainly maize) and 62 per cent of the world's soy beans. Though a small producer, the United States is the world's leading rice exporter. US corporations, operating in the relatively unregulated US market, dominate international grain trade.

One out of three US farm acres produces for export, and about one out of five for export to developing countries. US farmers depend on developing countries for about two-fifths of their export market. Developing country food imports increased threefold between 1960 and 1977, and the bulk of this increase came from the United States. The $20 billion of US food imports, mainly from developing countries, included mainly beverages, sugar and tropical fruits and vegetables.

In addition to its leadership in production and trade, the United States also holds a major share of world stocks of such basic food products as wheat flour, coarse grains and oilseeds (mainly soy beans). These stocks are vital for providing food aid and emergency assistance to refugees and for responding to harvest shortfalls and natural disasters. Not only regular US food exports, but also the large proportion of food stocks held in the United States, are important factors in pursuing US interests in the Third World.

The enlarging market for US grain in the developing countries is intensifying pressure on the US agricultural resource base, leading to questions as to the United States' ability to keep pace indefinitely with the role of 'feeding the world' as residual supplier. Competition for agricultural land, rising production costs and input prices, reduction in soil productivity, growing energy dependence, lowering of underground water tables, environmental deterioration, crop vulnerability due to monoculture (especially of grains), levelling off of research activity and climatic changes have all led to a narrowing of that resource base. Although dramatic scientific and technological breakthroughs might possibly produce another 'green revolution', a gradually declining production growth rate is more likely for the next decade or two.

A significant consequence of US current dominance in food is its potential for playing a leadership role in maintaining global food security and improving the international food system. If current worldwide production patterns continue, it will become steadily more difficult for the United States to meet the rising international demand for cereals, especially in the Third World, without a sharp escalation in prices. The United States, therefore, has a direct self-interest stake in helping developing countries increase their food production and improve its distribution. Food aid buys time and can assist development, but it cannot over the long-term make up for food deficits in the developing countries.

Energy

In the energy field the shoe is on the other foot. In that area the US interest is to obtain sufficient supplies of energy at predictable prices (which is not necessarily the same as low or unchanging prices) for adequate but prudent consumption by industrial and individual users.

US consumption of energy historically has not been prudent. Several decades of abundant supplies and declining real prices led to wasteful consumption patterns. In 1978, *per capita* consumption of energy in the United States, almost 11.374 kg of coal equivalent, was nearly double that of the average consumption of industrialized countries (7,060 kg) and over seventy times that of low-income countries (161 kg). The oil supply constraints and price rises of the 1970s have not until recently altered US consumption patterns, largely due to the domestic US energy policy which through the regulation of price of domestic output maintained consumer prices at levels well below those incurred in other countries. US oil consumption relative to output now has begun to decrease sharply, due to conservative measures and domestic recession. The recent decision to deregulate the domestic price of oil should accelerate this trend.

The problem of high US consumption of energy, which is based on the historical abundance of energy resources available to Americans, has had negative effects on nearly all other areas of economic relations with both developing and developed countries. US imports of oil and petroleum products, totalling $59 billion in 1979 ($53 billion of which came from developing countries, primarily members of OPEC), has been the leading factor contributing to US trade deficits. These aggregate deficits in turn have at times led to the depreciation of the dollar and have reinforced protectionist sentiments towards non-oil imports. Consumption patterns cannot be changed overnight, but reduced US demand for energy is clearly in the best interest of the United States, other industrialized countries and developing countries. This point has been made with increasing frequency and decreasing subtlety over the past several years.

Increased US dependence on OPEC energy supplies has already led the US to alter its attitude towards and strategy in the Middle East and Persian Gulf and to exert massive diplomatic efforts to resolve the Arab-Israeli conflict, although a final solution agreeable to all has yet to be reached. The United States is also attempting to improve its often-neglected relations with Mexico, which has the potential for becoming a major world supplier of energy.

In the longer run, energy shortages, whether in terms of physical supplies or in the form of high production costs, have the potential to dampen the growth prospects and welfare of all countries. The United States, like other countries, therefore has an interest in the expansion of world energy production, the attainment of greater energy self-sufficiency by the developing countries, and the implementation of necessary domestic conservation measures. This implies the need for much greater emphasis on investment in and research and development of conventional and alternative sources of energy.

The Role of International Investments

US investments in the Third World are large, highly visible and important to both host and home countries. These investments provide the United States with significant levels of raw materials, manufactures and income.

Over 21 per cent of cumulative US foreign direct investment at year-end 1976 was in developing countries, or about $29 billion out of a total of $137 billion. In 1979 the total value was $44.9 billion, an increase of 18.6 per cent from 1978. In the 1970-9 period, US investments (excluding investments in the petroleum sector) grew at an average annual rate of 29 per cent in developing countries while the figure for developed countries was 16 per cent. Almost 37 per cent of total US direct investment income in 1980 originated in developing countries. The Third World provided by far the bulk of *net* US service transaction earnings, some $22.7 billion or 66 per cent of the 1980 total, much of which was accounted for by direct and other private investment income. In addition to growth in direct investment, US private bank lending to developing countries has rapidly expanded in recent years. US banks account for some 60 per cent of total commercial bank claims on non-oil middle-income counries. US bank claims on developing countries amounted to $96.8 billion at the end of 1980, growing at an average rate of about 30 per cent per year following the oil crisis. Interest from these loans constitute large and growing shares of US banks' overall revenue.

Foreign investment by US firms, and its costs and benefits both to the United States and to the host country, has been the subject of intense debate over the past decade. Those who contend that foreign investment promotes American interests hold that capital flows have the effect of encouraging exports as well as imports, in addition to providing returns to investors, thus giving the United States a 'piece of the action' that would otherwise go to other countries' firms if capital outflows were restricted. To these advocates, foreign investment benefits the United States by encouraging efficiency, raising the quantity and quality of employment, and providing access to needed raw materials. However, opponents of this view argue that foreign investment undermines American interests. To them, the multinational corporations (MNCs) export capital and technology and thereby 'displace' domestic investment, employment and growth.

In spite of these contradictory assertions of American interests, official policies have with few exceptions favoured the free flow of capital and technology. The government promotes US investment in the Third World, both as a means of achieving the 'positive' US gains described above and a method of inducing capital formation in developing countries. This policy almost certainly will be expanded and given priority by the current Administration.

While its overall approach towards US investments in developing countries has been one of *laissez-faire*, the US government has intervened when it perceives American economic or strategic interests to be at stake. Most policy measures are directed at objectives in functional areas such as trade, balance of payments and taxes, which relate to US investment in all countries. The Hickenlooper Amendment, which provides the legal basis for automatically cutting off bilateral assistance to countries which expropriate US property without prompt and adequate compensation, has been used only once, but political and economic pressures have been applied in cases where US investments were seized. As an added protection to US investors in developing countries, the Overseas Private Investment Corporation (OPIC), an independent government organization, provides insurance against certain non-commercial risks. Finally, the United States pursues its foreign policy goals and ethical concerns via investment policies, including anti-corruption regulations, restrictions on investment in 'unfriendly' nations, anti-boycott legislation, etc.

Foreign Assistance

Each year requests for foreign assistance appropriations are put forward on the basis of two premisses: promoting the general US interest in world development and stability, and advancing specific US interests (including security interests) in the Third World. In the regional breakdown of the flow of US economic assistance (including security supporting assistance, development assistance, Public Law 480 and other programmes such as the Peace Corps), the Middle East is the largest recipient region, which, with Egypt, Israel, Syria and Jordan, accounts for almost one-third of total US economic assistance. This is a direct result of the significant US geo-political interest in the Middle East and the Persian Gulf regions. South Asia, with India, Pakistan and Bangladesh among the ten top recipients of US aid, is another major recipient region, with assistance being primarily geared towards promoting development efforts in the area. The Philippines and Indonesia receive large amounts of American aid, in the former case because of historical ties and as compensation for military bases. Direct domestic gains from the US aid programme are ensured by the fact that three-quarters of the budget of the Agency for International Development (AID) is spent in the US to purchase American goods and services. The food assistance programme administered under Public Law 480 also is of direct benefit to US agriculture.

In addition to these and other related interests, the United States benefits indirectly from economic growth and progress in developing countries through commercial transactions with developing countries. Finally, and not insignificantly, the United States has a humanitarian interest in eliminating the worst aspects of global poverty, meeting the basic human needs of the world's poor, and improving the condition of political, economic and human rights world-wide.

The positive interests outlined above are confronted by the fact that aid is viewed in the United States largely as a cost, with actual or potential benefits largely ignored. This view is reinforced by the current climate of budgetary stringency. Other opponents of aid claim that the humanitarian aspects of foreign assistance are not being met, that aid recipients demonstrate little goodwill towards the United States and that pressing domestic problems deserve prior attention. The strategy of those who hold these views has been to limit overall assistance and to place conditions on aid disbursements. Allocating only 0.20 per cent of GNP to official development assistance, the United States ranked very low compared to other donor countries in 1979.

Within the agencies charged with administering foreign assistance, several conflicts arise with respect to US interests. One such conflict is that between aid for economic development purposes and aid to promote security interests, which affects the functional and geographic allocation of funds. Another divergence exists between short-term specific US interests which lead to policies like tied aid, and broader long-term interests which might suggest more efficient use of capital transfers. Administrators must also cope with differences which emerge between humanitarian and strategic objectives, which have direct impact on the questions of aid flows to authoritarian regimes or countries ideologically opposed to the United States. These conflicts result in a rather eclectic US policy which is not satisfactory to either developing countries or American constituencies.

The advent of the Reagan Administration has cast into sharp focus questions concerning the role of foreign aid. Previous American governments had begun to shift emphasis to multilateral aid institutions, most particularly the World Bank. The Reagan approach puts more emphasis on bilateral aid due to the feeling by some in the Administration that multilateral institutions are too large, support governments and programmes not congruent with American interests, and are not in control of their donors. In addition, the increased emphasis on security policy leads to a shift towards direct and indirect military assistance and/or aid to countries in which the United States has security interests.

International Institutions and Systems

The United States played an instrumental role in the establishment of post-Second World War institutions involved with economic, political and security relations. Many systems and organizations dealing with economic matters (particularly those which emerged from Bretton Woods) and strategic concerns (e.g. NATO, SEATO, etc.) were largely of US design, and the creation of the United Nations system received a strong US endorsement.

Some of these institutions have been more successful than others with respect to their impact on US interests. Debates over whether or not individual institutional arrangements and practices have been skewed in favour of the United States have been long standing and will continue. All of these systems have evolved over time, some to the liking of the United States and others to American disfavour. The US Administration and/or Congress have reacted strongly to institutional developments or policies perceived as negative to US interests: examples include the temporary US withdrawal from the International Labour Organization (ILO), attempts to block multilateral bank loans to countries of which the United States disapproves, and efforts to withhold or restrict general or functionally-related funding of the United Nations and its operations.

Looking beyond specific conflicts and functional detail, one can conclude that the United States' three principal interests have been well served by these institutions. Those objectives are the avoidance of another major world war, the prevention of another major depression, and the reconstruction of the economies of the Second World War combattants. Against those standards the post-war system has performed rather well, and while the conflicts and crises experienced in recent years cannot be considered inconsequential, they pale against the possibilities of major war or economic collapse. Indeed that is part of the reason that the United States resists any but marginal changes in these institutions.

Over the last several decades, an additional goal has been added to those listed above, improving the prospects of the world's poorest people so that their citizens can some day overcome the certainty of starvation, disease and indignity. The goal of development is clearly in the interest of the United States in that a large portion of the world's population faces conditions akin to those of war and depression on a permanent basis.

Third World countries have achieved different degrees of progress in their development efforts, and international institutions have contributed to this progress. But it has not been enough, and insufficient progress in the Third World has fomented increasing calls for reforms in international economic and political institutions. The United States has in large part resisted the NIEO proposals on the ground that they will not significantly promote development, but also to some degree on the basis that the proposals are not considered in the US interest.

The United States does not totally oppose institutional reform, as evidenced by its support of recent changes in the structures and operations of the GATT and the IMF, but rather pursues a policy by which reform is gradual and is implemented in such a fashion as to minimize or avoid altogether any reductions in the level of US influence. To this end the United States has been loath to relinquish the significant control it exercises in 'functional' international institutions such as the IMF, the GATT and the World Bank. The US reaction to the increasing militancy and perceived 'anti-Americanism' of the developing countries in forums such as the UN system has been to retreat to organizations viewed as less hostile. Finally, the decline of US economic hegemony, ongoing balance-of-payments deficits, and reduced confidence in the dollar and the role it plays in international finance, have combined to place the United States in a defensive position *vis-à-vis* both developed and developing countries. The natural strategy for a country with a defensive posture is to maintain as much control as possible, avoid sweeping systematic change, and limit actions which appear to have the effect of further deterioration on its position.

The Political Process

The preceding sections have dealt with perceived and actual American interests in the developing countries. This section analyzes some of the influences on the formulation of American policies towards the Third World, including the influence of bureaucratic politics, the growing role of Congress in foreign policy issues and the impact of pressure groups and public opinion.

Bureaucratic Politics

The Executive Branch of the federal government has no centralized structure either for making decisions or implementing policy on the broad range of issues that concern the developing countries. Functional areas of responsibility are dispersed widely among federal departments and agencies which in turn guard their independence and influence. Interdepartmental rivalries and conflicts are inevitable, often resulting in the fragmentation of policies.

The Department of State oversees relations with individual governments in the developing countries but gives the developing countries as a group secondary priority to relations with the industrial countries or with the Soviet Union. The Department maintains control over bilateral development assistance through its domination of AID. The Department's interests, however, extend beyond economic development and into other issues of foreign policy. As a result, it often views development assistance as a political instrument to be used for short-run purposes of gaining influence or otherwise affecting events, a view which at times has caused major conflicts with AID and will be more marked in the immediate future.

United States participation in the international financial institutions and contributions to multilateral assistance efforts are managed by the Department of Treasury, which also formulates American policy on international monetary issues. The administration of the PL-480 (Food for Peace) Program is jointly shared by AID and the Department of Agriculture. Trade policy, on the other hand, is negotiated by the Office of the United States Trade Representative in the White House, but the administration of trade policies and programmes is divided among a myriad of departments and agencies, including the International Trade Commission, the Export-Import Bank, the Departments of Treasury, State, Labor, Agriculture, Commerce, etc. The Department of Defense oversees military sales, but other departments, primarily the Department of State, have an influence in this process. Investment policies fall within the domain of Treasury and Commerce, but there is also a separate Overseas Private Investment Corporation, and the Department of State maintains some measure of say in this area.

With such a diffusion of power the role of individuals often becomes exceedingly important and the question of who within the bureaucratic structure dominates and who does not varies from time to time and from administration to administration. In the Nixon Administratration the struggles between the Department of Treasury and Department of State on policy concerning the developing countries were legion. The then Secretary of Treasury William Simon and his subordinates felt very strongly that the proposals of the developing countries for a new international economic order were contrary to American interests and indeed to the laws of economics. Secretary of State Henry Kissinger and Under Secretary Charles Robinson, however, were prepared to compromise with the developing countries for both economic and political reasons. Kissinger, probably because of his dominance over foreign policy-making in the United States in those years, was able to prevail over Treasury but not without mammoth bureaucratic struggles, which often resulted in US policy being enunciated too late to be effective. Under the Carter Administration, much of the decision-making on North-South issues was concentrated in the Department of State, but within the Bureau of Economic Affairs rather than the Bureau of International Organization Affairs or the Agency for International Development. Again the problem of co-ordinating policies with other agencies arose. Treasury resistance to centralizing decisions on foreign assistance crippled reorganization attempts, and laborious efforts to negotiate positions *within* the Executive Branch were difficult and time-consuming.

Within the American federal system there are usually two textbook solutions for dealing with policies that involve a number of cabinet departments and agencies; either all existing programmes are combined in one separate 'super agency', or the policies are co-ordinated within the White House. Both approaches have been tried in recent years. In 1973 a Development Coordination Committee (DCC) was created (by Congressional action) within the Agency for International Development to co-ordinate many of the diverse programmes relating to United States' interests in the developing countries. The DCC was not effective either in the Nixon and Ford years or under the Carter Administration.

The 1979 Carter Administration plan for the reorganization of the US foreign aid programme, which arose due to Congressional pressures, attempted to streamline US policy-making *vis-à-vis* the Third World. This plan established the International Development Cooperation Agency (IDCA) to administer and co-ordinate – but not operate – most US foreign aid programmes. IDCA oversaw the activities of AID, the Overseas Private Investment Corporation (OPIC), and some of the Administration's input into the development efforts of the United Nations and the multilateral and regional development banks and agencies. The Director of IDCA was principal adviser to the President on international development matters and also advised the President on all trade, science and technology and other matters significantly affecting the developing countries. The Director reported to the President, and, on foreign policy matters, to the Secretary of State. These arrangements proved at best half a loaf. The mandate of the new agency did not include authority over the multilateral development banks and the relationship with AID took many months to work out.

The other strategy — co-ordination through the White House — also has been tried with varying degrees of success during the past few years. The Carter Administration restructured the National Security Council staff to oversee relations with the developing countries, but co-ordination of governmental policies has proved difficult. The underlying problem was a lack of priority for North-South issues on the part of the President and his chief advisers, and the consequent small amount of time and attention given to these concerns. Without the interest of the Chief Executive, or at least of his designated surrogate in the field of foreign affairs, no amount of organizational tinkering will serve to change the low priority accorded to relations with the developing countries. The result has been a lack of coherence and follow-through on most North-South issues.[9]

The Unique Role of Congress

The US Congress plays a role in the determining of American foreign policy that is perhaps unique among the industrial countries. The American constitution provides that authority over foreign policy — including power over war, treaties, appointments and commerce — be shared between the Executive and the Legislative Branch. In addition, Congress wields effective control over budgetary authorizations and appropriations, including foreign assistance expenditures. This wide range of powers gives the Congress opportunity to negate Executive Branch initiatives if it so wishes, or alternatively, to put forward its own programmes. It is well to remember, however, that power may be more widely dispersed within Congress than within the Executive Branch. For example, 13 of 19 standing committees have some responsibility for foreign economic expenditures and legislation, and almost 50 sub-committees have some jurisdiction over issues significantly affecting developing countries.[10] In contrast with parliamentary democracies, party discipline is weak. Douglas Bennet, a former Senate staff member and Administrator of AID has pointed out that: 'Partisanship does not bind the majority in Congress to the White House as much as the separation of powers separates them.'[11]

American history is replete with examples of Congress thwarting the international programmes of American presidents, the most notable example being the Senate's rejection of the Treaty of Versailles after the Second World War. In the post-1945 period, however, Congress shared the general Administration perception of American interests in the developing countries, and as a result, supported large military and economic aid programmes, as well as a series of security treaties linking the United States to other countries.

Since the mid-1960s, however, the congressional perception of its role in foreign affairs has undergone a considerable change. Here too, the Vietnam War was the major catalyst with particular congressional concern over the 'blank check' that had been voted by President Johnson in the Tonkin Gulf resolution. The aftermath has been the passage of a series of measures designed to limit the authority of the Executive Branch to commit American troops and engage in armed conflict. Congressional concern over excessive use (or abuse) of power by the Executive Branch was increased by the revelations of the covert activities of the Central Intelligence Agency not only in Chile but throughout the world, and by the Watergate scandals. A growing number of legislators view these events as the pattern to be expected of an Executive Branch unchecked by legislative control, and as a result, Congress is taking a much more active interest in a variety of policy issues. For instance, Congress must approve all arms sales agreements over $14 million, has an overview on intelligence operations, and inform- ally approves all development co-operation grants made by AID before that agency enters into an agreement with a foreign country.

The recent record of Congress in foreign affairs is mixed. The Exec- utive Branch maintains that Congress has been mainly obstructive, but the record is not that simple; on some issues Congress has been far ahead of the Executive Branch, particularly in the area of international development policy. It was Congress, not the Executive Branch, that initiated the reforms of the American foreign aid programme to focus it on basic human needs in 1973. And it was Congress which put forth the proposals for reforming the organization of the US government to deal with development issues comprehensively. In addition, pressures to enhance human rights originated in Congress, as did the requirement that the concessionally-loaned food aid provided by the United States go predominantly to the poorest countries rather than to those coun- tries in which the United States has a strategic foreign policy interest. There is, however, a negative side to this participation — the growth of a variety of special interest amendments to foreign policy legislation.

It is not likely that the trend towards greater Congressional activism will be revised despite the shift in party control of the Senate. The new willingness of Congress to vote military expenditures and cut domestic programmes should not be taken as a sign of a fundamental shift in power between Congress and the Executive Branch, but rather as a sign of ideological agreement at this moment. Congressional resistance to military aid to El Salvador and the sale of radar warning aircraft to Saudi Arabia are clear indications that it will not surrender its recently won power.

The Domination of the Budget Process

Decision-making within the American government is particularly shaped by the process of formulating, authorizing and appropriating the annual federal budget. The budget itself over time has become the main vehicle for determining federal policies, particularly in terms of defence and domestic social policy.

This budget process works well except for areas of public policy that are not large budgetary items. Discussions of policy towards the developing countries tend to be dominated by the annual foreign aid legislation. Unfortunately aid is only a small part of overall transactions between the United States and the Third World, and is a diminishing part of overall American economic transactions with developing countries, dwarfed by trade, investment and private bank lending. Nevertheless, it consumes an inordinate amount of time and attention of both the Executive Branch and Congress as the aid bill winds its way through the legislative process.

Interest Groups

A variety of organized interest groups affect decisions of American policies towards the developing countries. *Trade unions*, for instance, which generally have provided the leadership for social reform in the United States, remain a potent political force despite the fact that the overall rate of unionization of the US labour force has fallen from 33 per cent in the mid-1950s to 23 per cent. Many unions, however, have shifted their outlook on relations with the developing countries for reasons of both self-interest and altered domestic economic conditions. Until the mid-1960s, when the US was in a strong international position with a monopoly on capital- and technology-intensive products and continuous trade surpluses, the unions favoured free trade and open markets. But as the trade balance swung into deficit, the US manufacturing sector diminished relative to the service sector and capital continued to flow out of the country, some unions altered their stance. The organized labour movement still continues to support aid to the developing countries, but would like to see it focused on the poorest countries. But many unions worry about the transfer of technology leading to the loss of American jobs. Indeed, outflows of private capital, whether government subsidized or not, are seen as exporting US jobs to the Third World, and technology transfers are seen as selling the 'US heritage'.

The position of individual labour unions on trade issues, for instance, varies widely depending on the industry. Unions in those industries hit hardest by imports from the developing countries (textiles, shoes and electronics), strongly favour restrictions on trade while those whose members benefit from exports (aerospace, agricultural implements, chemicals and farm products) urge more liberalized trade. All unions, however, do agree strongly that the interests of the labour movement are not taken into account in the formulation of international economic policies, particularly as they concern the developing countries.

On the whole, the *business sector* tends to have fewer reservations than labour about the adverse effects of trade liberalization since, in most cases, it is more mobile and thus better able to adapt to changing circumstances. However, the viewpoint of individual firms or industries depends on the nature of their business. A number of firms benefit directly from relations with the Third World, whether as a source of their raw materials or as a market for their manufactured goods. And US banks generate significant amounts of profits on their lending activities in developing countries. Others, however, threatened by the competition of imports from the developing countries, have become increasingly protectionist. This is particularly true of the steel, electronics and textile industries.

The business community carries considerable weight in the political process. Corporations act collectively through the Chamber of Commerce, the National Association of Manufacturers, industry associations and the Business Roundtable, a group of high level corporate leaders. In addition, individual corporations and business leaders influence policy-making through contributions to political campaigns.

The impact on overall US policy towards the developing countries has been mixed. Business organizations have long supported programmes of foreign assistance and individual corporate leaders have spoken publicly on the importance of growth in the developing countries to progress in the United States. But the major efforts usually are put into specific programmes of direct interest to particular corporations. Thus the auto and steel industries have lobbied for protection against foreign imports, while major exporting corporations have favoured expansion of export credits and trade liberalization measures.

The strategy of US business has been remarkably pragmatic in practice. Particularly in the past five years, corporations have adapted to governments utilizing a variety of ideologies, provided that business needs for profit and predictability are met. One sees in this regard the rapid growth of American interest in investments in mainland China and arrangements with such 'radical' states as Algeria and Libya for oil and liquified natural gas. And American oil companies are quite prepared to co-operate with a Marxist regime in Angola when the Executive Branch continues to be strongly opposed to relations with that government on ideological grounds.

One sector of the US business community has a particularly strong interest in relations with developing countries and a strong influence over US policies — American agriculture. Farmers and agribusinesses have long supported food sales and aid to the Third World, but have also reacted against rising imports of competing products and against commodity agreements considered detrimental to the interests of US producers.

Attitudes of US economic sectors have been affected by the lack of adjustment mechanisms. While the United States is in many ways in a stronger economic position than some of the other OECD countries, it lacks a basic set of policies to deal with domestic economic dislocation, whether caused by trade with the developing countries or by other reasons such as migration of industry within the United States. Adjustment policies are inadequate at several levels. For instance, the United States is the only industrial country (except for South Africa) without some type of national health care scheme, and the provisions of American law allowing workers to transfer their pension credits when they switch jobs are still rudimentary. Beyond that, however, there is a lack of co-ordinated government policies to deal with the changes implied in a rapidly evolving world economy. Existing trade adjustment assistance, for instance, is entirely inadequate. It first became law in 1962, but *no* benefits were paid under that scheme until 1969. Even now the federal programmes designed to provide trade adjustment assistance are unable to meet the needs of workers (a very small percentage) who lose their jobs due to import competition.

As a result, there is a strong feeling in the American labour movement and parts of American business that the costs of economic dislocation and change fall most heavily on workers, communities and firms; many, therefore, are not prepared to support policies which appear to have an adverse effect on American labour.

Minority and ethnic groups also exert an influence on American foreign policy towards the developing countries, often much more effectively than indicated by the size of the groups. As one US Senator recently has written: 'The "secret weapon" of ethnic interest groups is neither money nor technique, which are available to other interest groups as well, but the ability to galvanize for specific political objectives the strong emotional bonds of large numbers of Americans to their cultural or ancestral homes.'[12] The impact of the Jewish constituency on American policy in the Middle East is perhaps the best-known example. But in recent years a similar role has been played by other groups: for instance, Americans of Greek descent have blocked resumption of American arms aid and sales to Turkey, pending a resolution of the Greek-Turkish dispute over Cyprus. In this case, a relatively small constituency with well-placed Congressional support could block a major programme of support for a NATO ally seen by the President as crucial to America's interests. There is also a growing interest among black Americans regarding US policy towards Africa, as a result of raised consciousness over civil rights within the United States. Pressure from black Americans has not yet reached a point equal to that of the American Jewish community, but there is a growing unwillingness among American blacks to see the United States continue to support white-dominated regimes, particularly in Southern Africa. Their influence was indicated by President Carter's decision not to lift economic sanctions against Zimbabwe-Rhodesia. In addition, the emergence of what is now known as 'Mex-America' (the Mexican community within the United States) and the growing strength of Spanish-speaking voters in some crucial states, particularly in the southwest, means that American policies not only towards Mexico but also towards the rest of Latin America may at some time in the future be subject to domestic pressures not dissimilar to that exerted by American Jews on the Middle East.

Other interest groups have a varying impact on formulation of US policies towards the developing countries. Consumer groups, interested in the benefits to be derived from low-cost imports of manufactures from the Third World, are growing in number but are not very influential in policy circles. Religious and other public-interest organizations lobby for increased aid and other measures to support the developing countries. These groups have grown in importance and in impact since the food crisis in the early 1970s and the subsequent World Food Conference. They have become the nucleus of a nascent development lobby which has succeeded in increasing public support for foreign aid in the United States at a time when most pressures are running in the other direction.

Finally, there are the so-called 'single issue' pressure groups that can apply a positive or negative influence on American policy. These operate in such areas as human rights, population or the environment. The effective environmental lobby, for instance, pressured Congress and the Administration for increasingly strict environmental standards for industry in the United States. One result has been some relocation of 'polluting industries' to the developing countries whose standards are not as stringent and where investment is welcome. This in turn has led environmental groups to press for the application of domestic environmental standards for all US programmes of aid, export credit financing and investment insurance.

Public Opinion

In the early 1970s it was fashionable to say that Americans once more were becoming isolationist and withdrawing from responsibilities in the world. This conclusion was based on the diminution of concern with Cold War problems and the consequent unwillingness to consider using military power to accomplish US objectives. It is now apparent, however, that this shift in opinion was not so much towards isolationism *per se*, but rather towards a growing concern with domestic problems, complemented by an increased belief that détente with the Soviet Union and China was both desirable and possible. In the latter years of the 1970s, successive polls on foreign policy issues clearly showed that Americans did not want to withdraw from the world, but that their attention had turned to economic problems which have strong domestic implications. For instance, a recent survey[13] of possible foreign policy goals for the United States by the Chicago Council on Foreign Relations elicited the following suggestions in order of priority: maintaining the value of the dollar, securing adequate supply of energy, protecting jobs of American workers, world-wide arms control and combating world hunger. The only two non-economic goals (other than arms control) within that same ranking were 'containing Communism' and 'defending our allies' security'.

In recent months, there has been a resurgence in concern about the actions of the Soviet Union and about America's military security. Stimulated by the Soviet invasion of Afghanistan, Russian activity in Africa and growing Soviet military power, support for increased defence expenditures and for a more aggressive US posture seems to be growing. This does not, however, translate into approval of direct military intervention in areas such as Central America, indicating that the impact of the American experience in Vietnam remains strong.

Developing-country issues in general have, however, a low priority for most people in the United States. There still is a considerable gap between the public and the leadership in understanding the growing US economic interdependence with the developing countries and the need to make adjustments over the long term. Therefore, public opinion — as opposed to special interests — has its greatest influence in setting the general atmosphere as in the current furore over government spending and inflation.

Americans do, however, strongly support humanitarian programmes aimed at the developing countries. Surveys which have attempted to assess American attitudes towards poverty and development concluded again and again that Americans feel a responsibility for contributing directly to programmes which reach poor people within the developing countries. For this reason, support for the concept of basic human needs is considerable, and for this reason also the humanitarian lobby within Congress has had an impact. Finally, it is worth noting that on a *per capita* basis, voluntary contributions by Americans to agencies with programmes in the developing countries are higher than most other developed countries.

One final note concerning American attitudes towards developing countries is in order. Currently there is no viable movement on the left on either domestic or international affairs that has influence in the United States. In fact, the main critique of current US policy comes from the conservatives. There is no major pressure from the left being exerted on US policy-makers, and no effective force pushing them to take more far-reaching steps concerning the developing countries. There is, therefore, a comfortable certitude about taking centrist positions when issues concerning American relations with the developing countries arise.

The Reagan Administration: a Shift in Perspective

The preceding sections have attempted to sketch in the multiple aspects of US interests in the developing countries. The complex admixture of interests, tangible and intangible, that come into play on any specific US-Third World issue makes it very difficult to assess the extent to which the general philosophy of any US administration (which theoretically defines and pursues the collective US interest) is translated into policy. Indeed, one would be fortunate to find any administration which both had a comprehensive view of the Third World and adopted a consistent set of policies to match that view.

To a large extent, the special perspective of the Reagan Administration represents the culmination of a basic shift in the 'official' view of US relations with the developing countries. Parts of this shift were already taking place prior to the election of the current administration. Some portions of this perspective do not deal directly with the developing countries, although their implications for US-Third World relations are strong and clear. Rather the philosophy is a world view in which the developing countries have their special place.

The perspective − and position − that seems to be emerging is based on a shift in interpretation of four key issue areas, each of which has historically been a contentious aspect of US foreign policy. As such, shifts in interpretation have usually resulted in changes in policy approach. The four core issues are the following:

(1) The intentions of the Soviet Union, and the appropriate US response to Soviet actions.
(2) The appropriate level of US military power and employment of power in the Third World.
(3) The trade-off between change and stability in developing countries.
(4) The desirable strategy to pursue US economic interests abroad.

The Role of the Soviet Union

US foreign policy since the mid-1940s has been dominated by two divergent views of the international role of the Soviet Union. Proponents of the first school believe that the Soviet Union is an international revolutionary state committed to unrelenting ideological warfare powered by a messianic drive for world domination. The second school, while not ignoring competition with the Soviet Union, de-emphasizes the role of ideology and views the USSR as a traditional great power attempting to expand its reach within the existing international systems in a defensive rather than offensive strategy.[14]

Those who feel that the Soviet Union is bent on endlessly expanding its power believe strongly that competition with the USSR *must* remain the central focus of all US policy; other issues are of secondary importance at best or must be viewed in light of the relationship with the Soviet Union. On the other hand, those who see the Soviet Union as a powerful but essentially defensive nation-state suggest that other foreign policy issues should be dealt with on their own merits, apart from an overriding concern with their implications for US-Soviet relations.

In recent years, US concerns over the Soviet 'threat' have risen considerably, with important implications for US-Third World relations. Soviet activities in Afghanistan, Ethiopia and Southern Africa have been seen as evidence of their renewed expansionist drive, and many are worried about the Soviet's potential for cutting off the West's supply of oil from the Persian Gulf area. In an era of increasing Soviet assertiveness, the relative decline in American military power is seen as an invitation to Soviet adventurism, particularly in the Third World.

This viewpoint has been particularly marked in the initial pronouncements of the Reagan Administration, which have emphasized the need for increased defence spending. According to Secretary of State Alexander Haig, a 'major focus of American policy must be the Soviet Union, not because of ideological preoccupation, but simply because Moscow is the great source of international insecurity today ... Soviet promotion of violence as the instrument of change constitutes the greatest danger to the world.'[15] From this perspective flow a series of decisions about alliances with developing countries, policy priorities and the allocation of assistance between security and development programmes, with priority obviously given to the former.

The Level and Use of Power

America suffered a series of military and economic setbacks in the 1970s, leading to a reduction in US influence and loss of US pride. While some of these events were inevitable, they have in sum precipitated a backlash — growing public sentiment that the United States must pull together and restore its military and economic strength. The emerging consensus became dramatically apparent during the 1980 presidential campaign, and the Reagan Administration seems intent on carrying through its programme to revitalize American power.

A closely related issue is the question of the use and applicability of force in US relations with the developing countries. There are indications that we are entering a period of greater advocacy of the use of American power and, where necessary, military force, to defend and further US interests.

> Our first and overriding obligation clearly is to defend the interests
> of those existing liberal democracies that are our natural allies. To
> achieve this, however, we must be ready to defend our strategic and
> economic interests as a world power, willing and able to use the
> necessary force to do so. This earth will be a place where American
> ideals are respected only if the world respects our *interests* — which
> it is not likely to do if we show no respect for our own interests.[16]

This type of sentiment has been reflected in policy terms in the
current emphasis on increased military expenditures and capabilities,
the negotiation of base agreements and the creation of a rapid deployment force to enhance the capacity to move US troops quickly to any
part of the world. The geographic focus is for the moment the Persian
Gulf, but by extension, these policies have implications for other areas
of the Third World, especially in the Caribbean area and in Central
America.

Change versus Stability

Another derivative of heightened concern over Soviet 'meddling' in the
Third World is a growing feeling that change in developing countries
is dangerously destabilizing and therefore more often than not inimic-
able to American interests. While those who hold this view will acknowledge that not all change in these countries is caused by the Soviet
Union, they are concerned about the opportunities that instability
opens up in developing countries for increased Soviet influence. For
this reason, a distinction is being drawn between 'totalitarian' and
'authoritarian' regimes, with the latter being offered more tolerant treatment because they are somehow less oppressive and because stability in
many Third World nations deserves a higher priority than personal
liberty.

The line of reasoning favouring a greater emphasis on stability is
given support by a Rand Corporation report which analyzes the
growing strength of the developing countries and their demands for a
fundamental shift in political and economic power. The report pre-
dicts that in the next decade we are likely to witness a deterioration
or even breakdown in the international system.

> . . . the diffusion of military power and growing reluctance of the
> industrial democracies to use force in defense of their national inter-

ests will increase the propensity of medium- and small-powers, especially in the Third World, to resort to violence where their interests clashed with those of the United States, Japan, and Western Europe.[17]

The taking of American hostages in Iran offered strong corroborating evidence for this view.

Economic Issues

Views on economic issues involving the United States and developing countries are far less crystallized than those related to security matters. This is due in part to the current concentration on restoring domestic economic strength and in part to the view that international economic matters are basically subordinate to international security considerations.

Many policy analysts have always viewed US relations with the developing world — with the exception of certain countries and issues — as peripheral to the economic interests of the United States.

> our fate does not otherwise depend on the changes occurring in the Third World. If oil is the great exception, we can otherwise accommodate ourselves to a Third World that remains quite unstable for an indefinite period. Even more, we can remain relatively indifferent to most of the change taking place in the developing countries. This indifference expresses in turn an indifference to the prospects that much of the developing world may find us historically irrelevant as we find them less than vital to our interest.[18]

From this standpoint the existing economic order has worked well and there is no compelling reason to change it.

Exceptions to this attitude include the importance of bilateral relations with major regional powers such as Brazil and Mexico, and an emerging concern about access to natural resources. The economic interest of the United States is coming to be seen mainly as access to energy and raw materials, which again relates to the issue of US power.

> The industrial democracies' growing dependence on imports from volatile regions in the Third World — from the Middle East in the case of petroleum, or from southern Africa with respect to vital minerals — demands that all NATO members pay close attention to developments within these regions. If instability in these areas is

sparked by internal conflicts or external meddling the consequences for the world could be disastrous. The growing resource power of the Third World reflects a broader trend of diffusion of power, indeed a transformation of the post-World War II international environment.[19]

Thus economic interdependence is viewed less as an opportunity than as a problem to be overcome; hence the current interest in stock-piling oil and strategic materials. In this context, the United Nations has become little more than a forum for Third World attacks on the industrial nations; proposals for structural change not only make little economic sense but are contrary to the interests of the United States and its industrial-country allies. In the mid-1970s failure to achieve much progress in multilateral forums on the economic issues of the so-called North-South dialogue have considerably raised the frustrations of Americans (as it has those of participants from the developing countries, of course) and prompted Daniel Patrick Moynihan, former US Ambassador to the United Nations, to suggest that the United States 'go into opposition'.

> We are witnessing the emergence of a world order dominated arithmetically by the countries of the Third World. This order is already much too developed for the United States or any other nation to think of opting out. It can't be done . . . What then does the United States do? The United States goes into opposition . . . [20]

Whether by design or by circumstance – by the beginning of the 1980s, the United States was increasingly viewed as playing such a role.

During the course of its first six months in office, the Reagan Administration has shown that it is at least as sceptical as its predecessors over global economic negotiations and efforts to effect basic institutional reforms. In fairness, most policy decisions were held in abeyance pending the Administration's overall review of US-Third World relations, and the President and his Cabinet Secretaries did agree to participate in the Mexico North-South Summit. At the Summit, the United States agreed to join in some form of 'global negotiations', but only if several strong conditions were met.

If anything can be said with certainty about the Reagan Administration's views towards North-South economic issues, it is a clear and strong preference to leave the management of international economic transactions to market mechanisms and the private sector. This is a direct corollary to the Administration's domestic economic philosophy which favours a reduction in the role of the government both as an economic entity and as a regulator of private market transactions. This would suggest that in the international economy, the appropriate government actions would be those which reduce undue incentives and impediments to private flows of goods, services and capital. This approach runs counter to many of the Third World demands for greater government intervention which are felt necessary to redress existing inequities in the international system.

Conclusion: Needed – a Broader Definition of US Interests

There is no one particular national viewpoint on US interests in the Third World but rather – as this paper has shown – a multiplicity of interests that are complex, overlapping and often even conflicting. Understanding and reconciling those interests poses one of the major challenges for American foreign policy in the coming years. What is certain is that the United States does have a considerable stake in the development of the Third World in and of itself. Relations with the developing countries cannot be treated solely as a derivative of relations with US industrial-country partners, or even as a mere function of US relations with the Soviet Union. This is because many of the problems facing the United States – particularly in the economic, social and environmental spheres – will persist regardless of what happens in the confrontation between East and West.

The United States needs to develop a broad definition of its interests with regard to the developing countries, a definition that encompasses and balances its own political, security, economic and humanitarian objectives and is sensitive to those of other nations. The reason for this is simple and compelling: power bears with it a proportionate level of responsibility. If the United States were now to turn its entire attention to a narrowly defined, primarily self-serving series of objectives, the considerable amount of respect still accorded to the US would surely begin to deteriorate.

Pursuing a broad definition of interests does not imply that the US should neglect its own specific interests. On the contrary, the will and vigour with which the Reagan Administration is seeking to restore American economic and military strength is admired by many foreign leaders, although perhaps privately. The concern is whether all of the legitimate interests are being served adequately in a period when but a few are sought purposively.

In seeking a comprehensive definition of US interests, it is useful to return briefly to the four central issues which were raised earlier. First no one can dispute the fact that what transpires between the United States and the Soviet Union will ultimately determine whether or not the world stays at peace, at least in the foreseeable future. One can, however, point to a sufficient number of trends and events affecting North-South interests (wars, famines, embargoes, the positive aspects of commercial relations, etc.) that have *not* involved the Soviet Union, to indicate the need to differentiate between issues and geographic areas before concluding where the actions of the Soviet Union are important and where they are not. For example, there are certain areas in the Third World where Western interests are crucial and where actual or potential Soviet influence is an important ingredient, as in the Persian Gulf, and other areas such as Central America or Southern Africa where the problems are more complex and the influence of the Soviet Union more tenuous. Approaching all issues and areas through the 'East-West prism' could in many cases prove counterproductive. One can also point to the rather uneven record of the Soviet Union in maintaining its presence in those developing countries, such as Indonesia, Ghana and Egypt among others, where the Soviets have invested vast resources and efforts with very little or no enduring influence.

Looking at the use of power, one cannot disagree with the reality that the United States must be prepared to defend its key interests if these are challenged. However, it is necessary to acknowledge the fact that the United States has lost power in a relative sense, and while still a superpower, is surrounded by countries of growing influence and importance, both in the industrial world and in the Third World. In fact, this is to a large extent the result of successful past US policies to rebuild Europe and Japan and to support independence and development in the Third World. As a result, the proper US strategy is to exercise what one analyst termed 'power without hegemony' — that is, to provide leadership at a time when the relative economic and political position of the United States has changed.

The use of military power to achieve America's objectives in the developing countries is not always viable in terms of either efficiency or morality. A classic example is the US involvement in Vietnam, for which the US received no benefits and bore high costs. The handling of the hostage crisis in Iran is another case in point. The debate over the efficacy of American military involvement in Central America is a current illustration. A recent Brookings Institution study identified

215 incidents since the end of the Second World War (185 of which were in developing countries) where US forces were used for political purposes, and concluded that the use of military force to achieve political objectives has only a short-run effect and is no substitute for long-run-diplomacy.[21] Stanley Hoffman has observed that: 'Military power is of little use, either when the objectives we try to achieve are economic or when the threat to our economic security could be worsened by sending in the Marines.'[22] In sum, there are a range of other non-military elements of national power — primarily strong economic and diplomatic relations — which can be much more effective than military force and need to be emphasized if peace is the ultimate objective.

Turning to the question of change versus stability, one can observe that while change may be destabilizing, it also is inevitable in a rapidly evolving world. And it does not necessarily work against longer-term US interests. One of the great strengths of the American system is its adaptability and capacity to absorb the destabilizing effects of change. This strength needs to be translated into the international system. The United States faces a

> world undergoing rapid change, with growing expectations, better education, quickened communication; a world in which neither the United States nor any other country commands a preponderance of power or a monopoly of wisdom. It is a world of conflicts, among nations and values, among social systems and emerging new interests. It is a world in which competitive superpowers hold in their hands our common survival, yet paradoxically find it beyond their power to order events.[23]

In such a world, change should be managed and channelled as peacefully as possible; accommodation to change is necessary everywhere, but especially in sensitive areas such as Southern Africa and Latin America. The peaceful transition in Zimbabwe and the negotiation and ratification of a new agreement with Panama over the governance of the Panama Canal provide recent examples of successful accommodations to change.

Finally, in examining and pursuing US economic interests, the importance of the developing countries to America's economic well-being should not be overlooked. It also should be acknowledged that interdependence is as much an opportunity as a challenge to the power of the United States. As previously noted, developing countries constitute a large and growing market for US goods and will become increasingly important as suppliers of raw materials. Third World growth, as well as resolution of a series of global bottlenecks in food, energy and raw materials, can contribute considerably to growth in the industrial world at a time when demand in the North seems to have reached a plateau.[24]

At the systemic level there are several ways to serve US economic interests, particularly in terms of reactions to the various proposals for change put forward by the developing countries. Many Americans feel that the current international economic system is working fairly well, not only for the rich countries but also for the poor – and that what is needed is not a new order but rather some gradual reforms in the existing order. This assessment may have held true until the recent past, but there are now enough strains building in the international economy – stagnation of trade flows, accumulation of large current account imbalances, increasing debt servicing problems – to indicate that the capacity for the current system to manage these problems may not be sufficient indefinitely. It is not alarmist to recognize the need for reforms, whether engineered in some form of global economic negotiations or carried out within existing institutional structures.

The preceding comments have addressed what appears to be the emerging US approach to its relations with the developing countries, suggesting that a broader view of American interests is necessary. These arguments may not seem particularly compelling in the short run; indeed, long-term problems always seem to be superseded in priority by immediate concerns. This does not, however, negate the urgent need to find a balance between the legitimate US concerns about military security on the one hand, and the pressing need to achieve global co-operation to deal with a series of major international problems. The ability or inability to balance these two agendas may mark the success or failure of American foreign policy in the 1980s.

The fact that all nations – East and West, North and South – face a set of political, economic, social and environmental problems which cannot be resolved without extraordinary co-operative measures, has become increasingly apparent over the past decade. Overcoming many of these problems is beyond the ability of any single nation state, and many do not lend themselves to bilateral approaches.

The sources of interdependence are both physical – for example, the spread of ocean pollutants or the depletion of the earth's protective ozone shield – and social – for example, the economic, political and perceptual effects of events that the Middle East and the United States have had upon each other.[25]

Because of the complexity of problems in areas such as nuclear proliferation, the oceans and the environment, outer space, energy and food, multilateral action is imperative, and the role of the developing world becomes crucial. Since these problems transcend national boundaries the US interest lies in the creation of a series of co-operative international mechanisms, whatever their form. Unless solutions are found,

> the world in 2000 will be much more crowded, more polluted, less stable ecologically, and more vulnerable to disruption than the world we live in now . . . Barring revolutionary advances in technology, life for most people on earth will be more precarious in 2000 than it is now — unless the nations of the world act decisively to alter current trends.[26]

A Malthusian type of global apocalypse may not be inevitable, but the events of the 1970s provide enough evidence that greater international efforts are required to reduce even the slightest chance of such an outcome. The 'national' interest in such efforts may be difficult to calculate, but is nevertheless obvious.

Perhaps the most important US interest to be pursued, a derivative of concern about the future, deals with the world as it now is and what it could be. This is the humanitarian ideal of the United States — an interest in helping to build a world with greater human dignity, well-being and freedom. Americans have been fortunate to be blessed with greater amounts of these 'assets' than most other nations, and it has been abhorrent to many — though not all — sections of American opinion that their relative prosperity should co-exist side by side with the extremes of poverty in the Third World. Hence there is a fundamental moral obligation to assist in the removal of at least poverty's worst aspects, if not poverty itself.

The United States still has the ability to calculate its own needs and implement policies aimed at maximizing its own benefits from international transactions and relations, even at the expense of others. Unique among the industrial countries, the US probably could benefit from a self-serving approach, at least in the short run, even if this meant running the risk of further dividing the international system and alienating the developing countries. Alternatively, the United States could take a long-run view of its relations with the Third World and consider improvements in those relations as investments for future returns, even if short-term costs must be borne. To do so, however, American attitudes, policies and governmental structures fashioned in an era of abundance and relative isolation from the outside world will have to be changed to fit an era of limits.

The United States no longer holds the dominant position that it enjoyed after the Second World War; that period was most likely an aberration from the standard patterns of international relations. The United States faces a fundamentally new situation in the world, despite the fact that the US remains among the world's most powerful nations and is uniquely situated to exert leadership in the world.

If the United States and other countries do not begin now to seek solutions to common problems, they all face slower growth, higher prices and a world system more vulnerable to disruption. On the other hand, by addressing concerted attention to these problems, it is possible to restore growth and stability and measurably increase the well-being of people everywhere. Positive sum outcomes are possible, with benefits accruing to all, if national interests are defined and sought appropriately. Herein lies the real US interest.

Notes

*With the assistance of Devinda R. Subasinghe and Carol A. Grigsby.

1. Alexis de Tocqueville, *Democracy in America*, Vol. II, Book II, Chapter III (Vintage, 1954) K5B, p. 108.

2. Robert Packenham, *Liberal America and the Third World: Political Development Ideas in Foreign Aid and Social Sciences* (Princeton University Press, 1973), pp. 112-60.

3. Robert Lampman, 'Measured Inequality of Income: What Does It Mean and What Can It Tell Us', *The Annals of the American Academy of Political and Social Science* (September 1973), pp. 90-1.

4. Roger D. Hansen, 'The Emerging Challenge: Global Distribution of Income and Economic Opportunity' in James W. Howe and the Staff of the Overseas Development Council, *The U.S. and World Development Agenda for Action 1975* (Praeger for the ODC, 1975) p. 159.

5. Leslie H. Gelb, 'After Ottawa, Allies Still Far Apart on Third World', *The New York Times* (26 July 1981), p. E3.

6. Nelson M. Blake and Oscar T. Barck, Jr., *The United States in Its World Relations* (McGraw-Hill, New York, 1960), p. 458.

7. William R. Cline, *Imports and Consumer Prices: A Survey Analysis* (The American Retail Federation and the Retail Merchants Association, 1979).

8. Jere Behrman, 'International Commodity Agreements: An Evaluation of the UNCTAD Integrated Commodity Programme', in William R. Cline (ed.), *Policy Alternatives for a New International Economic Order: An Economic Analysis* (Praeger for the ODC, 1979), p. 68.

9. These problems are not inherent in relations with developing countries, they

are present in all aspects of American foreign economic policy. I.M. Destler in *Making Foreign Economic Policy* (The Brookings Institution, 1980) provides an excellent analysis of these problems using specific case studies.

10. Robert H. Johnson, *Managing Interdependence: Restructuring the U.S. Government* (Overseas Development Council, Development Paper Number 23, 1977), p. 4.

11. Douglas Bennet, 'Congress in Foreign Policy: Who Needs it?', *Foreign Affairs*, vol. 57, no. 1 (Autumn 1978).

12. Senator Charles McC Mathias, 'Ethnic Groups and Foreign Policy', *Foreign Affairs* (Summer 1981), p. 996.

13. *American Public Opinion and U.S. Foreign Policy, 1979* (The Chicago Council of Foreign Relations, 1979).

14. These two schools of thought and their impact on American foreign policy in the post-Second World War period are analyzed by Daniel Yergin in *Shattered Peace: Origins of the Cold War and the National Security State* (Houghton Mifflin, 1977).

15. Alexander M. Haigh, Jr, speech to the American Society of Newspaper Editors, Washington DC (24 April 1981), text in *The New York Times* (25 April 1981), p. 4.

16. Irving Kristol, *Wall Street Journal* (18 January 1979).

17. Guy J. Pauker, *Military Implications of a Possible World Order Crisis in 1980s*, a Project Air Force Report prepared for the United States Air Force (Rand Corporation, November 1977), p. 73.

18. Robert Tucker, 'The Foreign Policy of Maturity', *Foreign Affairs* (December 1979), pp. 479-80.

19. Alexander M. Haig, Jr, 'The Alliance of the 1980s', *Washington Quarterly* (Winter 1980), p. 134.

20. Daniel Patrick Moynihan, 'The United States in Opposition', in *Commentary*, vol. 59, no. 3 (March 1975), pp. 40,41.

21. Barry M. Blechman and Stephen S. Kaplan, *Force Without War: U.S. Armed Forces As a Political Instrument* (The Brookings Institution, 1979), p. 517.

22. Stanley Hoffmann, 'The New Orthodoxy', *The New York Review of Books* (16 April 1981), p. 24.

23. Cyrus R. Vance, Harvard Commencement Speech (5 June 1980), p. 2.

24. For a detailed analysis see John W. Sewell, 'Can the North Prosper Without Growth and Progress in the South?' in Martin M. McLaughlin and the Staff of the Overseas Development Council, *The United States and World Development: Agenda 1979* (Praeger for the ODC, 1979), Chapter 2, pp. 71-6. Also see *1979 Review Development Co-operation: Efforts and Policies of the Members of the Development Assistance Committee* (OECD, 1979) p. 23.

25. Joseph Nye, 'Independence and Interdependence', *Foreign Policy* (Spring 1976), p. 132.

26. Gerald O. Barney, Study Director, *Global 2000 Report to the President; Entering the Twenty-First Century*, a report prepared by the Council on Environmental Quality and the Department of State (US Government Printing Office, 1980), p. 1.

3 CANADA AND THIRD WORLD DEVELOPMENT: TESTING MUTUAL INTERESTS*

Bernard Wood

Canada: Distinctive Interests on North-South Issues?

More than most of the industrialized nations, Canada is visibly torn between its interests in the global *status quo* and in a basic re-ordering of the international economic system. Even the country's international 'identity' has sometimes seemed to be at issue in the major North-South debates of recent years.

Because Canada's own economy remains heavily resource-based and is dominated by foreign investment and imported technology to a greater degree than other industrialized states, there are special temptations to assume an identity of interest with some of the Third World's demands for a New International Economic Order. On the other hand, the cultural and ideological permeation which has accompanied Canada's economic linkages and defence alliances (particularly with the United States), means that Canadian attitudes and perceived interests internationally are often too-readily identified with those of the dominant Western industrial powers. With these dual dangers of the over-simplification and misperception of Canadian interests, remarkably little serious analysis has been carried out, even within limited areas of North-South relations (such as international commodity trade, the surveillance and direction of transnational business activity, or the relationship between development aid and trade promotion). Even more apparent, and a reflection of some of the gaps in domestic policies, is the absence of comprehensive, integrative strategies for Canada-Third World relations. None the less, heightened debate on issues such as 'de-industrialization' in Canada,[1] the need for national industrial strategies and Third World competition in both manufactured goods and resource sectors, now provide an environment in which more comprehensive perspectives may be able to take root.

However, under conditions of chronic economic slack and demoralization (combined with unprecedented centrifugal pressures from the increasingly aggressive provincial governments), Canada's mutual interests with developing countries are defined and pursued in some

94

extraordinary ways. In a longer-term assessment of Canada's international and global interests, it is especially important to take into account the diverse, and sometimes surprisingly narrow, approaches to mutual interests which may be taken by different Canadian spokesmen. In particular, it is essential to view these mutual interests in a much wider context than that of the aid relationship which, for Canada, is frequently still the most direct and visible link.

In late 1977 it was the President's committee of the Canadian International Development Agency (CIDA) that listed 'the pursuit of mutual benefits' as the first strategic guideline for CIDA officers. The President amplified in the following terms, on this 'adaptation' of the Canadian aid strategy:

> The recent evolution of the Canadian economy as well as its short and medium term prospects require that CIDA strive to ensure that its activities maintain or generate employment and economic benefits in our own country. We must also aim at strengthening mutually beneficial bilateral relationships between our developing partners and Canada. This goal must be achieved while not neglecting our essential mandate which is international development.[2]

In cognizance of the intense pressures reflected in this kind of statement (and their potential impact on Canadian perceptions of 'mutual interests' with developing countries), it is important to establish more clearly where Canadian interests lie.

By most of the usual indices, Canada must be considered to be among the richest and most highly-developed of nations.[3] It is noteworthy that in recent years Canada has joined the Western Summit powers but, like Italy, falls just outside their inner circle. Canada is the next most important Western actor to be considered when the United States, the European Economic Community (acting as a unit) and Japan have set their directions. In a forum such as the Multilateral Trade Negotiations, Canada's position can be important, particularly as it influences the balance among giants (Canada is still the largest trading partner of the US). On the other hand, the Canadian impact apparently can safely be ignored in setting Western policies for an OECD 'steel cartel'.

While Canada's freedom of action has always been shaped, for good or ill, by continental realities,[4] Canada's breadth of vision has sometimes not only been unconstrained, but even somehow bolstered by the overwhelming US presence. John W. Holmes has traced the ways in which Canada has maintained a vigorous commitment to multilateralism and collective international action, true to Lester Pearson's view:

> as a Canadian that our foreign policy must not be timid or fearful of commitments but activist in accepting international responsibilities. To me, nationalism and internationalism were two sides of the same coin.[5]

Others, however, have seen a waning of Canada's prudential internationalism from the disproportionately energetic Canadian response to 'community interests' in the post-war period. One seasoned American observer has commented that:

> Canadian diplomacy in recent years has in fact reflected a rather narrow conception of Canada's problems and interests. In multinational meetings, Canada has been less and less likely to propose general solutions or to act as a middleman. Instead, when multilateral proposals were made by one of the 'big three' or by international secretariats, Canada would seek to differentiate itself and to seek exceptional treatment or the inclusion of a Canadian reservation.[6]

In some areas, however, and for a variety of reasons, multilateralism remains a constant in Canada's external action and promotes interaction with other countries (many in the Third World) whose size and vulnerability incline them too to seek 'safety in numbers' and in a diversity of international links and contacts.

This 'multilateralizing' imperative has found tangible expression in Canadian support for international trade and monetary regimes, UN peace-keeping activity, multilateral development programmes; NATO membership and the search for a 'Contractual Link', with the European Community and in leading participation in both the Commonwealth and *la Francophonie*. Canadian commitment in several of these fields promotes specific contact and sometimes commonality of interests with Third World countries. Canada has come to see the Commonwealth and *Francophonie* associations, in particular, as invaluable linkages, cross-cutting the North-South divide. Thus it was at the Commonwealth Heads of Government meeting in Jamaica in 1975 that the Canadian Prime Minister sharpened his government's perception of the demands of the New International Economic Order and undertook a firm moral commitment to try to accommodate them. Although the government machinery failed to follow up this top-level commitment adequately, the theme remained close to the centre of Canadian foreign policy statements, at least until the disillusioning 1977 outcome of the Conference on International Economic Cooperation in which Canada, as co-Chairman, had worked at the thankless task of trying to achieve some bridging of North-South differences.

Although Canada lacks the colonial or other long-standing Third World links of other industrialized countries, Canadian relations with the Third World have grown to substantial proportions even beside Canada's much closer overall relationships with other Northern countries. In 1977, the Third World (including oil-exporting countries) accounted for nearly nine per cent of total Canadian exports and over 11 per cent of imports, while 23 per cent of the stock of Canadian-based foreign direct investment was found in Third World countries at the end of 1975. By one significant non-economic yardstick, that of immigration to Canada, Canada clearly had established closer Third World connections. By 1977 Third World arrivals (at 48 per cent) almost equalled those from traditional European sources and the United States.

Canadian perceptions of the Third World and the relationship, however, have been slow to change since the initial impetus given by the creation of the Colombo Plan in 1950 to assist newly-independent nations of Asia. Throughout the 1950s, development assistance continued to be the focal point of interaction; the Colombo Plan led to similar efforts for the Commonwealth Caribbean (one region of long-standing links) in 1958 and for Commonwealth Africa in 1960, the same year that an External Aid Office, to be responsible for the Assistance programme, was established within the Department of External Affairs.

Canada's basic outlook towards the Third World during the 1960s followed the pattern established in the previous decade. New regions were included within the development assistance programme – Francophone Africa in 1961 and Latin America in 1964 through the Inter-American Development Bank, and in 1970 on a country-to-country basis. As a reflection of an increased emphasis on development assistance, a new structure, the Canadian International Development Agency was created to administer the programme. The 1969 Pearson Commission report, *Partners in Development*, aroused special interest in Canada because of the chairmanship of former Canadian Prime Minister Lester Pearson, but its stress on 'non-aid' measures to promote development failed to make much impact. The 'aid stereotype' built up during the 1950s continued to predominate, and even the strengthening of the 'Group of 77' after UNCTAD I and the enunciation of demands that would eventually evolve into the call for a new international economic order, failed to shift public or official perception in any decisive way.

In 1970, the beginning of a new 'Development Decade' and the expectations held for the still-new Trudeau Government gave hope to some of the most interested Canadians of a promising new era in Third World-Canada relations. As a result of the foreign policy review initiated in 1968, the Government's *Foreign Policy for Canadians* was published in 1970. It noted the trade and investment opportunities in the Third World, pinpointed some of the hard choices to be faced in 'seeking social justice for the developing nations', and recognized that the 'progress of the developing countries can be affected through every aspect of their relationship with the more-developed countries'.[7] This foreign policy review explicitly anticipated the eventual pressure for structural changes in the world economy without, however, presenting any accompanying indications of a positive Canadian response to this pressure. The review also ratified the compartmentalization of the 'non-aid' relationships affecting developing countries outside any integrated development assistance approach. For example, the discussion of international development policy tacitly dismissed these other issues, such as trade investment and monetary relations, as those 'whose primary consideration lie outside the Canadian development assistance program'.[8]

In the course of the 1970s the basic Canadian approach to the Third World continued to exhibit similar characteristics. The rhetorical response from Canadian officials to the NIEO demands formulated at the Sixth Special Session of the UN General Assembly has often been eloquent and supportive. An excerpt from Prime Minister Trudeau's speech at the Mansion House in London in March 1975 perhaps best exemplifies this:

> The demands of developing countries have been carefully formulated and powerfully articulated. They reflect a sense of frustration and anger. Those countries seek no piecemeal adjustments but a comprehensive restructuring of all the components – fiscal, monetary, trade, transport and investment. The response of the industrialized countries can be no less well-prepared and no less comprehensive in scope. But we should be very wrong, and doing ourselves and our children a great disservice, if we regarded this process as an adversary one. We would be foolish as well, for solutions are not

beyond our reach.[9]

With this kind of declaration, Mr Trudeau gave recognition to a profound long-term mutuality of interests, long before the theme of 'interdependence' became common international parlance. Even in its own principal foreign policy guidelines, however, his government continued to find it impossible to translate such wide vision into an integrated approach to North-South relations. The gap between rhetoric and policy, let alone practice, was strongly evident in the government's five-year *Strategy for International Development Cooperation* released in 1975.[10] While the document's first section, 'Analysis', looked towards 'new relationships' with the Third World and the role of 'non-aid policies in development', the operative section of 'policies' was directed almost exclusively to aid issues. As will become apparent below, subsequent measures have also fallen far short of achieving the 'comprehensive and organic approach to development' promised in the *Strategy*.

Consistent with this continuing 'aid-fixation' in Canadian policy, it is only in the area of development assistance that Canada's record in North-South relations has been notably forthcoming.[11] At least until the later years of the 1970s, the government was making steady efforts to move towards the international aid-volume target of 0.7 per cent of GNP and was firmly committed to putting priority on aid to the poorest countries. Even in the assistance field, however, Canada has remained particularly unresponsive to the need for 'untying' aid procurement, resisting even the limited proposals to open up aid contracts for developing-country bidding. One Canadian initiative, however, which went beyond conventional aid measures on one important front, and placed Canada among the most responsive donors, was the 1977 decision to write off aid-related debts owed to CIDA by some of the poorest debtor-countries.

However, in relation to providing access to the Canadian market for manufactured and processed goods from the Third World, the Canadian record is far from one of leadership. While Canada protects the 'traditional market share' of suppliers such as the United States, Third World imports have been heavily restricted, in spite of obligations under the GATT and the Multi-Fibre Arrangement. Canada was, like the United States, tardy in its introduction of the Generalized System of Preferences and failed to give any evident priority to Third World interests in Multilateral Trade Negotiations.

In the area of commodity trade, it is even more difficult to explain the ways in which Canadian interests appear to have been defined and pursued. While there was early and lively interest, at the highest levels of the Canadian government, in the Integrated Program for Commodities and the Common Fund, Canadian negotiators have sometimes been among the 'hardest-line' OECD bargainers on these issues. Canadian resistance here has consistently been explained in the root opposition to interventionism and to cartels and producer-only agreements in international commodity markets. Yet there was apparently official encouragement for Canadian participation in a uranium cartel in recent years, and some legislators appeared receptive at one point to going beyond present consultative arrangements to the possibility of establishing a wheat producers' cartel.

To provide a basis for assessing Canada's interests in Third World development in the 1980s and beyond, it is important to try to understand the domestic background to this past performance and then to analyze several aspects of Third World-Canada relations in greater depth.

The Changing Domestic Realities

In the two decades after the implementation of the Colombo Plan, Canadians experienced steady growth in their standard of living. The generally buoyant international conditions and the rising fortunes of the United States − Canada's prime customer − led to a prosperous Canadian economy. The last years of the 1960s were particularly golden as a number of factors − the initial impact of the 1965 Canada-US Auto Agreement, the increase in Canadian competitiveness due to the devaluation of the Canadian dollar and the influence of the 1963-6 flood of investment − combined to produce boom conditions in Canada. New realities in the 1970s drastically changed this picture. Internationally the price increase in key commodities, notably oil and food, the world-wide recession in 1974-5, and the sluggish growth in the US economy exerted both inflationary and recessionary pressures on Canada. At home, the continued labour force expansion (the most rapid in the OECD countries) contributed to a major increase in the unemployment rate, while the dramatic rise in the Canadian dollar from 1970 to 1974 and a subsequent surge in wages and salaries led to a marked deterioration in Canada's competitive position. Soon the perceived poor business climate in Canada, particularly in comparison with the United States, began to inhibit further rapid business expansion in Canada.[12]

The upshot of these conditions has been a slow-growth economy, together with the highest unemployment levels since the Second World War, resurging inflationary pressures, a massive current account deficit (more than $7 million in 1979) and a resultant fall in the Canadian dollar to near-record lows, all accompanied by worrisome levels of external borrowing.

Given this economic climate and prospects for 'more of the same', it is likely that the current economic retrenchment, with its cautious policy measures, will continue. This approach presumes that the downturn is essentially cyclical, and that the best alternative is to 'ride it out' while tempering its impact. However, many observers now contend that economic recovery will not be so straightforward and that Canada is experiencing the repercussions of structural economic weaknesses.

Whether in fact they are 'cyclical' or structural, economic troubles in Canada will continue to have a major impact on Third World-Canada relations. Pressure against government expenditure has already resulted in substantial cutbacks in CIDA's budget (by $100 million in 1978-9 and $133 million in 1979-80), with some far-reaching implications for Canada's development assistance programme, notwithstanding the recent decision to achieve a '0.5% of GNP' target for aid by 1985. The stagnant economy, together with high levels of unemployment, rapidly mounting current account deficits and massive external borrowings, compound the existing pressure for greater protection of Canadian manufacturers. Another effect has been rising criticism of the export of Canadian capital and of the investment insurance in Third World countries offered by the Export Development Corporation, concerns about the relationship between immigration and unemployment, and a more general trend to national introversion among both the populace and the policy-makers.

Although economic pressures may exert a predominating influence on the policies affecting Canada's relations with the Third World, domestic political and social factors also help shape the policy-making process. The increasing number of provincial forays into international affairs, for example, has led to some federal-provincial conflict in this area and, in some instances, limited the options of the federal government.

In Canadian society generally, the mounting pressure to restrain government, that has already resulted in reductions in Canada's development assistance allocations, may have impacts on relations with Third World countries. Any measures (e.g. in the trade or investment fields) which call for government initiative to redirect or even monitor relationships that have been the preserve of the private sector are likely to be highly vulnerable to the critics of government interventionism. Whether or not new development policies actually involve new expenditures, they will be tarred by some as 'giveaways', the kind of bureaucratic largesse which can no longer be tolerated.

Policy-makers and Interest Groups

Not only do the economic, political and social pressures outlined above directly influence Canadian foreign policies, they also may indirectly affect the ways in which policy decisions are made.

Traditionally, foreign-policy decision-making in the government of Canada has been fragmented, with each department predominating in its functional sphere. During the early years of the Trudeau decade an attempt was made to transcend these strict departmental biases through an improved central co-ordination machinery and a more vigorous Cabinet committee system.[13]

In the initial stages of the Trudeau mandate, the overall responsibility for foreign policy co-ordination rested with the Cabinet, but eventually the Department of External Affairs had to try to maintain a co-ordinated system. The External Affairs Department is unfortunately not well-equipped for such a mandate – it is only peripherally involved in some of the processes it is charged with co-ordinating.[14] The growing linkages between domestic and foreign policy which have brought a number of domestically-oriented departments into the conduct of external relations have also made the objective of a well-coordinated foreign policy more difficult to attain. In recent years an attempt has been made to upgrade and expand the expertise of the Department to strengthen its leadership with co-ordination roles, and the 1980 decision to integrate the Canadian foreign service was also intended to promote coherence.

Until 1974, scant consideration was given to the need to provide special co-ordination for Canada's policies towards the Third World. But the sense of urgency given to North-South issues by the OPEC oil price rise in late 1973, and the fractious Sixth Special Session of the UN General Assembly in April 1974, prompted government action. In response to the obvious requirement to pay greater heed to these matters, the government set up the Interdepartmental Committee on Economic Relations with Developing Countries (ICERDC) and gave it a mandate to:

(1)   direct a continuing review of policies as they affect Canada's economic and other relations with developing countries;
(2)   consider the consistency of Canada's international economic and other policies with Canada's development policies; and
(3)   ensure the preparation of policy positions for major international meetings affecting Canada's economic and other relations with developing countries.[15]

Originally it was expected that the committee would function as a major actor in the preparation and co-ordinaton of Canada's response to the North-South issues and, in fact, it did play an important role in the preparation for the 1975 Commonwealth Conference in Kingston, Jamaica (mainly because the Prime Minister had a lively personal interest in the meeting). Since that time the committee has been largely moribund. It no longer functions at the deputy minister level, it meets infrequently, it has neither a standing secretariat nor its own research staff and it has consequently let the responsibility for policy research and formulation again fall to individual departments. In addition, its focus in practice on conference preparation has made its work reactive rather than innovative and has militated against both policy co-ordination and long-range planning.

Responsibilities for specific policy issues thus revert to the departments that have traditionally viewed the matter as being within their functional sphere, and the sought-after comprehensive approach has been lost. As a result, the Departments of Finance, External Affairs and Industry, Trade and Commerce generally have the dominant influence in setting Canadian policy. Even at the formal interdepartmental level these three 'core' departments often control the proceedings through a combination of expertise, fiscal control, historical functional responsibility and political leverage.

Issue-oriented departments and agencies (Agriculture; CIDA; Energy, Mines and Resources; Employment and Immigration; and the Ministry of State for Science and Technology) do have inputs in their areas of expertise through informal links with the three core departments, but their contribution is intermittent and not consistently influential. CIDA's lack of power, especially on non-aid issues, is particularly noteworthy as it is evidence of the continued separation of development and trade issues. CIDA apparently was somewhat instrumental in the decision to initiate the General Preferential Tariffs in 1974, but this was a rare exception.[16] Perhaps a better example from the recent past is the responsibility CIDA was given for UNCTAD V interdepartmental deliberations: the development potential of land-locked countries (viewed as one of the lowest-priority agenda items).

Once issues reach the level of the Cabinet or Cabinet committees for final decision, with the guidance of the Privy Council Office, departmental interests are tempered somewhat by political party priorities and by the regional-constituency interests that many Cabinet ministers are required to represent. Such regional representation can be particularly critical on issues of major importance to one region of the country (e.g. textile imports for Quebec, grain exports for the Prairies). The Minister perceived to be responsibile for presenting the region's viewpoints is likely to be subjected to additional pressures from interested groups or individuals.

Finally, the participation of the Prime Minister must be considered. Even in a situation where a prime minister has had an avowed interest in North-South issues he has not generally been able to play a sustained role in this area. Prime Minister Trudeau and his special foreign policy adviser were instrumental in the decision to support UNCTAD's integrated commodities programmes in principle,[17] for example, but were frustrated in their efforts to elicit the necessary follow-up analysis and action from the federal departments most concerned.

Given the vast array of competing interests at both the bureaucratic and Cabinet level, it is perhaps not surprisng that the government has been unable to formulate a consistent approach to its relations with the Third World. To date, policy co-ordination efforts have proved unsuccessful; North-South issues are still being dealt with in a traditional fragmented fashion.

It is clear that the decision-making process depicted above has discouraged any widespread public input in foreign affairs and hampered the efficacy of those who have sought to influence policy. A parliamentary structure which centres power in the Cabinet and the upper echelons of the bureaucracy, a weak and underdeveloped parliamentary committee system and no traditional support for access to information or the public's 'right to know' (most particularly in regard to external relations), all make the task of interest groups more difficult and the practice of foreign policy more esoteric.

Interest Groups and Third World Relations

Meanwhile, however, many concerns previously in the domain of domestic policy — environmental control, energy and resource conserva-

tion, exploitation of the seabed, scientific and technological developments — are now cross-border or global issues. 'Foreign policy' matters
such as international trading relations, Canadian direct foreign investment and international development co-operation efforts, are seen to
have a more direct linkage to domestic issues, and particularly domestic
economic concerns.[18] This has brought a number of domestically-
oriented departments into the conduct of foreign affairs and given
internationally-oriented departments, agencies or branches a higher
domestic profile.

Grappling with these changing ground-rules, both at the federal level
and between different levels of government, a number of domestic
interest groups have a significant and continuing influence on the ways
in which Canada's interests in Third World development are defined and
pursued.

Business and professional associations, ranging from very small and
issue-specific industry groups to such inclusive groups as the Canadian
Manufacturers' Association or the Canadian Chamber of Commerce,
would seem to be one of the most effective sets of interest groups. In general, they have a substantial membership base, both the financial resources and the professional staff required to prepare in-depth briefs, and
sustained contact with the policy-makers (which is reinforced by govern-
ment-supported programmes to facilitate personnel exchanges between
the private and public sector). In addition, the role of business groups
seems to be enhanced during periods of poor economic performance
when the public and the government look to this sector as the engine of
recovery.

Due in part to their financial and professional resources, these groups
are able to pursue their interests through a variety of avenues: some
have formal yearly consultations with the Cabinet; they serve on government advisory boards or task forces; they are often requested to comment
on proposed legislation; they present briefs to parliamentary committees; they have informal direct links with the bureaucracy; and
many have the resources to employ full-time government relations or
public relations officers or to use freelance lobbyists.[19]

It would be simplistic however to suggest that the business community has an overwhelming influence on policy questions. In fact,
this community feels that it is neglected and impotent; that the government has intruded too far into business; and that the public and the
policy-makers have many misconceptions about the business community.[20]

Although the business organizations and associations are far from monolithic (and sometimes pitted against each other), both 'horizontal' and 'vertical' groups (those limited to an individual industrial sector), are a powerful force in the formulation of Canadian policies affecting developing countries.

The labour movement in Canada has at times been very active on North-South issues: especially through the Canadian Labour Congress (CLC) — and the latter's strong links with the International Labour Organization and the International Confederation of Free Trade Unions — it has expressed support for many of the Third World's NIEO demands;[21] in conjunction with other ICFTU members it has taken a vocal stand on human rights violations.[22] (It is perhaps noteworthy that a Canadian, former CLC President Joe Morris, was the trade unionist appointed to the Brandt Commission on international development issues.)

The poor economic climate in Canada, coupled with high unemployment, has recently caused a policy revision by much of organized labour in Canada. The CLC has now assumed a more protectionist position on trade policies where such protectionism may be damaging to Third World interests. Although certain strong sectors of the labour movement (such as the paper workers' and wood workers' unions) had long defended trade liberalization measures, basing themselves on the clear export interests of their members as much as on any principle, they have been forced to mute this position because of the more insistent voices of import-threatened unions. The Congress' 1978 *Policy Statement on GATT* appears as something of a watershed. Although it upholds unobjectionable principles, the declaration also had undertones of a marked shift towards the traditionally more protectionist position of 'Big Labour' in the United States.[23]

The differences among non-governmental organizations (NGOs) in Canada have led to varying approaches to Third World issues and even to dissension within the community. Most of the major NGOs can be categorized according to the focus of their activities; whether their prime focus is development education, development programming or some combination of these two. There are obvious differences among those whose prime concern is development programming and those who concentrate on development education questions; but there are also differences within these two categories with regard to the type of development programming approach to be taken and the scope of development education activities. For example, whether such activities should be internationally-oriented or focused on a fundamental analysis of Canadian society — its power structures, its values and the life styles it fashions.

Interestingly, conflicts can also occur within individual NGOs, especially those whose activities cover a wide spectrum. For example, debate has arisen within the religious community over donations made to liberation movements in southern Africa through the World Council of Churches' Program to Combat Racism. This Program has caused rifts both between and within churches — dissension which attracted considerable national attention and prompted attacks on CIDA for its support of voluntary organizations that help fund liberation groups.[24]

Such controversies are, of course, to be expected in dealing with the basic questions of values at stake in the Third World, but beyond a certain point, the heated debate and uncertainty of direction that characterize the voluntary sector limit its effectiveness. In addition, the groups that make up this sector do share some common weaknesses. First, they tend to have relatively unstable memberships, meagre staffs and limited research capabilities. Secondly, their resource base is usually slight, often forcing them to rely on government funding. And thirdly, their contacts with government are intermittent although they are generally given a sympathetic hearing through the parliamentary committee system and within the bureaucracy.[25] Nevertheless, these groups have on occasion had significant impact on policy, particularly aid policy, through their own aid programmes, through their network of supporters and through their somewhat more informal links with CIDA.

An examination of the few national lobbying efforts mounted by the voluntary agencies illustrates some of the constraints they face in their efforts to influence policy. When they were able to focus on an emotional issue (the stark and compelling vision of world famine, or the vivid injustice of apartheid) and relevant remedial measures (food aid and reserve stocks, or withdrawal of government support for business ventures)[26] they were able to attract both media and public support, and their campaigns were effective. On the other hand where their focal point was a tedious negotiating process on very technical matters and their rallying cry a 'common fund' for commodity stabilization, they were unable to appeal to the non-specialized public. The Canadian NGOs showed limited enthusiasm for basing a lobbying campaign on UNCTAD V, but were prepared to mount quite a significant effort again for the 1980 special session of the UN General Assembly on Development.

There are a number of other specialized or professional organizations that do, at times, attempt to exert influence in specific North—

South issues/areas. Universities can be a source of specialized and policy input, and also have their own interests to pursue in relation to overseas co-operation projects or the inflows of foreign students. Policy inputs of various kinds can come from the independent and quasi-governmental policy-research centres or 'think tanks', which have come to occupy a significant place in Canadian public policy debate. Groups representing farmers (the Canadian Federation of Agriculture and the National Farmers' Union), consumers (the Consumers' Association of Canada), scientists (the Association of the Scientific, Engineering and Technological Community of Canada) and internationalists (the Canadian Institute of International Affairs and the United Nations Association), all have particular interest in certain Third World-Canada relationships, and have at times mustered significant influence.

Any examination of non-governmental influence that was restricted to coverage of groups and organizations would be very incomplete. Vast segments of the Canadian population are not members of such groups or organizations (although at times they may be mobilized by them) and must therefore be considered apart from the organized interests.

With regard to Canada's relations with the Third World, however, the public seems generally ill-informed or uninterested, a situation not helped by the usually superficial and second-hand international coverage of the Canadian media. Domestic issues reign supreme. And at the head of these are the current twin economic problems of inflation and unemployment; even domestic political concerns are secondary.

Obviously, any foreign policies that may attract interest are those with direct impact or relevance to Canadians. Hence immigration and refugee questions, the effects of manufactured imports from Third World countries and problems related to the Canadian aid programme have caught the public's eye, and lower-profile issues have been met with indifference. Canadian internationalists have also fallen into the habit of responding to the cycles of international conference activity so that, over a period of years, they will have covered issues as vast and complex as the environment, world food, the role of women, disarmament and others. While these issues are unquestionably interlinked and vitally important, it is not clear whether this cycle of conference participation can continue to accomplish more than general consciousness-raising in Canada. When so much of the study and organization involved falls frequently to the same small nucleus of citizens, and when public input is so often obscured in the negotiation of final intergovernmental positions, the participation process can become frustratingly ritualistic.

Surprisingly though, the public's basic support for the Canadian aid programme has remained strong. A 1977 poll indicated that the majority of respondents considered aid to the Third World a necessity (81 per cent) and a duty (69 per cent). There are indications, however, of declining public confidence in CIDA. The lack of public reaction to CIDA budgetary cuts and a softening of support for increased aid may be the response to the substantial amount of criticism that CIDA has received in Parliament and in the media over the last two years. More recently, the Canadian Exporters' Association has been able to take encouragement from a national magazine poll which hinted at a widespread public readiness to link Canadian aid more tightly to the country's trade objectives. The Association reported to its members:

> 56% of Canadians, the survey reveals, believe that priority in aid programs should be given to our trading partners, and not necessarily to the poorest LDCs . . . These figures tend to support the view of the Association that if Canadian aid is to be increased as a percentage of GNP, more public support will be required, and that this is more likely to be achieved if, and this can be done, aid and trade objectives can be made mutually more self-supporting without denigrating either.

The Third World and Canada: Competition and Complementarity

While many global diagnoses and prescriptions in recent years have been able to demonstrate the interrelatedness of a vast range of issues and the 'interdependent' interest of all rich and poor countries in reform, it is helpful to be much more selective in analyzing the stake of a secondary actor such as Canada. Here the key question concerns the possible mutuality and conflicts of interest between such a country and the Third World: first, in fields which are of primary importance to Canada; and secondly, in fields where Canada is of unusual importance, actual or potential, to the developing countries.

Keeping in mind the ethical stake of Canadians in more equitable world development (as articulated by Canadian leaders), and the general importance of co-operative international decision-making to a trade-dependent nation locked in an asymmetrical continental relationship, it is possible to isolate a small number of central issues for Canada on the Third World's agenda. For different reasons, these topics should include: world food and agriculture; private foreign investment and technological development; Third World imports and industrial adjustment; commodity trade and development; and concessional development assistance and debt.

It is only when these issues are analyzed in specific terms that the complex web of Canadian interests in Third World development begins to become apparent, as do some of the intricate ways in which they are perceived, articulated and acted upon. It becomes clear that the central problems are those of the time frames in which interests should be analyzed and weighed, and the accessibility and reliability of the information required for such judgements. Perhaps the most interesting feature of the current Canadian situation is that the 'time frame' problem now goes far deeper than the classic long-term/short-term trade-offs. From a purely domestic perspective, the pressure for basic and rapid change is now building on a number of fronts. For example, in the areas of industrial policy and mineral resource development, it is more and more widely recognized that further temporizing can only worsen some serious Canadian problems. However, in any fundamental rethinking or new initiatives in these areas Canadians must, for the first time, come to grips with the new realities of Third World countries as both serious competitors and customers.

World Food and Agriculture

In relation to world food supply, food trade and security, Canada is a major power internationally and has a wide range of relationships with many Third World countries. The future directions of world food production are of primary importance for Canada, touching as they do the vital interests of an economically-vital, well-organized and vocal agricultural sector in Canada. For the poor of the Third World, these issues can be the key to self-reliant development to survival itself.

Canadian official statements acknowledge that greatly increased self-sufficiency in food supply is the only long-term hope for overcoming continuing world hunger and malnutrition, but concrete Canadian policies and practices do not yet reflect a consistent emphasis on the promotion of agricultural development and self-reliance in the developing countries.

Through the official aid programme, Canadian support of multilateral agricultural research and production assistance has been vigorous, and has been complemented by a heavy emphasis on agriculture in the work of the International Development Research Centre. Although the aid agency (CIDA) has given priority to rural and agricultural development for at least a decade, only a small fraction of Canadian bilateral aid is allocated to the direct promotion of food production, in large part because this type of aid requires such intensive planning and management and is difficult to mesh with the policy of 'tying' Canadian aid to the provision of Canadian goods and services.

Direct food aid, which has in recent years accounted for roughly 20 per cent of total Canadian development assistance, is increasingly controversial, with very serious questions as to whether it actually advances or retards the cause of Third World development. While official Third World representatives have fairly consistently pressed for higher levels of concessional food supply (albeit with important provisos such as much greater use of multilateral channels), more and more concern has been expressed about the potential disincentives of food aid to indigenous food production, and the perpetuation and reinforcement of cash crop dependence in developing countries.

Canada was widely applauded at the time of the World Food Conference for its multi-year pledge of specific and substantial quantities of food aid. This pledge was given at a time when commercial sales opportunities were very attractive and when dollar-level pledges were being eroded by rising prices, so it was seen as a very forthcoming Canadian response to the perceived crisis in world food supply. It is noteworthy that voluntary agencies in Canada had mounted a large-scale and effective lobbying campaign to help achieve this result.

Since that time, the pendulum of much 'developmental' opinion has swung. Although the cushion of world food reserves remains perilously thin, there is no sense of crisis and, instead, a determination exists to avoid excessive or perennial dependence on food aid. After commissioning a major interdepartmental review of food aid, the federal government has still been unable to arrive at a firm long-term approach but has established the Food Aid Coordination and Evaluation Centre within the aid agency to monitor and plan these programmes. It is significant that when overall cutbacks were imposed in CIDA in mid-1978, Canada's Food Aid Convention pledge was an easy target for reduction — from 750,000 to 600,000 tonnes annually. The commitment remained unchanged for 1980-1. The voluntary sector has also shifted substantially away from support of food aid. The stance of the important inter-church and non-governmental organizations (in Canada the Canadian Council for International Cooperation) coalitions to this form of assistance is now almost uniformly critical.

Contrary to what might be expected, the vested Canadian interests in food aid programmes are rarely overwhelming. Farmers themselves are often not vigorous advocates, deriving only some two per cent of their total income from food aid spending and being sensitive, from their own experience, to the possible disruption to local markets result-

ing from food imports. Nevertheless, traditional support and pressure
for food aid is kept alive by farm organizations, political representatives and some of Canada's powerful agricultural marketing boards. As
a general rule, their advocacy of food aid seems strongest when market
prospects for their particular commodities or regions are weakest and
the availability of surpluses is still a more powerful determinant of food
aid levels and composition than is any careful study of needs. This tendency, to treat food aid as a 'residual' outlet for supplies that are surplus
to domestic or international commercial demand, is well established
and it has benefits as well as costs. There seems to be little likelihood
that the Canadian agricultural community will attempt to claim a legitimate long-term Canadian interest in production for food aid purposes.
In this sense there will not be a Canadian lobby for continuing direct
food dependency. Nor have Canadian farmers yet seen any conflict
between their interest in world markets and the promotion of much
greater food production and a higher degree of self-sufficiency in poor
countries. Rather than obstructing the development of potential competition in Third World countries (as has occurred in some other donor
countries), Canadian farmers have so far been active participants in
the Canadian aid programme. Resistance has been encountered to some
Third World food imports directly into the Canadian market, and it is
conceivable that strong competition in some of Canada's traditional
food export markets would give rise to some degree of Canadian backlash. As a general rule, however, Canadian food producers are probably
prepared to recognize their interest in promoting rising incomes in poor
countries (even through more self-reliant agricultural growth) without
fear of inadequate global demand for their own products.

If improved measures for global food security are seen as an appropriate way of countering cyclical and regional food shortages, and
avoiding the dangers of long-term dependence on food aid, it has been
in the negotiation of food security plans where Canada's vital interests
as a major food exporter have come most strongly to the fore and into
conflict with the immediate goals of the Third World bargainers. In
international wheat negotiations, Canada, as a producer, has been concerned with maintaining its commercial markets, prices and earnings,
without having to bear an excessive share of stabilization costs. Like the
US therefore, Canada has differed with importers, including Third
World countries, on the size and pricing of reserve stocks and on cost-
sharing and special dispensations for unilateral stocking by Third World
countries. The Canadian position has been tough, and talk of a 'wheat
cartel' has been kept alive as a threat in the event that multilateral

negotiations fail to achieve satisfactory results. The issue of wheat reserve negotiations has received very little attention from the voluntary sector in Canada, probably because it is too complex to engender widespread interest. Meanwhile, farm organizations, though not opposed to reserves in principle, are extremely vigilant in protecting their members' interest — they are extensively consulted both in Canada and as observers at the actual negotiations.

Foreign Investment and Technological Development

Canada is the world's fifth largest home base for direct investment flows to the Third World, and simultaneously has the world's most heavily foreign-permeated investment structure at home. Not unrelatedly, Canada has a relatively weak indigenous scientific and technological capability and is heavily reliant on imported technology, skills and know-how for its industrial growth.

At least superficially, on the basis of these characteristics, Canada has a great deal in common with developing countries in areas which rank high on their list of priorities for action. It is therefore important to assess how these issues have actually been dealt with by Canada at home and internationally and where common and mutual interests with developing countries may actually lie.

Canada is deeply and firmly linked into the international investment network. The stock of foreign investment in the country (C $39.8 billion 1977) ranks it as the leading host to foreign equity capital, while Canadian investment abroad of C $10.5 billion (1975) places Canada among the major exporters of foreign investment. The Third World hosts 23 per cent of Canadian foreign investment, most of it in non-manufacturing sectors, with Brazil and the Caribbean area accounting for the largest shares.

While this stake of Canadian-based firms in Third World countries is unquestionably important, it cannot be said to determine the direction of Canadian policy on international investment issues. The Canadian interest is much more crucially affected, for good or ill, by the country's role as an importer of capital. It remains one of the most heated and enduring debates of Canadian society as to whether that interest lies in tighter monitoring, regulation or limitation of investment on the one hand, or enthusiastic hospitality for foreign investors on the other. There is a steady flow of argument from both sides as to the performance of foreign-owned firms in job-creation, research and development, resource-upgrading, export development, transfer pricing and every other aspect of corporate behaviour. After decades of discussion, in 1974 the federal government finally set up a screening mechanism, the Foreign Investment Review Agency (FIRA) which seems to satisfy none of the protagonists. Economic nationalists point to its very high rate of approval of take-overs and new projects and view it as a toothless sham. Other critics, including on occasion provincial governments, claim that it is an awesome deterrent to international capital and blame FIRA's actions or its mere existence for the loss of numerous potential investments to other jurisdictions.

With this degree of dissension among Canadians, it has not yet been possible for governments to carry into the international debate any clear general view of the Canadian interest in incoming or outgoing investment flows and their possible regulation. In the absence of such a view, a *laissez-faire* attitude tends to prevail. In relation to Canadian-based investment overseas, the only concern formally acknowledged by the Canadian authorities is a very narrow one for balance of payments implications, since the Canadian government has never taken an active role in disputes between Canadian-based firms and foreign host governments. The broad assumption that Canadian investment is of benefit to developing countries is reflected in small incentive schemes from CIDA, and its assumed benefits to Canada have been used to justify substantial investment insurance and related export financing and insurance by the Crown-owned Export Development Corporation.

Ironically, it is perhaps only through the emergence of developing countries as serious competitors to Canada for resource and manufacturing investment that the Canadian policy of complacent non-interference will be fully tested. In recent years, competing Third World investments in nickel and copper by Canadian companies have aroused lively controversy, and the shift to offshore manufacturing operations shows every potential for doing the same. Although there is a real danger that this competition will give rise to some backlash against the Third World, it may also be expected to drive home the Canadian interest, shared with host governments, in being able to ensure less disruptive movements of investments or, at the very least, much better knowledge by governments of the operations and intentions of the powerful transnational enterprise.

If this concern about investment export should dovetail with new pressure in Canada to achieve greater control over existing and incoming transnational investment, it will almost certainly generate much more vigorous Canadian participation, with developing countries, in attempts to devise new international rules. Even in these circumstances, however, Canada's adherence to market principles and a broader Western interest, together with a genuine ambivalence about its own and Third World interests, are likely to preclude Canadian support for the most interventionist of 'code of conduct' proposals for investment. One recurrent sentiment in various Canadian circles is that the encouragement of Canadian transnationals will be a key element in Canada's own economic future.

The degree of foreign ownership in Canada, and the dearth of industrial research and development activity (to some extent associated with it), place tight limits on the country's potential contribution to technology development in the Third World, since most technological development and transfer takes place in the market sector. Just as Canada's 'market' role in technology development has been weak (with the possible exception of some strengths in a few resource sectors and international engineering and consultancy services), so has the integration of technology development in the Canadian aid programme. However, Canada has established a distinctive role in Third World science and technology development through the independent International Development Research Centre (IDRC). The Centre, with its untied support of research in Third World countries, has already made a major contribution to innovation and to the promotion of both skills and institutions in developing countries. After IDRC's first decade, some Canadian developmentalists see a crucial Canadian interest in maintaining the essential character of the Centre and adapting its support programmes to emerging research priorities in Third World countries, while others are exerting new pressures to tie IDRC's work much more closely to Canadian policy and Canadian skills. While the Centre's budget represents only about four per cent of Canada's official development expenditure, the Centre's future directions may reveal a great deal about the interpretation of the Canadian interest in Third World development.

Third World Imports and Industrial Adjustment

It is only with the emergence of Third World countries as a force on the international trade scene in recent years that the inevitability and powerful implications of a new international economic order have begun to be brought home to thoughtful Canadians. Some have so far seen only the competitive impact of 'low cost' imports, mainly from semi-industrialized countres, on some of the labour-intensive sectors and less-developed regions of Canada. Still other observers are slowly coming to recognize that Third World markets are of substantial global importance, especially for a trade-dependent nation with only a small assured market of its own and a neighbouring superpower shaping much of its economic system.

Taken together, these trends, and the need to re-examine traditional Canadian trade and industrial policies, should provide the basis for searching discussion of Third World-Canada trade prospects. So far, in fact, the lively Canadian debate among advocates of 'continentalism', 'technological sovereignty' and 'import substitution' strategies has given only incidental attention to the actual and potential impact of Third World countries as competitors and customers. These trade relations have thus usually been left in the much more short-term framework of industry-by-industry problems or as a subordinate issue in the multi-lateral trade negotiatons under the auspices of GATT.

Over the years since the 'Group of 77' began forcefully presenting the developing countries' needs and demands in the trade field, Canada's practice with respect to Third World exporters has been fairly typical of the industrialized countries, although Canada's trade regime has generally retained unusually high tariff 'peaks' while relying less than most OECD countries on non-tariff barriers. In spite of the early recognition of the importance of 'trade-not-aid' measures in the 1970 foreign policy review, little progress has been made in improving market access for Third World countries or initiating the industrial restructuring which would make such improved access politically and socially acceptable. Instead, Canada, like other industrialized countries, has consistently resorted to the defensive protectionist response, which, though invariably presented as 'temporary' or 'transitional', in fact tends to become entrenched because there are not adequate constructive adjustment measures available to substitute for this protection.

For a variety of historical and other reasons, Canada's imports of manufactured goods from Third World countries represent a more modest share of total imports (three to four per cent) than they do in the other major industrialized Western countries. However, Canada's Third World imports are more heavily concentrated than the OECD average in traditional labour-intensive consumer goods, with the result that the impact of this competition falls most heavily on Canada's own least-favoured regions, workforces and industries. Thus, in the field of textile and clothing trade, after Canada had been relatively restrained in applying import controls over the first few years of the Multi-Fibre Arrangement (MFA), domestic criticism and concerted pressure from business and labour ultimately became irresistible and a much tougher line was initiated in 1977.

The barrage of domestic criticism reveals a startling and significant gap between prevailing Canadian and foreign perceptions of the balance of benefits in trade relationships and policies. A prevalent Canadian assumption has been that Canada alone has been playing by the 'rules of the game' and carrying more than its share of the 'burden' of low-cost imports – Canadian critics refer to 'boy-scoutism' and 'naiveté'. Seasoned outside observers, meanwhile, bemoan a new Canadian narrowness and reticence to provide multilateral leadership, with one US official stating that a Canadian position in the recent GATT talks (with particularly adverse effects on the Third World) was 'just another example of how Canada refuses to accept the doctrine of equal pain in these negotiations'.

As distinct from the perceived defensive Canadian interest in 'protecting' the home market from Third World products, the Canadian record in capturing a share of growing Third World markets is markedly less successful than that of other Northern exporters. The analysis of evolving trade flows shows that Canada's export 'basket' to the Third World tends to be directed towards the slowest-growing markets and characterized by a product concentration in goods with the slowest growth in trade. Whatever the reasons or cures for the relatively laggard Canadian performance in taking up commercial opportunities in the Third World, it is clear that in view of the economic pressures in Canada this lack of 'return' now seriously inhibits greater responsiveness to Third World needs for import access.

It is in the area of market access that lobbying activities have been more sustained and intense than in any other field of Canadian relations with the Third World, and a very substantial block of opinion sees Canadian interests ranged against those of developing countries. It is in this field too that it is vitally important to distinguish between immediate regional, sectoral or occupational interests on the one hand, and wider and more long-term national interests on the other. Quite apart from the consumer interest in improved import access, there is a widening consensus on the need for industrial strategies and the rationalization of Canadian industry in order to assure the country of a viable economic futue. It is clear that expanding access for Third World imports and at the same time developing new, competitive export capabilities to penetrate their growing markets, will be an essential part of any medium to long-term national economic interest for Canada. From the viewpoint of both equity and political realism, the dislocation and costs involved in this adjustment cannot be allowed simply to fall on the workers, industries and communities most affected. New mechanisms are required to spread these adjustment costs, like the benefits, among all sections of the Canadian community.

Commodity Trade and Development

Commodity trade issues, which have become the centrepiece of North-South negotiations in recent years, have been especially revealing of Canada's hesitancy and ambivalence in defining and pursuing its interests both at home and abroad. Is the Canadian interest predominantly that of a raw materials-producing nation, a consuming nation or, on the other hand, is it possible and legitimate for Canada to resist the 'integration' of different commodity markets into any common approach, but assess and pursue national interests on a case-by-case basis? It is basically the latter course which Canadian negotiators would claim to have pursued, but even this claim should be subjected to careful examination.

At the highest political level the Canadian government had seen merit, and presumably at least a long-term shared Canadian interest, in comprehensive measures to stabilize and improve the essential commodity earnings of developing countries. On balance, technical, political and psychological factors seemed to favour joint action on the commodities of major export interest to developing countries. Research had tended to show that consuming countries as well as producing countries could benefit well economically. With exports of the 18 UNCTAD commodities of $2.5 billion in 1976, and imports of only $1.6 billion, Canada was especially well protected in such a scheme.[27] Yet the federal departments most concerned, and industry lobbies in Canada, have persistently pressed for a case-by-case approach to commodity markets with the result that the Canadian approach has been hesitant or obstructive at key stages in the discussion of the Integrated Program and the Common Fund.

In very broad terms, it is possible to group the Canadian responses to commodity discussions according to the types of interest which come into play. First, those imported products which may be termed as having minor economic importance to Canada (e.g. jute, hard fibres and bananas) have not been viewed favourably by Canadian officials as candidates for buffer stocks. Instead, support has been expressed for establishing international organizations to facilitate research and development, diversification and market promotion of the relevant commodities. Secondly, in cases where there are already producer-consumer agreements in place and where imported products (e.g. tin) have important linkages with Canadian industry, or where the commodity plays a substantial role in Canadian consumer preferences (e.g. coffee), Canada has discharged its consumer-member obligations. Thirdly, in cases where no agreement exists and where Canada is a major importer and processor (e.g. natural rubber and bauxite markets), the Canadian position has been typified by the desire for stable commodity prices and a negative response to synthetics-harmonization. Finally, in cases where Canada has significant export interests (e.g. copper, iron ore, vegetable oil and oilseeds) Canadian representatives have advocated greater trade liberalisation for processed commodities and have tended to lobby against international commodity agreements equipped with stocking facilities and export controls.

Apart from the recognized common interest with other producers in securing improved trade access for proposed materials, it is in those commodities where Canada has a major export interest (especially copper and iron ore) but has consistently hung back from producer co-operation, that the perception of Canadian interests seems especially confused and inconsistent. While Canadian resistance on these commodities is sometimes put in terms of 'free market' rhetoric, this never seems to be a concern when it comes to discussion of international arrangements for grain.

More importantly, Canadian positions appear to have been heavily influenced by the country's intimate overall economic ties with the principal consumer-nations, and by the dominant position of consumer-country transnational firms in the sectors involved. For example, in 1972, foreign-controlled enterprises accounted for over 20 per cent of shipments from Canadian nickel and copper mines, and nearly 80 per cent of those from iron-ore mines. Even where direct industry ownership of commodity firms does not inject foreign priorities into Canadian decision-making, Canadian attitudes and negotiating positions are inevitably shaped by the tightly-woven web of cross-border relationships between commodity-consuming industries. With 50 per cent of Canadian manufacturing industry being foreign-owned (and, perhaps, especially vulnerable to dislocations and head-office decisions) it should come as no surprise that the responses of Canadian business and labour to commodity agreements, or to greater Third World processing, are often indistinguishable from those of their counterparts in other Northern countries. In fact, there have been suggestions that because of their commanding flexibility, Canada is pitted against potential new Third World producers in competition for investment. Under such conditions, the argument runs, the greater stability and security of investment which might come through strong international agreements could actually be inimical to Canada's interests.

In the whole range of Canadian positions on commodity trade issues, the overriding question is whether Canadian responses are consistent with either global or Canadian interests. It seems clear that the Trudeau Cabinet, frustrated in its attempts to generate a consistent and constructive response to Third World commodity demands, and shaken by the government's unpreparedness to cope with new competition in nickel and copper production, was not satisfied that either Canadian or legitimate international interests were being properly served. The Cabinet in 1978 ordered a comprehensive review of Canadian commodity interests and policies, a review which reportedly failed to produce an adequate base for grappling with both Third World concerns and Canada's own employment and export prospects.

'Aid', Debt and Monetary Relations

International development assistance, or 'foreign aid', receives a disproportionately large share of Canadian attention and opinion on Third World-Canada relations, and is popularly viewed as a purely one-way flow of resources, providing 'benefits' to 'recipients' through 'sacrifices' on the part of 'donors'. Gradually the more complex balance of actual benefits in the aid relationship has emerged more clearly, through a number of quantitative and qualitative measures, reflecting both Third World needs and demands and the accepted experience of the donor group and the international community.

For a country like Canada, even if 'aid' is substantially less important than other relationships, it is still the most important instrument explicitly concerned with promoting or supporting development in the Third World. Fundamental shifts in the Canadian approach to the quantity or quality of 'aid' may therefore signal vital trends in Third World-Canada relations generally.

The volume of Canadian aid expenditure over the past 15 years has almost doubled as a proportion of Canadian GNP, but the effort, and official commitment, have waxed and waned constantly over this period. While never binding itself to reach by a specific year the Pearson Commission's target of 0.7 per cent of GNP, the Canadian government has been unequivocally pledged to move steadily towards it. It seems clear that the present precipitous slide in allocations could lead to the unspoken abandonment of that goal. The development assistance programme is now seen as a major government expenditure whose effectiveness is subject to question (for very different reasons) by every sector of opinion, including the committed 'development community'.

On the traditional 'quantitative' and 'qualitative' yardsticks of aid performance, the Canadian record has been better than the donor average, but there are now strong indications that policy could shift to attempts to extract greater short-term benefits for Canada. Specifically, the movement to give priority to the basic needs of the poorest groups and countries could be slowed, or partially reversed, in order to give greater attention of the middle-income countries considered to be of much greater commercial interest to Canada. In line with such a shift, even the financial terms of Canadian aid, which have been mainly 'near-grant' soft loans, would be tightened up for these more commercial purposes. With pressures to add or retain 'middle-income' recipients, additional obstacles are placed in the way of the essential concentration of Canadian aid effort, already dispersed over an unmanageably large number of countries. The benefits which could be reaped from concentration, with increased field capability would lie in improved effectiveness and greater co-operation with selected governments which are themselves committed to more just development patterns.

Unfortunately, another Canadian interest in greater concentration of aid has begun to emerge in recent discussion. For the first time, there is some official sentiment (reflected publicly in the work of the Economic Council of Canada) that Canadian aid can and should be used consistently to exert political 'leverage' over recipients. While not unknown in past Canadian programmes (and now partly motivated by a desire to promote the observance of human rights), some of this new political interest in aid seems to signal Canada's accession to a kind of 'great power' status and values in the aid field. Its proponents tacitly or explicitly aim to shift the political benefits of aid to Canada from those of long-term goodwill and international co-operation to a much more immediate focus on usable 'credits' in Canada's political and commercial accounts with developing countries.

This same growing concern for a 'return' on aid is also evident in two other areas: the continuing insistence of the 'tying' of aid to Canadian goods and services, and new pressures to reduce the share of Canadian aid directed to multilateral agencies and programmes. In the case of the 'country-tying' of aid, where Canada ranks as a laggard ninth among the Western donors in the quality of its efforts, it is noteworthy that policy can be steered by the most short-term benefits (even with disproportionately high indirect costs) or in fact by disproved but ingrained popular assumptions about Canadian interests and benefits. The most glaring problem here is Canada's refusal so far to 'untie' its aid to allow Third World countries, other than the recipient, to bid on projects under the Canadian bilateral programme. After pledging to do so immediately in its 1975 *Strategy for International Cooperation*, the government has steadily backed away from this modest liberalization under active pressure from a narrow business lobby. The success of this campaign in obstructing a firm government commitment (even while evidence has emerged steadily on the high costs of tying to recipients and its very limited and short-term economic benefits to Canada[28]), is evidence of the power of a poorly-armed business lobby in times of domestic economic austerity. Meanwhile, the tying approach seems more and more to interfere with the implementation of the substantive *Strategy*, which emphasizes 'basic needs' and grass roots activities for which Canadian goods and services may often prove inappropriate or overpriced. The refusal to untie for Third World procurement is also embarrassing evidence of unwillingness to use available instruments to promote the development of production and trade within the Third World itself.

The new interest in reducing the multilateral share of Canadian aid is generally linked to the concern for both economic and political returns from aid expenditures. In the past, Canada has consistently been one of the mainstays of support for multilateral aid efforts and a significant influence among donors for growing contributions with minimum strings attached. Even without the impact of cutbacks in the aid budget, the opposition of business critics (against this form of 'untied' aid) and 'influence-minded' foreign policy planners was already pressing for some reduction in the multilateral share. Canada achieved the Pearson Commission's recommended minimum multilateral contribution of 30 per cent early in the 1970s and reached a level of half Canada's total aid disbursements in 1977, an exceptional year for several reasons. With the very limited success of Canadian suppliers in procurement under these programmes (in relation to Canadian contributions) and the recognition that Canada's influence over their direction was small, such pressure was predictable. However, in a situation where the aid agency must undergo harsh, general cutbacks, and where the bilateral, voluntary agency and industrial co-operation programmes all have relatively well-established consituencies, inside and outside bureaucracy, fighting to preserve their share of the budget, multilateral programmes are uniquely and dangerously exposed. The effectiveness of multilateral development programmes in general is by no means established in the public mind, and in some important circles there is an undocumented assumption that such programmes are necessarily more bureaucratized than are direct bilateral schemes. As in the case of UN peacekeeping activities and international trade negotiations, multilateral aid obligations will now test the depth of Canada's post-war commitment to multilateral co-operation. The marked reduction in 1979 of Canada's share of the Sixth Replenishment of the International Development Association (IDA), the 'soft-loan' window of the World Bank, was a key and influential bellwether of Canadian directions.

The debt relief issue of recent years has been one where real differences of interest emerged early among different groups of Third World countries, with important impacts on the negotiating response of Northern countries. As the homebase of a substantial international banking community, Canada's policy with respect to commercial debt has always been influenced by the determination of private bankers to stand publicly by the inviolability of outstanding obligations or, in the face of unavoidable default, to negotiate terms of rescheduling in private. In fact, this kind of approach to the handling of commercial debt problems, with some modifications, has basically satisfied most of those Third World countries with a significant commercial debt concern since they feel it is important to maintain their commercial creditworthiness. With Canadian bank holdings of Third World debt roughly estimated (in mid-1978) to be at least £3 billion, and with the existence of an extensive web of Canadian banking operations in Third World countries, it is not surprising that the Department of Finance, the lead department in these areas, remains conservative and unlikely to welcome any substantial change in the *laissez-faire* approach to commercial debt problems.

The Canadian government has, however, participated in the various 'clubs' organized to negotiate the terms of official outstanding debts of selected Third World countries. In these instances, finance officials and other creditor agencies represented, are said not to consult beforehand with Canadian commercial creditors since there is considered to be some element of competition in securing the most satisfactory terms for rescheduling.

For no clear reason, the same broad lines of approach applied to commercial and non-aid-related debt relief also seem to have been typical of the responses to early calls for generalized relief of the poorest countries' aid debts. Only after considerable interdepartment pressure, and inputs from Parliament and outside researchers, was the government finally willing to countenance the cancellation of the limited aid-related debts of the poorest countries in the final stages of the Paris Conference on International Economic Cooperation, when positive initiatives were badly needed. Because of the relative generosity of

Canada's aid lending terms, this particular problem was not a major one and is unlikely to recur.

Traditionally, Canada has exercised an influence in international monetary affairs out of proportion to its strict stake in these global issues. The country also shares some important objectives with the Third World in monetary reform, such as the replacement of gold and other reserve currencies by the SDR and the major international *numeraire* and reserve asset, the enhancemement of IMF lending facilities; and the enactment of special measures to improve facilities and representation for Third World countries. On other issues, however, the Canadian policy favours flexible exchange-rates and Canada has adhered to a very rigid perception of the IMF as a provider of balance of payments assistance. With government expertise and influence localized in the Department of Finance and the Bank of Canada, and non-governmental input to date restricted to the fairly narrow concerns of the private banks, the need for expanded public understanding and debate on monetary and debt issues is going to be crucial in reflecting the Canadian stake in both development and monetary stability.

Into the 1980s

Even this brief review of some of the Canadian interests involved in Third World relationships reveals a striking range of possibilities. The evidence does not support the most simplistic assertions that Canada may have a generalized identity of interests with Third World countries, but it also demands a re-examination of the prevalent assumption that Canada 'fits' comfortably into another group of nations whose interests lie in resistance to many Third World demands. Even more than most OECD countries, Canada has solid reasons to abandon the view of North-South dialogue as a 'zero-sum game' to be handled through a strategy of obduracy and frugal philanthropy.

'Aid', indeed, can be seen to be a relatively small part of the total Canadian response to the Third World, but a critical one in its reflection of the seriousness and clarity of Canadian purpose. It also tests, under adverse economic conditions, the capacity to act strategically with decency, rather than merely to capitalize on every tactical advantage.

There is competition, to be sure, between certain Canadian and Third World interests and, interestingly, even some of the competitive elements make Canada quite distinctive. In groping towards a satisfactory *modus vivendi* with the transnational corporation, or in attempting to secure a minimum of order in international commodity markets, Canada's perspective must be similar to that of some Third World countries, and on some points they will be formidable competitors to be reckoned with. The competitive potential of developing countries in manufactured trade has begun to have a profound impact in Canada, but the opportunities for expanded Canadian exports to these buoyant markets have not yet been properly recognized. With both imports and exports, the new impact of the Third World helps expose fundamental changes required in the Canadian economy itself — some of them long overdue and strikingly consistent with the emerging regional and sectoral opportunities for Canadian industrial strategy.

The complexity of some of these relationships, however, and the imperfect and cumbersome machinery for identifying and pursuing Canadian national interests, dictates a long process of analysis, debate, bargaining and adjustment within the Canadian community. On the strength of the analysis here, there is a clear Canadian interest in moving urgently, before the costs of change rise higher and opportunities slip away. There is also still a Canadian stake in moving co-operatively, through multilateral action where possible, since the traditional Canadian commitment to collective international response is as firmly rooted as ever in the Canadian interest.

Notes

*The text for this paper was completed by the author in mid-1980 and does not necessarily reflect in all respects the current state of Third World-Canada relations.

1. 'De-industrialization' is viewed by the Science Council of Canada as the most important symptom of a possible long-term economic decline now facing Canada. See for example, John N.H. Britton and James M. Gilmour, *The Weakest Link: A Technological Perspective on Canadian Industrial Underdevelopment*, Background Study No. 43 (Science Council of Canada, Department of Supply and Services, Ottawa, 1978).

2. Michel Dupuy, 'Directions for the Agency', *Papers and Documents* (Canadian International Development Agency, Ottawa, December 1977), p. ii.

3. In terms of its GNP, Canada ranks sixth among the OECD nations, seventh in *per capita* terms. In terms of indicators designed to measure progress in more human terms, such as the Physical Quality of Life Index (PQLI) developed by the Overseas Development Council of Washington, Canada ranks above the average of the high income countries with an index of 97 (out of a possible 100) on life expectancy, infant mortality and literacy.

4. The integrated North American defence system, formalized through NORAD and NATO, continues to act either as a source of latitude or as a constraint in different political/military situations. The theme of formal continental economic integration, which has recurred throughout modern Canadian history, is again stirring lively debate between 'continentalists' and 'nationalists', a debate

which commands serious attention by policy-makers and the public.

5. Cited in John W. Holmes, *Canada: A Middle-Aged Power* (McClelland and Stewart, Toronto, 1976), p. 67.

6. H.B. Malmgren 'The Evolving Trade System' in H.E. English (ed.), *Canada-U.S. Relations* (Praeger, New York, 1976). A current illustration of the continuing Canadian capability for multilateral leadership has been in the Law of the Sea negotiations, but here Canada itself has stood to gain so substantially that its multilateral initiatives can be seen somewhat differently.

7. Canada, Department of External Affairs, *Foreign Policy for Canadians* (The Queen's Printer, Ottawa, 1970).

8. Canada, Department of External Affairs, *International Development: Foreign Policy for Canadians* (The Queen's Printer, Ottawa, 1970), p. 19.

9. A recent study of Trudeau suggests that 'in more formal, prepared speeches he is often attempting to provide intellectual leadership without signifying any accompanying intention to legislate'. This pattern seems to apply closely in the field of international development. George Radwanski, *Trudeau* (Macmillan of Canada, Ltd., Toronto, 1978), pp. 124-6.

10. Canada, Canadian International Development Agency, *Strategy for International Development Cooperation 1975-1980* (Information Canada, Ottawa, 1975).

11. See The North-South Institute, *Canada North-South 1977-1978, Vol. 1: North-South Encounter: The Third World and Canadian Performance* (The North-South Institute, Ottawa, 1977), pp. 6-7.

12. Canada, in this period, became a net exporter of equity capital.

13. These changes are treated in greater detail in G. Bruce Doern, 'Recent Changes in the Philosophy of Policy-making in Canada', *Canadian Journal of Political Science, v. IV (June 1971), pp. 243-64.*

14. John J. Kirton, 'Foreign Policy Decision-making in the Trudeau Government: Promise and Performance', *International Journal*, vol. XXXIII. no. 2 (Spring, 1978), pp. 287-311.

15. Members of ICERDC are: the Departments of Agriculture, Consumer and Corporate Affairs, Finance and Industry, Trade and Commerce; the Ministry of State for Science and Technology; the Treasury Board; CIDA; the Privy Council Office; and the Prime Minister's Office.

16. In fact, ITC and Finance, which dominate on trade issues, tend to see the formal committees as an unwarranted intrusion, to be avoided if possible. David Protheroe, 'Making Trade Decisions in Canada 1968-1978', unpublished thesis, the Norman Paterson School of International Affairs, Carleton University (Ottawa, 1979).

17. For more general background on Trudeau's role in the Cabinet see Radwanski, *Trudeau*, especially Chapter 9.

18. The 1970 Foreign Policy Review explicitly recognized these linkages by noting that: 'External activities should be directly related to national policies pursued within Canada, and serve the same objectives.' Canada, External Affairs, *Foreign Policy for Canadians* (The Queen's Printer, Ottawa, 1970), p. 9. The merger of the Department of Industry with the Department of Trade and Commerce in 1969 had also been intended to strengthen the ties between domestic and international activities.

19. The list of former senior bureaucrats who now head business associations or operate consulting firms is impressively long.

20. These views were reflected in Roy MacLaren, Chairman, Task Force on Business-Government Interface, 'How to Improve Business-Government Relations in Canada', a Report to the Minister of Industry, Trade and Commerce (September 1976).

21. See Canada, House of Commons, *Minutes of Proceedings and Evidence of the Subcommittee on International Development of the Standing Committee on External Affairs and National Defence*, First Session, Thirtieth Parliament (issue no. 14) (12 February 1976).

22. *Canadian Labour Comment*, vol. 7, no. 3, (16 February 1979).

23. Canadian Labour Congress, 'Policy Documents', 12th Constitutional Convention, (Quebec, April 1978), p. 30.

24. Canada, House of Commons, *Minutes of Proceedings and Evidence to the Standing Committee on External Affairs and National Defence*, Fourth Session, Thirtieth Parliament (issue no. 3) (1 December 1978), pp. 25-9.

25. Hearings of the Commons Standing Committee on External Affairs and National Defence are replete with praise from members of all parties for the 'grass roots' work of NGOs, frequently juxtaposed with 'over-bureaucratized' official aid.

26. For more details on this example see Donald Page, 'Does Don Jamieson Read All Those Letters You Write?' *International Perspectives* (May/June, 1978), p. 25. It is noteworthy that Page suggests that Canada's South African policy will, in the future, continue to respond to pressure from the public: 'even now the strength and implementation of the proposed changes may rest in the balance . . . ', p. 25.

27. Data provided by UNCTAD-OECD Division, Department of Industry, Trade and Commerce, Ottawa.

28. Since 1975, in fact, serious studies have been carried out, within government and elsewhere, but their results have been downplayed or classified within government. Media and public attention have also increasingly focused on the negative impact of aid tying.

4 JAPAN AND THE THIRD WORLD: COINCIDENCE OR DIVERGENCE OF INTERESTS*

Ronald Dore

In a number of senses, Japan differs more from the leading OECD countries than those countries differ from each other: in internal economic structure, in international involvements and in cultural predispositions and views of the outside world. I begin with the last.

Perceptions as Revealed in the Press and Other Media

Most Japanese have an acute sense of the alienness of abroad. Foreign countries are places for adventure and interesting experiences, for discomfort and even for danger, places in which to try to make one's mark but not, except in tiny Japanese enclaves, places in which to feel at home or to relax. The possibility, for instance, of friendships based on common tastes or professional or business interests transcending national boundaries seems much more remote to most middle class Japanese than to most members of the European middle classes. It is a rare Japanese Marxist economist at an international conference who feels more at home with French Marxists than with fellow Japanese economists of capitalist or neo-classical persuasions. Barriers of language and custom and sentiment often seem impenetrable, even to those who have experienced higher education and are well acquainted with European history and literature.

The other side of this sense of separateness is not a lack of human sympathy for poverty in the poor countries, but a lack of much sense that it is any of Japan's responsibility. Japanese can on occasion individually respond generously to appeals for disaster relief: Schweitzer is as much a Japanese as a European hero. But since the renunciation of 'co-prosperity sphere' ambitions, the initial automatic assumption of responsibility for the plight of foreigners does not come easily, as recent policies towards Vietnamese refugees have demonstrated.

A number of particular circumstances help to explain the difference in this regard between the Japanese and Eurpean middle classes. First, in spite of $7,000 *per capita* national income and $22 billion reserves, the Japanese do not feel rich. And with very good reason. There *is* a difference between having and not having a century of accumulation of residential and social infrastructural capital. The Japanese official or businessman used to travelling in jam-packed commuter trains from his modest two-bedroomed suburban home, is frequently reminded of this fact when he is in Europe and America, whether visiting the homes or (government servants especially) the offices, of his opposite numbers, or wandering in the parks or galleries or museums. (The 1979 Trade White Paper specifically makes that point in a table showing that Japan has flush toilets in only 31 per cent of houses compared with 98 per cent in Britain; only 13 doctors for 10,000 inhabitants compared with America's 17; only 1.5 square metres of park space per Tokyo inhabitant compared with 23 in London.[1])

Secondly, although the Japanese too have a colonial experience it did not have the same effect in breeding a sense of paternal responsibility as grew out of the European assumption of a 'civilising mission' in Asia and Africa. The Japanese *did* see themselves as having a mission to develop the decrepit kingdom of Korea and neglected Taiwan. They did so by extending to those colonies the fruits of newly imported modernity. But in terms of intrinsic culture – at the level of what Europeans thought they were doing in transferring the rudiments of Christian civilization to Africa – Korea and Taiwan were, if anything, more ancient and authentic exponents of the Confucian-Buddhist East Asian culture which they all shared in common.

Thirdly, Japan is very much a socially mobile nation with many of the problems which attend such social mobility. For a century Japan has been working its way up from a lowly position in the international status ladder. At the individual level, while a Japanese abroad may share the same sense of the alienness of foreigners as do members of the British working class, in any misunderstanding with a foreigner, whereas the descendants of Imperial Britain are likely to assume that it must be the foreigner's fault, the Japanese is more likely to assume that the fault is his. It is the Japanese who, as the arrivistes, have had to learn to conform in the course of a century-long national endeavour to secure a position of respect in the international community. ('He spoke of "civilization" [i.e. Western civilization] as a kind of bitter medicine that Japan had to swallow' said Beatrice Webb of the Japanese Prime Minister in 1911.)[2] There was one period, 1937-45, when the Japanese abandoned the conformist, 'ingratiating' path to status and made a bid to remake the world, or a part of it, in their own image. But that ended in a disaster, in a foreign occupation and an even more overt and universal acceptance of the need to conform to the norms and assumptions of foreign countries.

One consequence of such an historical experience (combined, perhaps, with a special sensitivity to status distinctions in interpersonal relations within Japan) is an acute consciousness of the world as a stratified system. For the Japanese the 'significant others' are the top nations whose company Japan has recently come to keep. All peoples are more sensitive to the standing of their nation in countries generally deemed to be above them in the international pecking order than to their standing in 'lesser' countries. It is just that the difference is more marked in Japan. So much so that perhaps the most common perception of Japan's position in the North-South context is that Japan has an obligation *vis-à-vis* the other *rich* countries to 'share the burden'. This comes out clearly in a Foreign Ministry pamphlet published by a satellite quango of the Foreign Ministry and written by the Director of the Ministry's Economic Cooperation Bureau. He begins his exposition of the foreign aid question by reference to Japan's low position in the DAC league table (aid as a percentage of GNP and the grant element proportion) and quotes the Prime Minister as saying that the record was 'embarrassing' and that Japan should aim to reach the DAC average as soon as possible in order that she should be seen to be taking her fair share in 'the common effort'.[3] The same theme is echoed in the 1978 Foreign Ministry 'White Paper' on aid.[4]

Among the general public, as opposed to Foreign Ministry officials, other considerations seem more important – at least if the results of annual government opinion surveys are to be believed. The proportions definitely against aid have been regularly very small – only seven per cent in 1979 thought that aid should be stopped or kept as small as possible. Forty per cent thought that Japan should expand aid, 34 per cent that she should be content to 'keep it at an ordinary level'. When the last two categories were asked for their reasons, 17 per cent gave the need to avoid being isolated from the other OECD countries, over 50 per cent cited Japan's dependency on imported resources and between 35 per cent and 40 per cent mentioned each of mutual dependence, humanitarian duty and contributions to world peace.[5]

The reference to resources reflects a widespread sense of Japan's vulnerability and accounts for a note of wary defensiveness found in some Japanese reactions to the Third World – a note well caught in the following passage from another popular foreign Ministry exposition (1973) of the underlying reasons why Japan should give foreign aid.

We cannot for ever sustain a selfish 'I'm all right Jack' attitude to the poor countries and their need for capital and technology in order to develop, particularly those Asian countries with which we have close connections. We already attract the none-too-flattering jibe that we are 'economic animals' and we can expect such resentful reactions to be even more widespread if that were the policy we adopted. It is even not impossible to imagine a large-scale anti-Japanese movement leading to a boycott of Japanese goods, and then, far from being able to solve our current structural problems we would have to give up all prospect of economic development and reconcile ourselves to a low standard of living and massive unemployment on our tiny island. At any rate we would lose far more than the umpteen thousand houses [that the critics of foreign aid say could be built with the money],[6]

Concessions or aid to the Third World, then, are less likely (it *is* a matter of more or less) to be seen as a means of winning friends than as a means of appeasing potential enemies. Japan did not feel she could afford the gesture of cutting off aid to put pressure on the Vietnamese over the refugees, but stepped up aid to Thailand instead — partly to provide reassurance lest the continuance of aid to Vietnam gave offence. The considerable space devoted to Tanzania in the 1977 White Paper on international trade[7] and the attempts to step up aid to Tanzania were explained by a Foreign Ministry official as having to do with Tanzania's position, along with Japan, as an elected member of the Security Council, and Tanzania's role as a leading castigator of industrial countries with extensive dealings with South Africa and a suspected role in breaking Rhodesian sanctions. Tanzanian attacks on Japan in the Security Council during 1977 had, he thought, been somewhat tempered as a result.

In the same vein, a journalist commenting on the Prime Minister's tour of Southeast Asia in the autumn of 1977 spoke of a regular aid cycle, beginning with export-promoting aid, leading to an expansion of Japanese exports, a growing Japanese export surplus to the recipient countries, growing resentment of that surplus, anti-Japanese manifestations and further aid as appeasement.[8]

Two further reasons for Japan's underlying attitudes are suggested in the pamphlet by the Director of the Economic Cooperation Bureau quoted earlier.[9] The first is the absence in Japan of the Christian tradition of charity — and he quotes Mr Pronk, the former Dutch Aid Minister, in a lecture in Japan as giving this a dominant place in Dutch motives for aid. Secondly, having had the experience of developing their own country in a short space of time by sheer hard work and with little external assistance, Japanese are less inclined to think that the world owes the developing countries a living and more inclined to think that they ought to do more to help themselves.

Divisions of Opinion: Politics

So far I have written about 'the Japanese', and generalizations of this kind about attitudes and assumptions *are*, perhaps, more justified about Japan than about any of the other rich countries except the small Scandinavian ones. There is a homogeneity about Japanese society — three major newspapers being virtually indistinguishable in style and editorial opinion, for example — which is rare in modern nation-states. That said, there are of course political and other differences. As between the Socialist and Communist Parties on the one hand, and the ruling Liberal Democratic Party on the other, the overwhelmingly important dividing issue in foreign policy concerns Japan's stance towards the US. That automatically involves sharp opposition, too, on any Third World issue in which the US is involved — e.g. Vietnam. Where the US is not a dominant factor, however, as in relations with China, there is a greater identity of outlook: before the resumption of Japanese-Chinese relations, for example, Socialist leaders were involved from time to time in carrying messages to Peking and even in informal negotiation.

Nor do other non-US-involved Third World issues achieve much prominence in the central political and ideological debates. Socialists share very much the same feelings of alienness and non-connection *vis-à-vis* Africans as other Japanese. The Socialist Party does not, therefore, feel strongly about Japan's relations with South Africa or Zimbabwe. First, UN resolutions have little bite with the Japanese left. Since the 'UN equals US' equation was established during the Korean War on their doorstep a quarter of a century ago, there has been little predisposition among communists or socialists to see the UN as the potential framework of a more just world order. Secondly, the Japanese left is most deeply serious about capitalism and the need to abolish it. Foreign aid and other manifestations of Japanese 'positive' policies towards the Third World are likely to be seen simply as the imperialist expansion of Japanese capitalism and as such something to be wholly deplored rather than discriminatingly judged according to some kind of 'contribution to Third World development' criterion (though a socialist member did launch a private member's bill in the Diet in 1973 to restrict aid to non-democratic governments). Thirdly, having not, for twenty years, seen themselves as potential members of an alternative government, socialist politicians have not been much motivated to think seriously about, for instance, energy problems or long-term security problems. In line with this general politics-in-command orientation, the Socialist Party tends to be more interested, for example, in non-aligned meetings than in 'Group of 77' meetings. There is a tendency, too, for particular alignments to determine the policies advocated – attitudes towards the old or the new Cambodia, Vietnam, Angola, etc. being much affected by the current balance of feelings towards Moscow and Peking respectively.

The one political grouping which adopts a general stance towards North-South issues of the kind common in the moderate left in Europe, is the Democratic Socialist Party. Its Chairman is a leading member of a newly formed Committee for North-South Relations which organized a pre-UNCTAD symposium attended by a number of Asian Ministers, in March 1979. With only 32 of the 511 Lower House seats after the 1980 election, however, the DSP does not carry much weight.

Of potentially greater importance is a division of sentiment within the ruling Liberal Democratic Party which emerges at times of tension between US and Third World countries. This is between the dominant group which sees Japan's future as lying with the United States, and the Afro-Asian group which reflects not so much Pan-Asian sentiment as a co-Asian resentment against a Western world which will never accord Japan the status which she deserves on her merits, and insists that, in the end, Japan's future must lie in throwing in her lot with other non-Caucasian peoples. Since the end of the Vietnam War and the normalization of US relations with China, the world has not seen the kind of tensions which catalyze these differences and they have remained muted. But any tendency towards the general spread of protectionism and a division of the world into trading blocs might give a renewed importance to this kind of 'Afro-Asian' view and increase what now seems a remote possibility – that its exponents, in alliance with left-wing parties, could become a dominant political force.

Divisions of Opinion: Bureaucracy

It is generally agreed that the politician/bureaucrat power balance is tipped rather more towards the latter in Japan than in most other democracies. The divisions of interest within the bureaucracy are, therefore, of more than passing importance.

There is no single ministry responsible even for overseas aid, much less for dealing with developing countries in general. Aid and technical co-operation matters are decided in a four-ministry council — the Foreign Ministry, the Ministry of International Trade and Industry, the Ministry of Finance and the Economic Planning Agency. Of these, the first two are the most concerned, the Foreign Ministry being the administrator of the aid budget and also the controller of the Japan International Cooperation Agency (JICA), which deals with technical assistance, while MITI is the chosen spokesman for Japan's industrial and trading interests which (as one might guess from the lists of 'most used telephone numbers' stuck on the walls of its aid departments' offices) have a considerable influence on policy. The EPA, in spite of the fact that it is the parent Ministry of the other aid organ, the Overseas Economic Cooperation Fund (OECF) which deals with loans and capital grants, does not have a similar power base and has the reputation for being 'academic' — i.e. taking more long-term and enlightened, but therefore 'unrealistic', views of issues such as restructuring. The Ministry of Finance is the least 'concerned' — the other Ministries complain of its parochial preoccupation with domestic issues — but, with its control over the purse, arguably the most powerful. These four ministries are joined for all aid project decisions by relevant functional ministries. The Ministries of Transport or Construction are involved for almost every large project; the Ministry of Agriculture for any project concerned with rural development. Sectional interests, e.g. the Ministry of Agriculture's protectionism, may be reflected in the attitudes which these ministries take in any such project meeting, though a more common concern is said to be to find lucrative technical assistance assignments for senior bureaucrats with blocked promotion prospects.

There is a considerable degree of straightforward (non-policy-related) bureaucratic rivalry between the two main ministries concerned with aid and development matters — a rivalry exaggerated by Japanese groupiness according to Rix who sees 'identification with the primary work group' of a specifically Japanese kind as 'the fundamental barrier to active coordination across ministerial boundaries'.[10] MITI has for some years published a detailed annual survey of *Economic cooperation: the current situation and its problems*; the Ministry of Foreign Affairs had been content with a shorter special section of its annual survey of foreign affairs, but in 1978 it produced its own independent survey, *Economic cooperation: the current situation and outlook.*

(The MITI survey for that year opens with the claim that 'this is the only systematic source of information concerning economic cooperation in Japan'.) In the rivalry between the two ministries, the Foreign Ministry has been the source of the most tenacious resistance against proposals to establish a special ministry, or, later, agency, to deal with aid matters, and with aid accounting for 56 per cent of its budget (1979-80) could not afford the blow to its standing in the expenditure league table which such a departure would entail.

These rivalries apart, there are, it seems different emphases between the two main ministries in their perceptions of problems and these differences are reflected in their respective Year Books. The Foreign Ministry's 1978 report contains a strong statement of the need for foreign aid with emphasis on Japan's 'good neighbour' reputation, her low standing in the DAC GNP ratio league ('if we look back on our reactions to North South problems, it can hardly be denied that — chiefly because of the unclarity of our basic beliefs on these matters — we have been lacking in consistency and not up to the standards of other advanced countries'), as well as Japan's long-term interests in a more secure and peaceful world.[11]

The MITI document, by contrast, expresses none of this discomfiture, points out that Japan is the third largest DAC donor before it mentions that it is 14th in the proportion of GNP devoted to aid, and begins its discussion of aid policy by identifying the growth of Japan's trade surpluses as the factor which has intensified pressures on Japan to increase the volume of her aid.[12] This difference in approach has a long history.[13]

It is perhaps consonant with this difference in approach, and difference in sensitivity to currents of opinion in the 'international development community', that the Ministry of Foreign Affairs' document treats the basic human needs strategy as an important revelation (while warning that given the greater difficulty of implementing such aid projects there should be no sacrifice of the greater priority which is to increase the total amount of aid). The MITI document on the other hand, suggests that while 'aid in the welfare field' should be considered along with industrial development, 'this emphasis on BHN should·not lead to any undervaluation of economic growth; the satisfaction of basic needs can only be achieved on the basis of growth'.

Not all individuals in either ministry necessarily conform to the ministry ethos, of course, but the differences suggested above do represent something real. Foreign Ministry officials are much more likely to be on the receiving end of criticisms of Japan's 'poor performance', and to feel the force of what the bureau chief calls in the pamphlet quoted earlier 'the good neighbour logic' (the duty to fulfil obligations *vis-à-vis* the *other rich countries* by taking one's share of the aid burden). They are also more likely to develop a genuinely internationalist outlook. Both the Foreign Ministry pamphlets quoted earlier and the Ministry's White Paper urge that the Japanese need to become more internationalized, not in the mere sense of acquiring cosmopolitan sophistication, but by developing a sense of shared humanity with all peoples on the globe.

Business Official Relations

One common view of Japan suggests that to look for the reflection of any kind of conflict of interest in her external relations is a waste of time. Japan Incorporated moves with a rare unity of purpose; its heart throbs with a single beat. In its extreme form that is nonsense, but undeniably co-operation between business and government in matters of external relations is closer than in most other OECD countries – and the partnership involves a larger element of government leadership – i.e. it is not just that the businessman abroad can sometimes call on political support from his embassy to get a concession on a contract; businessmen are also expected to rally round to support policies thought to be in the interests of Japan as a whole. The pressure on Mitsubishi to establish a white elephant ethylene plant in Saudi Arabia to 'bind' the Saudis to Japanese interests is an example (though in the end such pressure succeeded only when government guarantees made it worthwhile for Mitsubishi to succumb). The manner in which the entire Japanese community in Indonesia was mobilized to prepare for Prime Minister Fukuda's visit in August 1977, is another example; likewise the manner in which the ambassador in smaller African countries can, depending on his personality, see himself as head prefect of the Japanese community and not hesitate to scold those among his 'charges' whose behaviour he considers not likely to enhance the regard in which Japan is held. A more important manifestation of this close business-official relationship is in the large role played by consulting firms in the project identification and appraisal surveys on which the selection of projects for aid is based. Many of the same firms are subsequently successful in tendering for the project they have designed. Since country programming is rudimentary (total aid volumes are fixed only for a few consortium countries such as Indonesia) and aid commitments are on a project-by-project basis, these business firms play a major part in determining the direction of aid.[14]

The capacity for concerted action is even more marked in those projects, like the major Asahan project in Indonesia or a similar aluminium project in the Amazon, which are concerned with the development of resources of acute interest to Japan. The Amazon project sponsored by the OECF is being run by a consortium, 40 per cent of whose funds is provided by the Japanese government, the rest by a wide variety of firms – five aluminium smelters, ten trading companies, five aluminium rolling firms, five engineering firms usuing aluminium, three window frame makers and one bank.

That this spirit of co-operation operates to the very considerable advantage of Japanese businessmen, and not only to those directly engaged in the consulting business, is a fair inference from the pattern of aid distribution. To begin with, a very high proportion of aid is bilateral: only 5 per cent of 1977 aid was in the form of grants to multilateral agencies, compared with the DAC average of 15 per cent. A similar concern with promoting specifically Japanese interests can be seen in the distribution between countries. The Foreign Ministry at least tries to set country priorities in a formally rationalized way. The aid division of the Ministry and the various regional divisions each rank prospective aid recipients according to a number of criteria including their poverty and the trade they do with Japan. The two rankings are then amalgamated and are supposed to provide guidelines for the global amounts of projects approved to each country. That 'importance to Japanese business' rather than 'poverty need' plays the predominant part in the weighting is suggested by the rank order of leading recipients in 1975-7. Indonesia, well in the lead with US $547 million of concessionary aid, is followed by South Korea with $196 million, then more closely by the Philippines, Egypt and Bangladesh in that order. However, aid to Indonesia was falling and that to Bangladesh gaining during the period – an indication that in response to criticism of Japan's 'commercial' aid policy, the 'poverty need' criterion has been gaining in importance. 1978-9 figures would probably show that trend even more markedly.

Priorities in Japan's Agenda

If, then, it does make more sense in Japan than it might elsewhere to talk about the consciousness of the 'typical' politician or businessman, in what light do the problems of the Third World impinge on that consciousness? Any attempt to rank the 'salience' of different aspects of Japan's relations with the Third World in general public discussion is bound to be impressionistic. My impression of that ranking is therefore offered tentatively.

    1. TWCs as sources of raw materials.
= 2. TWCs as political actors, as part of the audience which assesses Japan's international 'performance' and determines her international standing, and consequently the 'clout' she can exercise in UN, GATT, IMF, OECD, etc. The Third World is the lesser part of that audience, as compared with the OECD countries, in terms of 'moral authority', but still important — being able, for instance, to give Bangladesh the seat Japan wanted on the Security Council.
= 2. TWCs as a field for Japanese investment.
= 2. TWCs as a market for Japanese goods.
    5. TWCs as a source of manufactured imports, enforcing structural adjustment on Japanese manufacturing,
    6. TWCs as the source, directly or indirectly, or threats to Japan's security.

Perhaps the most striking thing about this ordering is the central importance attached to resources and the low place accorded to the industrial restructuring problem (though the latter is rapidly rising in the attention scale, if primarily as a reflection of debates elsewhere). Let us consider some of the elements in turn, beginning with the economic items.

Resources

Japan is more dependent on raw material imports than any other of the rich countries, and since 1973 official publications have reflected the extent to which the oil crisis heightened awareness of that fact. Oil from developing countries provided 94 per cent of Japan's mineral fuel, and over 70 per cent of all primary energy sources in 1979.[15] Dependency on developing countries for food and other raw materials is of lesser proportions (37 per cent and 42 per cent respectively in 1976)[16] but the oil dependency alone gives Japan a larger share of trade with developing countries than any other leading industrial power. (Imports: 55 per cent in 1976 — 42 per cent before the 1973 oil crisis added $14 billion to the oil bill — compared with 44 per cent for the US and 35 per cent for the UK. Exports: 46 per cent compared to 35 per cent for the US and 36 per cent of the UK, according to the Ministry of Foreign Affairs classification of OECD statistics.)[17]

As far as oil is concerned, this dependency will continue for some time to come. Consumption reductions will not be easy. Japan remains a relatively frugal oil consumer using 67 per cent of its total consumption (3.08 tons *per capita* per annum) for industry, compared with 47 per cent of US consumption (8.72 tons *per capita*; UK, 55 per cent and 3.78 tons respectively).[18] Nuclear alternatives are subject to very strong environmental democratic procedure constraints. Projections for 1985 suggest that *if* energy saving measures succeed, imported oil might reduce to 66 per cent of total energy sources, which given expected consumption, would still be an increase in total volume of 50 per cent over 1975.[19] After the Tokyo summit and Japan's acceptance of the target of a mere 6.3 million barrels per day of imports in 1985, revised plans for alternatives (including large imports of LNG and coal) had by 1980 adopted the − admittedly hopeful − aim of reducing reliance on oil imports to 50 per cent by 1990.[20] Some diversification to Mexican and, if Congress relents, Alaskan oil might be possible, but with no basic change in Japan's overwhelming dependency on Middle Eastern producers.

On the other hand there is some slight lessening of the sense of vulnerability which prevailed in early 1974. IEA sharing arrangements, the enlargement of stocks from 50 to 85 days consumption (with 90 days as the target for 1980) and the slow build-up of a 'presence' in the Middle East (Mitsubishi's ethylene plant in Saudi Arabia mentioned earlier for instance) have provided some small comfort.

As for food, the self-sufficiency of the Japanese economy was calculated to be about 73 per cent in 1972, is expected to rise to 75 per cent in 1985, though in cereals self-sufficiency was only 42 per cent, and is expected to fall to 32 per cent. The scare of 1974 produced plans to revive production of wheat and barley and to double-crop marginal land, but it is obvious that very considerable efforts whould have only minimal effect on the self-sufficiency ratio,[21]

As a food importer, Japan has every interest in promoting the development of food self-sufficiency in developing countries and even of promoting their capacity to export (especially aminal feed) to Japan − one aim of proposals by the Ministry of Agriculture and Forestry for a special agricultural aid fund in 1972-3.[22] In this capacity however, Japan might stand to lose from the industrialization of developing countries if it turned them into food importers and so added to the upwards pressure of international food prices. There is no evidence, however, that this in any sense enters into policy (except perhaps to provide an extra edge of keenness to Japan's assistance to agricultural development in Southeast Asia not present in her aid for industrializa- tion). In any case many countries, like Japan, actually increase *per capita* food production with industrialization.

Although Japan does not share the same vulnerability with regard to any other raw material source, the 'oil shock' has generated a general sense of insecurity about the political vulnerability of raw material supplies leading, perhaps, to greater efforts to diversify sources. It has also led to a greater willingness to entertain LDC demands for help in developing downstream processing, though several other consi- derations enter here. The recession after 1974 was also a searing experi- ence for some Japanese producers, notable copper refiners, who found themselves caught with contracts to purchase copper ore, from sources they had helped to develop, on a scale way above what the market could absorb. Most of the agreements were renegotiated and have sur- vived, but nevertheless the experience induced a certain caution about the 'Japanese finance plus long-term purchasing agreements' for mineral development.

This has not, however, prevented some subsequent large-scale devel- opments, such as the Amazon aluminium project already mentioned, and a number of other similar projects in which Japanese companies have gone beyond financing and entered into direct venture partnerships, usually with parastatals of the host government – in Malaysia, Peru, Indonesia and Zaire as well as Canada. The Trade White Paper attributes these developments to growing nationalism on the part of Third World governments prompting them to resist the approaches of the Euro- American majors who had dominated the extractive industries hither- to.[23] Heightened nationalism sells its resources more dearly. Alcan had been involved in abortive negotiations with the Brazilian government before the Japanese Amazon scheme started. The Japanese consortium was able to meet the Brazilian terms chiefly because it could command much better financing guarantees from the Japanese government than Alcan could offer. Staking priority claims on raw material resources has a high place in Japanese government assessments of expenditure-worthy objectives. Also relevant is a greater Japanese willingness, for energy and environmental reasons, to accept – even seek – downstream primary processing.

The ties of dependency which, through these mechanisms, do link Japan to developing countries link her, however, only to a minority of those countries, and not at all to the poorest. Africa (which at present provides six per cent of Japan's metal raw material imports) could disappear from the globe with little lasting effect on Japan's resource position. Partly because of distance, partly because of political/cultural problems ('You got your first English-Swahili dictionary in the 1830's; the first Japanese-Swahili dictionary − a translation of an English one − was done by a mining company in the 1960s'), few ventures on that continent have proved a success. The copper venture in Zaire, started in the early 1970s with some enthusiasm, has since run into difficulties and is marking time.

Overseas Investment

At March 1979, Japan had about $11 billion of direct investment in Europe, North America and Oceania and $15 billion in the rest of the world. (Whereas the American $168 billion (December 1978) and West Germany's $36 billion (June 1979) were heavily directed, in a ratio of about 3 to 1, towards the industrialized countries.) Of Japan's $15 billion investment in the Third World, about a third was in mining and nearly half in manufacturing.

Japan's overseas investment, according to Kojima, has been 'trade-oriented', that is to say has consisted very largely of the export to other countries of industries in which Japan was losing comparative advantage. This contrasts with a good deal of American MNCs investment abroad which has been 'anti-trade-oriented' in as much as it is the industries in which America has the greatest competitive advantage which have gone overseas in order to duck under the trade barriers of countries with active import-substituting industrialization policies.[24]

However, whether there is such a clear difference between Japanese and American overseas investment policies may be doubted. A MITI survey found recently that overseas Japanese subsidiaries in the electrical equipment industry sold 75 per cent of their output locally, eight per cent back to Japan and 18 per cent to the rest of the world. The proportions were not so very different in other branches of manufacture. Precision machinery firms exported the largest amount back to Japan − 36 per cent − apart from the resource industries.[25]

Investment primarily motivated by a desire to capture local markets or circumvent trade restriction has probably predominated in the investment in Central and South America, amounting, in manufacturing, to about $2.7 billion investment by the end of 1978. By then Singapore had become the favourite platform, lacking the political problems of Taiwan, still small in export volume and hence not as likely as South Korea to attract US protectionist counter-measures, closer to Middle Eastern oil than Hong Kong and in the middle of the large ASEAN market, with a splendidly pro-business political climate – and, above all, a labour force of Sinic culture with Sinic work habits. Industrial emigration to Singapore is beginning to take the form of transfers of industrial complexes, not just of single firms. Larger firms have been followed by their parts-supplying smaller subcontractors.

Malaysia is thought to be the likely next favoured country if Singapore becomes saturated, but there is as yet little disposition to move very much further afield. There is a system of loans designed to stimulate overseas investment by small firms which is confined to ventures, not in the established NICs, but in the next wave of proto-NICs; Thailand, Indonesia, etc. The demand is never large enough to absorb the funds available.

Nevertheless, there is little doubt that this kind of investment will steadily increase. Japan has succeeded better than many anticipated in scaling down her growth rates. During the 1977-9 period, when investment rates in manufacturing at home were a good deal lower than in the high-growth periods but savings refused obstinately to fall (still around 22 per cent of GNP in 1978), there were additional measures to liberalize movements of capital overseas.[26] The savings surplus had its counterpart in a balance of payments surplus, and although each substantial oil price rise turns the trade account into deficit for a year or two, the long-run exporting strength of the Japanese economy offers the prospect of surpluses conducive to overseas investment as a feature of Japan's normal condition.

There are a number of other reasons, too, for expecting investment to grow:

(1) Labour cost differentials will increase and gastarbeiter solutions are not acceptable.
(2) The financial logic of corporation growth – the micro-economic counterpart of the excess savings just mentioned. The overall internal financing ratio of Japanese companies (retained earnings plus depreciation as a proportion of fixed home investment) slowly reached, then exceeded, 100 per cent in the early 1970s – the point reached by US corporations, at the start of their overseas expansion at the end of the Second World War.[27] The lower post-recession growth rates, with profits recovered but fewer opportunities for home investment, may even have raised the

ratio further.

(3) The overvalued yen (which the competitiveness of Japan's exports may well keep overvalued) makes capital export attractive.

(4) The organizational imperative. Broadening pyramids of civil service-like managerial hierarchies within corporations mean intensifying competition for top jobs as growth slows down. Having too many chiefs may create the need for foreign indians.

(5) A younger, more culturally adaptable generation of managers may well make Japanese firms more genuinely transnational and so less subject to political constraints to growth.

(6) The focusing of competition between the major firms in each industry on market shares is carried over into their overseas operations and produces a bandwagon effect, partly through economic calculation — to get a fair share of overseas markets — partly because successful overseas operations become a matter of prestige.

(7) By the same token that 'virility test' is coming to seem more and more difficult as political uncertainties in the Third World seem to grow. The Iran débâcle has prompted much talk of what is called 'country risk'. The government had to provide US$100 million of aid to persuade Mitsui to resume its part in the joint-venture petrochemical plant it was, until the revolution, building in Iran with the National Iranian Oil Company and already, after the Iran-Iraq war stopped the project a second time, Mitsui is talking of the need for further infusions of funds if the project is ever to be restarted.[28]

(8) It should also be said that in a recent influential summary statement of the prospects for the 1980s, the development of local downstream processing of primary materials in LDCs, and the transfer to LDCs of labour-intensive industries losing their comparative advantage, rank only third and fourth in the list, after 'market-securing investment in heavy engineering in the advanced industrial countries to circumvent their protectionism and increased competition from the NICs' and 'spreading risks in the high-volume export industries to get a better balance between home-demand, exports and overseas production'.[29]

Export Markets

The export performance of the Japanese economy is legendary. The addition of $14 billion to Japan's oil bill was handsomely paid off —

and a surplus of similar proportions generated — by a rapid expansion of exports which carried the export/GNP ration from nine per cent to 14 per cent in a few years. Apart from paying for oil, exports have played a large role in sustaining growth. The 1977 Trade White Paper[30] calculated, through an input-output table, the contribution of different segments of final demand to overall increase in income. Exports come out best. One extra unit of exports implies a 2.2 unit increase in total income compared with coefficients of 2.1 for fixed domestic capital formation and 1.7 for private consumption. The assumption that exports are 'a good thing' is likely, therefore, to survive the present phase in which the hypercompetitiveness of Japanese exports is seen as a source of problems.

There is, too, in the minds of MITI policy-makers, a strong identification of 'progress' with two trends:

(a) increasing weight of sophisticated machinery and chemical products in Japan's exports (typified by the increase in machinery exports from about 20 per cent of the total in 1960 to 45 per cent of the vastly larger total of 1975); and
(b) increasing horizontal specialization in trade with rich country peers.

The second militates against a central concern with LDC markets, but the first, of course, argues a strong Japanese interest in promoting the industrialization of LDCs in order to increase their demand for capital goods — rather than seeing them as markets for Japanese light industry products and as such, countries which should be deterred as far as possible from substituting imports. It is noticeable that the 1977 Trade White Paper gave considerable attention to the export of plant, and to the need for measures to provide special credits, etc. to promote the work of engineering consultants so that they can act as more effective intermediaries between developing countries and Japanese plant manufacturers.[31] So far Japan seems to have been doing well out of the expanding trade of the NICs. The four Asian NICs plus Brazil and Mexico took 18 per cent of Japan's exports in 1979, compared with 15 per cent in 1975. Imports from these countries were respectively nine per cent and seven per cent of total imports and the discrepancy has been a source of friction, particularly with South Korea *vis-à-vis* which Japan's trade surplus in 1979 reached $3 billion.

Industrial Restructuring

The question of export markets is intimately related, of course, to the whole question of structural adjustment within the Japanese economy. Of all the industrialized economies, Japan is perhaps the one where public opinion, at least, is best prepared for large-scale restructuring. Discussion of such matters and of the need to switch towards more knowledge-intensive (or technology-intensive) high-value-added branches of production has a longer history in Japan than in, say, the UK. MITI established a 10-man Industrial Restructuring Section as early as 1973, long before the current scare about the employment effect of microprocessors, and the discussion was only marginally influenced at first by the growth in competitive export capacity of the NICs. It sprang, rather, from environmental concerns – the sense that, with the pollution tolerance threshold falling rapidly, Japan was running out of factory sites – aided perhaps by the fact that the futurology of the 1960s was taken more seriously in Japan than elsewhere. That in turn was partly because the Japanese are more technology-minded anyway, partly because of the experience-extrapolation factor. The Japanese had already seen, not just in their lifetimes but in a mere decade and a half, a very substantial shift in the centre of gravity of domestic manufacture from light to heavy and chemical industry. It came naturally to them to accept that the process of restructuring would continue in the future: they were less likely to suffer from '*plus ça change*' cynicism than those whose experience was of more slowly growing economies and had more confidence in their ability to cope with change.

Add to this that Japanese economists and policy-makers tend to *believe* in free trade and comparative advantage: exports played a large role in Japan's growth; they spent a couple of decades arguing against GATT Article 35 restrictions against Japan; they would have a lot to lose in exports to Europe and the US from any general onset of protectionism to which restrictions on their part against LDC imports might contribute. As the matter is put in the 1976 version of MITI's major perspective planning document – produced by what is significantly called its 'Industrial Structure Council': the vitality of the Japanese economy has depended on its increasing openness to the international economy and this characteristic should be maintained.[32] The 1980 update (written, note, for internal not external consumption) declares that the first principle of Japan's industrial policy should be: 'By establishing an appropriate international division of labour between the advanced and the developing countries to work for a harmonization of the world economy and to contribute to its development.'[33]

So, the doctrine that Japan must be forward-looking and positive, move rapidly out of declining low-technology labour-intensive industries and into the advanced industries, is so universally accepted that to be against it is like being against motherhood. The actual record is a little more ambiguous. Three categories of industry need to be distinguished: heavy energy-using basic and processing industries, surplus capacity industries and import-threatened industries.

Willingness to support the transfer of downstream processing industries to developing countries has been widespread in principle, patchy in practice. Some of the forward-looking projections of the early 1970s, such as those of the Japan Economic Research Council and MITI's Industrial Structure Council, foresaw a much reduced growth in steel production in Japan, for instance, largely on the grounds that Japan had run out of sites — and needed to reduce energy import requirements. Southeast Asian countries had higher pollution tolerance thresholds, and Japanese firms would find it advisable to locate new plants there. Even then, one of the Employers Federations (Keidanren) argued that Japan must continue to be a supplier of steel, fertilizer and petrochemicals to Asia, and that increasing technology-intensity (agreed to be a condition of progress and growth) could just as well come in those industries — reducing costs, pollution, energy and space requirements — as in fancy electronics.[34]

That debate took place at a time when steel-making capacity was nearing 140 million tons and home demand was expected to be 180 million tons in 1985. The recession and the switch to low growth have altered the picture. With capacity still around 140 million tons and production only just climbing back to 110 million in 1978, it was expected that most of the growth of production needed for the planning future could be achieved by expansion and re-equipment of existing sites in Japan, without need of steel imports. The possibility that cheaper steel imports will actually begin to compete with Japanese production seems not to enter into such discussions.

In other industries with lesser excess capacity problems, however, there are more positive plans to promote the development of processing facilities overseas. An example is the aluminium industry whose excess capacity is in high-cost inefficient equipment which the smelters are not unhappy to sacrifice. The projections underlying the decision to go ahead with the large government-backed joint-venture projects in the Amazon and Asahan were based on the projections in Table 4.1, confirmed by an agreement between the industry and MITI to scrap 0.53 million of the existing 1.63 million tons capacity. Recent oil price rises making energy availability an even more important determinant will doubtless accelerate this process and extend it to other industries.

Table 4.1: Aluminium Projections 1977, 1980 and 1985 (million tons)

	1977	1980	1985
Home demand	1.51	1.86	2.40
Home production	1.19	1.11	1.14
Imports	0.47	0.75	1.25
(of which, from overseas subsidiaries)	–	0.22	0.57

The second group of industries are those which have been legally designated for special government treatment as 'structurally depressed industries': artificial fibres, ferro-silicon, spinning (cotton, artificial fibres, synthetics), wool spinning, corrugated cardboard, open hearth and electric furnace steel-making, ship-building and ammonia/urea. It is clear, however, from a MITI report on these industries[35] that competition from the NICs is not their main problem: the spinners, for instance, actually increased their exports between 1973 and 1977 and saw a halving of imports in volume, a decline from 18 per cent to 12 per cent in terms of total home demand. They are the victims not of import competition but of the gearing down of the economy to lower growth rates. They are stuck with the capacity in which they invested at a time when continuous high growth was expected, overmanned (in spite of considerable trimming of the labour force – by 43 per cent between 1973 and 1977 for cotton and synthetic spinning) and facing declining relative prices, partly because of intensified competition, backed by productivity rises in leading firms, partly because of new substitutes.

For these industries a special law of early 1978 permitted concerted measures to restore profitability by subsidizing the scrapping of obsolescent capacity – in the case of shipbuilding with carefully modulated measures to distribute the burden justly between small producers (expected to make 14 per cent capacity reductions) and large producers required to scrap 40 per cent. In the case of urea fertilizers, the overall reduction was expected to be 45 per cent of capacity. Unlike the pollution/energy problem industries, however, increase in imports have played no part in these plans.

The third group of industries are the most important – those such as garments, leather goods, etc. in which developing countries have established competitive strength. Here there is a puzzle. Japan is an open market: it does not impose quota restrictions or negotiate 'voluntary restraints' with LDCs in the manner of the US and European countries, except in the single case of Korean raw silk. Tariff levels are low — claimed to be lower on average than other OECD countries. And yet actual imports of manufacturers from developing countries are relatively small. Total imports of textiles, for example, were only $21 *per capita* in 1977 compared with $41 for the EEC as a whole and $50 for the US.[36]

The explanation is complex. In many textile fields, undoubtedly, Japanese firms have retained their competitiveness by determined cost-cutting adaptation, including a much more rapid rundown of the labour force than one might have expected. (Torei, with a large female labour force where 'lifetime commitment' is only a commitment until marriage, went from 13,000 to 8,000 employees in a few years). They are helped, too, by discriminating consumers inclined to believe, where clothes are concerned, both that 'Japanese is best' and that 'cheap is nasty'.

There has been adaptation too, in some of the industries like ceramics, still organized on a family firm basis. Although the manufacturers of Seto have lost nearly the whole of their china ornament market in the US to Taiwanese and Korean producers (mostly taught by Japanese entrepreneurs who set up overseas subsidiaries to take advantage of cheaper labour costs), they still retain almost total dominance in the domestic crockery market, where Korean imports have a very small market share. Bankruptcies have been few, and manufacturers seem to think that their capacity to automate in rather modest (and still pre-electronic) ways, plus quality, plus their superior grasp of the design preferences of the Japanese consumers, will see them through. Perhaps there are also 'understandings' with wholesalers which depend in part on a 'we Japanese must stand together' sentiment, perhaps backed by threats from the gentlemen (known as Sokaiya — or 'shareholder general meeting trouble experts') who can be hired for their expertise at giving lectures on moral obligations while making a meaningful display of their muscles and strength of character. This is sheer speculation, however, and it is unlikely that this kind of non-tariff barrier could operate in an industry as fragmented as the ceramics industry.

The prospects of restructuring to make room for imports from the NICs, need to be looked at industry-by-industry. In general terms, one might summarize the situation as follows:

(1)　There is a generally positive attitude on the part of bureaucrats and 'federation businessmen' towards the idea of restructuring, of getting out of the low-technology industries for the reasons mentioned earlier — the experience extrapolation factor and the belief in the advantages of free trade — plus two additional factors. The first is the concern with international prestige; the historical shift in the structure of industry has not only brought prosperity but also international status. At the top end, there is undoubtedly a large element of the Olympic spirit as well as pursuit of profit in the determination to get ahead in computers. If Japan succeeds in outstripping the US there, the aerospace industry will be the only field left to conquer in order fully to justify the title of Japan's recent best-seller (by an American sociologist) *Japan as Number One*.[37] Likewise, at the bottom end, there is even a feeling that Japan ought positively not to be seen to be demeaning itself by persisting in the low-technology industries, particularly the stigma industries like textiles, associated with Japan's cheap labour past. Secondly, the Japanese have reason to be confident that they will take a larger than proportionate share of the trade expansion accruing to OECD countries from the Third World. Japanese exports to the NICs have increased faster in recent years than those of either Europe as a whole or the US.

(2) Still at the same level of general policy, these favourable predispositions towards restructuring are occasionally reinforced by acceptance of a moral obligation to 'make room for' the developing countries in the world trading system.

Both in unofficial and official writings, one comes across the argument that Japan should recognize that the NICs have a right to be allowed to tread the path that Japan has trod — and should not have to struggle against the same odds as Japan did in the bad old Article 35 days.[38] But this is rare. Perhaps more typical are the sentiments of a businessmen's group, the Industrial Planning Round Table, which published a general survey of Japan's future in July 1978.[39]

The threat from imports from the Third World, the report said, coming on top of the loss of exports from import-substituting industrialization there, was a real threat. But the source of this problem is the illusion that the LDCs need all the latest rich country technology. They don't: the last thing they need is something that puts 99 traditional weavers out of work for every factory job created. Give them some really appropriate Ghandian technology 'for production by the masses, not for mass production' and everybody's problems would be solved.[40]

(3)   There is a tendency for the discussion of restructuring and the discussion of overseas investment to be treated as part of an identical process — i.e. to assume automatically that most of the imports from LDCs will be from Japanese subsidiaries, on a US-Mexico pattern. This assumption is (a) a potential source of friction; and (b) one of the elements underlying the favourable general attitudes towards restructuring which might well disappear as the NICs develop their own indigenous capitalism.

(4)   Still at the level of general attitudes, Japan differs from other OECD countries in that unemployment rates have never been high, and unemployment has not been a central electoral issue. The Komeito's recent electoral slogan listed 'The people's five anxieties: Pensions, Housing, Health, Education, Natural Disasters' — but not unemployment. However, as unemployment rates creep up from one per cent to two per cent and beyond, that situation might change. If it does, and unemployment levels acquire the central political significance they have in other OECD countries, that will introduce a whole new dimension into the discussion of restructuring in Japan. It may be a straw in the wind that, specifically, apropos of overseas investment, the Ministry of Labour's White Paper for 1977[41] offered a calculation of the total number of jobs lost as a result of Japanese firms establishing manufacturing plants abroad rather than in Japan. The calculation was said to include indirect employment effects, and on the plus side, the employment created through the export of plant and intermediates.

On the assumption that the total output of the overseas subsidiaries could have been produced in Japan, the net loss was 800,000 jobs. On the assumption that only the exported output of overseas subsidiaries could have been produced in Japan the net loss was 60,000.

The Ministry of Labour, however, does not assert the need for job protection above other considerations. It expects considerable employment effects on some industries. 'However, to attempt to restrain overseas investment for this reason, would be undesirable, not only from the point of view of international cooperation, but also because of the need to plan for a stable development of the national economy through, for example, the securing of resource supplies.'[42] The process just has to be orderly and controlled.

(5)   When one moves, however, from the plane of generalized attitudes to the likelihood of particular action in particular industries, other considerations enter the picture. First, the value placed on har-

mony, persuasion and the appeasement of those who throw tantrums, means that particular threatened groups can often hold society up to ransom even in the face of a 98 per cent consensus concerning what the overall social interest is. Narita Airport is a good example; the length of time taken to translate Kennedy Round agreements into tariff reductions, 1968 to 1972, is another. It is, moreover, a sustainable proposition that this veto power is stronger for organizations of small firms than for large corporate enterprises. The latter can absorb diversification costs; the former cannot. The smooth bureaucratic manager of the corporate enterprise does not adopt or threaten kamikaze tactics; the small businessman will, and even if he is poorer in campaign funds, he is likely to have more votes under his personal influence.

It is relevant, therefore, that the most immediately threatened industries do tend to have a high concentration of small firms: textile and garment enterprises have on average half the number of employees of the average American firm (14 per cent of all workers in 22 per cent of establishments, compared with 12 per cent of the workers in ten per cent of the establishments of the US).[43] Leatherwork is almost a monopoly of the former outcast *burakumin* group which − quite apart from the small-firm effect − has developed in many parts of Japan a skill in 'Mau-Mauing' governmental authorities well beyond the scope of most bureaucratic 'flak-catchers' to cope with.

(6)   Aid for 'structurally depressed industries' is an established good cause. But as between (a) helping the entrepreneur to diversify out of the industry; and (b) helping him to re-equip, cut costs and stay internationally competitive with the same product thanks to subsidised capital, the second, much less international-trade-promoting alternative is infinitely preferred by the assisted who thereby are spared having to learn a totally new technology, new markets, etc. There is a tendency for adjustment measures to gravitate in this direction. It was not so with the assisted rundown of coal in the 1960s, because the coal seams were so poor and the superior attractions of oil so obvious, but in spinning, the net effect of a series of adjustment measures since 1956 has been to increase production considerably. A recent general statement of the principles of adjustment policy, however, is quite clear about the need for state assistance to hasten the reduction of capacity when there are no clear prospects for long-run viability − particularly in industries concentrated in narrow geographical areas.[44]

(7)   The lifetime employment system obviously adds another obstacle to the running down of the work force in major unionized firms. However, over a period of a few years adjustments do seem to take place and on the other side, the inability to sack managers provides incentives for a firm to adjust to the situation by moving overseas and establishing subsidiaries in cheap labour countries.

Security Issues

In specific terms, Japan has a keen interest in maintaining peace in the Malacca Straits through which her tankers come − or in the Lombok Straits if the worst came to the worst. She also has a strong interest in the stability of the Korean peninsula and in avoiding any China-Taiwan conflagration. The Malacca concern may prompt a special willingness to make concessions to ASEAN demands. Korean policy likewise − not only economic concessions, but the willingness also to lose political prestige over the Kim Dae Chung affair − is partly inspired by fear of weakening the South Korean regime.

Beyond that, the publications of the Japanese Foreign Ministry on the subject of foreign aid do sometimes make the point that Japan being *more* dependent on raw material imports than any other OECD country has a *greater* interest in world peace. There is no reason to suppose, however, that the relations between Third World prosperity in general and world peace in general should seem any different to Japan than to any other country.

Summary: Options for the Future

Current Japanese perceptions of Japan's interests in seeing the Third World develop are, it is argued, rather unclear. Japan's dependence on *some* Third World countries is recognised, if regretted. As long as Saudi Arabia controls the oil, Saudi Arabia must be appeased, but it would be much better for all of us if it were under American occupation. There is little thought that the Saudis might become more 'reasonable' as they become richer. Other countries have a greater significance to Japan as export markets and fields for foreign investment and here − in Southeast Asia and South-Central America − there is a much clearer perception of the possibilities of all-round benefits from continued economic growth in those countries. As for Africa, the Indian subcontinent and the non-oil Middle East, however, there is little disposition to see much profit accruing to Japan from their development except in so far as that contributes generally to the buoyancy of world demand.

It is hard to see that these perceptions of where Japan's interests lie will change in the future, given the likely prospects for either a change in value priorities of the groups in power, *or* a change in the relative strength of the different groups which now influence policy. Nor does this writer have the wit or the hubris to discern where the reality perceptions of the Japanese (about what policies might have what consequences) might be mistaken. The present general pattern of perceptions would be intensified if new world protectionism and intensified nationalism led to a 'vertical' restructuring of the world with Japan forced to concentrate on consolidating an Asian sphere of influence, perhaps in consort with China.

That pattern would, on the other hand, be substantially modified by a second — remote — possibility, namely that the concern for Japan's 'international standing' might make attractive what one might call the 'super-Scandinavian option' — the adoption of a general 'friend of the Third World' policy in international affairs. It is doubtful, however, for the reasons listed earlier, whether the cultural bases for such a policy exist. There is, at any rate, very little sign of any interest in following such a line, even among potential members of alternative left-wing governments.

Notes

*The author is grateful for many corrections, comments and suggestions by members of the IDS Conference and of a seminar kindly organized at the Japan Economic Research Centre by Mr Saburo Okita. Also to Mr Saburo Ninomiya for much good advice and source materials. This chapter was completed in March 1980.

1. Tsūshō Sangyōshō (MITI), *Tsūshō hakusho* (White paper on trade) (1979), p. 334.
2. Letter, 8 August 1911, typescript copy in possession of Norman MacKenzie.
3. Kikuchi Kiyoaki, *Towareru Nihon no Keizai-kyōryoku* (Japan's economic cooperation in question) (Kokumin Gaikō Kyōkai, *Kokumin Gaikō*, no. 48, 1977), pp. 4-5.
4. Kikuchi Kiyoaki (ed.), *Keizai-Kyōryoku no genkyō to tembō: Nambokiu mondai to kaihatsu-enjo (Economic cooperation, the present situation and prospects: North-South problems and development aid)* (January 1978), pp. 168-9.
5. Gaimushō, Jōhō-bunka-kyoku (Foreign Office Information Department), *Kaigai seikei jōhō* (Overseas political and economic news), no. 337 (November 1979).
6. Japan, Ministry of Foreign Affairs, *Nihon no Keizai Kyōryoku (Japan's econome cooperation)* (1973), quoted in Yamamoto Tsuyoshi, 'Keizai ampo e

no kiseki' ('The path to economic security'), *Sekai* (January 1978), p. 102.

7. Tsūsho Sangyōshō (MITI), *Tsūshō hakusho (White paper on trade)* (1977), pp. 166-71.

8. Tsuyoshi, 'Keizai ampo e no kiseki'.

9. Kikuchi, *Towareru Nihon no Keizai-kyōryoku*.

10. Alan Rix, *Japan's Eeonomic Aid* (Croom Helm, 1980), p. 270.

11. Kikuchi (ed), *Keizai-Kyōryoku no genkyō to tembō*, pp. 168-70.

12. Tsūshō Sangyōshō (MITI), *Keizai Kyōryoku no genjō to mondaiten (Economic cooperation: the present situation and current problems)* (1978), pp. 141-2.

13. Rix, *Japan's Economic Aid*, pp. 35-40.

14. Ibid., Chapters 6 and 7.

15. Herbert I. Goodman, *Japan and the World Energy Problem*, Occasional Paper of the Northeast Asia-United States Forum on International Policy (Stanford University, July 1980), p. 24.

16. Ministry of International Trade & Industry, *White Paper on International Trade* (1977), p. 79.

17. Kikuchi (ed.), *Keizai-Kyōryoku no genkyō to tembō*, p. 357. The *White paper on trade* gives 58 per cent for 1976, and aggregates the EC figures as 22 per cent for imports and 18 per cent for exports. Tsūsho-Sangyōshō (MITI), *Tsūshō hakusho (White paper on trade)* (1978), p. 289.

18. S. Okita, 'Energy Five Years Later', mimeo. paper for the International Monetary Conference (London, June 1979) and *Observer* (24 June 1979).

19. Sangyō-kōzō Shingikai (Industrial Structure Council) *Sangyō-kōzō no chōki-bijion (Long-term vision of Japan's industrial structure)* (1978), p. 469.

20. Tsūsho Sangyōshō (MITI), *80 nendai no Tsūsan-seisaku Bijyon (Perspective on trade and industry policy for the 80s)* (April 1980), pp. 65-6.

21. K. Kojima, *Japan and a New Economic Order* (Croom Helm, 1977), p. 137.

22. Rix, *Japan's Economic Aid*, p. 52.

23. Tsūshō Sangyōshō (MITI), *Tsūshō hakusho* (1978), p. 314.

24. Kojima, *Japan and a New Economic Order*, p. 58.

25. Tsūshō Sangyōshō (MITI), *Tsūshō hakusho* (1979), p. 398. The representativeness of the survey sample is not indicated.

26. For example, a tax concession in 1978 permitted tax exemptions for a loss-risk reserve fund equivalent to 30 per cent (in the case of extractive industries 100 per cent) of new overseas investment. (Tsūshō Sangyōshō (MITI), *Tsūshō hakusho* (1978), p. 893.)

27. Miyazaki Yoshikazu, 'The Changing Nature of Corporations', *Japan Quarterly*, vol. 24, no. i (January-March 1977).

28. *Japan Times Weekly*, 22 November 1980.

29. Tsūshō Sangyōshō (MITI), *80 nendai no Tsūsan-seisaku Bijyon*, p. 52.

30. Tsūshō Sangyōshō (MITI), *Tsūshō hakusho* (1977), p. 352.

31. Ibid., pp. 402-17.

32. Tsūshō Sangyōshō (MITI), *Sangyō-kōzō no chōki-bijion (Long-term vision of the industrial structure)* (1976), p. 144.

33. Tsūsho Sangyosho (MITI), *80 nendai no Tsūsan-seisaku Bijyon*, p. 121.

34. Kojima, *Japan and a New Economic Order*, p. 141.

35. Tsūshō Sangyōshō (MITI), *Kōzō fukyō sangyō no jittai ni tsuite (On current conditions in the structurally depressed industries)* (January 1978).

36. See *ESP*, no. 80 (December 1978), p. 19.

37. Ezra Vogel, *Japan as Number One* (Harvard University Press, 1979).

38. Okita Saburō, *Happō-yaburi no keizai-senryaku (Economic strategy for a nation with no defences)* (1978), p. 18; and Tsūshō Sangyōshō (MITI), *Keizai Kyōryoku no genjō to mondaiten*, p. 202.

39. Sangyō-Keikaku Kondankai, *Sangyō-boeki Kozo no Kaikaku (Reform of the industrial and trade structure) Keizai Oraisha,* 1978.
40. Ibid., pp. 90-1.
41. Rōdōsho, *Rodo hakusho* (1977), p. 109.
42. Ibid., p. 112.
43. Sangyō-kōzō Shingikai, *Sangyō-kōzō no chōki-bijion*, p. 103.
44. Tsushō Sangyōshō (MITI), *80 nendai no Tsusan-seisaku Bijyon*, p. 135.

5 AUSTRALIA'S INTERESTS IN THIRD WORLD DEVELOPMENT: THE PERSPECTIVE OF A RESOURCE EXPORTER

Stuart Harris

Introduction

As with any developed country, Australia's interests in Third World development combine economic, political and strategic interests. In several respects, however, Australia's interests differ from those of other developed countries. In part, this stems from Australia's continuing problem of reconciling its history and cultural affinities with its geography; in part it arises from similarities between its economic structure and that of a developing country.

The term 'interest' encompasses here the notion of interconnectedness in the sense of links which are convenient but not crucial, as well as dependence and interdependence relationships, mainly bilateral, which on one or both sides are crucial, economically or politically.[1] It also embraces multilateral interests of a complementary or competitive nature.

Two of Australia's interests in Third World development are held in common with other developed countries; first, like most developed countries, Australia trades extensively with developing countries and this trading interrelationship will grow. Investment and other economic relationships are also expected to expand with Third World development. Secondly, Australia shares an interest in global political and economic stability that is considered at risk with inadequate economic development in the Third World.

On the other hand, Australia has interests in Third World development which differ from those of developed countries generally, or are more important to it. First, Australia is heavily dependent upon commodity exports and shares many of the interests of developing countries that apply generally to commodity exporters, while at the same time competing with them in specific commodity markets.

Secondly, Australia, as with other small economies, gains from an effective system for organizing international relationships and would benefit to the extent that the system's effectiveness was enhanced by

156

greater participation within it of Third World countries.

Thirdly, for economic and strategic reasons, Australia has an especial interest in the political and economic stability of the Asian-Pacific region to which economic development is judged to contribute. Moreover, if energy, food and raw materials increase as problems for developing countries, greater attention might be directed to Australia's attitudes to development and trade in its abundant resources.

Fourthly, Australia's geographic proximity to Third World countries puts a premium on good relations with countries in the Southeast Asia and Pacific region with regional groupings such as ASEAN.

This paper analyses the strength of these interests, and their acceptance and manifestation in policy responses or in public attitudes.

Economic Background

The large-scale post war European immigration programme helped lift Australia's population to over 14 million people, but its limited population relative to its continental area and to its available natural resources, as well as its cultural background, influences Australia's attitudes and its perceptions of countries in close proximity.

Australia's resource endowment in relation to population is substantial.[2] For most major minerals large resources are known. The principle exception is crude oil where around one-third of requirements is currently imported; this proportion will increase in the near future, though resources of coal and oil shale from which substitute liquid fuels can be produced, as well as of uranium, are extensive.[3] In world terms, however, known resources of only a few commodities – bauxite, mineral sands, lead, zinc, phosphates, uranium, iron ore, nickel and manganese – constitute more than a few per cent of global reserves/resources.[4]

Similarly, its usable land resources – much of Australia being desert – are already substantially utilized in supporting the existing population settlement and an agricultural export trade which, globally, is not particularly large; in recent years, its grain production has accounted for about one per cent of world production and about ten per cent of world grain exports. Scope for expanded production through increased acreages is, on present technology, limited.

The Australian economy remains substantially based on resource trading. Agriculture has dominated for most of its history, although exports of some mine products have been important for more than a century. Unlike most primary commodity exporters, however, average real incomes in Australia have always been relatively high, although instability in foreign exchange earnings had provided problems for domestic economic management. Despite attempts to reduce such vulnerability and to increase the employment base, mainly through tariff assistance to manufacturing, about 80 to 85 per cent of total exports are still of agricultural and mineral commodities — shared about equally.

In the earlier post-war period and pre-war, agricultural exports were pre-eminent, directed mainly to markets in Europe, notably Britain. Growing agricultural protection in Europe and North America, Britain's economic decline, reduced Commonwealth preferences and Britain's entry into the European Economic Community impelled the diversification of markets. They remain largely developed country oriented but for some commodities, notably grains, Third World countries continue to constitute major and growing outlets, as they do for minerals.

The Australian economy seemed to have achieved some independence from the world economic system. Contrary to common experience, exports have not increased relative to national income and, at some 13 per cent of GNP, are not especially high in world terms; the relief after 1960 from the severe balance of payments difficulties of the 1950s and the relative stability in world economic activity in the 1950s and 1960s also seemed to support that view, as did the discovery of large domestic oil deposits. Diversification in the export sector, including the mining expansion, not only reduced instability in foreign exchange earnings but also increased interest in the Asian-Pacific region and heightened Australia's dependence upon the Japanese market — which seemed, however, to have infinite capacity for expansion. Recent experience, however, has reminded Australia of its ties with the world economy and the sensitivity to demand fluctuations that its increased reliance on minerals exports implies.

Thus, in pursuing its economic objectives of full employment (increasingly flexibly defined), economic growth and rising living standards and reasonable stability of prices, and its political goals, it has accepted that it must re-examine its international policies, including their consistency. Except occasionally, as with industrial protection and refugees, however, international issues generally remain of limited public interest.

Australia's dependence on overseas sources for capital investment and for technology is also relevant. Australia has been a substantial net importer of capital throughout its history. Foreign capital inflow post-war has been substantially on private account, however, and growing foreign ownership and control, particularly of resources, stimulated considerable debate about the extent to which Australia's development implied increased loss of sovereignty.

In 1974-5, based on value-added, 52 per cent of Australian mining, including oil, was foreign-owned and 59 per cent was foreign-controlled.[5] Foreign ownership and control is lower but still substantial elsewhere in the economy. Given public concern about foreign ownership, particularly of resources, foreign investment controls have been tightened. Nevertheless, the foreign investment and multinational corporations issue that concerns developing countries, has parallels in Australia.

Other Australian similarities with developing countries include dependence upon overseas technology, with only a small indigenous industrial research and development effort; dependence upon overseas shipping services, with a very limited ocean transport capacity; and an interest in increasing raw material processing.

Not all of these lead to sympathy with developing country policies. For example, despite concern at the non-competitive operations of overseas shipping conferences, there is limited support for a greater Australian ocean transport capacity and officially Australia feels its trade could be disadvantaged under the proposed UNCTAD shipping code.[6]

Political Background

For much of its 200 years or so existence, Australia was a British outpost in Asia. For the last 40 years or more, it has become increasingly an outpost of the United States-led West. It has normally regarded the Asia-Pacific area mainly as representing threats: from an expansionist Japan, from China, from other European or colonial powers including once again Russia, or from cheap Chinese or Fijian labour and subsequently cheap Asian labour generally.

This has substantially shaped its attitudes. Since the First Fleet, 'Australians have steadfastly believed that they needed a major external guarantor', first Britain and then the United States.[7] Apart from Japan and China, it was the colonial powers, or those influencing the various colonial empires in Asia, that were the concern rather than regional countries themselves. Yet this need for a protector has influenced Australia's international policies for much of the twentieth century, and the strong support given the United States over Afghanistan may partly be designed to encourage the United States back into the Pacific.

The limited concern with Third World countries outside Asia and the Pacific reflects their small effect on direct diplomatic or strategic interests, though major exceptions include South Africa and Zimbabwe. With some important exceptions, the line-up on non-regional issues has been with the West. In trade particularly, however, interests in Third World development have been wider both where political interests are judged to reinforce market interests and more generally in relation to international trade institutions.

Within the Asia-Pacific region, the common suggestion that Australia has to choose between being European or Asian puts the choice for Australia incorrectly, but Australia does have to define how far it will resist its inevitable involvement with Asia. Changes in strategic and geo-political balances, including detente, Vietnam and Afghanistan, have made such a redefinition inevitable, including a reassessment of Australia's relationships with the Third World.

This reassessment will be slow. In a recent report on Australia's Third World link, a minority view was entered against insistence that Australia is a Western country. This is partly presentational: the concern that 'the Third World tends to see "the West" as its adversary — in terms of its colonial past, its economic exploitation, its resistance to their demands and sometimes for its grudging concessions',[8] a burden of historic responsibility Australia need not assume. In part, it is substantial. Even this conservative report, however, argued against Australia striving to defend every Western interest in the Third World as its own, 'an error into which it can be argued (Australia has) fallen in the past . . . . '[9]

Australia's international role diminished in the post-war years. As signatory to the Atlantic Charter, a significant participant at Bretton Woods and Havana, and emerging from the Second World War with food production capacity at a time of shortages — and for a time a role in leading the smaller nations — Australia had a significant international voice. Its power passed fairly rapidly, however, with the end of the Korean War, the restoration of European agricultural productive capacity and the emergence of the Cold War — the big nations' game. The rise of Communist China weakened Australia's independence because of Australia's perception of the implied need for protection from the threat it offered.

For much of the post-war period, Cold War concerns with political 'stability' in the region largely determined Australia's international attitudes. China was not recognized diplomatically, despite the establishment of commercial links and large wheat sales, and Soviet influence was feared. Given Australia's concerns at Cold War politics in Asia, fears of downward thrusts of communism and feelings of insecurity engendered by isolation, the need for United States' protection and the strong commitment to anti-communism in domestic politics was unsurprising.

It meant, however, emphasis on the *status quo* in world affairs, suspicion of independence movements, generally hostile reactions to revolutionary movements and a preference for, at times, distasteful but 'dependable' governments. This strengthened pressures for pushing Australia into adopting the gradualist, Western approach to economic development with distaste for, and fear of, radical change, and influenced the domestic political climate and Australia's stance internationally. The dependency implied was generally accepted on the assumption that Australia was also needed and that economic gains would be shared; perhaps also that the costs would not include actually participating in policing or preventative actions. When these assumptions became in doubt and involvement in the Indonesia/Malaysia confrontation and in Vietnam was called for, problems arose domestically. Similarly, given its dissatisfaction at developments in its trading and economic position, Australia faced continuing conflict between strategic needs for the Western alliance and economic needs for better terms of economic exchange.

Problems as to an appropriate response also arose from the growing recognition of China, the emergence of detente, America's pullback from Asia and the Nixon doctrine, and then re-emerging world food and raw material shortages. The Cold War had buttressed the Western self-interest case for helping developing countries. Once the Cold War eased, this self-interest argument for aid also substantially passed. In Australia, as elsewhere, the domestic interest in Third World development to ward off communist influence lost its urgency.

Australia has often seen itself as a bridge between the West and developing countries, mainly because of shared trade problems. This role was encouraged by developed countries at times — not to any evident Australian benefit; as a recent inquiry witness put it, the role of a bridge is to be walked on.[10] Nevertheless, Australia subsequently saw itself with a leadership role among developing countries — within regional arrangements such as ASPAC or ASEAN, or by way of the Commonwealth Heads of Government meetings (CHOGM) — again partly but not wholly in the regional context. Some of Australia's leadership initiatives, however, such as for a form of alliance between

Australia, US, China and Japan, against USSR influence in the region, stimulated ASEAN suspicion that Australia was siding with China.

Japan's regional role has been important in the light of history and of Australia's long-standing fears of Japan. Japan's low-key post-war stance has offered less problems than if Japan had a military presence and used more thrustingly its economic strength in the region. Its inevitable economic power has given Japan difficulties, and fears existed that Australia might agree to be part of a three-party approach in Asia, using Australia's goodwill and Japanese economic strength; it was never clear that the Japanese took this seriously, or that Australia's goodwill was marketable in this way. Nevertheless, misgivings existed in Asia about Japan's economic influence, and they still do with respect to the various Pacific Community initiatives, but the earlier desire in the region for closer ties with Australia to counterbalance these concerns seems to have diminished.

Australia's relations with Africa were complicated by links with South Africa and, until UDI in 1965 facilitated formal disentanglement, with Rhodesia. Trade and investment links with South Africa remain, but the significance of the independent African states and of world opinion generally, has led to a changed — if still somewhat ambivalent — attitude.[11] Various factors have been influential: East Africa's political-strategic relevance; Africa's growing political importance, particularly as the Cold War moved into, and remains in, that continent; growing domestic disapproval of apartheid; doubts about South Africa's survival; African membership in the Commonwealth and Prime Minister Fraser's personal support for Zimbabwe's independence. The importance of African Commonwealth members has been recognized by Australia's Aborigines, who have internationalized their domestic disputes with Australian governments, lobbying African Commonwealth leaders and the United Nations.

Australia's Trade and Economic Interests

At Bretton Woods and Havana, Australia substantially co-ordinated its approach to economic and political issues. Subsequently, economic and political aspects of Australia's foreign relations tended deliberately to follow largely separate paths. The advantage gained from not invoking Australia's foreign relationships in each commercial negotiation involved at times, however, some risk of inconsistency in overall policy.

With a gradual weakening in the international trade and payments system, with greater bilateralism likely to characterise future trade, and with developed and developing countries seeking new 'rules of the game', links between political and economic aspects of Australia's relationships, including those with Third World countries, have again become important.[12] This may be seen more clearly in the light of Australia's trade interests in Third World development.

In 1977-8, some 24 per cent of Australia's exports went to developing countries. Perhaps reflecting the commodity composition of Australia's exports, this is smaller proportionately than that of either the United States or Japan. Imports from Third World countries constitute a slightly smaller proportion (20 per cent), but have grown from around 14 per cent in the late 1960s/early 1970s, only partly due to oil imports. Growth in trade with developing countries in the longer term has been more marked, particularly in the Pacific (see Table 5.1).

Table 5.1: The Changing Direction of Australia's Trade 1957 to 1977

Exports to	1957	1967	1977
	%	%	%
EEC (9)	50	26	15
North America	7	15	12
Japan	13	21	33
CPE's (excluding China)	3	3	4
China	1	4	4
Developing countries	17	23	24
(ASEAN)	(2)	(6)	(6)
Other (including New Zealand)	9	8	8
	100	100	100
Imports from:			
EEC (9)	51	35	25
North America	16	30	24
Japan	3	11	20
CPEs (excluding China)	*	*	*
China	1	1	1
Developing countries	22	16	21
(ASEAN)	(5)	(3)	(6)
Other (including New Zealand)	7	7	9
	100	100	100

*Less than 0.5 per cent.
Source: United Nations, *Yearbook of International Trade Statistics,* various issues.

Of Australia's exports, Third World markets in Asia and the Middle East, long-standing markets for grains, are expanding for dairy products, meat, sugar and fruit. Further growth is expected with economic expansion in those areas. Australia's mineral exports go mainly to Japan but markets are developing for products such as iron ore and coal in newly industrializing Asian countries, such as Korea, Taiwan and the Philippines.

For imports, the picture is mixed. Imports of some traditional regional products, such as jute and sisal, have declined and so did imports of crude oil from Indonesia, with Australia's own oil discoveries; manufactured imports, including textiles, footwear and clothing, have increased.

These changes reflect Australia's trade shift from Europe to the Pacific region. Exports to Europe have declined from almost 50 per cent of the total to about 14 per cent over the last quarter of a century. The Pacific region has therefore considerable economic importance to Australia. Australia's trade balances with ASEAN countries and Japan favour Australia, a point argued by those countries in seeking greater access to Australian markets.

Australia has growing interests in the Third World outside Asia and the Pacific, particularly in the Near and Middle East. Trade with Egypt, Saudi Arabia and, until the overthrow of the Shah, Iran, was growing with potential for further development.

Australia's imports from developing countries have increased in the past decade or so faster than Australia's total imports, with some help from preference arrangements and programmes assisting exporters to Australia. Some 70 per cent of developing country imports enter duty free but imports of protected items are particularly sensitive issues in, at times, acrimonious discussions between Asian countries and Australia.

Australia's trade with developing countries has increased more slowly than their total trade growth. The relationship between Australia's export growth and developing-country growth rates in general depends upon various factors, including their general trade propensities, the industrial development strategy followed — such as how far it involves using iron ore, coal or non-ferrous metals — and the import policies followed on agricultural items. Sometimes, general attitudes towards Australia will be important: for example, in recent years the Philippines has tried to divert iron ore imports away from Australia.

Complicating direct trading relations with Third World countries has been the disposal of surplus agricultural products by developed producers, particularly the EEC and the United States. EEC surpluses have long been dumped in what Australia regards as its traditional Asian markets. United States' food surpluses were even more sensitive an issue, involving continuing conflicts with recipients over the levels of commercial sales consistent with accepted guidelines requiring minimum impact on normal commercial sales.

In the other direction, Australia still has important economic interests in some regional Third World countries. Foreign investment links with developing countries are small but growing. The development of offshore manufacturing links in Asian countries, reflecting the ultimately inevitable structural adjustment in Australian industry, is likely to resume in the future. As well as some investment in developed countries, principally the United States and Britain, most Australian investment has gone to New Guinea, followed by Indonesia, Malaysia, Singapore, the Philippines, Thailand and Fiji. Investment, mainly in the service and finance sectors, has also gone to various Pacific Islands, notably Tonga, the Cook Islands, the Solomon Islands, New Hebrides and New Caledonia.[13]

Not surprisingly, capital inflow from developing countries is limited, though some Asian funds are at times associated with foreign investment projects. It is often unclear, however, whether such funds are from the United States or other developed countries using locations such as Hong Kong, Singapore or Bermuda for tax purposes. Also unsurprisingly, Australia's economic dominance is at times important — as in Fiji — and some companies have localized their operations to improve their image.[14]

Apart from oil, Australia does not as yet have a dependency relationship in trade or investment with developing countries. Australia does not depend so vitally on developing country markets that major difficulties would exist in their absence nor do developing countries depend that heavily on Australian markets. Supply dependency — Australia's imports of Middle East oil, Middle East and Asian imports of Australian food — is greater, but the genuine interdependence of Australia's trade links with Japan, for example, is not reflected in developing country interrelationships.

Relative Resource Endowments

Australia's resource endowment and its sparse population have led to fears that heavily populated Asian countries will invade Australia to gain control of these resources. An alternative proposition is that the limited utilization of Australia's resources will encourage China, for example, to lead a Third World propaganda attack on Australia as a rich country refusing to share its wealth with poor countries, and demanding that its under-utilized land be allocated to those starving in Asia.[15]

Invasion is hardly plausible; agricultural development in largely unoccupied Northern Australia would be difficult without Australian help. Even with help, scope for such development based on cheap Asian labour is limited; Indonesian fishermen have landed on Australia's northern coasts for centuries and, if feasible, would have established agricultural settlements by now.[16] For minerals, an invasion to obtain supplies seems beyond the present or prospective capabilities of developing countries in the region.

Australia's moral responsibility to exploit such resources is at times invoked. Government spokesmen have accepted that if Australia does not exploit the offshore resources of the 200 mile exclusive economic zone (EEZ), others will be entitled to do so. This may be consistent with thinking emerging in UNCLOS but, if extended onshore, the principle would have wide implications, such as whether or not Australia should mine its uranium. Again, however, the practical possibilities are limited.

Apart from immigration policies, discussed below, Australia's interest in Asia's population growth is greater because of Australia's size and sparse population. Flood argues that substantial migration from these countries to Australia would not solve regional population problems, but that regional population growth will increase pressures on Australia to develop its resources at rates compatible with their needs rather than Australia's wishes.[17] Others argue that although Australia could be criticized for under-utilizing its resources, more likely targets are its financial and trade policies.[18]

Australia's food aid relations with development countries, where potential problems could exist, have three important aspects. First, Australia is interested in ensuring basic food security needs are met. As a food exporter, however, substantial pressure is applied during food shortages to supply food on concessional terms. Australia has tended to concede such concessional arrangements, but argues that this distorts its aid giving and imposes on food exporters burdens that should be shared by developed countries as a whole. Secondly, as noted earlier, important in the past were food surplus disposals — from the United States, in particular — and Australia's attempts to protect its traditional commercial markets in countries such as India, Pakistan and Malaysia strained the relationships between recipient countries and Australia. Eventually, this was eased by declining food import needs of countries such as India and expanding markets elsewhere for Australian wheat, particularly in China. Nevertheless, serious food problems in Asia would lead to difficult to resist pressures on Australia to provide concessional food.

In multilateral food aid and food security forums, in seeking to defend its commercial interests while meeting the reasonable requirements of developing countries for food security, Australia is commonly neither in the developed country camp, which declines to share the food aid burden, nor are its interests those of the developing countries.

A further issue, important at times, is access to phosphates. Supplies for phosphate-deficient Australian soils have largely come from Nauru, Ocean and Christmas Islands, with not entirely happy perceptions among those concerned of the methods used or the phosphate prices paid by developers, which usually included the Australian government.

The International 'Rules of the Game'

Given its relative economic and political weakness and its geographic isolation, Australia has supported strongly multilateral arrangements for regulating international affairs, including international economic affairs. It actively participated in shaping the post-war system of rules for international trade and payments, in part because Australia had frequently found its economic interests differing from those of developed countries.[19]

Subsequently, Australia found the international rules for trade and payments were not being applied effectively to trade in primary commodity exports and commodity trade liberalization was not occurring. In GATT, this drew it into conflict with the largely commodity-importing developed countries.

Australia has in consequence seen itself in general sharing the common problems of primary product exporting countries and sharing therefore many developing country interests — more stable conditions of trade, better market access in industrialized countries, some acceptance of the inadequacies and uncompetitiveness of primary commodity markets and better commodity prices (to offset, for example, downwards pressure on world prices from US and European agricultural protection).

As UNCTAD took shape and solidified the developing country approach, however, the issues of temperate agriculture became less and less the major international trade issues, nor were the developing countries with interests in temperate commodity trade the major powers in the Third World.

Attempts were made in UNCTAD and GATT to establish a separate category of 'middle zone' countries, neither developed nor developing — but primary commodity exporting, net capital importing countries. While neither successful, nor without criticism in Australia,[20] this reflected genuine frustration at a world otherwise divided merely into developing and developed countries.

From this Australian attitude also emerged policies such as the accelerated removal of revenue duties on tropical products and Australian preferences for developing countries introduced in 1966. The latter arose from the assumption that some preference arrangements were inevitable; that once a momentum had developed Australia's arguments about special circumstances would not be heard; that its middle zone argument — that its help must be consistent with its economic structure and not as a developed country — must be demonstrated positively; and that it might help to prevent preferences being established in primary commodity trade. It was also accepted that its tariff policies made Australia vulnerable to criticisms from developing countries.

More recently, it supported the developing countries' case for a Common Fund, changing its initial strong backing of developed country positions. It has also attempted in UNCTAD V to lead in attacking protectionist tendencies in world markets.

Undoubtedly, there are mixed motives behind these attempts to differentiate Australia from other developed countries. They have a logic in the different characteristics of the Australian economy. There is also a more general logic which applies to smaller developed countries as a whole.

The rule of law internationally is, in effect, a contractual arrangement which will be adhered to by those seeing themselves deriving benefits in return for adhering to that contractual arrangement. The developed countries have benefitted from the existing system and as necessary, as through the codes of conduct developed in the Multilateral Trade Negotiations (MTN), they have changed them in line with their interests. The MTN, as with previous GATT negotiations, mainly helped manufactured goods trade. Little improvement occurred in commodity trade and the trading system which affects it. Yet this was initially more affected by exemptions; it failed to cover increasingly important areas such as imperfect competition, investment and state trading; and it was increasingly ignored by industrialized countries.[21] This has been as much a source of dissatisfaction for Australia as for developing countries.

The developing countries, however, have a more general dissatisfaction with the existing system and institutions. They want fundamental changes, and commodity trading arrangements have not been the only target. The significance of this general dissatisfacton is that unless sufficient gain from the existing world economic system goes to developing countries, and they accept that that is so, they are likely to extend their opposition to such a system and take action increasingly inconsistent with it.[22]

Concessions to developing countries may be necessary therefore to maintain an effective market system and related institutions including accepted 'rules of the game' for international trade and payments. Without such arrangements, existing trends towards bilateralism in trade and other economic interchange, a situation in which small countries tend to be disadvantaged, will be reinforced.

In these 'rules of the game' for commodities, in particular, Australia's general interests are similar to those of developing countries. Yet in the trade to which these rules related, Australia's interests are frequently competitive. Australia's major competition for iron ore markets in Japan is Brazil; Australia is a major competitor of the West Indies in bauxite and alumina, as it is of many developing countries for sugar.

In seeking international collaborative arrangements on commodities Australia has tended to take the developing country position except, as with wheat, where the principal exporters are mainly developed countries. In international forums, however, it has opposed the principle of price indexation or producer group pricing, though its actions, as with other major producers, demonstrate that it no more follows its own statements of principle than do other countries. Nevertheless, as a consumer, it actively encouraged negotiation of agreements on cocoa and coffee and one on tin at a time when Australia was still a net importer.

Decisions to participate in the bauxite, iron ore and copper groups were taken largely on general foreign policy grounds, demonstrating sympathy with developing countries. On commodity policy grounds, Australia would probably not have joined, not from a satisfaction with the markets or pricing arrangements for the commodities involved but in part because unilateral pricing action, as for bauxite, is against the principle of consumer-producer co-operation which Australia has espoused; more important perhaps is that somehow such producer group action is not considered 'legitimate' even though it was accepted as appropriate for grains, sultanas, zinc or uranium, where participants have been largely developed countries. In addition, industry opposition was strong and overseas ownership is important for bauxite and copper.

Nevertheless, membership of the three commodity producer groups has been maintained despite the change to a government generally more sympathetic to industry and less sympathetic to developing countries. Australia has not followed the pricing action of other bauxite producers, though Australian producers benefit from their price raising effects since Australia alumina thereby becomes competitive in United States markets. Problems in relations between Australia and the other bauxite producers could arise in the future. A major question in any price support arrangement concerns the level and location of investment; industry investment expansion underway in Australia may substitute for investment in developing country locations.

Global Relations

Australia's relationships with Third World countries are influenced by its perceived vulnerability in three respects: the first, its trade policies have already been discussed; secondly, in its immigration and racial policies; and thirdly, in its regional and bilateral relationships.

Some commentators suggest that together with Australia's immigration policies, its internal policies towards its Aborigines could lead to retaliatory action by developing countries. Australia's historical perception of very large populations and related scarcity of land in the region, the problems that emerged from importing Chinese and Kanaka labour and the general fear of 'difference', generated a widely accepted policy of selected racial immigration known as the White Australia policy. While this policy could be rationalized as avoiding the social problems that a rapid mix of different cultures would imply, support came largely from a racial bias that was no less objectionable because critics of the policy were commonly from countries with equally biased racial policies. Despite especial difficulties with India in the 1920s and the Philippines in the 1940s over immigration issues, concerns about these policies were probably less among neighbouring developing countries than in the United States and especially Japan or among newly independent African states. Nevertheless, its operation and its heavy-handed application 'poisoned our friendships and damaged our name in every part of the world'.[23]

During the 1960s, discrimination was gradually eliminated from Australia's immigration and the White Australia policy was formally dead by 1966. Its removal was hastened by the Whitlam Government which was concerned to remove the racist image that it considered Australia's involvement in Vietnam had reinforced.[24] Even critics accepted that by the early 1970s, although some underlying biases still exist, it had largely ceased in practice.

The current policy of taking skilled migrants from Asian and other Third World countries, as well as from Europe, has been criticized as contrary to developing country interests even though contributing to the ease within Australia of removing colour discrimination. With reduced immigration levels, removal of colour discrimination may also have been easier since the criteria — such as family links and skills in short supply — still offer greater barriers to citizens of developing countries.[25] Nevertheless, attitudes to the proportionately large numbers of refugees from Vietnam have generally been acquiescent.

Other issues, such as nuclear power, world food scarcity, fisheries policies, more general law of the sea issues and, ultimately, Antarctica impinge on Australia's total concerns with the Third World. Even here, however, their main interest is in their regional or bilateral impact.

Australia's support is commonly sought for various matters not of its direct concern. Among the economic issues, the Common Fund was important while more generally, African issues — Zimbabwe, Namibia and apartheid in South Africa — have dominated. On these issues, Australia's policies both under Labor and the subsequent Liberal Government in 1975, have tended to support developing country attitudes. It is symptomatic, however, that Australia has taken many Third World policy initiatives in CHOGM: this was so on the Common Fund and also, in 1977, for an enlarged food aid initiative.

The unproven assumption that global instability is reduced by increased economic development underlies much of Australia's approach to Third World development. Nevertheless, without reasonable development, it is accepted that scope for outside interference or Third World countries' needs for 'great and powerful friends' or for foreign ventures to distract attention from internal events, is large. A common view, also, is that the capacity for settling differences by compromise, rather than confrontation with the dangers that entails, is greater with general economic growth. There has been some questioning in Australia of the appropriateness for developing countries of the Western development model, and the association with Western values that it implies, but so far the debate has not developed a workable alternative nor been influential.

Regional Relations

Recent changes important to Australia's perspectives on regional Third World countries have included the reduced United States military presence in Asia; détente; improved relations with China; the exacerbation in Asia of Soviet-Chinese rivalry; and instability arising from the military interventions by Vietnam, China and the USSR.

Cold War fears of world communism and the threat of China for a long time made military and strategic aspects of regional interrelationships dominant. Economic aspects were important, as SEATO's economic programmes and Australia's aid programmes indicated, but Whitlam moved to a more overly economic, technical, cultural and political approach to Asia, a shift in emphasis which continues. This shift in emphasis has not led to increased aid or other assistance, however, though it shows up in concerns that the region's generally rapid economic development would be adversely affected by export instability or by global protectionism. There is also some concern over the energy problem's effects on developing countries in the region, including the Pacific Island countries, and their economic viability and political stability. The position is also complicated by Australia's strong reaction to Afghanistan. Politically, Australia has common interest with ASEAN countries that 'no one power should dominate the region again'.[26] Even though heavily dominated by regional issues, therefore, Australia's policies again see those issues in a global — but suspiciously Cold War — context.

Australia has welcomed regional groupings and, recently, particularly those with an economic orientation. While the South Pacific Forum and regional Commonwealth meetings are important to Australia, the major group is ASEAN — consisting of Malaysia, Singapore, Thailand, Philippines and Indonesia. Australia's relationships with ASEAN, however, have not been easy.

ASEAN countries reacted adversely to Australia's actions in restricting imports of 'sensitive' items in 1974 and subsequently. These measures, covering most textile yarns, fabrics, clothing and accessories, footwear and plywood, hit new industries unfavourably compared with their treatment by other developed countries[27] and led to fears that other exports would be affected and developing country preference margins reduced, as they were on flat glass and ceramic sanitary ware.

Trade with Australia is not generally large in these countries' total trade. Considerable irritation arose, however, particularly in Malaysia, Thailand, Singapore and the Philippines from their treatment, as new exporters, compared with Hong Kong and Korea, under Australia's quantitative controls on 'sensitive' imports; and from the barriers such controls imposed on reducing their trade imbalances with Australia. In being politically sensitive to Australia's domestic industries, Australia was seen as insensitive to the developing countries in the region, even though the growth in ASEAN exports to Australia of 'sensitive' goods has exceeded Australia's total import growth and the growth of imports of 'sensitive' items from all sources.

Difficulties re-emerged with the dispute over Australia's airlines policies. As an issue, its substance remains hard to assess but an attempt by Australia to negotiate bilaterally was seen as an apparent attempt to divide ASEAN and achieved a cohesion previously lacking among the ASEAN countries.

Nuclear power and fishery policy issues are important in the region but not specifically as developing country issues. Attitudes to the use of nuclear power in neighbouring Third World countries differ little from those which would apply if they were developed countries. Similarly, fishery policy issues do affect South Korean and Taiwanese fishing in waters adjacent to Australia but in ways comparable to those affecting Japan.

Bilateral Relations

The two prime areas of Australia's bilateral interests with developing countries, in which economic developments and their related political implications are of crucial importance, are New Guinea and Indonesia. Relations with other countries — such as Singapore and Malaysia — are also considered important but increasingly in an ASEAN context.

New Guinea is of particular strategic importance to Australia. Initially, its role as a colonial administration in an era of decolonization was an offset to a favourable Australian image as an ex-colony itself. Nevertheless, the close and generally amicable relationship maintained with that country is not only relevant to the direct bilateral relationship but in a wider Third World context.

The more complex relationship with Indonesia has experienced some strains. The generally favourable view of Australia by Indonesia — arising from the immediate post-war support given to the independence movement in Indonesia — remained until the 'confrontation' period of Sukarno, though even then serious antagonism was avoided. Restoration of good relations was followed by a coolness over Indonesia's assumption of control over West Iran and its treatment of East Timor, and that issue remains sensitive both to Indonesia and in Australia. Economic ties with Indonesia are not large and trade and investment difficulties have discouraged many firms; trade, however, has continued to expand. Politically, good relations are important with Indonesia because of its proximity and its size — a population of over 200 million by the turn of the century — rather than its Third World character, although that is a complicating factor.

Australia's post-war concerns to contain China suggest a strategic significance for India as a counterweight but such an overt relationship would have risked Pakistan's friendship and the growing trade with China. Yet, India was important in the balance — and its development and stability therefore crucial — while China remained a theat. It is once more important to the region's stability — less as a democracy in a largely undemocratic area, than as a country bordering the USSR — in an area vitally affected, in the Liberal Government's eyes, by the Afghanistan invasion.

The importance of bilateral economic relations in the region is illustrated by the fact that as well as that with New Guinea, Australia has bilateral trade treaties with Korea, Thailand, Vietnam, Philippines, Malaysia, Indonesia and Singapore. With developing countries outside the region, Australia has such treaties only with Iran, Brazil and Nigeria.

Foreign Aid

Australia's foreign aid is mainly oriented to bilateral and regional links; New Guinea receives nearly three-quarters followed by Indonesia. Southeast Asian countries receive the bulk of the remainder of Australia's bilateral aid along with South Asia (through the Colombo Plan) and a number of developing African countries, through the Special Commonwealth African Assistance Plan.

Australia's commitment to the OECD 0.7 per cent of GNP target was reaffirmed in 1976. Aid continues to fall short of this target, however, but the 0.5 per cent achieved compares reasonably in the international league. Australia emphasizes the quality of its aid which is provided almost completely as grants and three-quarters of which is untied.

Aid is not a major public issue in Australia. Technical issues are argued among officials and academics and a small articulate group representing voluntary organizations, the latter also doing most to raise public awareness on the issue. Apart from operating schemes such as volunteers abroad in Asia, the Pacific and parts of Africa, non-government aid agencies have a small but important aid role, supplying goods and services ($28 million in 1978).[28]

The heavy dominance of budget support aid to New Guinea reflects past relationships and perhaps an original emphasis on aid designed to make participation by non-Australian agencies in New Guinea management unnecessary.[29]

Following an extended, though specialized, debate on aid administration within the Australian bureaucracy, attempts were made to isolate aid administration from direct foreign policy influence, with a more professional, development-oriented approach. The present compromise arrangements, a largely professional agency within the Department of Foreign Affairs, probably reflect reasonably Australia's perception of aid as ultimately a foreign policy instrument but to be used flexibly enough to permit its professional administration.

Again limited discussion has taken place on the 'basic needs' focus on aid, but it is not a major issue in Australian aid administration. The preponderance of programme aid is to New Guinea, where the wealthy elites that lead to pressures for a basic needs approach are not evident; and food aid by its nature tends to meet basic needs.

Public Perceptions of the Third World

Public perceptions of these issues are wide-ranging, constantly changing and influenced by history, culture, education and the like. Moreover, attitudes to the Third World or Asia are often a by-product of other influences, such as emphasis on the communist threat in Asia in the post-war domestic political debate. Similarly, current emphasis on Australia's economic difficulties, for domestic political reasons, influences attitudes to aid or to refugees.

The Third World is an issue of high public interest only infrequently and then usually incidentally to subjects such as sport with South Africa, miltary action in Vietnam, coloured immigration or Asian refugees. The fact that public opinion polls seldom consider Third World development issues suggests that they are not generally at the forefront of public attention.

Moreover, the maturing of Australia is itself a recent phenomenon. In 1945 a majority thought Australia's foreign policy should be part of a common Empire policy,[30] while in 1966 nearly two-thirds (61 per cent) of a public opinion poll sample supported Australia's involvement in Vietnam.[31] Relaxation of coloured immigration tended to get majority, though gradually declining, acceptance on a 'present levels' basis in polls through the 1960s and early 1970s in which non-European permanent settlers were increasing;[32] it has now apparently ceased to be an issue.

Similarly, aid has been difficult to politicize other than in specific circumstances – such as for emergency food relief. Aid appears more acceptable in specific cases – for New Guinea or Indonesia, although in 1966, eight per cent of polled respondents were willing to pay ten per cent more tax to aid Asian countries as a whole.[33]

Other pressure groups have neither a sustained nor, usually, a comprehensive attitude to Third World development, and trade unions and business groups have emphasized factors affecting their own immediate interests. Trade unions are concerned primarily with employment effects of low cost imports and of immigration in the face of high domestic unemployment. An exception has been their strong interest in trade union development in Third World countries. A related concern with human rights has been evident recently with respect to countries such as Chile and Malaysia.

Business interests are often pursued through business co-operation committees, such as with Indonesia, Korea or the Philippines. Groups such as Chambers of Manufacturers maintain their traditional opposition to competitive imports, but a blanket approach is increasingly difficult as members' interests diversify into overseas investment, importing components or in offshore manufacturing and into food and minerals exports. Consumer groups give some support to the importation of manufactured goods but they have limited influence on diffuse issues of a general nature.

Government policy attitudes are determined substantially by the interplay of bureaucratic interests though major initiatives normally require a positive ministerial interest. The Third World constituency is normally represented by the Department of Foreign Affairs, but other departments are involved. In Australia's Westminster-type system, most departments reflect their constituency's interests such as transport, agriculture and mining — or a viewpoint, such as the Treasury's opposition to government intervention except where the Treasury has a responsibility.

While a specialist department is normally the major influence on a specific topic, broader issues are determined by Foreign Affairs, Treasury, Trade and Resources and perhaps the Prime Minister's Department. Given their close links with Western financial interests and support for market forces, the Treasury supports strongly the orthodox Western financial approach, and opposes the market interventions it sees in the NIEO. Other bureaucratic attitudes have been somewhat ambivalent. Foreign Affairs has a positive political response while Trade and Resources, despite some recognition of a general community of interest, moves reluctantly from pure pragmatism even on resource trade issues.

Increased awareness of the Third World's importance has been reflected in policy statements by the government more than in public perceptions, and in the establishment of two inquiries concerned with Third World relationships. In 1979, a Committee (Harries) reported to the government on Australia and the Third World.[34] A Senate Joint Committee also reported on Australia and the New International Economic Order.[35] Both reports emphasized changes needed in Australia's attitudes to the Third World, including the strong interest of these countries in increased markets in Australia. The Senate Committee report also emphasized the influence Australia could have on attitudes among developed countries themselves.

Conclusion

Historically, Australia has seen itself threatened by developing countries and has sought the protection of developed countries. Its cultural links tie Australia to developed countries while its affluence, its advanced economic institutions and its technological base are developed country characteristics. Moreover, despite its similarity of interests with the Third World on some issues, on others, and as a rich nation, its interests often compete or conflict with those of developing countries. Australia tends to see itself as of the West, even if — no doubt like others — with a difference. Yet it has had increasingly to take Third World development more seriously.

Policy attitudes probably remain predominantly orthodox but, from recent public debate, increasingly enlightened. The Harries report, reinforced more strongly by the Senate report, argued that Australia should distinguish between the interests of the West, which it should support and those of particular members of the West, which it normally should not. Both argued for compromise, for co-operative approaches to Third World views and for ways to satisfy the practical possibilities underlying Third World objectives. This is an improvement on Australia's previous frequent uncritical acceptance of Western attitudes, often leading in rejecting Third World proposals without offering constructive alternatives. Yet, although Australia's stated political attitudes may now be constructive, responses in practice on economic issues remain unhelpful. Although Australia's economic and political relations are now once more interlinked, Australia has a much smaller strategic role as counterweight to the great powers and is increasingly judged in the region by its contribution to the trade and development efforts of Third World countries, even if outside Asia its political attitudes are more important. Yet its renewed interests in Third World development evidenced in policy statements have not reflected themselves in economic terms. Support for the Common Fund was already in place, but aid has not increased. Some downwards pressure on industrial tariffs may ultimately eventuate but decisions made in 1980 were discouraging.

Frequent entreaties for outward-looking Third World policies have not been paralleled in Australia's policies nor, with the deterioration in the post-war international co-operative system, and the West's inward-looking attitudes, do the chances of outward-looking approaches globally seem high. Moreover, outward-looking policies alone are insufficient for the Third World. There are disadvantages as well as advantages for developing countries in their links with developed countries; these disadvantages may have to be reduced before positive gains are recognized by developing countries. Arguments for an outward approach which start by largely denying any disadvantages are unlikely to achieve that.

For various reasons Australia's position warrants a constructive, moderately reformist, approach less aligned than currently with the West which, while improving world productive efficiency, would make some concessions to income and power distribution inequalities of the Third World.[36] First, the Third World's case against the existing international system has some substance. Secondly, reduced protection would benefit Australia directly and, by international example, indirectly. Thirdly, Australia benefits from accepted rules for international relationships, which developing country support would reinforce. Fourthly, it cannot avoid close relations with Third World countries. Finally, rational accommodation with the Third World will improve world stability. If power is shifting to developing countries, orderly negotiated changes might be desirable; even if Third World countries fail to achieve greater power, Australia could be vulnerable in that failure, with its resource abundance, its geography and its immigration and racial policies.

The Harries report argues that Australia should support measures mutually beneficial to developed and developing countries alike. The debate, however, is largely about what policies benefit mutually the Third World and the West. If, like the Harries report, few imperfections are acknowledged in the existing system, few changes are mutually beneficial; unsurprisingly, mutuality arguments favour the *status quo* in such circumstances. This is even more so if each issue is decided on its merits as the Harries report proposed for economic issues: long-term national interests — which the Senate report emphasized may have to be pursued at the expense of short-run interests — will then normally be ignored. Most importantly, whether or not there are mutual benefits is ultimately decided by the West. The mutuality argument therefore either simply reaffirms the West's power or it lacks policy value since it begs all the important questions.

Even then, limited moves by Australia in supporting its interest in Third World development such as support for the Common Fund, stimulated surprise and scepticism among Western spokesmen. If the West continues to assume that Australia's interests in Third World development are identical to its own a constructive approach by Australia to the Third World could involve some cost in terms of Western relationships. Australia has therefore a long way to go in clarifying its interests in Third World development. It is a major step that the debate has at least started.

Notes

1. For a detailed discussion of the concepts of interest and interdependence, see R.O. Keohane and Joseph S. Nye, *Power and Interdependence: World Politics in Transition* (Little, Brown & Co., Boston, 1977).
2. See Stuart Harris and Ian Reynolds, 'Population and Natural Resources' in *The Population of Australia*, (Economic and Social Commission for Asia and the Pacific monograph, Bangkok, forthcoming).

3. National Energy Advisory Committee, *Liquid Fuels in Australia: Long Term Needs, Prospects and Issues*, NEAC Report No. 9 (AGPS, Canberra, 1980).

4. See Stuart Harris, 'Future Minerals and Energy Trade' in Peter Hastings and Andrew Farran (eds.), *Australia's Resources Future* (Nelson/AIIA, Melbourne, 1978).

5. The latest data are those given in Australian Bureau of Statistics, *Foreign Control in the Mining Industry, 1976-77* (Canberra, 27 July 1978).

6. Department of Transport, 'Submission to the Senate Standing Committee on Foreign Affairs and Defence on 'The New International Economic Order – Implications for Australia' (Canberra, 1979).

7. For a useful discussion of these general issues, see T.B. Millar, 'India, Japan, Australia and the Security of Asia', *Australian Quarterly*, vol. 39, no. 3 (September 1967),pp. 7-19.

8. The dissenting view was entered by Mr J. T. Smith, in Committee on Australia's Relations with the Third World, *Report: Australia and the Third World* (Harries Report) (AGPS, Canberra, September 1979), pp. 191-2.

9. Ibid., p. 104.

10. John Stone, Secretary to the Treasury, 'The New International Economic Order – Implications for Australia', Senate Standing Committee on Foreign Affairs and Defence, Transcript of Evidence (1980), vol. 2, p. 1048.

11. This point is developed more fully in J.D.B. Miller, 'Australia and the Indian Ocean Area' in Gordon Greenwood and Norman Harper (eds.), *Australia in World Affairs, 1966-70* (Cheshire/Australian Institute of International Affairs, Melbourne, 1974), p. 430.

12. The basic change in the international situation that this reflects is discussed in Stuart Harris, 'Changed International Resource and Trade Relationships: The Economics/Politics Link Renewed' *World Review*, vol. 19, no.1 (April 1980), pp. 17-31.

13. Greater detail can be obtained from Australian Bureau of Statistics, *Foreign Investment: 1977-78* (Canberra, 29 August 1979).

14. More detail is given in Senate Standing Committee on Foreign Affairs and Defence, *Australia and the South Pacific*, Parliamentary Paper No. 41 (AGPS, Canberra, 1978).

15. These ideas have emerged in various forms but were perhaps expressed most starkly by Alfred Sauvy, *Zero Growth?* (Praeger, New York, 1975), p. 126.

16. A point made clearly by Robert O'Neill in 'The Strategic View' in Peter Hastings and Andrew Farran (eds.), *Australia's Resources Future* (Nelson/Australian Institute of International Affairs, Melbourne, 1978), p. 217.

17. See P.J. Flood, 'Population Growth and Foreign Policy', *Australian Outlook*, vol. 32, no. 1 (April 1978), pp. 53-64.

18. This proposition was argued, for example, in Australian Population and Immigration Council, *Immigration Policies and Australia's Population* (a Green Paper) (AGPS, Canberra, 1977), p. 23.

19. Australia's attitudes and role at this time are described in J.G. Crawford, *Australia's Trade Policy, 1942-1966* (ANU Press, Canberra, 1968).

20. As, for example, in H.W. Arndt, 'Australia – Developed, Developing or Midway?', *Economic Record*, vol. 41, no. 95 (September 1965), pp. 318-40.

21. These issues have been discussed at greater length in Stuart Harris, 'Commodity Problems and the International Economic Order: What Rules of What Game?' in Peter Oppenheimer (ed.), *Issues in International Economics* (Oriel Press, London, 1980).

22. This point is developed in more detail in Stuart Harris, 'Australia and the New International Economic Order', *Australian Outlook*, vol. 32, no. 1 (April

1978), pp. 22-40.

23. Kenneth Rivett, 'Race, Immigration and the Borrie Report', *Australian Quarterly*, vol. 48, no. 3 (September 1976), pp. 12-22.

24. These developments have been discussed in Charles Price, 'Beyond White Australia: The Whitlam Government's Immigration Record', *Round Table*, vol. 65, (1975), pp. 369-77.

25. See, for example, Rivett, 'Race, Immigration and the Borrie Report'.

26. J.M. Fraser, Australian Prime Minister, *Statement on the World Situation* (Canberra, 1 June 1976).

27. This issue has been discussed at greater length in Clive Edwards, 'Asean-Australia Trade Relations: A Survey of Current Issues' (Department of Economics, ANU, Canberra (mimeo.), September 1978).

28. More details of Australia's international aid are given, for example, in Senate Standing Committee on Foreign Affairs and Defence, *The New International Economic Order: Implications For Australia* (AGPS, Canberra, 1980), pp. 35-9.

29. See discussion on this point in Anthony Clunies Ross, 'Foreign Aid' in Gordon Greenwood and Norman Harper (eds.), *Australia in World Affairs, 1966-1970* (Cheshire/AIIA, Melbourne, 1974).

30. Australian Gallup Polls (Roy Morgan Research Centre, Melbourne, August 1945).

31. Ibid., September 1966 (Poll No. 183).

32. Ibid., August 1971 (Poll No. 2285) and November 1972 (Poll No. 2363).

33. Ibid., November 1966 (Poll No. 185).

34. Committee on Australia's Relations with the Third World, *Report: Australia and the Third World*.

35. Senate Standing Committee on Foreign Affairs and Defence, *The New International Economic Order*.

36. These reasons have been discussed in greater detail in Harris, 'Australia and the New International Economic Order'; and in Stuart Harris, 'The Brandt Commission Report and its Significance for Australia', *Australian Outlook*, vol. 36, no. 1, April 1982.

6 BRITISH INTERESTS AND THIRD WORLD DEVELOPMENT

Vince Cable

Introduction

Rich country policies towards poorer countries are often rationalized in terms of morality but are almost certainly inspired in practice by what are thought to be national interests. Attempts to modify these policies therefore need to be preceded by a clear understanding of these interests. This is particularly true in the case of the UK whose government, together with that of the United States, has been to the fore in opposing Third World proposals to reform international economic relations.

Study of British policy-making in relation to a group of countries as heterogeneous and loosely articulated as the Third World is bound to be problematic. As the government minister currently responsible for North-South negotiations defined his job: 'we in the FCO deal overwhelmingly with individual countries and when you deal with individual countries you find that they are more interested in their individual problems than they are in this whole set of subjects'.[1] In addition, there are problems of consistency. Within the last 16 years there have been four changes of government. Although policy towards developing countries (LDCs) has been well in the background as a political issue, each new administration has changed the status and functions of the Ministry of Overseas Development and the emphasis of external policy in general. It is often difficult, furthermore, to establish what the policies actually are. British sensitivity on matters of official secrecy is extreme; thus, officials consistently refuse to disclose to parliamentarians the existence let alone the deliberations of committees dealing with even the least contentious aspects of overseas economic policy and, specifically, aid.

The concept of 'national interests' poses many problems and some of particular relevance to Britain. Britain acts as host to a sophisticated international financial and services market in 'the City' some of whose activities – for example, 'offshore' eurodollar banking – reflect truly transnational rather than 'national' interests. Similarly, Britain is also the nominal country of origin of some of the world's leading transnational companies.

Even where 'national interests' are unambiguous they are not necessarily unique. Many of the interests of industrial countries are common, even if they are not always perceived as such. British 'interests' are primarily determined by the fact that, like most other industrial countries, Britain runs a substantial surplus on trade in manufacturers and services with LDC countries, imports from them a wide range of raw materials, foodstuffs — and increasingly, competing manufactures — and is a net exporter of capital and a net importer of labour. But there are some differences of emphasis and some distinctive British interests — for example, as a result of Britain's energy self-sufficiency.

Britain's International Role

The major influences moulding policies in relation to LDCs stem from several interrelated historical developments: relative economic decline (which some would argue is becoming absolute); the liquidation of Empire and its legacies; and an economic and political realignment towards Western Europe.

Relatively poor economic performance has greatly limited the scope for an expensive, wide-ranging, foreign policy and not only in the development field. A leaked Foreign Office dispatch by a retiring ambassador caught the flavour of recent pessimism: 'we are not only no longer a world power, but we are not even in the first rank even as a European one. We are scarcely in the same league as the Germans or the French. We talk of ourselves without shame as one of the less prosperous countries of Europe. The prognosis for the foreseeable future is discouraging.'[2] Concretely, this decline is manifested in a gradual fall in relative living standards, and most acutely in the deteriorating state of manufacturing industry.

The implications for policy are several. First, Britain is, simply, becoming less important. The relative influence of Britain — as a market, as an aid donor, as a member of the IMF — is shrinking to reflect relatively diminishing economic resources. Secondly, experience of relatively poor international trade performance has engendered considerable pessimism about Britain's ability to benefit from a reform of relations with LDCs, even when this has elements of self-interest for Western countries as a whole. This has been a strong reason behind scepticism about the 'pump-priming' character of improvements in developing countries' commodity earnings capacity, or an expansion of untied multilateral aid and heightened sensitivity to the 'threat'of new sources of industrial competition. Thirdly, a major influence from public opinion, especially on attitudes to 'aid', is the widespread feeling in Britain that it is no longer a 'rich' country, despite the exploitation of oil. Finally, while Britain's relative decline has been gradual and long-term, it has been punctuated by short-term financial crises, as the balance of payments has carried the strain of accommodating Britain's declining international competitiveness. And the current preoccupation with inflation is perhaps best understood in terms of frustration, building up over a long period, at the inability of the economy to meet even modest expectations of growth. Governments have struggled in each crisis to 'get the economy right' and this has become a prior condition, not a rationale, for more positive policies in relation to LDCs.

The next major influence is that, as the main *ex-colonial power*, Britain has links with the Third World which are of a quite different character from those of the developed countries which had no empire, and more far-reaching than those of countries like France or Holland, which did. The Commonwealth ('old' and 'new') is still important, out of proportion to its role in the world economy, as a market for British goods and as a recipient of British private investment. Decline has, however been rapid and the political significance of the Commonwealth in Britain is now minor. There are still some unsolved problems and residual obligations which absorb a good deal of political attention and goodwill: Hong Kong, the Falklands.* Other aspects of the imperial heritage are intangible. Some are negative (racism and a generalized resentment towards 'ungrateful' countries which Britain 'built up' and to which it then 'gave' independence). Others are more constructive. There are, for example, large numbers of British expatriates who have worked in the tropics, or still do, in fields such as civil engineering, tropical medicine or teaching. Although this paper records the colonial heritage as a distinct influence from the relative economic decline, some would argue that they are interrelated: that, for example, the traditional internationalism of the City of London has diminished the role which it could be playing in financing British industry.

It was preoccupation with the need to reverse relative economic decline and also to find a post-colonial, political role which together led to *membership of the EEC* and which is now in itself a major influence on British external policy. Britain no longer has an independent trade policy, at least on the import side. Tariffs and preferences, quotas, anti-dumping procedures and farm levies are now negotiated and

*This was written before the Falklands war.

administered through the Community. The effect of the Community has recently been to restrain the British from pushing too strenuously for restrictions against LDC products, except in agriculture. British governments have also had to accept, with some adaptation to meet Commonwealth interests, the Community's geo-political concentration on Africa and the Mediterranean basin rather than on Asian or Latin American countries. More generally, Britain is now a constituent member of the world's largest trading group, the EEC, and is in a strong position to influence its policies towards the rest of the world for good or ill.

National and Sectional Interests and the Decision-making Machinery

To take the analysis of 'interests' further, the paper looks first at the influences — from public opinion and competing political ideologies — on the formation of a 'national' view, then at the sectional and pressure groups which are particularly influential, and finally at the decision-making machinery which connects these various component parts.

Public Opinion

A major constraint on government policy in a democratic society is what the public will stand. A survey of public opinon in 1969 showed that there was a good deal of sympathy (over 60 per cent) for the proposition 'that Britain had a duty to help poor countries'. The survey also showed that 'public knowledge and understanding of aid tended to be rudimentary and that most people regarded aid as charity'.[3] A second survey in 1976 retested public attitudes and found that only 47 per cent of the sample were in favour (with varying enthusiasm) of the UK giving help to poor countries as against 62 per cent seven years earlier;[4] 39 per cent were against (with the balance undecided) as against 29 per cent in 1969. Several reasons were established for the change. The first was a feeling that Britain was now too poor or had too many problems of its own. There was a general syndrome of 'national introversion'. (This 'national introversion' does not only concern LDCs; separate Gallup polls have found that the percentage of the British people who think foreign policy a major issue for this country declined from 48 per cent in 1960 to eight per cent in 1970, and to five per cent in 1980.)[5] Secondly, the 1976 survey established a close correlation between hostility to LDCs and racial hostility to immigrants, especially amongst older people and in less educated and low-income groups.

Thirdly, arguments based on Britain's self-interest appeared to cut little ice. Those who favoured aid did so largely for humanitarian reasons and they were not influenced by political and economic arguments. Those opposed to aid were not impressed either; they largely disbelieved claims that there is any real benefit to Britain.

Ideological Cross- Currents

Development ranks low down in the priorities of the general public and this is reflected in Parliament. There, the subject of North-South relations is largely non-partisan and inconspicuous, debated infrequently. Interest has been confined largely to a dozen or so committed MPs from both sides of the House mainly those working through a Commons Select (Sub) Committee.

In the Labour Party, much of the old internationalist commitment has ebbed in the wake of the powerful tide of Britain's industrial and political decline. To the extent that there is any interest in relations with developing countries on the increasingly important 'left-wing' of the Party it is heavily influenced by the view that the world economy is dominated by multinational companies and most LDCs by 'elites' and that not much can usefully be accomplished by reformist measures. The 'right' of the party, and the Liberals have for the most part been less interested in developing countries than in Europe. All told, this is not very promising material, and the party's attempts in office to fashion positive policies have stemmed mainly from a handful of dedicated ministers and a rather weak sense of generalized goodwill from the remainder. None the less, interest has revived within the last few years, and speeches from most sectors of the party now stress that support for developing country aspirations is a touchstone of socialist internationalism.

In the Conservative Party there has been a shift to the 'right', to people who believe in less government, strict monetary control and the need to let resources be allocated by market forces. 'Global Keynsianism', 'planned international restucturing' and more aid have no part in their scheme of things. Another ingredient in the thinking of much of the Tory 'right' is a populist economic and political nationalism often tinged with racial feelings in a Third World context. Even the hard-line 'free market' members of the present Cabinet, including the Prime Minister, show no sympathy for the view that 'free markets' might apply to trade in agriculture or textiles, or to untying aid or that there should be free international movement of labour (into Britain) as well as of capital out. Populism of this kind helps to capture the mood of 'national introversion' and the feeling that 'charity begins at home'. Reinforcing this conviction is the traditional conservative view, given intellectual coherence by the writings of, *inter alia*, Professor Bauer and Mr Enoch Powell, that resource transfers to poorer countries are not only bad for the donor but also for the recipient, weakening the spirit of self-help. These instincts are, in the present government, having to be balanced against the more traditional sentiments of post-war Conservative administrations: concern for the country's image abroad, and for exercising leadership in world affairs. But to the extent that there are differences in view, they are essentially differences in the degree of generosity of outlook rather than in perception of national interests.

Interest Groups

Contemporary Britain is often likened to a 'corporate state' in which big business and unions dominate.Whether or not that is accurate (and both of these groups are unhappy under the present government), they are clearly important influences.

The CBI is a loosely federated body which represents *business opinion* albeit somewhat uneasily. Some powerful business groups – farmers and textile manufacturers for example – operate primarily through their industry federations. The main multinational companies and City institutions also have independent political and official influence. But the CBI comes nearest of any body to expressing the views of manufacturing industry as a whole. A unifying theme is that 'British relations with the Third World must be based on the principles of the free circulation of goods and of the "social market economy" – free and fair competition'.[6] This has led the CBI to a forthright rejection of more dirigiste features of the NIEO. Its specific preoccupations have concerned the 'threat' of 'unfair' Third World imports, the encouragement of private overseas investment in LDCs and a greater tying of overseas aid to UK exports.

Protectionist pressures among CBI members are currently strong. In one of the few genuinely controversial debates ever held at an annual CBI conference, there was a successful revolt in 1980 by delegates, led by the footwear manufacturers, against the relatively free-trading line of the platform. The British Institute of Management is a less substantial body than the CBI but its Chairman recently also gave an eloquent statement of this current preoccupation of British manufacturers: 'the Western world must control its trade with the Far East and the Eastern Bloc before the products of their managed economies and their highly organised societies and cultures (which we shall never be able to match) destroy the manufacturing base in all so-called advanced countries'.[7]

The CBI has also argued strongly for the encouragement of overseas private investment, urging that there is 'an illogicality in promoting a policy of official aid to developing countries while discouraging private investment'. The CBI's view on aid is it should be 'increasingly devoted to projects of benefit to Britain's trading interests'. In particular it should be increasingly tied, switched to non-Commonwealth countries where there are 'commercial and investment opportunities' and concentrated more in infrastructure projects in countries which are 'rich in natural resources but lacking in communications'. In general, the message from businessmen is that British development policies have been too disinterested and now need to be tougher in order to promote British interests (or, at least, theirs).

The influence of the *trade unions* on overseas policy is more circumscribed, but the TUC's views are of some interest because of the influence of trade unions on the Labour Party. The TUC takes as a major theme the need for a revival of economic growth and the mutuality of interest between Britain and LDCs achieving that end.[8]

On the emotional issue — for trade unions — of market access, the TUC tries to be balanced: 'a policy which severely limited access to industrial countries markets would be very damaging, although safeguard measures of a temporary and selective character are essential. Measures to promote adaptation and change will also be required.' The TUC has, however, been exercized by the 'unfairness' of low wages (private and social) in some developing countries which are 'the underlying cause of "disruption" in trading patterns. Clearly one of the main advantages of less-developed countries in world trade is low labour costs . . . If minimum labour standards are not maintained social progress will be penalised by a decline in trading competitiveness.'

The interest groups described are essentially those of producers. Formal *consumer groups* are not so influential. To a large extent they do not need to be; with a well organized, outward-looking, retail and importing system, consumers have a considerable countervailing power to producer interests. When, however, they have been threatened with the loss of this option — as with textiles and farm produce — the widely diffused consumer interests have proved difficult to mobilize politically.

Within the *non-governmental 'development lobby'*, the British based charities and volunteer organizations — Oxfam, War on Want, Christian Aid, Save the Children Fund, Voluntary Service Overseas, Action in

Distress — have acquired an enviable reputation for providing useful development assistance without strings and for their ability to draw on a wide and sympathetic public, particularly at times of disaster. Inevitably, however, the total resource transfers effected by these groups, an estimated £25 million in 1977, are small in relation to the government's own budget (about five per cent). The Church also has an influence. Public attacks by the Archbishop of Canterbury on government cuts in overseas aid, especially when echoed by the Catholic Primate, are bound to cause ministers concern, even in a country which is not deeply religious.[9]

There are the campaigning groups (such as the World Development Movement and the Catholic Institute of International Relations) which have been influential where concern can be sharply focused (as for example on the conditions in Sri Lankan tea estates or in Bolivian tin mines). There is in addition a large back-up of specialist development studies academics. Despite this cumulatively substantial collection of committed groups and individuals, their influence on wider issues of North-South relations, other than aid, has been small.

The Co-ordination of Decision-making

Interests do not exist in isolation and have to be geared to the decision-making machinery.[10] One of the criticisms of British governments in the North-South context has been that machinery does not work well. Policy, it has been argued, is characterized by *ad hoc* and short-term policies: 'your (parliamentary) committee has been quite unable to establish any capacity or administrative arrangement for long term strategic interdepartmental liaison on foreign economic policy: much less have they been able to establish the means by which British foreign economic policy is co-ordinated with British domestic economic affairs'.[11] This comment however subsumes two different criticisms.

The first is that the bureaucracy does not function well in pulling together the various strands of policy. There are some areas where the fragmented nature of departmental responsibilities encourages a piecemeal approach to policy. Commodities, for example, fall to the Department of Trade (general trade policy and Common Fund negotiations), Industry (metals), Agriculture (agricultural commodities), ODM (Stabex), Treasury (IMF Compensatory Finance Facility and anything which requires public money), Energy (oil) and The Foreign Office (North-South co-ordination). But criticism of poor co-ordination is largely misplaced. On the contrary, Britain is, in this narrow sense, well served, especially by the *Foreign Office* which has particular responsibility for co-ordination. A leading academic analyst concluded: 'coordination for the sake of consistency has been considered important' and 'it can hardly be said that British policy in the world has been notably erratic or seriously at odds with itself'.[12]

There is another more telling criticism that there is an absence of any long-term strategic design, both because of a general diinclination to think long term and because the pressures of short-term events and domestic interest groups overwhelm whatever efforts there are. In the case of North-South relations, the problems have been compounded in several ways.

First, the various policy strands have never been pulled together in one independent ministry. It was the view of those (a working group of Fabians under Lord Balogh) who originally pioneered the ideas of a *Ministry of Overseas Development* before 1964 that it should be a department concerned with all aspects of policy affecting the Third World. It never became so. Even as a Ministry of Overseas Development (ODM) with a minister in the Cabinet, it was always primarily an aid ministry. At present, the Overseas Development Administration (ODA) is subordinate to the Foreign Office and its head is a (rather junior) Foreign Office minister, while another Foreign Office minister is responsible for North-South negotiations. The last (Labour) Minister of Overseas Development did manage to increase the aid budget in relation to GNP and public expenditure, despite mounting economic difficulties, and developed a clear poverty-focused aid philosophy. But the 1974-9 experience demonstrated the Ministry's precarious dependence on one active minister (and to a lesser extent on the political support of a left-of-centre government); departmental influence on wider North-South issues was limited even then.

Secondly, the definition of British external economic interests has undoubtedly been hampered by the absence of a department concerned with long- or medium-term economic planning. Responsibility for economic policy, both in its internal and external aspects, has rested with departments whose recognized field of competence is in short-term economic management (the Treasury) or in management of commercial policy in liaison with manufacturing industry (Trade and Industry). *The Treasury* is immensely influential. This is partly because of its control over public expenditure and, in particular, annual aid expenditure ceilings and control over aid items. Attempts to assist departmental planning through medium term (five year) 'real' spending targets have invariably been superseded by changes in government and short-term crises requiring emergency 'cuts'. The Treasury is also the 'lead' department on the currently crucial issue of international financial reform, acting on the advice of the Bank of England. Its essentially conservative stance is partly explained by a considered view of the kind of international monetary order which is in Britain's interests, but is also influenced by immediate preoccupations: the possible effect of 'indexing' oil producers' financial assets on UK capital inflows and the exchange rate; the possible effect of aid-linked SDR issues on the Public Sector Borrowing Requirement.

Those departments concerned with commercial policy have had, in Britain, no long-term strategic design to guide them either. Even Labour's interventionist 'industrial strategy' was not a strategy in any real sense; it deliberately eschewed choices between industries and was not based on intersectoral planning. The *Department of Trade* has recently moved more to the centre of the stage, reflecting the priority given by LDCs to trade issues and its responsibility for UNCTAD. Departmental philosophy could best be described as 'working with the grain' of British business interests in trade matters.[13] There has, within the department, been something of a change in emphasis in the 1970s away from non-interventionist to mercantilist ideas largely because of the growing importance of trade with developing and Communist countries and because of the influence of British businessmen who believe (to quote the CBI) that 'there is a greater willingness on the part of governments in other countries to bring about . . . the propagation of interests of national industry . . .'[14] A further strong influence in this direction is the *Department of Industry* which sees its main job as relaying to Whitehall the views of British industry much of which feels threatened by 'unfair' international competition. Such have been the pressures on these departments that perhaps the two most aggressively free market and free trading ministers in the current Conservative government have in practice been responsible for a baffling array of import restrictions[15] (mainly on imports from Third World countries) and Mr Nott (the then Trade Minister) assured the House of Commons that 'we have substantially increased the number of quotas and restrictions we have inherited (from Labour)'.[16]

Finally, as the above illustrations show, there has been a general tendency in the main departments not only for short-term tactical considerations to prevail over longer-term thinking but for domestic pressures to prevail increasingly over international interests and obligations. Other departments are even less sensitive to the wider international ramifications of domestic policy: the *Home Office* (immigration control); *Education* (overseas student fees); *Agriculture* (farming and especially sugar). The main countervailing influence is provided by the Foreign Office, the Whitehall department other than ODA where there is likely to be the greatest appreciation of the usefulness of 'goodwill' in international relations, of maintaining some sort of 'dialogue' with potentially hostile and important developing nations and also of international order in the widest sence. But there are considerable limitations on the influence which the Foreign Office can bring to bear. Moreover, North-South questions (except those which are very specific such as Zimbabwe and the Middle East) rank well below those concerning Britain's interests in the EEC and NATO. And there are genuine doubts, reflected in its inability or unwillingness to protect the budget of the ODA and more generally in the rather dismissive Foreign Office memorandum on Brandt,[17] as to whether Britain's long-term interests (rather than prestige and image) are in fact well served by a positive approach to development matters. To the question of real national interests we now turn in detail.

Developing Countries as Markets

The centrepiece of the 'mutual interests' approach to North-South relations is the belief that developed countries have as markets, creating jobs and profits in their exporting industries and that they will be willing to support measures designed to raise purchasing power in LDCs. The idea is not a new one. The British aid programme had its origins in the Colonial Development and Welfare Act which, in the inter-war depression, was an attempt to match the needs of the colonies (initially the Caribbean) with British exporters' excess capacity. Certainly, today, there is evidence of the importance to Britain of exports to LDCs. Including OPEC, these accounted for £10.6 billion of exports in 1980, 23 per cent of the total, this proportion having risen from 20.5 per cent in 1972 (after a long period of decline from 32 per cent in 1960).[18] This amount of production is equivalent, directly, to approximately one million jobs, overwhelmingly in manufacturing. In some categories — construction equipment, aircraft, textile machinery, electrical machinery — exports to LDCs account for over a quarter of all goods sold. But there is a singular lack of enthusiasm for proposals to enlarge the purchasing power of developing countries. Is this due to an ability to see or pursue 'true' national interests or is there something wrong with the mutual interests argument?

The first and most obvious difficulty is that the proposals involve changes which cut across other perceived national economic interests. Exports are of concern because of jobs which they directly generate or because they alleviate an external payments constraint on internal economic expansion. The present UK government does not, however, regard unemployment − rather than inflation − as its main priority and with a high exchange rate it has no reason to regard the balance of payments as an effective constraint on economic growth. Like other Western governments, moreover, it no longer sees the world, as did the Brandt report, in Keynesian, expansionary terms. The objection is partly that Britain would have to contribute to any additional concessional transfers and 'we are under very strict budgetary constraints at present because we feel that the problem of inflation has been neglected in the past'.[19] But there is also a more general view that 'the OECD countries cannot correct the underutilisation of capacity by a massive extra injection of spending'[20] (because of the generally inflationary consequences and specifically because it creates an economic climate in which oil exports can more easily raise real oil prices). Even if the government was converted to more expansionary policies, it could find ways of reflating the British economy which were more popular (by cutting taxes) or more directly linked to UK economic interests (by supporting investment in UK industry as a whole). This is not, however, quite the end of the story. Foreign aid could be selectively slanted to favour UK industries and regions where particularly high excess capacity and unemployed labour would minimize the inflationary consequences, and maximize the employment benefits. The extent to which recent aid programmes have contributed to these objectives was recently brought out by a detailed micro-level survey conducted in 1977.[21] The survey concluded that almost two-thirds of (tied and bilateral) aid orders appeared to have contributed additional business and almost three-quarters were to firms with spare capacity (even at a time of relative buoyancy). Regions with high unemployment, especially Scotland, appear to have benefited; 55 per cent of aid orders went to high unemployment areas of Scotland, mainly Clydeside.

A second reason for scepticism about resource transfers derives from experience of a declining share of world exports, indicating the inability of British exporters to profit from generalized measures taken to enlarge developing countries' purchasing power (though, clearly, with tied aid, this would not be a relevant consideration). Trends in World Bank procurement under competitive tender are, however, fairly reassuring. In the 1970s, UK exporters obtained roughly the same share of new orders as their share of overall OECD manufactured exports (about nine per cent) and as their share of subscriptions (roughly ten per cent for IDA). The British market share was particularly high in soft loan (IDA) credits to low income areas: South Asia and East Africa. But the position is less happy at the margin and especially in the NICs of the Far East and Latin America.

Thirdly, the notion that developing rather than industrialized countries are the growth markets of the future is a confusing one for businessmen and governments. In the wake of Empire, they have been gradually and painfully reorienting themselves in the opposite direction especially towards Europe. While there has been recognition of the importance of exports to OPEC countries, the dominant perception is one of the marginal and generally less dynamic character of Third World markets. This perception is reinforced by the experience of rapid growth of exports to Western Europe (whose share of UK exports rose from 32 per cent in 1960 to 53 per cent on 1977) and the declining importance of non-oil LDCs (25 per cent to 13 per cent in the same period) and of the Commonwealth (34 per cent to 14 per cent). The current lack of importance to Britain of even some of the most significant LDCs is striking. Less was sold in 1978 to Brazil than to Finland or New Zealand, only fractionally more to the whole of Latin America (or to all 'Centrally Planned' economies) than to Denmark or Norway, less to China or Indonesia than to the Netherlands Antilles or Bahamas. Reinforcing this set of priorities, the head of the British Overseas Trade Board recently observed that 'within the export drive the Board has felt it right to concentrate upon the major industrial markets – Western Europe, North America, Australia and Japan . . . There is a tendency on the part of some of our companies to go for Third World markets as a kind of easy option. We do not think we ought to pull out of these markets but it is misguided not to go for European markets now that we are in Europe.'[22] Developing country markets are also usually considered more problematic. Businessmen complain about political uncertainty, bureaucratic inefficiency, corruption and poor communications. Many have become disillusioned, after exploring abortively for riches in the new El Dorados: Iran, Nigeria, China, Brazil, Venezuela. Other things being equal, the government would also prefer to avoid deep entanglements with countries which, in trade, do not observe the 'rules of the game' while 'we have been reluctant to buy exports either through much easier ECGD loans or by additional aid. We normally give priority to what we get paid in cash.'[23]

Finally the crude aggregate figures for British export 'interests' are

Table 6.1: UK Share of Procurement from World Bank Loans (%)

	All LDCs	East Africa	West Africa	European LDCs North Africa Middle East	Latin America	East Asia	South Asia
BRD procurement up to 1980	9.8	26.3	14.5	9.0	5.2	5.3	19.4
1980	6.1	16.4	9.0	7.3	4.2	4.7	5.8
DA procurement up to 1980	13.8	19.6	9.0	11.5	4.2	5.3	15.2
1980	12.0	17.5	5.8	16.5	1.2	1.5	12.4

Source: World Bank.

misleading in several ways. Over half of British exports to LDCs are to OPEC and most of these to a small number of rich states such as Saudi Arabia. And over 10 per cent of British exports to LDCs are arms sales. (The total British overseas arms sales in 1978 were officially estimated at £900 million, which may be a 50 per cent underestimation. Of this sum, roughly three-quarters has been channelled to developing countries.)[24] British governments, especially the present one, have given high priority to arms sales as 'a means of reducing and recouping R & D expenditure, sustaining defence industries through lean periods . . .'[25] But this is hardly what Brandt envisaged by 'mutuality' of interest.

Thus, it is not too difficult to explain the apparent paradox that, despite substantial British 'interests' in Third World markets, both businessmen and government are currently restrained in their enthusiasm for policies following in the path of the Brandt report. Prolonged stagnation in Western economies may eventually force a radical reappraisal of interests and priorities, but not yet.

Developing Countries as Industrial Competitors

Competing 'low cost' imports, especially from developing (and communist) newly industrializing countries (NICs), have been a source of growing worry in Britain. In response there has been a shift away from traditional liberal access at a time when developing countries have been giving higher priority to access questions. Although the influence of the French within the EEC has probably been stronger, the British (under both Conservative and Labour governments) have played a leading role in steering the EEC to more restrictive policies with regard to import quotas for textiles and clothing, to more restrictive ceilings under the Generalised System of Preferences, and on the 'selective safeguards' issue in the GATT, Tokyo Round, talks.

This recent history is not explained by exceptionally rapid market penetration by LDCs. Britain has experienced rising import penetration from NIC manufacturers at a rate no greater than that for manufactured imports as a whole. The share of eleven major NICs in British manufactured imports between 1963 and 1977 remained at around seven per cent (while their share of OECD manufactured imports as a whole in this period rose from three per cent to eight per cent).[26] Nor is it attributable to a protectionist ideology. Although there is currently strong support for import controls in the Labour Party and a protectionist tradition in the Tory Party, the present government has succumbed to pressures for extending selective curbs at a time when its own ministers including Ministers of Trade are vigorously denouncing them in principle: 'import controls would treat the symptom rather than the disease and they would do so in a way which would be likely to make the situation worse. They would put up prices thereby fuelling inflation and restricting consumer choice.'[27]

The most obvious explanation for the current inconsistency between declared national interests and actual policies pursued is rising unemployment. The current Secretary of State for Trade, John Biffen, has described as one of three major causes of rising unemployment: 'the challenge to the industrial world from the new economies emerging in the Far East' (the others being higher oil prices and the government's own anti-inflation policies).[28] Most evidence, including that published by government economists, suggests, however, that, in relation to other factors impinging on job loss, the influence of competition from newly industrializing countries has been overall, very small except in one or two narrowly defined subsectors of the garment industry. None the less, it is easy to see how workers should try to resist any additions to unemployment, while there are obvious political attractions to governments in shifting responsibility for unemployment somewhere else.

A second reason for resistance to trade induced change is pessimism, based on Britain's slow growth, and current industrial uncompetitiveness, that if certain sectors are 'given up' in the name of 'comparative advantage' this will not necessarily lead to 'positive adjustment' into more productive activities. Neither of the two main parties have been willing in government to try to combat this pessimism with the kind of active restructuring policies advocated by international agencies and practised to some degree by other countries, notably Japan. The Conservatives are opposed on principle to 'picking winners' and can reasonably point to disastrous errors of government involvement in the past; while the last Labour government's industry strategy was based on the idea of improving the performance of the weakest firms within established industries.

A third factor is political. Producer lobbies are powerful in Britain as in all industrial countries. The textile lobby is able to point to the concentration of much textile employment in Lancashire, where there happens to be a large number of marginal parliamentary constituencies; and to the relatively large number of garment workers in Northern Ireland, which is politically sensitive for other reasons. The influence of the employers is probably even more important (workers in formerly labour intensive industries such as cotton textiles and jute have, after all, been displaced in large numbers by modernized equipment designed to 'save' the industry from 'cheap' import competitions). In the case of textiles the otherwise fragmented lobbying efforts of separate federations representing the many small firms have been rendered much more coherent by the large man-made fibre companies, ICI and Courtaulds, whose interest lies not only in textiles production but in protecting downstream outlets for their fibres. One distinctive feature of British experience is the relatively low degree of direct involvement by British manufacturing firms in various forms of specialization with developing countries (subcontracting, offshore processing or overseas investment in all stages of LDC export industries) which might assist, for capital, the process of adjustment in troubled industries. Even in the electronics industries, where there has been a substantial 'internationalization' of production, British industry has been defensive, having failed to secure a base in Southeast Asia. A contrary influence is the retail sector, especially the large stores, which in Britain are well organized for international sourcing and an influential lobby in their own right (though one major chain, Marks and Spencer, has backed stricter import controls, having found that its purchasing arrangements with British firms were causing it to lose ground to other retailers which 'shopped around').

Fourthly, protectionist sectional interest groups have been helped in mobilizing support by a feeling among businessmen that Britain (and now the EEC as a whole) is uniquely liberal in trade matters and should demand more in terms of reciprocity: 'The EEC should be more aware of the costs involved in pursuing a liberal common commercial policy and should seek greater benefits for its own industries.' Also, it believes that the 'EEC has to bear greater burdens than for example its US counterpart in terms of imports from LDCs' and 'although currently one of the weaker members of the Community, the UK continues to bear an unfair burden as regards imports from LDCs'.[29]

The main restraining factor on protectionism in general has been fear of direct retaliation. Developing countries, however, have rarely offered such a threat — though recent action by Indonesia against UK exports had a profound effect, meriting extended comment in Parliament by the Prime Minister and a modification of the use of 'trigger' quotas under the MFA. This apart, the pressures on governments to act are severe. Here is a case where British national economic interests appear to have substantially diverged from actual policy, for political reasons which are, alas, all too compelling.

Invisible Earnings and Trade in Services

Services have not been a dominant issue in North-South negotiations. But invisible earnings would be a substantial additional element in UK exports resulting from additional purchasing power by LDCs. Invisible earnings are equivalent to about half of visible export earnings and contribute around ten per cent of GNP. Amongst important net earners are the international traded financial services of the City (net earnings £1.4 billion in 1977, up from £440 million in1970— and overseas construction (£620 million earnings in 1977, up from £84 million in 1970) — see Table 6.2. The role of developing countries in British service exports is impossible to quantify, since there are no current statistics detailing source of earnings. But some services are almost entirely geared to developing country markets (e.g. overseas construction and brokerage in tropical commodities) and it is a plausible hypothesis that Commonwealth markets in general are disproportionately important.

Table 6.2: British Invisible Trade (£ million)

	1970 Gross	1970 Net	1977 Gross	1977 Net
A. Overseas earnings by the 'City'				
Insurance Lloyd's underwriting	122		333	
Brokerage commission	50		185	
Other underwriting	30		42	
Overall insurance activity (including investment net earnings)		+297		+909
Commodity trading	87		229	
Banking Financial services	48		293	
Overall net earnings (including interest on sterling liability and foreign currency assets and overseas investment)		+90		+254
Brokerage Baltic exchange	47		155	
Total	85		235	
Total City earnings (including others)		+605		+1,747
of which financial services		+439		+1,372
B. Other invisible earnings				
Royalties	142	+34	430	+100
Overseas construction	84		618	
Overseas students expenditure	67		309	
Civil aviation		+50		+244
Shipping	402	−76	1,035	+21

Source: *UK Balance of Payments* (HMSO, 1977).

It has not been in the British interest to stir up dissatisfaction by drawing attention to the substantial benefit which Britain derives from trade in services with LDCs. But in view of the increasing interest of UNCTAD and some developing countries in shipping and insurance, there is increasing concern in the City about LDC competition. Insurance business is particularly important to Britain; it accounts for half of the net overseas earnings of the City, a large part of which is accounted for by Lloyds members' underwriting activities – mainly reinsurance. The growth of reinsurance has largely compensated UK concerns for the loss of direct insurance business in LDCs with the spread of controls and take-overs of foreign companies. The newly established national companies have invariably required reinsurance because of the narrow spread of risks in limited domestic markets, and have turned to London. There is now a competitive growth of Third World reinsurance corporations such as those currently being launched on a multinational basis in Asia and Africa. There is also concern about developing country ambitions in shipping and in particular about attempts to reorganize the cartel system of conference lines in such a way that LDCs are guaranteed a larger market share. Agreement has been reached to share out liner trade under a UN code, but because of the likely inability of LDCs to meet their agreed quota (40 per cent), it is probable that crosstraders, including British shippers, will retain substantial business for a while. There is now a demand for similar changes in the more significant bulk cargo trade which could raise the cost of sea transport as well as affecting the UK share of trade. In services, as in manufactures, developing countries are no longer simply markets but also competitors.

Private Direct Investment

The extent to which Britain has an interest in direct overseas investment was explored comprehensively in the Reddaway report a decade ago.[30] The broad conclusion was that the 'true' return from overseas investment by manufacturing companies was greater than the opportunity cost (i.e. the return from investing at home). The report also pointed to the substantial exports associated with overseas investment. Two factors have subsequently strengthened the role of overseas investment as a British 'interest'. The first is a widening gap between returns on domestic and foreign investment. The second is the changing nature of the balance of payments problem, and in particular the effect which exchange controls had in helping to keep up an uncomfortably high exchange rate. Controls have now been removed entirely.

The Empire (and South America) once took a lion's share of British foreign investment. Even as late as 1962, developing countries accounted for over 40 per cent of British overseas private foreign assets (£1.3 billion). The share had fallen to 25 per cent by 1974, valued at £2.4 billion, representing scarcely any increase in real terms (see Table 6.3). These figures are not complete (they exclude oil and insurance) or up to date and there are familiar valuation problems. But a clear feature of this period is relatively declining investment in developing countries, and net disinvestment in some Commonwealth countries. Since the mid-1970s, however, there has been a redirection of overseas investment back towards LDCs, especially to OPEC countries, and a slower growth of net investment in the EEC and 'other developed countries' including South Africa. Several big companies – notably Dunlop and Unilever – are now substantially expanding their LDC operations.

The British interest does not lie, however, in having the overseas assets but primarily in the stream of incomes flowing from them. British net invisible earnings from existing overseas investments in developing countries (excluding oil and insurance) averaged annually £675 million in the 1974-7 period, a substantially larger amount than the annual level of net investment there (£400 million). The evidence points to LDCs yielding higher net rates of return than elsewhere. In 1974 developing countries accounted for 35 per cent of UK overseas investment earnings but only 25 per cent of the assets. Over the 1974-7 period developing countries accounted for 25 per cent of new investment but 33 per cent of earnings. In addition there are royalty payments from technical or management collaboration arrangements; there was a surplus of about £60 million in such a trade with LDCs in 1977.

The other major feature of overseas investment in LDCs is the shift from resource-based activity to distribution and manufacturing. Overall, the LDC share of British overseas investment in resource-based activities fell from 29 per cent in 1962 to 15 per cent in 1976. The decline of mining investment has been of particular concern – with only two per cent of UK net overseas investment since 1974. The attitude of LDC governments, especially in Africa, has been blamed by the mining companies, though there are, clearly, other explanations.[31]

Private direct invesrment will almost certainly form an increasingly important component of British interests in LDCs, given both the ideological support of the present government and the financial advantage of acquiring overseas assets when the exchange rate is high and profitable outlets, in the UK, few. Foreign investment is being presented also as one way in which Britain 'can greatly contribute to the advancement of the developing countries'.[32] Proposals for the mandatory international regulation of multinationals are generally regarded, by government and private sector, as an unacceptable price to pay. Foreign investment is, instead, being promoted primarily by encouraging LDCs which welcome investors by seeking investment protection agreements and offering political risk insurance.

Bank Lending: the 'Debt Problem'

British banks have been heavily engaged in the business of lending to LDCs (mainly recycling OPEC funds). It is somewhat misleading, however, to talk in terms of British patriality where banking is concerned. Many 'British' bank operations in the City are of an 'offshore' character conducted in foreign currencies and by the subsidiaries of overseas, mainly US, banks, which happen to operate eurodollar business from London. In 1977, developing countries accounted for £32 billion out of £83 billion of 'British' overseas bank lending (as defined by the UK authorities).[33] On a much wider definition of UK banking interests, developing countries (oil and non-oil, but excluding offshore banking centres) accounted for about 18 per cent of overseas bank claims and 30 per cent of liabilities, the balance being accounted for by recycling of OPEC deposits to other countries.[34] Approximately two-thirds of (gross) LDC claims are accounted for by five countries (if we exclude the large sums relent through the Bahamas and the other offshore centres).

The British interest in this matter has several aspects. There are the net invisible earnings of the banking community. They are not particularly large, however, in relation to overall invisible earnings (about £280 million net in 1977) and not all of this is derived from eurodollar business. Much accrues from the retail activities of the banks overseas. But it is in practice impossible to separate out one element of gain from a large interrelated complex of activities which are comprised by an international financial centre. What is more central to the national interest is that the system of international payments financing does not go off the rails. This is partly because large-scale debt default would create serious repercussions for the British banking system to the extent that British banks are involved (and, even if they are not, because of general confidence factors). It is also important because the financing mechanism is inextricably tied up with the economic performance —

Table 6.3: Returns on Overseas Investment (£ million)

	(1) 1960 Stock	(2) 1974 (Stock)	(3) $\frac{(2)-(1)}{(1)}$ Growth %	(4) 1974 (Net earnings)	(5) 1974-7 (Net investment)	(6) 1974-7 (Average net earnings)	(7) $\frac{4}{2}$
World	3,404	10,118	197	1,490	4,993	2,084	14.7
Commonwealth	2,049	4,501	120	616	1,628	859	13.7
Developing	1,274	2,413	89	465	1,233	675	19.3
Oil-exporting	162	319	97	67	326	166	21.0
EEC	273	2,197	705	268	1,014	351	12.2
North America	785	2,214	182	308	1,412	607	13.9
Other developed	923	2,968	311	408	1,009	602	13.7
South Africa	290	997	237	214	459	234	21.5
South America/Caribbean	277	464	68	125	246	153	27.0
Africa	414	737	78	127	494	184	17.2
Middle East and Iran	14	64	357	22	50	58	34.3
Other Asia	519	868	64	152	319	209	17.5

Note: Overseas investment figures exclude oil and insurance.
Net earnings are after payment of overseas tax and depreciation. They include profit of overseas branches plus UK companies' receipt of interest and profits from overseas subsidiaries and associates.
Source: Derived from MA4, *Overseas Transactions* (HMSO, 1977) and M4 (1974 supplement).

in real terms — of borrowing and lending countries.

The most immediate significance of a substantial lending to LDCs by UK-based banks has been to help define the official stance on the question of debt. Reflecting the views of the Bank of England and of the City itself, the government has opposed generalized debt relief. Commercial debt, it has been argued, may be dealt with by rescheduling, but that is a matter for consideration case by case, by private creditors, in a way that does not undermine the sanctity of the debt contract. The majority of UK bank claims on developing countries relate, in any event, to a handful of countries — Brazil, Mexico, Venezuela and Korea notably — which are willing and apparently able to conduct borrowing on entirely commercial terms. 'Aid debt' has been dealt with as a separate issue by writing off much of this debt and setting the cost against the aid budget. In 1978 the British made a significant initiative on 'aid debt', making a retrospective adjustment of terms covering £900 million owed by 17 of the poorest countries. Since the cost was charged against aid appropriations there was no net flow of resources to LDCs (though there was a benefit to them from untying, or, in the case of India, freedom to use the sum of debt relieved for local (rupee) costs). The position on commercial debt remained firm, however. This policy combination has considerable attractions for the City. It is generous to poor countries. Also, by shifting to the UK Exchequer the cost of servicing debt by poor countries it helps to ensure that private loans are repaid.

With the renewed increase in oil prices and the need for large-scale additional financing by non-oil LDCs, the recycling — and associated debt problem — has once more come to the fore. The British government view, echoing the City, is that 'the international capital market can continue to play the primary role in recycling OPEC surpluses to finance these deficits'.[35] But major banks are becoming increasingly concerned about the major non-oil LDC borrowers, and correspondingly cautious. To the extent that the British government is looking for means of supporting commercial recycling, it is in terms of strengthening the IMF. Still having one of the largest quotas in the IMF, and thereby one of the largest voting rights, Britain has been in a position to influence the course of discussion. This influence is being directed to 'increased access to the IMF for countries in need and for extra sources of finance for larger drawings' while avoiding more radical proposals such as linking SDRs to aid.[36] While supporting administrative 'flexibility' in Fund conditionality, the British government strongly supports the principle: 'Agreement on an economic programme will not only release IMF funds but often enable the country concerned to attract private finance as well' (though Labour ministers, with unhappy memories of the IMF, would perhaps argue differently). There is little support for proposals from LDCs for new institutions or changes other than gradual adaptation, to the IMF. And any suggestion of guarantees or interest rate subsidies for private lending is dismissed as an 'unacceptable extension of the State role into the realm of private banking'.[37]

A final consideration affecting government policy towards international financial issues is that sterling is an international medium of exchange and store of value. Until recently, the main problem was that the 'overhang' of private and officially held sterling balances led to periodic crises of confidence in sterling. Arrangements to 'fund' official sterling balances have greatly reduced their importance. The problem now is the different one of embarrassment at the enthusiasm of foreigners for holding sterling as a 'petro-currency'. One major reason for hostility to indexing oil producers' financial assets is that 'if the terms were sufficiently attractive that could lead to a very large inflow of funds into the UK with effects on the exchange rate that we might not necessarily welcome'.[38]

Commodities

The commodities issue is not as important for Britain as some of those discussed above. Britain is becoming significantly less dependent on LDCs for many important raw materials as imports are replaced by home products (oil and sugar beet), or by those of other OECD countries (food and minerals) or by technical substitutes. None the less, 30 per cent by value of foodstuffs imports and 50 per cent of non-renewable resources still come from LDCs.

Successive government responses to LDC demands for changes in commodity trade have eafned Britain a reputation as a 'hardliner'. This is explained mainly by its fear that ambitious attempts to regulate commodity markets would directly lead to a pushing up of prices and legitimize the idea of price 'indexation' at the expense of commodity importing countries like Britain: 'the idea of indexation, the principle of it, could very easily spread to . . . commodities . . . and that action would lead us into very considerable difficulties'.[39] Hence, there has been concern to channel discussion of commodities into a 'case by case' approach, in which consumer interests would have proper consideration and a limited stabilization objective maintained. There has been no evidence, however, of any pressing national interest even in reaching individual agreements. Arguments about the 'ratchet effect' of unstable prices or, more generally, a widespread advantage from more stable commodity prices have evoked little apparent interest and do not appear to have figured prominently in representations by industrial raw material users. So far, Britain has opposed a copper ICA. It has been, reluctantly, prevented from supporting the International Sugar Agreement by EEC policy. It supports in principle rejoining the cocoa, tin and coffee agreements or a new rubber agreement, if agreement can be reached on price bands.

The (then Labour) government was undoubtedly swayed, particularly in the early stages of negotiation on the Common Fund, by advice from private sources that the proposal was contrary to their and, by implication, the national interest. Dr Jeremy Bray MP referred to the influence of a 'great many old war horses from some of the international companies who are not perhaps the most disinterested parties'.[40] Complementary views came from the City brokers who deal in futures on the London Commodity Exchange (sugar, cocoa, rubber, coffee, etc.), the Metal Exchange (copper, tin, lead and zinc) and the Baltic Exchange (grains, oils and fats), and are opposed to governments meddling – as they see it – in commodity trade, especially when it would diminish the role of the London market.

Britain is particularly dependent on LDCs for imports for metal and mineral requirements. In several cases, developing countries are the dominant source of supply (bauxite and alumina, copper, tin, niobium, phosphates) and they account for an important share of others (iron ore, manganese, chromium, cobalt, molybdenum, tungsten, sulphur and silver). The dependence is, however, lessening. Between the years 1964/5 and 1974/5, UK consumption of metals actually fell for all but five out of 23 leading metals and minerals due to slow industrial growth and a gradual process of technical innovation and product substitution (the main exceptions being chromium, cobalt (five per cent annual import growth) and potash (5 per cent also)). This meant that the UK 'could stay within its traditional obligations without mounting an aggressive search for new supplies as the Japanese and to a lesser extent the Germans and French have been compelled'.[41] There has also been a gradual switch of investment and procurement to more 'secure' sources, mainly Canada, Australia and the US.

Since price-raising fears have receded in metals in the short run with the failure of producer cartels the emphasis of debate about policy has shifted to questions of long-term supply. The British government, like others in the EEC, has been lobbied and apparently persuaded by mining companies, and other industry groups such as the CBI, that national interests are involved in reducing the degree of political risk in Third World mining investment. This lobbying helped determine the EEC negotiating position on the Lomé Convention to seek investment guarantees. It has also coloured policies towards the Law of the Sea. Britain has opposed in the United Nations measures which might have undermined the willingness of private corporations to invest in deep sea extraction.[42]

Another aspect of the supply security question is the attempt on the part of developing countries to force the pace of export processing by withholding exports of raw materials from the world market. British processors have been particularly concerned about trends in hides and skins, and similar problems are building up with petrochemicals, tropical timber and bauxite. But neither on this question nor on that of long-term supply has there yet emerged a strong feeling that LDCs can deliver a satisfactory 'quid' in return for the 'quo' of concessions in commodities negotiations.

Food

Britain differs substantially from the rest of the EEC in the low level of self-sufficiency in food items, especially in several products for which developing countries are major suppliers (oils and fats, sugar, fresh fruit and vegetables and beef). There is a tradition of openness to food imports going back to the mid-nineteenth century. This has, in the past, created a complementarity of interest between developing country (and other) exporters and British consumers in agricultural matters. The UK can still normally be relied upon to put up a strong case for extending tariff preferences on agricultural items or reducing the protectionist element of the CAP (e.g. tobacco, rice, vegetable oils). The most important issue has been sugar, where the interests of consumer and cane-producer countries are reinforced by those of substantial British companies (Tate and Lyle and Bookers in cane production, Beresfords in importing). Moreover, Britain's sugar refineries are geared to imported cane and several are situated in politically sensitive areas.

But the British position is gradually changing. The CAP has reinforced a tendency in British agriculture, already evident long before EEC entry, towards increased national self-sufficiency, at least of final output. Greater self-sufficiency was the declared policy of the 1975

White Paper on agriculture (*Food from our Own Resources*). The effects are to be seen in sugar. British acreage under beet, which is subject to quotas, has been expanded substantially in recent years while it is being contracted in Germany and France, the justification given that British production is more efficient within a given EEC output. This expansion has created a strong beet lobby. Cane sugar exporters are not only being threatened by import substitution in the UK but also by the closure of Tate and Lyle refineries which are based on cane imports. The old consumer/cane producer/domestic processor coalition is still there, but it is being eroded by the force of domestic agricultural interests.

More generally, the British government has given positive support to two Brandt proposals: to conclude a Wheat Agreement with internationally co-ordinated reserve stocks, and to increase emergency food supplies (including use of the EEC's surplus food stocks as food aid). The British government has also used the occasion of the Brandt report to rub in the message that individual developing countries should give 'increased priority to food and agricultural production', a matter primarily of concern to these countries themselves.[43]

Energy

Britain has advanced within a short period from being almost entirely dependent on oil imports to virtual self-sufficiency in energy. It is, apart from Canada and Norway, the only OECD country in this position. It now imports fuels only for specialized purposes (coking coal) or in order to achieve a better mix of crudes for its refineries, or of products. This radical change in economic status has not, however, significantly altered the British government's perceptions of national interests in a North-South context. A member of a Parliamentary Select Committee looking at the energy implications of Brandt was driven to complain: 'every answer we have had this afternoon has been wholly negative on these points that OPEC apparently places great importance on'.[44] Other than solidarity with other industrialized countries, the main reason is the feeling that the effects of higher OPEC prices in deepening recession in the West and in aggravating inflation outweigh any national advantages which Britain derives from the effects of higher prices. None the less, the government has sought to maximize the advantages of higher prices, such as they are, and North Sea oil prices consistently follow those of Nigerian light crude. Moreover, there is a longer-term recognition by the government 'that the long term trend of oil prices is upward in real terms'[45] and (by the nationalized British National Oil Corporation): 'some commentators have seen oil prices as being higher than they ought to be. We do not accept this and agree with the Brandt Commission that prices should reflect long term scarcity.'[46] The British government also echoes Brandt's call for measures to promote energy conservation and new supplies.

Oil made a net contribution to the balance of payments of £4 billion in 1978 (to rise to £9 billion by 1985). It has thus helped to alleviate the balance of payments problem which has always, in the past, been invoked as a reason for not pursuing more imaginative policies in the aid and trade field. In practice, however, oil has created its own problems: in foreign exchange markets it has driven up the exchange rate, helping to reduce imported inflation but eroding further the competitiveness of manufactured exports and import substitutes. The effect has been to intensify the state of crisis in the weaker, labour-intensive, import-competing industries, and also in export industries. This in turn has triggered demands to protect exports (by increasing aid-tying) and import-competing industries (from 'low cost' developing country competition).

Finally, the North Sea has led to a declining direct interest in developing-country oil development. The North Sea has acted as a 'pull' on the oil companies while nationalism in OPEC countries has acted as a 'push'. Shell is now mainly concerned with buying and distributing others' crude and its former LDC oil interests (e.g. Venezuela) have been nationalized. BP has been more involved in overseas production, but it has now lost its Nigerian assets and is overwhelmingly concerned with the North Sea and Alaska. There have been tentative links between BNOC and the new state oil companies in LDCs but this is on a modest scale. None the less, the opportunities being opened up for British firms — oil companies, mining equipment specialists, power stations contractors — by energy developments in the Third World are seen as important 'national interests'.

Beyond Economics

Strategic interests are now — in terms of direct military security — almost exclusively confined to NATO and to the maintenance of the relationship between the United States and Europe on which the alliance depends. The global networks of defence interests and obligations which Britain was party to – SEATO and CENTO – ceased to have much meaning for Britain following the decision, on economic grounds, to withdraw, very largely, from 'East of Suez' in the late 1960s. Events in Afghanistan and the advent of a Conservative government have, however, given renewed support to those arguing for more explicit commitment to pro-Western governments in those parts of the Third World in which growing Russian influence is feared, especially in the Gulf states and Southern Africa. This could involve a military presence in future.[47]

The main change in the last two years has been a declaration of intent to make the (diminishing) aid budget subject to a clearer bias towards friendly or politically important developing countries; thus, as stated by the Minister of Overseas Development, 'I don't think there is anything incompatible in using aid to further foreign policy. Our foreign policy is a very good one and it is in the interests of the peace of the world.'[48] What lies behind this policy is a wish to get away from the previous strong emphasis of British aid on India and other very poor countries (like Tanzania) which are now seen as somewhat peripheral to British interests, ideologically unsound or insufficiently appreciative.

Another strand in British political interests is the lingering wish to try to influence world events and to retain great power status. One residual piece of big power status lies in being a permanent member of the Security Council and this has undoubtedly extended the British role in international affairs: 'permanent membership has obliged the UK to involve itself more in the UN's activities generally than is justified . . . by national interests.'[49] There is a corresponding wish to be part of the North-South action. In 1976, one of Britain's major objectives in the CIEC talks was to have a separate seat. Fear of being snubbed by exclusion from any further summit is currently one factor making for public attempts at politeness towards the idea of a 'dialogue'. The enthusiasm at a top political level for wielding influence through summitry does however contrast vividly with other, more humble but perhaps more effective, ways of wielding influence, as through the authority of BBC External Service broadcasting, which, like the aid budget, is currently under threat of serious cuts in its operations.

An additional (if related) political objective is a concern for the country's image overseas. William Wallace has described how concern for 'image' is a powerful factor in explaining the size of the aid programme: 'any government of an industrially developed country which wants international respect must support an aid programme maintained not so much in the hope of exerting influence as from a recognition that any significant reduction would damage Britain's image abroad'.[50]

Such political concerns are probably a brake, at present, on even deeper cuts in the aid budget, and on the use of more abrasive language in criticizing the demands of LDCs. But aid and trade performance, and the stance taken on the New International Economic Order in international gatherings, are of only modest importance in determining the way in which Britain is judged, politically, abroad. Of much more importance are the treatment of Britain's own black and brown population and the development of foreign policy in relation to such problems as 'apartheid' and the Palestinian question.

Conclusions

To the extent that it is possible to pull together the various strands into an overall assessment of how the British government views its interests in developing countries, the conclusion is not too encouraging from a mutual-interests standpoint. The current British government simply does not relate to the Keynesian framework of economics which underlies much of the Brandt analysis. There is little interest, either, in proposals for intergovernmental regulation of commodity markets, or of the transfer of technology, or restructuring, on other than a commercial basis, of contractual debt. Liberalization of markets is closer to its ideological heart but where this might help developing countries (lifting restrictions on imports of competing manufactures and agricultural goods and, above all, people) there are major political obstacles and some genuine, if exaggerated, frictional costs. The virtual ending of any British need for imported energy, the increasing self-sufficiency (albeit at great cost) of European and British agriculture, and the disengagement of British and other Western mining companies from developing countries, have substantially weakened formerly strong sources of economic interdependence. Political interests have waned with winding up of Empire and the ending of all but nominal military involvement. What is known of public opinion also indicates some hostility or, at least, indifference. The present government has signalled its attitude towards North-South relations in general by representation at conferences which is low in level and negative in tone and by even sharper cuts in the aid budget than in public expenditure in general. Although its tone was more conciliatory and its policies, on aid notably, more generous, the last Labour government showed no evidence of being persuaded that an accommodating approach to the demands of LDCs was in Britain's interest. This background helps to explain, in large part, the cool government response to the Brandt report. Foreign Office ministers have since made more positive noises, but not due to any real reappraisal of 'interests'; rather because of a greater sensitivity to the country's image overseas and in deference to the strength of 'moral' feeling — in the Church, Parliament and in some sectors of public opinion.

However, there is evidence, which this survey has tried to bring together, that there are some British interests in developing countries which are of growing and perhaps underestimated importance. The share of LDCs as a market for British exports of goods and services is increasing again after decades of decline. Private foreign investment in developing countries is now of growing relative importance and is given high priority by the present government. There is a strong interest in stabilizing the international monetary system not least because of the heavy involvement in LDCs by UK-based banks and the role of sterling as a petrocurrency. There are signs that austere monetarism is giving way to greater concern for economic expansion at home and abroad. It might be said that all of these aspects of interdependence are well known and understood and are best dealt with problem by problem and country by country, corresponding to the reality that developing countries differ greatly in outlook, economic potential and political importance. It is at this, modest, level that the Brandt report may prove to have been useful; not in persuading this, or other, British governments that a radical new international economic order is in their interests — of which there is little prospect — but in promoting an outlook towards LDCs which is somewhat more positive, long sighted and generous in spirit than before.

Notes

1. House of Commons Foreign Affairs Committee, *The Brandt Commission Report: HMG's Response* (Minutes of Evidence, 5 August 1980), para. 1313.
2. Dispatch by Sir Nicholas Henderson, reproduced in *The Economist* (2 June 1979).
3. I. Rauta, *Aid and Overseas Development* (HMSO, 1971).
4. T.S. Bowles, *Survey of Attitudes Towards Overseas Development* (HMSO, 1978).
5. 'A Cognitive Lag', *New Society* (2 October 1980), p. 3.
6. CBI Evidence to the First Report of the Select Comitttee on Overseas Development, *Trade and Aid*, vol. 2 (1977/8), pp. 290-349.
7. Leslie Tolley, 'Can Our Industry Survive?', *Guardian* (17 December 1980).
8. TUC, *Economic Review* (1979).
9. E.g. speech to Church of England General Synod: 'I fear we are in danger of subjugating the international imperative to the domestic imperative, and if that

is so then it may prove to be a very dangerous and foolish mistake.'

10. See William Wallace, *The Foreign Policy Process in Britain* (George Allen & Unwin, 1975).

11. 'First Report of the Select Committee on Overseas Development, *Trade and Aid*, vol. 1 (1977/8), p. viii.

12. F.S. Northedge, *The Coordination of Interests in British Foreign Policy*, mimeo. (LSE, December 1980).

13. Department of Trade testimony, *Trade and Aid*, vol. 2 (1977/8), pp. pp. 38-76.

14. CBI evidence to the Select Committee.

15. Quoted in 'Protection by the Back Door', *Guardian*, January 1981.

16. Statement in House of Commons, 30 July 1979.

17. *The Brandt Commission Report* (HMSO, July 1980).

18. 1979 and 1980 (preliminary figures) suggest, however, that the market share has fallen back to 22 per cent, with a sharp cut back in demand from OPEC countries.

19. *The Brandt Commission Report: HMG's Response*, para. 1297.

20. *The Brandt Commission Report*, p. 6.

21. N. Dobson and R. May, 'The Impact of the Aid Programme on British Industry', *ODI Review*, no. 2 (1979).

22. Evidence of Sir Frederick Catherwood, *Trade and Aid*, vol. 2 (1977/8), p. 382.

23. Ibid.

24. See Laurence Freedman, *Arms Production in the United Kingdom: Problems and Prospects* (Chatham House Research Papers, 1978).

25. Ibid.

26. Foreign and Commonwealth Office, *The Newly Industrialising Countries and The Adjustment Problem* (Government Economic Service Working Paper No. 18, 1979).

27. Quoted in 'Protection by the Back Door'.

28. Interview with Frances Cairncross, *Guardian*, 7 October 1980.

29. CBI evidence to the Select Committee.

30. W.B. Reddaway, *The Effects of UK Direct Investment Overseas* (Cambridge University, Department of Applied Economics Occasional Papers, 1979); J. Dunning, *The UK's International Direct Investment in the mid 1970s* (Lloyds Bank Review, April 1979).

31. Address by Vernon Smith and Response by M. Faber and R. Brown in *ODI Review*, no. 1 (1981).

32. *The Brandt Commission Report*, p. 4.

33. Based on *UK Balance of Payments* ('Pink Book') (HMSO, 1979).

34. Based on Bank of England, *Quarterly Bulletin*, 4 October 1979.

35. *The Brandt Commission Report*, p. 7.

36. Ibid., p. 8.

37. Ibid., p. 27.

38. *The Energy Implications of the Brandt Commission Report* (Minutes of Evidence, 28 October 1980), para. 1067.

39. Ibid., para. 1066.

40. Dr. Bray, House of Commons Debate, *Hansard*, 13 June 1977.

41. P. Crowson, *Non-Fuel Minerals and Foreign Policy* (Chatham House Research Papers, 1978).

42. Ritchie Calder 'Futures', *Guardian*, 12 March 1981.

43. *The Brandt Commission Report*, p. 9.

44. *Energy Implications*, para. 1068.

45. *The Brandt Commission Report*, p. 9.

46. *The Brandt Commission Report: HMG's Response* (Minutes of Evidence, 4 November 1980) (Memorandum of BNOC).

47. E.g. *A Global Strategy to Meet a Global Threat: A British Initiative* (The British Atlantic Committee, March 1981).

48. Press report of Lords' discussion on government statement, 20 February 1980.

49. CPRS, *Review of Overseas Representation* (HMSO, 1977), p. 10.

50. Wallace, *The Foreign Policy Process in Britain*, p. 190.

RICH COUNTRY INTERESTS AND THIRD
WORLD DEVELOPMENT: THE FEDERAL
REPUBLIC OF GERMANY

Manfred Nitsch

The General Position of the Federal Republic of Germany *vis-à-vis* the Third World

The Federal Republic of Germany is a child of the post-Second World War international order. Hitler's attempt at world dominance had left Europe divided and in ruins; the German Reich was broken up, and the Federal Republic if Germany was founded on the Western side of the Iron Curtain.

The regaining of international recognition, integration into the Western alliance and the East-West conflict dominated West Germany's foreign policy in the early years. Further dimensions were added when détente and Willy Brandt's Ostpolitik normalized relations with the socialist countries of Eastern Europe and opened the doors of the United Nations for both German states in 1973, which made them more or less normal members of the global community.

The general position of the Federal Republic of Germany *vis-à-vis* the international order in general and the Third World's claims for a 'new' order in particular is strongly shaped by its short history of rather successful economic reconstruction and democratic social and political development.

The Administration, the parties backing the government, and the parliamentary opposition, as well as an overwhelming part of the mass media and most professional economists perceive German interests as being served best by the existing international order. The need for 'improvement' is, of course, admitted, but no essentially 'new' order is envisaged that would be worth striving for.

The liberal credo prevails that economic exchange is always in the interest of both partners. Thus mutual interest is more often assumed than proven, when North-South economic interaction is analyzed. Demands from Third World speakers opposing this basic philosophy are often interpreted as being ill-advised, 'ideologically biased' and not in consonance with the self-interest of the developing countries.

215

There is a basic belief that it is the economic strength of the industrialized countries which pulls the Third World out of misery and underdevelopment, and that more could and should be done in using this strength. Any radical criticism, however, relating underdevelopment to the structure of the international economic order is viewed with incomprehension if not with open hostility.

Due to the fact that Germany had already lost its colonies after the First World War, ex-colonial ties in the economic field as well as personal North-South relations and understanding for anti-colonial feelings and struggles are less important for West Germany than for its West European partners.

Not only is there no widespread feeling in favour of 'another development' and of post-colonial emancipation; it is equally hard to grasp that more state control and more national self-reliance as well as more intergovernmental economic relations should provide the ways out of underdevelopment.

For Germans, because of their experience in the Third Reich, nationalism and powerful government control stand rather for warmongering and totalitarian repression, and intergovernmental economic deals stand for clumsy and unfortunate attempts of crisis management in the 1930s. The German Democratic Republic's less successful economic reconstruction in a Soviet-type economic order, going hand in hand with the suppression of civil liberties, tends to reconfirm these views. If the developing countries now demand more government control for the sake of economic development and nationalist emancipation from global interdependence, it looks like a step back rather than forward in the eyes of those who went through the last 50 years of German history and who tend to judge the world by their standards.

An important point can be stressed in this connection. There is a strongly perceived German interest in the maintenance and enlargement of the globalistic elements of the world's overall structure. As far as the Third World also has an interest in these elements — e.g. access to markets, investment in raw materials production, research on alternative energy sources, transfer of technology, foreign loans and aid — a certain mutuality of interests can reasonably be expected. Above all, the more general objectives, such as the maintenance of peace, the avoidance of arms races, and the restoration or protection of the world's ecological balance are to be listed here.

For the pursuit of its global interests, two pathways are open to the Federal Republic of Germany, best described by Stanley Hoffmann's alternative for the USA, *Primacy or World Order*. The strategy of 'primacy', which in the German case could only be a shared primacy, along with other Western countries, would imply a further increase in importance of trilateral summitry, a defensive line against the have-nots and the Eastern bloc, a certain flexibility in the co-optation of single 'important' Third World countries, and a defence of the established international economic order. Realpolitik considerations seem to point in this direction, the more so because of the Federal Republic's rather successful international 'pyramid-climbing' after the Second World War, already referred to. The 'world-order' strategy, on the other hand, looks much more burdensome, it would imply more formal inter-governmental co-operation and more dirigisme in economic matters. Yet, in spite of strong voices from the side of the hardliners, Stanley Hoffmann's plea with regard to the USA in favour of this strategy applies also to the Federal Republic of Germany, and it is indeed sometimes listened to and echoed. In a programmatic speech, the Minister of Foreign Affairs recently declared that a 'revolution of foreign policy doctrines' is necessary: 'We must build an order of cooperation which is looked upon as just from both sides, also from the side of the de-veloping countries,'[1] emphasizing, however, that the reform of the world economic system should be 'marktkonform' (conforming to market economy rules).

The aim of building a truly universal world order is threatened in times of East-West tensions. Bloc identity on both sides of the German-German border is probably stronger than in countries with an intact national identity. It is therefore understandable that German interests are often defined in terms of bloc interests, which by their nature tend towards zero-sum games and which tend to overrule other, less intense-ly felt, and more diffuse long-term objectives. Short-term political and strategic interests have increasingly threatened the pursuit of develop-ment goals in the last few years so that the Minister of Economic Co-operation, Rainer Offergeld, even declared in Parliament that 'develop-ment policy is not alliance policy with different means'.[2]

Beside the globalistic and the Western bloc levels, there is on the level of the European Community a strong set of interests to be reck-oned with when exploring spheres of mutuality and of conflict in North-South relations. It is on this level that understanding can be gained for the Third World countries' demand to control transnational corporations, to increase their bargaining position and to take effective control over their own economies. According to a very fundamental policy paper, the Tindemans Report of 1975 on the future of the Euro-pean Community, one of the strongest motives for European integration is the growing sense of a 'two-fold spiral of impotence': towards the outside, because the Eurocentric age is gone, and towards the inside because economic processes can no longer be controlled by national governments.

This sounds very similar to the assertions of the Third World. Thus the attitudes of West Germany and the Third World towards (collective) self-reliance, state control, priority for internal integration and a certain distance to bi-polar big power politics turn out to be not as far apart, if the European level is taken into consideration, as German policy statements emphasizing the globalistic and the Western bloc levels seem to suggest.

The list of general German interests to be considered in the North-South context would be incomplete, if confined to global interests, bloc interests and interests of gaining or regaining control over one's destiny on the European as well as on the national level. A fourth field of interest on the subnational level must be added, namely the direct concern with poverty, marginality and human rights.

This humanitarian concern does not lend itself to easy articulation. In spite of its rather diffuse and undirected motivational character it cannot be ignored as a driving force behind aid lobbying, stemming from a challenge to show or to restore the moral decency, if not superiority of one's system, from a perceived threat to one's own community (in the face of unemployment, gastarbeiter ghettos in German cities, less prosperous new European Community members and increasing flows of refugees and asylum-seekers from the Third World) and from a fundamental fear that recent progress in the direction of human rights, equality and democracy as universal principles might be discredited again. After all, Germany's Nazi past lies only 35 years behind, and a revival of old anti-egalitarian ideologies or an emergence of new ones (e.g. technocracy or socio-biology) is not impossible, if grossly inegalitarian socio-economic structures persist.

In addition, the belief in automatic 'trickle-down' is fading so that a reorientation of development policies towards a more direct attack on poverty and towards basic needs[3] has become acceptable also, with the argument that otherwise no mass markets for German exports would develop in the future. The recognition of a potential conflict of interest between short-term hard-selling export promotion and long-term market development helps the anti-poverty arguments, but does not invalidate the position that the humanitarian concern is to be considered a special field of interest in its own right.

This general assessment of interests determining the position of the

Federal Republic of Germany *vis-à-vis* Third World development shows a pattern which is not uncommon to policy analysis when 'national interests' are differentiated: each field of interests – the globalistic interests as well as the bloc interests, the control interests on the national and the European levels and the humanitarian interests – has not only its own legitimacy, but also a certain social base and an ideological justification of its own. Its pursuit, however, can be blind to the point of running amok; and if carried too far, sight is lost of the others. The permanent task of any government is to balance them. No 'optimum' combination can be reached, which would be an optimum for all, because individual and group value judgements are involved which cannot be aggregated to a consistent welfare function. A certain minimum can, however, be rather safely assumed below which it would be difficult to reach a democratic consensus.

Public Opinion and Policy Formation

The Third World is seen with mixed feelings in the Federal Republic of Germany: it is considered only fair and proper to do something against hunger and poverty in the world; as referred to above, this striving for decency can be interpreted as a diffuse interest in genuine development. On the other hand, the more the living conditions in the Third World are perceived as intolerable, the more those countries come to stand for 'chaos' threatening the islands of prosperity.[4] Fear and anxiety, however, lead to the will to dominate the threat and to hinder rather than to foster the emancipation and development of the Third World.[5] It is this emotional ambiguity in public opinion between solidarity with and domination of the Third World, on which the more compact and outspoken interests play, when trying to influence policies.

Recent public opinion surveys indicate a growing interest in development policy and an increasingly positive general attitude towards aid.[6] The importance is reckoned to increase further in the future.[7] A large part of the adult population (44 per cent) declares to be ready to sacrifice a certain amount of income increase in favour of aid. At the same time, however, the gap between positive attitudes towards aid in general and towards German development policies in particular is widening. Especially those with secondary and higher education are overwhelmingly in favour of aid in general (93 per cent), but only a slight

majority (57 per cent) shows a positive opinion of German development policies – the gap of 36 per cent in 1979 having widened from 21
per cent in 1975.[8] Among average young adults (18-25 years) 81 per
cent of which favour aid, the gap amounts to 25 per cent and it is increasing, too. This reflects the highly critical spirit of the development
community, i.e. those who are actively interested in development
problems – the action and youth groups and the non-conformist
academic voices – who argue that more of the same is no solution.
For them, more exports of often inadequate technology, more
investment in passenger car production, more bureaucracy-to-
bureaucracy aid, more cheap-labour manufactured imports and more
fruit, vegetable, dogfood and flower imports from developing countries
rather look like a strategy for the perpetuation, if not universalization
of poverty, combined with little islands of prosperity and cosmopolitan life syles.

The report of the 'Brandt Commission' has given a certain backing to
those forces in politics and administration who want to reorient at least
aid policies, if not policies in general *vis-à-vis* the Third World, towards
self-help groups. The 1980 Guidelines reflect this shift of emphasis,
even though the differentiation is still between countries rather than
between social strata. It remains to be seen whether actual policies
towards the Third World will be affected by these arguments. Those
policies have as a rule been determined less by specific development-
oriented interest groups pressing for certain activities with the backing
of development-committed public opinion, but rather by the outcome
of overall economic and foreign policies, shaped by the general constellation of forces within German society and within the international
system.

The most influential economic interest group in West Germany is
the industrial export sector[10] which has succeeded in creating a general
'export mystique'. International competitiveness is often referred to as
if it were the final objective of all policy. The successful dynamism of
export-led growth in the post-Second World War period (see Table 1.2)
has given rise to the belief that free trade and free factor movements
are in the general interest in Germany as well as abroad and that the
primordial German interest in world development lies in the growth of
export markets.

The pressure in favour of globalistic economic interests is hardly
mitigated within the Federation of German Industry (Bundesverband
der Deutschen Industrie) which groups together the national industrial
branch associations, because protectionist pressure is primarily exerted

on the level of the European Community, where trade policy decisions are made. On the national level, industry is supported in its free-trade, anti-dirigiste and pro-private business lobbying by the Federation of Wholesale and Foreign Trade (Bundesverband des Deutschen Groß und Außenhandels), grouping among others the big importing firms (exporting is largely done by the big industrial firms direct without the use of traders), by the Federation of German Banks (Bundesverband Deutscher Banken) and by the Association of Industry and Commerce (Deutscher Industrie- und Handelstag), the top-level organization of local and district chambers of industry and commerce.

More on the protectionist side are to be found the German Farmers' Association (Deutscher Bauernverband) and the private as well as the public local and regional groupings and entities which are affected by industrial or agrarian restructuring in problem-ridden regions.

The position of the trade unions and their top-level federation (Deutscher Gewerkschaftsbund) is rather complex with regard to policies towards Third World development. For a long time, the pattern of grand coalition between capital, labour and management favouring liberal policies prevailed. During full employment, even migration from non-EEC countries was welcomed (for reasons explained later under Other Issues). In the last few years, with a persistent unemployment rate of about four to seven per cent – high by German standards – the generally pro-free trade, pro-foreign investment and pro-migration position has changed towards a more diverse outlook, according to industrial branches.

It is increasingly understood, not only by the textile workers, but also within certain sub-branches of the metal workers' union, that a restructuring of the world's industrial geography according to the comparative advantage of cheap and plentiful labour in the Third World might hurt instead of help the workers on both sides: jobs are lost in industrial countries, and wages are frozen at low levels in developing countries; in addition, because of intense competition between countries for export-industrializing private investment, the state on both sides has to finance infrastructure investment with taxes on wages instead of profits. Considerations of this kind have been articulated in speeches and declarations,[11] but not yet transformed into policy prescriptions and lobbying in a specific direction, except for a call for 'social clauses' in international agreements which are to secure a certain minimum standard in working conditions.

On the government side, the various ministries and agencies pursue their policies rather independently. The rhetoric and the general line of argument in foreign economic policy is dominated by the Federal Ministry of Economics (Bundesministerium für Wirtschaft), a stronghold of neoliberal philosophy ever since the founding days of the Federal Republic of Germany when Ludwig Erhard was the first Minister of Economics. It is also responsible for commodities and energy as well as anti-trust policies.

At international conferences the Foreign Office (Auswärtiges Amt) generally heads the delegations and hammers out the formulae of compromise; the Ministry of Finance (Bundesministerium für Finanzen) along with the Central Bank (Deutsche Bundesbank) deals with the international monetary affairs; the Ministry of Economic Cooperation (Bundesminsterium für wirtschaftliche Zusammenarbeit) handles financial and technical assistance to developing countries and is responsible for a great deal of scientific and technological co-operation which in principle falls in the realm of the Ministry of Research and Technology (Bundesministerium für Forschung und Technologie). The Ministry of Food and Agriculture (Bundesministerium für Ernährung und Landwirtschaft) is responsible for agricultural policies and participates in their formulation on the European level; its programme of agricultural research is of interest to developing countries.

Co-ordination takes place in interministerial committees. Senior civil servants draw on the advice of interest group functionaries and scholars; they know their partners in the Third World, and they have developed routine ways to harmonize positions without really interfering with one another's domain. Only the very controversial issues reach the Ministers, the Chancellor and the Cabinet. The Chancellor's Office (Bundeskanzleramt) does not show a strong interest in development issues.

Since very little legislation is involved in international economic policy, the Parliament (Bundestag) is not very important, except for a general bias in the articulation of interests and the formation of policies: the Christian Democrats oppose the government coalition of Social Democrats and Liberals on the general line 'Freedom versus Socialism' (their slogan in the 1976 federal election campaign). Any concession to Third World demands to which the term 'dirigisme' might be attributed, is therefore not only hard to win over the liberal stronghold in the government, namely the Ministry of Economics, but also open to parliamentary attack by the opposition. In addition, the recent Soviet moves have led the Christian Democrats to perceive the North-South conflict as increasingly dominated by the conflict between East and West,[12] a view which is partly shared by the government and the public. From the right wing of the Bundestag a voice was even raised 'not to leave the U.S. alone' with the establishment of a military task force to protect Western interests in the Third World.[13]

For a different mix of motives, all parties in the Bundestag agree that an increase in aid is necessary, in so far as they tend to comply with the Third World's demands; they also agree, however, on the defence of a world economic order based on market-economy rules, more or less balanced by a certain protection of the weak;[14] thus the more fundamental demands do not find support.

On the whole, with a conservative opposition on its heels, the already conservative administration, supported by mainstream professional economists, is virtually immune against criticism voiced by proponents of the radical, the alternative life style and the structuralist positions who insist that Third World development is not the same as 'Westernization'. After the events in Iran, the tone of the 'Westernizers' has become a bit less self-assured, but the deep-rooted convictions are still unshaken.

In the formal policy-making process the only channels for the continuous articulation of alternative positions are a few left-wing Members of Parliament and some civil servants, especially in the Ministry of Economic Cooperation whose job it is to deal with partners in the Third World and with the development groups in Germany.

Many of these groups are attached to the German Churches (Catholic and Protestant) whose role in the discussion about policies towards the Third World is important. The Joint Conference of the Churches on Development in the Federal Republic of Germany (Gemeinsame Kommission der Kirchen für Entwicklungsländerfragen) regularly directs memoranda to the government before UNCTAD conferences and similar occasions calling for a more development-oriented response to the demands of the developing countries and for a more serious approach to the questions brought up by the alternative life-style movement. Furthermore, the German Protestant Churches have served as an important link — via the World Council of Churches (WCC) — between the national liberation movements in Africa and the German public. Although sometimes lukewarm and hesitant, or even — because of the problem of violence — highly critical of the WCC's policy, these churches have contributed to the questioning of the widespread belief that 'pro-Western-bloc' regimes are always in the West German interest, regardless of their internal structure.

In order to make the general points of the paper more specific, some of the major issues in North-South relations are taken up in the following section.

Issues

The International Division of Labour

The international trade relations between Germany and the Third World have traditionally been dominated by a liberal import regime for raw materials, cascading tariffs providing effective protection for commodity-processing industries, and export promotion for chemicals, transport equipment, machinery and other investment goods (see Table 7.1).

Table 7.1 shows a persistent complementary division of labour. Empirical investigations[15] into the causes show, not surprisingly, that in terms of factor proportions − the high level of skills, in terms of the product cycle − the high expenditure in R & D, in terms of import policies − the structure of effective protection and in terms of export policies − the undervaluation of the DM over long periods, can be considered the factors to be held responsible for this pattern.

The table also shows changes − a marked increase in the importance of oil at the expense of food and beverages and a dynamic development of manufactured imports, especially investment goods. On the export side, a certain decrease of chemicals and a slight further increase of investment goods can be detected. Consequently the OPEC countries have gained importance as suppliers as well as markets, not only in comparison with the other developing countries but also in terms of their shares in total German imports and exports.

Trade in commodities as well as manufactures has traditionally been left to private business, with the state following general pro-industrial export policies in the monetary field, in international trade negotiations etc., according to the institutional structure as described before.

The import flow of commodities was taken for granted which explains the lack of an official institutional infrastructure and the resulting reluctance to enter into commodity agreements. This applies also to oil which made it quite difficult to adjust to the post-1973 priority in North-South economic relations.

Since the foundation of the Federal Republic of Germany, energy policies had meant retreat from local coal in favour of cheap imported oil in order not to impede the international competitiveness of German industry. Without a privileged major national oil company, the German oil market has been dominated by the transnational oil companies with

Table 7.1: Structure of Trade (Imports and Exports) of the FRG with the Developing Countries, 1965, 1970 and 1977 (percentages)

Sectors	Imports			Exports		
	1965	1970	1977	1965	1970	1977
Agriculture, hunting, forestry and fishing	35.5	27.0	20.1	0.4	1.2	0.6
Mining, quarrying and energy	32.7	35.3	42.3	0.7	0.5	0.5
Coal mining	0.0	0.1	0.0	0.4	0.3	0.2
Crude petroleum and natural gas production	23.3	27.3	38.4	0.0	0.0	0.0
Metal ore mining	7.6	6.5	3.1	0.0	0.0	0.0
Other mining	1.9	1.4	0.8	0.2	0.2	0.2
Electricity, gas and water	0.0	0.0	0.0	0.0	0.0	0.0
Manufacturing	31.4	36.9	36.9	98.1	97.6	97.6
Basic materials	11.7	13.9	8.0	29.8	28.7	22.1
Construction	0.2	0.2	0.2	0.8	0.7	0.9
Metallurgy	8.1	10.2	3.5	9.8	7.4	5.6
Chemical	1.2	1.8	1.3	18.5	19.5	14.3
Mineral oil refining	1.4	0.6	1.8	0.3	0.4	0.4
Wood, pulp and paper production	0.9	1.0	1.1	0.4	0.6	0.9
Investment goods	0.9	2.6	5.9	60.4	59.6	65.9
Machinery	0.2	0.6	1.1	27.0	26.9	29.0
Transport equipment	0.3	0.5	1.1	15.2	14.9	16.2
Electric machinery and electronics	0.2	1.0	2.3	9.4	9.2	11.7
Measuring and controlling equipment, optical goods	0.0	0.1	0.5	2.8	3.1	2.6
Office- and data-processing machinery	0.0	0.1	0.3	0.9	1.3	0.9
Iron and steel products	0.2	0.3	0.6	5.1	4.3	5.6
Consumption goods	7.1	10.5	17.2	6.7	7.9	6.7
Glass, pottery, ceramics	0.1	0.0	0.1	0.6	0.6	0.4
Wood	0.5	0.4	0.5	0.3	0.3	0.5
Paper and paperboard	0.0	0.0	0.0	0.2	0.2	0.2
Printing	0.0	0.0	0.1	0.3	0.3	0.3
Textiles	3.0	3.6	4.0	3.0	4.0	3.0
Clothing	2.4	4.0	9.1	0.3	0.4	0.6
Leather- and foot-wear	0.8	1.4	2.2	0.4	0.6	0.8
Miscellaneous (musical instruments, sports, jewellery)	0.3	1.0	1.1	1.5	1.4	0.9
Food, beverages and tobacco	11.8	10.0	5.9	1.3	1.4	2.8
Other goods	0.4	0.7	0.7	0.8	0.7	1.3
Total	100.0	100.0	100.0	100.0	100.0	100.0

Source: OECD; taken from Schultz *et al.* (1980), pp. 53, 73.

only a minimum institutional superstructure. When the OPEC countries lifted the oil issues to governmental levels, the German government had first to create the political and administrative instruments for dealing with them.

Nevertheless, the general internal policy has remained to leave as much to the market as possible and not to interfere in pricing decisions, except for anti-trust reasons. Foreign policy with regard to oil has consisted in cautious bilateralism, multilateral negotiations within the European Community and the International Energy Agency, and in various attempts to bring energy into the North-South dialogue in various forums. The international energy relations are, however, not regarded as the model for a new international economic order, but rather as an exception to the rule of free trade.[16]

It is not surprising that a country with the history, the political structure and the economic record of the Federal Republic of Germany is a staunch advocate of free trade. During the 30 years of its existence as a state, it has developed from a marginal exporter to the world's biggest supplier of manufactured exports, running continuous trade surpluses until 1979 and specializing in some of the most dynamic and technology-intensive sub-branches, such as machinery, transport equipment and chemical and pharmaceutical products. The share of exports in the gross domestic product has steadily increased, reaching 20-25 per cent in the last few years (see Table I.2).

Most exports go to other industrialized countries which has given rise to the formula that West Germany is interested in the developing countries becoming industrialized countries, too. However, there might be a decisive difference beween *being* and *becoming* an industrialized country. The Germans and their neighbouring Europeans are the first to remember what enormous social upheavals, international tensions and wars went along with late-coming industrialization.

In spite of the mixed feelings with regard to the political side of development as a process, it can be said that West Germany has a strong and vested economic interest in access to overseas markets and, because of its particularly competitive capital goods sector, in as much worldwide investment activity as possible.

With regard to the internal economic structure of West Germany, however, the heavy reliance on industrial exports has led to the problem of 'over-industrialization'.[17] The term refers to a comparison between the Federal Republic of Germany and other industrial countries with a similar *per capita* income but a smaller share of industry in GDP; at the same time it refers to future trends in needs and demand, technical progress, relative labour costs, exchange rates, prices of raw materials, especially oil, and ecological factors, all pointing towards a relative decrease in production and employment in the industrial sector over the next decades.

The process of gradual 'de-industrialization' is not undisputed, especially not the question whether it is to be supported or fought by deliberate policies; however, stagnation of industrial employment (not output, which has increased all the time) was a fact in the 1960s and decreased by about 12 per cent in the 1970s.[18] So it is safe to assume that increasing manufactured imports from developing countries will hit branches with shrinking employment also in the future. Rough estimates for the years between 1970 and 1976 indicate that displacement of employment by productivity increases surpassed displacement by imports from developing countries at a ratio exceeding 20 to 1,[19] which means that the relocation of industries towards the South does not look like the prime mover of the process; but since technical progress at the factory level is hardly controllable, protectionism might look to many as a way out.

Gradual de-industrialization also tends to split the grand coalition already referred to between capital, labour, professionals and management, stemming from the years when West Germany was a favourite place for national as well as international industrial investment. Capital became increasingly mobile, benefiting from competition between countries with regard to tax incentives, exemptions from environmental control measures, cheap energy sources and cheap labour, and engineers and other professionals aspired to convert West Germany from one of 'the world's workshops' to one of 'the world's drawing-boards'. The blue-collar worker, finally, once the hero of Germany's reconstruction, the skillbearer behind export-led growth and the courted consumer of manufactured durables, is now in danger of being looked down upon as somebody whose job may or may not be mercifully protected, but who actually does no longer contribute significantly to national wealth and income.

As a reaction to these challenges posed by changing international economic conditions, second thoughts have arisen with regard to the benefits of an ever-deepening international division of labour. The needs of the internal market rather than competitiveness in foreign markets have therefore been emphasized as the guideposts for an 'alternative' economic policy.[20]

On the level of the European Community, as pointed out earlier, efforts are made to match again political and economic structures which had grown apart from one another, to a degree that the incongruency began to create a sense of powerlessness and impotence. On the national level, policies in the field of science and technology and of research and development activities are gradually led away from an uncritical instigation of 'progress', from an unquestioned emphasis on nuclear energy, and from a 'technological flight-ahead' philosophy.[21] This philosophy had already been denounced at an SPD Forum by the then Minister of Economic Cooperation, Marie Schlei, as a 'treacherous slogan'[22] revealing that those who use it do not envisage closing the gap between North and South, but rather perpetuating it, and that they are prepared to leave behind those who are not in a position to work at a drawing-board. On the other hand, concentration of the country's resources on activities in which West Germany has a comparative advantage, on the development of the most modern technology and on science-based production, has a strong emotional, political and economic appeal, since it suggests the possibility of staying ahead of the others.

The great public attraction of initiatives against nuclear plants as well as the emergence of 'green' parties indicate a growing concern for what the critique of technology and the 'alternative life style' movement stand for. The 'new values' — hailed in Sunday speeches, declarations and reports,[23] but as a rule denounced in everyday deeds and utterances — lead to a growing polarization between the 'Establishment' believing in the international division of labour, in transnational big business and big labour, in big government and big science, and that part of the young generation which embraces those new values. In contrast to the student generation of 1967/8, however, these young people do not engage in a heroic struggle, but are rightly called 'Aussteiger-Jugend'[24] ('drop-out youth').

At first sight this paragraph might seem out of place in a chapter on international trade. The definition of German interests in Third World development, however, differs so sharply between the groups in question, according to their Weltanschauungen in which international trade plays a radically different role, that reference to this very fundamental discussion[25] is necessary.

It is generally accepted that it would be naive to ignore the global economic, technological and communicational structures, and at the same time that it would be inhuman to overlook the 'little world' of the individual and his/her 'alternative' life in informal networks. If the motto becomes, to live with both, with an 'alpha-beta mix of technologies',[26] the point is reached where neither the 'International Division

of Labour' nor 'Small is Beautiful' is put on a pedestal to be wor-
shipped, but selectivity along human needs and interests becomes the
guiding principle.

Reference to the individual's various needs, motives and interests
opens a new perspective for the exploration of mutual as well as conflicting interests in North-South relations. Compassion and solidarity
exist side by side with greed, with the drive to dominate, etc. Interest
articulation not only takes place in the 'hard' spheres of politics and
economic advantage but also in the 'soft' sides of human life. Therefore
the question whose interests would be served by alternative life style
policies is wrongly put, since it is not a distinction between groups of
people which is at stake but a different emphasis on the various needs
and interests of every single person. Thus conflicting interests are not
only to be reckoned with between countries or country groups and
within countries (to be reconciled by governments under the heading of
a 'national interest'), but also on the individual level. If even the single
person tends to see the international division of labour with different
eyes on different occasions, the rather heterogeneous mix of export and
import policies and the contradictory views and activities in this field
become understandable, and it becomes clear that special compact
interests can play on a whole variety of motives.

A differentiated view of the interests of individuals, groups and
nations does not imply a defence of the *status quo* outcome of
decision-making processes, but it does mean a plea for valuing the
wisdom of incoherence. This can be contrasted with the espousal of a
more rigid, comprehensive scheme for the creation of a global social
market economy forwarded by the Academic Advisory Council to the
Federal Ministry of Economics in 1976,[27] which contains the main
traits of mainstream professional economic thought: 'In order to aspire
to a statically and dynamically efficient international allocation of the
scarce resources available', the authors plead for full integration of the
developing countries into the international division of labour, for the
removal of tariff and non-tariff trade barriers affecting products from
developing countries in the markets of industrial countries, and for the
establishment of 'investment guarantee zones' in the form of 'open
clubs' of countries ready to protect international private investment
from political risk. Separate from the allocation objective, distribution
goals are to be implemented by means of massive grants in the order of
0.7 per cent of GNP 'as a first step' and 'an increase in this percentage
at a later date'.

Criticism of this proposal has centred on two points:[28] a global market economy tends to serve as an auctioning mechanism depriving the poor of their very last goods and allocating the resources according to the skewed distribution of global purchasing power, especially when migration is excluded from the model. Secondly, redistribution by transfers on such a massive scale to alleviate the poverty of the hundreds of millions of people in the Third World, with the contributions of the few million rich in the industrial countries, is impossible in a world of nation-states and of existing welfare gaps. Allocation according to the rich's purchasing power and distribution according to the rich's transfer generosity would be looked upon as a double diktat rather than a strategy of development for the people and by the people in South and North.

The proposal has meanwhile been shelved, but it can still be considered typical of the kind of globalistic attitude prevailing in the Advisory Council and elsewhere in Bonn, whereas in Brussels the calls for a 'new protectionism'[29] have to be dealt with. As far as the globalistic interests of the Third World, such as market access, are concerned, the German voice in Brussels can certainly be considered a help. However, Bonn's free-trade rhetoric can probably only flower because West Germany's protectionist and state-control interests are discreetly taken care of in Brussels.

Direct Investment and Transnational Corporations

The economic history of the Federal Republic of Germany and the strong sense of belonging to the Western bloc tend to support a general belief in the mutuality of interests between transnational corporations, industrial countries and developing countries.

The rapid internationalization of the German economy after the Second World War, in the early days supported by aid (Marshall Plan), went hand in hand with a spectacular and rather continuous rise in incomes and with full employment so that the influx as well as the outflow of foreign investment were easily defended as a positive trait of modern economies. The German system of co-determination ('Mitbestimmung') of the workers and their trade unions in the management of national as well as foreign firms has further contributed to the general acceptance of a neo-capitalist welfare state system with big transnational corporations. Only very recently a discussion about the 'export of jobs' via capital exports has started; and with union members on their boards, German firms might turn out to be not quite as 'footloose' as their purely capitalist competitors. But that is still an open question. There is general agreement and convincing empirical material to support the view that up to now German direct investment abroad has stabilized and expanded exports rather than substituted for them, thus having a positive effect on employment.[30]

The already mentioned tendency to transfer the principles of the internal order into the international sphere makes the articulation of German interests in the field of international investment and trans-national corporations sound utterly conservative: the North-South dialogue is to be 'no one-way street', the protection of private property as a principle of international law is to be guaranteed, a good climate for foreign investment is essential for development, international codes of conduct should not be legally binding, etc. As long as the phrase 'New International Economic Order' was understood to mean only nationalist control, the term was anathema for private business and for the administration; second thoughts have, however, come up, since it has been realized that many of the NIEO characteristics might serve to streamline rather than to hamper the international division of labour.

On the other hand, the control over transnational corporations has recently received new attention and urgency in connection with the 'second oil crisis' and the events in Iran. Especially on the level of the European Community, a greater mutuality of interests between North and South can be expected to be perceived in this field in the future.[31] If globalistic streamlining and national or supranational control are seen not as a contradiction but as complementary traits of the complex problem of how to make the best of globalistic economic and techno-logical developments in a political and legal world of nation-states, a more pragmatic approach becomes possible in order to achieve a viable 'alpha-beta mix' here, too.

The Federal Republic of Germany was in general a net importer of investment capital until the middle of the 1970s.[32] This fact may help to explain the favourable attitude towards transnational corporations. Moreover, the change of investment flows in the mid-1970s was not very drastic; e.g. in 1978 the outflow of slightly over DM 6 billion was offset by two-thirds (around DM 4 billion) through investment inflows. With regard to stocks of direct investment, at the end of 1976 foreign investment in the Federal Republic of Germany (DM 63.0 billion) was still about 50 per cent higher than German foreign investment abroad (DM 43.4 billion),[33] whereas in 1980 the figures are reported to be nearly equal (DM 68 and 66 billion),[34] showing a marked speed-up of investment abroad.

With regard to developing countries, Germany has, of course, been a net exporter of investment capital for a long time. The particular circumstances of the reconstruction after the Second World War have made German firms, taken as a whole, develop two special features: first, a marked concentration on the home market and on exports which until now has led to a rather small importance of direct investment abroad when compared to total investment. Between 1972 and 1977 direct foreign investment amounted to 3.9 per cent of gross fixed investment (minus government investment and construction), and the share of the developing countries was only 1.2 per cent.[35] A second feature is the concentration of West German foreign investment in modern manufacturing, such as automobiles, chemicals and machinery rather than in raw materials.

German direct investment is thus less associated with the 'old', complementary international division of labour but is rather typical of the 'new' division of labour[36] (see Table 7.2). An exception can be seen in the enormous rate of increase in investment in petroleum and natural gas during the 1970s; from a very low level – still reflected in Table 7.2 – it went up to around DM 1 billion by the end of 1978[37] and has further increased greatly since then.[38]

Within the domestic economies of Third World countries, German firms concentrate on consumer durables and machinery, and with regard to the international markets, they are in the forefront in promoting the developing countries' export of modern manufactures. Their favourite locations are the more advanced newly industrializing countries (see Table 7.2).

This pattern has been shown most clearly in the case of Brazil, where about 40 per cent of German direct investment in developing countries is concentrated.[39] No wonder that the 'Brazilian Model' is highly esteemed in German business circles as well as in those academic circles which favour world-market integration as a development strategy.[40] On the other hand, Brazil is the favourite example for 'dissociationists' and structuralists pointing to the problems of maldistribution of income and wealth and to the persistence of poverty and dependence in spite of high rates of GDP growth[41] – the typical example for an unbalanced 'mix' and for a lopsided pursuit of interests.

Perhaps the structural characteristics of German foreign investment as promoting the 'new' international division of labour are responsible for the fact that West German trade union leaders are particularly active in the international trade union movement (as far as the non-communist unions are concerned), and that they increasingly

Table 7.2: Direct Investments of the FRG in Developing Countries by Industrial Branches and Countries, Accumulated End 1976 (DM million)

Industrial branches	Total	European	Non-European Total	NICs[a]	Others	OPEC
Mining, including oil	934	11	339	9	330	584
Manufacturing	7,442	1,836	4,926	4,149	777	680
Chemical industry	1,739	523	1,041	597	444	175
Mineral oil refining	381	194	13	1	12	174
Manufacture of plastic, rubber and asbestos products	105	52	51	48	3	2
Manufacture of non-metallic products	93	59	33	24	9	1
Iron and steel basic industries	460	25	424	422	2	11
Manufacture of machinery, except electrical	826	296	525	504	21	5
Manufacture of road transport equipment	2,018	163	1,746	1,723	23	109
Manufacture of electrical machinery	1,413	368	910	707	203	135
Manufacture of measuring, controlling and office equipment; optical goods[b]	108	39	67	56	11	2
Manufacture of food and beverages	58	10	47	33	14	1
Other industries	241	107	69	34	35	65
Construction	348	10	33	22	11	305
Wholesale and retail trade	426	86	232	111	121	108
Transport and communication	302	32	231	125	106	39
Financial institutions	296	28	262	216	46	6
Other services, other branches	1,768	425	1,250	544	706	93
Total	11,516	2,428	7,273	5,176	2,097	1,815

Notes: a. Newly industrializing countries: Brazil, Mexico, Argentina, Israel, Singapore, Hongkong, Chile, South Korea, Taiwan, Uruguay.
b. Including musical instruments, sports, toys, jewellery.
Source: Deutsche Bundesbank: taken from Schultz *et al.* (1980), p. 297.

realize that the German workers' interests lie in high wages and a widening of domestic markets in developing countries rather than in a dividing-up between capital and labour of extra profits from abroad.[42]

The West German government took up this view when referring to a 'social clause' in international agreements in its 1980 Development Policy Guidelines, as already pointed out.

The general line of policy, however, still is an indiscriminate incitement of direct investment in developing countries through investment protection agreements, double-taxation treaties, tax incentives, co-financing, etc. The specialized agency for fostering private investment in developing countries, the German Development Corporation (Deutsche Gesellschaft für wirtschaftliche Zusammenarbeit, formerly Deutsche Entwicklungs-Gesellschaft — DEG), has recently been greatly strengthened.

To sum up, in the field of direct investment and transnational corporations there is a certain, limited mutuality of interests between Germany and the Third World as far as the globalistic level is concerned, regarding access to markets and to modern technology as well as the interests pressing for a 'new' division of labour. The control interest which might also be called mutual, is dealt with on the European Community level. The interests to overcome poverty and marginality are still hidden in labour declarations, and they clash with the luxury character — for developing countries' standards — of most of the goods produced by German firms abroad (consumer durables and their inputs). Many observers would agree that 'growth without development' might be the proper term for what German business abroad, if unchecked, is interested in.

Aid

From the beginning of West German development assistance in the 1950s, the humanitarian motive and the diffuse interest in genuine Third World development have been linked to more immediate and compact interests, such as burden-sharing in the Western bloc, non-recognition of the German Democratic Republic, export and investment promotion and gaining international respectability.

In 1971 the Federal Government adopted a 'Development Policy Concept of the Federal Republic of Germany',[43] which emphasized 'economic and social progress in the developing countries' and 'the improvement of the living conditions of the population in these countries' as official objectives of German policy. Third World development was declared to be 'in the Federal Republic of Germany's own interest'.[44] Declarations of that sort did not kill the general belief in 'trickle-down', but they bridged the gap between the administration and the highly critical constituency of development policy which was largely influenced by the post-1967 student movement and New Left thinking.

After the resignation of Erhard Eppler as Minister of Economic Cooperation in 1974, the government's development policy was again brought into line with more narrowly defined German interests —

securing of supplies, exports and employment. But development-related thinking carried the topic of development as a German interest in its own right further, linking it to the ecological and 'alternative life style' movement. Without sight being lost of the specific problems and their magnitude in the Third World, 'development' and the direction of technological and social change became an issue to be concerned with everywhere in the world. On the conservative side, too, the last few years have seen a change in outlook. (The plea for an international social market economy with a transfer system, comparable to the domestic welfare system, has already been referred to.)[45] At first sight a broad consensus could thus be expected with regard to a massive increase in aid.

The aid performance, however, has been disappointing. The net flow of official development assistance (ODA) decreased from 0.45 per cent of GNP in 1962 to 0.27 per cent in 1977 (see Table II.4), which can partly be attributed to détente and Ostpolitik making West Germany less vulnerable to pressures from developing countries. The ODA percentage has since increased to 0.44 per cent, due to additional motives, such as the perception of matching idle capacities in the North with the needs of the South, as elaborated in the 'Brandt report', and due, at the same time, to a frostier East-West climate.

At the same time, some politicians have started to become concerned with the withdrawal of youth from politics and have sensed that a more enlightened and humanitarian approach to North-South relations could be a vehicle to bring them back. Together with a generation change in aid administration and with the basic-needs philosophy of international organizations such as the World Bank, all these factors have led to a new emphasis on aid as an instrument against absolute poverty.

The popular analogy — so dear to the German economists, free traders and aid administrators — between the internal welfare state and the global economy is revived; it suggests the feasibility of an all-out defence of the existing international market economy and at the same time of an acquiescence of the Third World, its governments and its poor, if only the aid budget could be increased. As pointed out before, in West Germany this analogy is quite attractive emotionally and in terms of administrative decision-making, but it is utterly misleading in terms of international politics and also of simple economic calculus: internally, the modern welfare state requires about 20 to 30 per cent of GNP in order to correct the distribution effects of a mature market economy by means of a tax and welfare system, not to speak of the poverty pockets and poor people which are still there. To reach comparable results on a global scale with 0.7 per cent or even 1.0 per cent of the GDP of the rich is impossible in view of the magnitudes of poverty in the Third World.

Politics also forbid much larger transfers: on the donor's side, the budgetary process is always related to the relative strength of constituencies, that is why in a democratic society there cannot be a massive redistribution in favour of non-voters — and, one may add, in a dictatorial regime this is even less likely. On the receiving end, the negative effects of budget aid are well known and would only be augmented if aid was increased substantially — and in a world of sovereign nations, governments cannot be circumvented.

Without aspiring to megalomaniac proportions, however, the positive attitude of the German public to help the poor could be combined with the transfer ideas of the developmentalists and the social market economists for some kind of 'development tax'. An additional indication of the willingness to accept an international transfer system can be seen in the fact that the analogy between development assistance and the Marshall Plan has become fashionable in West Germany (though particularly with regard to southern Europe).

The problem is, how to avoid the impression, be it right or wrong, that aid is the transfer of money from the poor in rich countries to the rich in poor countries. One step is the open declaration of aid as a grant for anti-poverty projects, minimizing links with other, generally more powerful interests; a second step is the withdrawal of aid from day-to-day foreign policy and a third is the need for competition and publicity for aid-channelling agencies in order to avoid bureaucratization and corruption.[46]

Suffice it here to point out that the general German interest in overcoming poverty and marginality and in enhancing the human rights could be served by some type of 'UNICEF aid' in the most direct way, even if it can only be a very modest and — in terms of the global economy — marginal element.

The magnitude of aid might rise considerably, and budgetary allocations have done so in West Germany during the recent recession, when linked to other interests such as employment. The matching of the supply and employment interests on the side of industrial countries and the demand for machinery and other imports on the side of developing countries has been hailed as the panacea for overcoming the present economic difficulties of the world. In a parliamentary hearing the German economic research institutes recently supported this view in unison,[47] and the German Council of Economic Exports endorsed it.[48] It is also one of the important lines of argument in the Brand report. Doubling the net resource transfer of all DAC member countries would reduce the number of unemployed by around 17 per cent and would bring down the unemployment rate by 0.9 percentage points.[49]

In the case of grants, the straight economics are simple: deficit spending and the production of exports for developing countries, instead of consumption, armaments or domestic public investment. As pointed out before, the problems lie with the democratic budgetary process which forbids such massive increases, particularly with a developmentalist constituency which no longer believes that the goods to be produced by the now idle industrial capacities and exported by Germany are necessarily good for development, and with an international market which would rightly scent aid-tying and call this type of export promotion 'dumping'. Furthermore, the transfer of resources to the South would rely even more on the business cycle in the North.

Another variant is the sale of goods on soft, hard or co-financed credit. With regard to private commercial financial flows, the Federal Republic already ranks high, since the one per cent objective for total net flows has been more than fulfilled in the last few years (1975, 1.18 per cent; 1976, 1.19 per cent; 1977, 1.12 per cent, 1978, 1.13 per cent, having doubled from 0.63 per cent in 1965[50]).

More net commercial credits also mean more debt, of course, so that in this field German interests in the management of the debt problem as well as trade interests are involved. By its very nature, credit only postpones problems. Thus the repayment of credits is associated either with higher prices or with higher volumes of imports or with both at a later date. If this is impossible or made impossible, a crash can always be postponed by prolongation, but a cancellation has to come one way or another. To keep uncollectable debt rolling may seem to lie in the interest of both parties; however, in the long run it hurts the interests of debtors and creditors alike, since mutual distrust is unavoidable. There is hardly any decision less likely to create political irritation and pressure than the answer to the question whose debts are to be written off first — or respectively repudiated — the friend's or the adversary's or the neutral's, the public or the private debts, the hard or the soft; what are the procedures in 'honourable' and not so honourable cases of bankruptcy?

As with other fields of interests and other mechanisms — with limited scope and to a certain degree — the idea of matching idle capacities here and obvious needs there makes sense, but if carried too far and if loaded with too many objectives and expectations it is likely to fail.

Other Issues

In addition to trade, investment and aid there are various other issues to be added in order to arrive at a more or less complete profile of German interests *vis-à-vis* Third World development.

In monetary matters, the German position (like that of most other industrial countries) is staunchly conservative, opposing efforts to convert the IMF into an institution for development finance, but at the same time augmenting its resources and with that its leverage in times of economic difficulties in individual countries.

According to textbook economics, the international monetary system has the function to smooth international trade and investment; as in domestic economic policy, the monetary authorities have to balance liquidity between the two perils of inflation on one hand and the stifling of economic activity by the lack of liquidity on the other. It cannot be expected that monetary authorities pursue objectives like self-reliance, human rights and the eradication of poverty. They do not have a Charter for it, nor the instruments, nor the spirit, and not even economic growth ranks high in their list of priorities. That is why central bank policies can only be judged in the overall context of the checks and balances of domestic economic policies.

In the existing international economic order, however, the institutional set-up is still so rudimentary that the monetary authority — the IMF — can exercise nearly unchecked power in the pursuit of its specialized objectives. Being the only international agency with 'teeth', since it is often followed by the private banks, it can reduce the United Nations institutions, with the exception of the Security Council, to talkshops; and the World Bank, which — long-term oriented as it is — could serve as a countervailing power to the short-term oriented IMF, is often following rather than controlling or balancing the IMF.

There are essentially three interests behind the IMF's behaviour, from the point of view of the German government and the Bundesbank;[51] price stability, access to markets for German exports and defence of Western influence. Because of German experiences with hyperinflation after the First and Second World Wars, price stability ranks particularly high in the objectives of economic policy. Not having secured 'stability' and having ceded to inflationary demands has long been a standard argument of attack against governments of different colours. This experience is transferred to the international sphere, and any plans which scent of the creation of money, such as the 'link', are opposed.

With regard to the usual IMF conditions of lending, export interests in opening the markets of the respective countries overrule development objectives, and since economic rationality is equalled with globalistic capitalist market economy rules in mainstream professional economic doctrine, the defence of strategic and political Western objectives follows quasi-automatically.

The Brandt report with its rather critical comments on the policies of the IMF has induced a certain scepticism with regard to the conventional wisdom; the *Guidelines of 1980,*[52] however, stress the need to strengthen the role of the IMF first and then add a small sentence about the social and political consequences of adjustment measures which should be taken into account. No basic change of policy is envisaged.

The over-accentuation of short-term globalistic and Western bloc interests at the expense of West Germany's long-term interests in viable and independent nation-states in the Third World, in the eradication of poverty and in human rights is thus not only the consequence of an institutional gap in the international structure, but also due to special German inflation traumas, liberal economic doctrines and the preponderance of interests which care little for development.

German economic interests in the armament trade are still rather limited, if compared to other industrial countries (see Table II.2). The importance of these interests, however, is growing because of the unemployment problem and because industrial co-production with other countries is increasing so that the principle of the Federal Government not to allow arms deliveries into 'areas of tension' ('Spannungsgebiete') can be circumvented. That is why a link between disarmament, arms transfer restrictions and development would still fit rather well into the German interest profile. But the time for achievements in this field may be running out.

The issue of migration has recently become a controversial one in public discussion in West Germany, because evidently there are deep-rooted problems. The official argument is that the Federal Republic of Germany is not a country of immigration and that foreign workers are here as 'guest workers' ('Gastarbeiter'). However, this official reading hides more than it reveals. In fact, the legal status of the non-EEC 'guests' and their families is rather insecure — neither once-and-for-all immigrants nor contractual migrants with a definite time limit. During the recent recession, the 'guest workers' (including foreigners from member countries of the European Community) turned out to be part of the employment 'cushion' or 'reserve army', and its share in the labour force decreased considerably between 1973 (when new recruitment from outside the EEC was stopped in October) and 1977 from 2.4 million (10.7 per cent of the labour force) to 1.9 million (8.8 per cent).[53] With an improvement of the cyclical employment situation in the middle of 1979, demands were heard again from the construction industry and from the hotel and restaurant business to allow in new guest workers from outside the European Community.

The disentanglement of interests in this field is not an easy task. The interest of business in relatively cheap unskilled labour is quite clear, but the position of the trade unions favouring the inflow of guest workers until 1973 needs an explanation.

Migrants helped to stabilize the traditional wage structure in which organized labour had an established interest: with the expansion of educational facilities, unskilled labour had become scarce in West Germany; its price was bid up in the labour market to levels close to that of skilled workers. Structural change in favour of unskilled and mostly unorganized labour was, of course, perceived as a challenge to skilled workers and employees and their unions. The positions are clear: those in favour of a hierarchic social structure will tend to favour immigration, while those in favour of an egalitarian society and those competing with immigrants in the labour and housing markets will oppose it.

Since this is a structural problem, the issue is bound to come up again whenever full employment is approached. For the time being immigration from the Third World will continue to be seen as an exception rather than a rule, as can be shown with regard to the generally hesitant reception of and the extreme right's terror acts against refugees and to the equally delicate questions of political asylum – a human right laid down in art. 16 of the West German constitution.

Thus migration turns out to be not only a question of hiring or not-hiring labour abroad, but it is increasingly looked upon as the manifestation of a growing gap between North and South with regard to economic amenities and human rights. Under this heading, an important mutual interest between West Germany and the Third World consists in rapid domestic development and respect of human rights in the South so that countries like West Germany are not flooded with refugees nor compelled to 'fortify' their borders.

The list of German interests *vis-à-vis* Third World development could be extended further, e.g. to tourism, transfer of technology, brain drain and terrorism, as well as to the more global problems such as disarmament, non-proliferation, global ecological balance and an institutional structure conducive to peace and development in a world order based on consent rather than on force.

Final Remarks

The profile of German interests in Third World development can be grouped in four fields: globalistic interests, Western bloc interests, control interests on the national as well as the European level, and humanitarian interests in human rights and the overcoming of poverty and marginality.

The resulting profile mirrors the Federal Republic's role as the world's leading exporter of capital goods; globalistic economic interests are the most powerful, articulating themselves in the doctrine of free trade and a favourable investment climate, which in turn tends to blur the line between global economic relations, regardless of economic and social systems, and economic relations within the Western bloc. The interests in a universal world order which comprises all nations can thus not be directly derived from narrow economic interests, but has to be related to peace and development as paramount though rather abstract objectives of policy which lack the backing of compact pressure groups.

When the profile of German interests is matched with the requirements of 'development' and its various facets and dynamic implications, only partial clear-cut mutuality can be detected, though a large field of diffuse common interests waiting for activation can be mapped out. Self-reliance in the articulation and the pursuit of interests on the side of the Third World remains essential, since it is obvious that German interests cannot be relied upon as strong enough for securing development outside the borders of the Federal Republic of Germany and its larger political and economic unit, the European Community.

Notes

1. Genscher (1979).
2. *Vorwärts*, Bonn, 31 January 1980, p. 14.
3. Bundesministerium für wirtschaftliche Zusammenarbeit (1980b).
4. See Hager (1975) and Noelle-Neumann (1977), pp. 93-4.
5. Duve (1971).
6. Very similar results by INFRATEST-Sozialforschung, Munich and EMNID-Institut für Meinungsforschung und empirische Sozialforschung, Bielefeld; see Bundesministerium für wirtschaftliche Zusammenarbeit (1979c) and EMNID.

7. EMNID, p. 11.
8. Bundesministerium für wirtschaftliche Zusammenarbeit (1979c), p. 5.
9. Ibid. (1980b).
10. For much of the following, see Kreile (1977).
11. See Buschmann (1977); Bundesministerium für wirtschaftliche Zusammenarbeit (1978) and ICFTU (1978).
12. Christlich-Demokratische Union (1980), thesis 1c.
13. Todenhöfer (1979).
14. Deutsches Institut für Wirtschaftsforschung (1980).
15. Wolter (1977).
16. Hermes (1978).
17. Schatz (1974) and Rogge (1979).
18. Sachverständigenrat (1979), p. 241.
19. UNIDO (1979), p. 51 and Dicke *et al.* (1976).
20. Arbeitsgruppe (1980).
21. See Hauff and Scharpf (1975) and Bundesministerium für Forschung und Technologie (1979).
22. Schlei (1977).
23. Such as Cocoyoc Declaration (1974); Dag Hammarsköld Report (1975); Bariloche Model (1976) and Laszlo *et al.* (1976).
24. Richter (1979).
25. See Weizsäcker (1978); Glotz (1979); Duve *et al.* (1980) and Habermas (1979).
26. This concept was introduced by J. Galtung in UNCTAD (1978); see also Galtung (1973); Senghaas (1977); Borges, Henke, Mutter and Nitsch in Technische Universität Berlin (1977) and Nitsch (1978a).
27. Bundesminsterium für Wirtschaft (1976) (quotations from the official English translation).
28. See Gagern (1977) and Nitsch (1978b).
29. Jeanneney (1978).
30. See Donges and Juhl (1979) and Wohlmuth (1980) and the material quoted there. For the opposition opinion see Fröbel *et al.* (1977).
31. See Holtz (1978).
32. See Schultz *et al.* (1980), pp. 128-59 and Deutsche Bundesbank (1978).
33. Deutsche Bundesbank (1979).
34. Institut der deutschen Wirtschaft (1980).
35. Schultz *et al.* (1980). p. 151.
36. See Fröbel *et al.* (1977).
37. Schultz *et al.* (1980), p. 138.
38. Bundesminister für Wirtschaft, *Tagesnachrichten*, 17 April 1980.
39. Doellinger (1979).
40. See Deutscher Bundestag (1974, 1977, 1979) and Donges and Müller-Ohlsen (1978).
41. See Senghaas (1977) and Grabendorff and Nitsch (1977).
42. See Buschmann (1977); ICFTU (1978) and Elsenhans (1979).
43. Bundesministerium für wirtschaftliche Zusammenarbeit (1971).
44. Eppler (1971).
45. Bundesministerium für Wirtschaft (1976) and Todenhöfer (1976).
46. For a detailed proposal, see Hirschman and Bird (1968).
47. Deutscher Bundestag (1979).
48. Sachverständigenrat (1979), pp. 170-92.
49. Deutsches Institut für Wirtschaftsforschung (1979).
50. Schultz *et al.* (1980), p. 100f.
51. See Shams (1980).

52. Bundesministerium für wirtschaftliche Zusammenarbeit (1980b). pp. 69-75.
53. UNIDO (1979), p. 6.

Bibliography

M.G. Adler-Karlsson, 'Umgekehrter Utilitarismus oder neue Lebensformen in den entwickelten Ländern', *Die Neue Internationale Wirtschaftsordnung in der Diskussion*, UN-Texte 21 (Bonn, 1976), pp. 93-102.

J.P. Agarwal, 'Zur Struktur der Westdeutschen Direktinvestitionen in Entwicklungsländern', *Die Weltwirtschaft*, no. 1, (1978), pp. 114-32.

Arbeitsgruppe, 'Alternative Wirtschaftspolitik', Memorandum, *Gegen konservative Formierung – Alternativen der Wirtschaftspolitik* (Köln, 1980).

Bariloche Model see Herrera, A.O. *et al., Grenzen des Elends* (Frankfurt am Main, 1977)

S. Baron, H.H. Glismann and B. Stecher, Ökonomische Implikationen einer Neuen Weltwirtschaftsordnung (Forschungsauftrag des Bundesministers für Wirtschaft, Kiel, March 1977) (mimeo.)

Bergedorfer Gesprächkreis (ed.), *Europa und die Weltwirtschaft – Politische und ökonomische Ansätze zur Lösung des Nord-Süd-Konflits* Hamburg, 1977).

J. Beyfuss, *Aussenhandel mit Entwicklungsländern* (Köln, 1978).

Willy Brandt, 'North-South-Dialogue – A New Dimension of Peace Policy', *Vierteljahresberichte*, vol. 73 (September 1978), pp. 197-202.

Bundesministerium für Forschung und Technologie (ed.), *Bundesbericht Forschung VI* (Bonn, 1979).

Bundesministerium für Wirtschaft (ed.), *Fragen einer Neuen Weltwirtschaftsordnung* Studien-Reihe 15 (Bonn, 1976).

Bundesministerium für wirtschaftliche Zusammenarbeit (ed.), *Die entwicklungspolitische Konzeption der Bundesrepublik Deutschland und die Internationale Strategie für die Zweite Entwicklungsdekade* (Bonn, 1971) and revised editions (1973 and 1975).

——, Entwicklungspolitik: Parteien und gesellschaftliche Gruppen', *Entwicklungspolitik*, Materialien no. 61 (December 1978).

——, 'Entwicklungszusammenarbeit zwischen der Bundesregierung und den christlichen Kirchen', *Entwicklungspolitik*, Materialien no. 62 (January 1979a).

——, *Journalisten-Handbuch Entwicklungspolitik 1979* (Bonn, 1979b).

——, 'Einstellungsdimensionen zur und Interesse an der Entwicklungspolitik', *Mitteilung für die Presse*, no. 83 (20 December 1979c).

——, *Vierter Bericht zur Entwicklungspolitik der Bundesregierung* (Bonn, 1980a).

——, *Die Entwicklungspolitischen Grundlinien der Bundesregierung – unter Berücksichtigung der Empfehlungen der 'Unabhängigen Kommission für internationale Entwicklungsfragen'* (Bonn, 1980b).

——, *Rückwirkungen der Entwicklungszusammenarbeit* (Bonn, 1980c).

K. Buschmann, 'Gefährdung oder Sicherung der Arbeitsplätze in den Industrieländern durch Industrialisierung in den Entwicklungsländern', *Dokumente der Fachtagung 'Entwicklungspolitik der SPD' am 1. und 2. Sept. 1977* (Bonn, 1977), pp. 151-9.

Christlich-Demokratische Union (ed.), 'Bundesfachausschuss Entwicklungspolitik der CDU legt Thesen zur Nord-Süd-Politik vor', *Pressemitteilung* (3 January 1980).

Cocoyoc Declaration see Bundesministerium für wirtschaftliche Zusammenarbeit, *Materialien Nr. 49*, (Bonn, June 1975), pp. 1-9.

K. Dadzie, 'Gemeinsame Interessen der Gewerkschaften in Industrie- und Entwicklungsländern', *Neue Entwicklungspolitik*, no. 4 (1978), pp. 5-8

Dag Hammarskjöld Report 1975, *What now — Another Development* (Stockholm, 1975).

C. Deubner, U. Rehfeldt, F. Schlupp and G. Ziebura, *Die Internationalisierung des Kapitals* (Frankfurt/New York, 1979).

Deutsche Bundesbank, 'Umschwung in der Bilanz der Direktinvestitionen', *Monatsberichte der Deutschen Bundesbank*, vol. 30 (October 1978), pp. 31-6.

—— 'Stand der Direktinvestitionen Ende 1976. Erste Ergebnisse einer neuen Statistik über die deutschen Direktinvestitionen im Ausland und die ausländischen Direktinvestitionen in der Bundesrepublik Deutschland', *Monatsberichte der Deutschen Bundesbank*, vol. 31 (April 1979), pp. 26-40.

Dehtsche Bundesregierung, 'Politik der Zusammenarbeit mit den Entwicklungsländern — 17 Thesen der Bundesregierung', *Entwicklungspolitik — Spiegel der Presse*, no. 23 (1979), pp. 706-8.

Deutsche Gesellschaft für Technische Zusammenarbeit (ed.), *Science and Technology for Development. Contributions by the Federal Republic of Germany* (Eschborn, 1979).

Deutscher Bundestag, 'Tätigkeit und entwicklungspolitischer Einfluss deutscher multinationaler Unternehmen in Entwicklungsländern', *Öffentliche Informationssitzung des Ausschusses für wirtschaftliche Zusammenarbeit Nov. 11-12, 1974* (Bonn, 1974).

——, 'Die Rohstoffproblematik im Nord-Süd-Verhältnis unter besonderer Berücksichtigung des Integrierten Rohstoffprogramms', *Öffentliche Anhörung des Ausschusses für wirtschaftliche Zusammenarbeit, May 23-25, 1977* (Bonn, 1977).

——, 'Nord-Süd-Verflechtung. Auswirkungen verstärkter Förderung der Länder der Dritten Welt durch öffentlichen und privaten Kapitaltransfer auf die Entwicklungsländer und die Industrieländer', *Öffentliche Anhörung durch den Ausschuss für wirtschaftliche Zusammenarbeit, April 23-25, 1979* (Bonn, 1979).

Deutscher Gewerkschaftsbund, *XI. Ordentlicher Bundeskongress des DGB, Hamburg, 1978: Beschlüsse und Anträge* (Düsseldorf, 1978).

Deutsches Institut für Wirtschaftsforschung, 'Aufstockung der öffentlichen Entwicklungshilfe nützt Entwicklungs- und Industrieländern', *DIW Wochenbericht* (May 1979), pp. 211-15.

——, 'Entwicklungspolitik im Spiegel der Parteiprogramme', *DIW Wochenbericht* (June 1980), pp. 247-54.

H. Dicke, H.H. Glismann, E.-J. Horn and A.D. Neu, *Beschäftigungswirkungen einer verstärkten Arbeitsteilung zwischen der Bundesrepublik und den Entwicklungsländern* (Tübingen, 1976).

C. v. Doellinger, 'A Study in International Economic Relations: The Brazilian-German Case', *Ibero-Amerika-Institut für Wirtschaftsforschung*, Diskussionsbeiträge No. 21 (Universität Göttingen, January 1979).

J.B. Donges and L. Müller-Ohlsen, *Aussenwirtschaftsstrategien und Industrialisierung in Entwicklungsländern* (Tübingen, 1978).

J.B. Donges and P. Juhl, *'Deutsche Direktinvestitionen im Ausland* — Export von Arbeitsplätzen?', *Konjunkturpolitik*, no. 4 (1979), pp. 203ff.

J.B. Donges, G. Fels, A.D. Neu *et al.*, *Protektion und Branchenstruktur der westdeutschen Wirtschaft* (Tübingen, 1973).

F. Duve, *Der Rassenkrieg findet nicht statt. Entwicklungspolitik zwischen Angst und Armut* (Düsseldorf, 1971).

The Federal Republic of Germany   245

——— (ed.), *Technologie und Politik 11* (Reinbek, 1978).

F. Duve, H. Böll and K. Staeck (eds.), *Kämpfen für die Sanfte Republik. Ausblicke auf die achtziger Jahre* (Reinbek, 1980).

H. Elsenhans, 'Für eine sozialreformerische Ausgestaltung der NIWO', *Entwicklung und Zusammenarbeit* no. 5 (1979), pp. 19-25.

EMNID Informationen, vol. 4 (1979), pp. 10-11, A37-A45.

B. Engels, K.M. Khan and V. Matthies, *Weltwirtschaftsordnung am Wendepunkt: Konflikt oder Kooperation?* (München, 1975).

E. Eppler, *Wenig Zeit für die Dritte Welt* (Stuttgart, 1971),

———, *Ende oder Wende* (Stuttgart, 1975).

———, 'Anfragen an unseren Lebensstil', *epd Entwicklungspolitik*, vol. 7 (1979), pp. 1-15.

G. Fels, *Der Standort Bundesrepublik im internationalen Wettbewerb* (Kiel, 1976).

D. Filip, R. Filip-Köhm, A. Geissler, C. Horn and H.-S. Ziervogel, *Abhängigkeit der Wirtschaft der Bundesrepublik Deutschland von Rohstoffimporten* (Gutachten im Auftrag des Bundesministeriums für Wirtschaft (DIW and Infratest-Industria) Berlin/München, 1976) (mimeo.).

F. Fröbel, J. Heinrichs and O. Kreye, *Die neue internationale Arbeitsteilung* (Reinbek, 1977).

M. Gagern, 'Marktwirtschaft und Armenpflege im Weltmasstab. Die Bundesrepublik Deutschland auf dem Holzweg' J. Tinbergen (ed.), *Der Dialog Nord-Süd (Frankfurt, 1977)*, pp. 102-15.

J.Galtung, *Kapitalistische Grossmacht Europa oder Die Gemeinschaft der Konzerne?* – *'A Superpower in the Making'* (Reinbek, 1973).

H.-D. Genscher, 'Perspektiven deutscher UN-Politik', *Vereinte Nationen*, no. 1 (1979), pp. 1-6.

H. Giersch (ed.), *The Changing International Division of Labour* (Tübingen, 1974).

——— (ed.), *Reshaping the World Economic Order* (Tübingen, 1977).

P. Glotz (ed.), *Die grossen Streitfragen der achtziger Jahre. Berliner Dialog über unsere Zukunft* (Bonn, 1979).

W. Grabendorff and M. Nitsch, *Brasilien: Entwicklungsmodell und Aussenpolitik* (München, 1977).

M. Greiffenhagen and S. Greiffenhagen, *Ein schwieriges Vaterland: Zur politischen Kultur Deutschlands* (München, 1979).

J. Habermas (ed.), *Stichworte zur 'Geistigen Situation der Zeit'; Vol. I; Nation und Republik; Vol. II: Politik und Kultur* (Frankfurt, 1979).

W. Hager, 'Angst vor der Dritten Welt?', *Europa Archiv*, no. 14 (1975), pp. 471-6.

V. Hauff and F.W. Scharpf, *Modernisierung der Volkswirtschaft* (Frankfurt, 1975).

H. Heck, 'Technologische Flucht nach vorn. Export und Arbeitsplätze von morgen', *Frankfurter Allgemeine Zeitung* (23 August 1975).

P. Hermes 'Aussenpolitik und ökonomische Interessen', *Aussenpolitik* no. 3 (1978), pp. 243-55.

A.O. Herrera and H.D. Scolnik (eds.), *Grenzen des Elends. Das Bariloche Modell* (Frankfurt, 1977).

H. Hesse, 'Die Diskussion über die Neuordnung der Weltwirtschaft', *Wirtschaftsdienst*, no. 10 (1976), pp. 501-7.

U. Hiemenz and K.-W. Schatz, 'Internationale Arbeitsteilung als Alternative zur Ausländerbeschäftigung – Der Fall der Bundesrepublik Deutschland', *Die Weltwirtschaft*, no. 1 (1977), pp. 35-58.

A.O. Hirschman and R.M. Bird, *Foreign Aid: A Critique and a Proposal* (Princeton,

1968).
Stanley Hoffmann, *Primacy or World Order* (New York, 1978).
U. Holtz, *Europa und die Multis* (Baden-Baden, 1978).
P. Hrubisch and H. Lahmann, 'Zur Einfuhrentwicklung der Bundesrepublik Deutschland von 1970 bis 1977', *DIW-Wochenbericht* (August 1978).
Ifo-Institut für Wirtschaftsforschung (ed.), 'Neue Weltwirtschaftsordnung – Auswirkungen auf die deutsche Wirtschaft', *ifo schnelldienst* (15 July 1977).
I. Illich, *Selbstbegrenzung* (Reinbek, 1975).
Informationszentrum Dritte Welt Freiburg (ed.), *Entwicklungspolitik – Hilfe oder Ausbeutung? Die entwicklungspolitische Praxis der BRD und ihre wirtschaftlichen Hintergründe* (Freiburg, 1978).
Institut der deutschen Wirtschaft, *Informationsdienst iwd* (17 July 1980), pp. 4-5.
International Confederation of Free Trade Unions, *The ICFTU Development Charter* (Brussels, 1978).
J.M. Jeanneney, *Pour un nouveau protectionnisme* (Paris, 1978).
Joint Conference of the Churches on Development in the Federal Republic of Germany, *Justice and Solidarity in the International Economic Order* (Hannover and Bonn, 1979).
R. Jonas and M. Tietzel (eds.), *Die Neuordnung der Weltwirtschaft* (Bonn, 1976).
M. Kreile, 'West Germany: The Dynamics of Expansion', *International Organization*, vol. 4 (1977), pp. 775-808.
H. Kunst and H. Tenhumberg (eds.), *Soziale Gerechtigkeit und internationale Wirtschaftsordnung* (München, 1976).
E. Laszlo *et al.*, *Goals for Mankind* (New York, 1977).
U. Müller-Plantenberg, 'Die Bundesrepublik Deutschland und die Neue Weltwirtschaftsordung' in V. Bennholdt-Thomsen *et al.* (eds.), *Lateinamerika, Analysen und Berichte 2* (Berlin, 1978), pp. 79-102.
M. Nitsch, 'Wissenschaft und Technologie für Entwicklung', *Lateinamerika-Institut der Freien Universität Berlin*, Diskussionspapiere No. 8 (Berlin, 1978a).
——, 'Zur Diskussion über die Neue Weltwirtschaftsordnung' in Stiftung Wissenschaft und Politik (ed.), *Polarität und Interdependenz* (Baden-Baden, 1978b), pp. 317-35.
E. Noelle-Neumann (ed.), *Allensbacher Jahrbuch der Demoskopie 1976-77* (München, 1977).
Organization for Economic Cooperation and Development, *Germany* (Paris, 1978).
H.-E. Richter, 'Was wir unseren Kindern vorleben. Die "erwachsene" Gesellschaft und ihre Unfähigkeit, die Aussteigerjugend anzusprechen', *Vorwärts* (17 May 1979) pp. 16-17.
H. Riese, 'Strukturwandel und unterbewertete Währung in der Bundesrepublik Deutschland', *Konjunkturpolitik*, no. 3 (1978), pp. 143-69.
P.G. Rogge, 'Weltwirtschaftliche Faktorallokation als Problem einzelstaatlicher Wirtschaftspolitik', *Kyklos*, vol. 32 (1979), pp. 331-49.
Sachverständigenrat zur Begutachtung der gesamtwirtschaftlichen Entwicklung, *Jahresgutachten 1979/80* (Bonn, 1979).
K.P. Sauvant and H. Hasenpflug (eds.), *The New International Economic Order* (Frankfurt, 1977).
K.F. Schade, *'Ohne neues Währungssystem keine neue Wirtschaftsordnung'*, *Die Neue Gesellschaft* (September 1978), pp. 739-43.
K.W. Schatz, *Wachstum und Strukturwandel der westdeutschen Wirtschaft im internationalen Verbund* (Tübingen, 1974).
M. Schlei, 'Die Entwicklungspolitik der Bundesregierung, eingebunden in die Gesamtverantwortung der Europäischen Gemeinschaft und der Industrie-

länder', *Dokumente der Fachtagung 'Entwicklungspolitik der SPD' am 1. und 2. Sept. 1977* (Bonn, 1977), pp. 144-50.

F. Schlupp, 'Internationalisierung und Krise – das "Modell Deutschland" im metropolitanen Kapitalismus', *Leviathan*, no. 1 (1979), pp. 21f.

A. Schmidt (ed.), *Strategien gegen Unterentwicklung. Zwischen Weltmarkt und Eigenständigkeit* (Frankfurt and New York, 1976).

H. Schmidt, 'The Struggle for the World Product', *Foreign Affairs* (April 1974), pp. 438-51.

——, Interview der Süddeutschen Zeitung (Franz Thoma), *Süddeutsche Zeitung* (24 June 1975).

——, 'The Internatinal Economic Order and the North-South-Dialogue', *Vierteljahresberichte*, no. 74 (December 1978), pp. 269-74.

S. Schultz, D. Schumacher and H. Wilkens, *Wirtschaftliche Verflechtung der Bundesrepublik Deutschland mit den Entwicklungsländern* (Baden-Baden, 1980).

K. Seitz, 'Die Europäische Gemeinschaft in einer Welt des Übergangs', *Europa-Archiv*, vol. 16 (1978), pp. 495-506.

——, 'Die Verhandlungen über einen gemeinsamen Rohstoff-Fonds', *Wirtschaftsdienst*, no. 7 (1978), pp. 93-7.

D. Senghaas, *Weltwirtschaftsordnung und Entwicklungspolitik* (Frankfurt, 1977).

R. Shams, 'Die Bundesrepublik Deutschland und die währungspolitischen Forderungen der Peripherie', *diskurs*, vol. 3 (1980), pp. 97-109.

A. Skriver, *Das Konzept der Hilfe ist falsch. Entwicklung in Abhängigkeit* (Wuppertal, 1977).

Technische Universität Berlin (ed.), *Technologische Grundlagenforschung für Entwicklungsländer* (Berlin, 1979).

L. Tindemans, 'European Union – Report by Mr. Leo Tindemans to the European Council', *Bulletin of the European Communities*, Supplement 1 (1976).

J.G. Todenhöfer, *Wachstum für alle. Plädoyer für eine Internationale Soziale Marktwirtschaft* (Stuttgart, 1976).

——, Interview, *Welt am Sonntag* (5 August 1979).

UNCTAD, *Development, Environment and Technology. Toward a Technology for Self-Reliance* (a Study by J. Galtung), TD/B/C. 6/23 (22 June 1978).

UNIDO, *Future Structural Changes in the Industry of the Federal Republic of Germany* (Study prepared by K.W. Schatz and F. Wolter of the Kiel Institute of World Economics in co-operation with UNIDO), ICIS, 103 (20 March 1979).

C.F. von Weizsäcker, *Wege in der Gefahr* (München, 1976).

——, 'Gehen wir einer asketischen Weltkultur entgegen?', *Deutlichkeit* (Darmstadt, 1978), pp. 73-113.

K. Wohlmuth, 'Die Bundesrepublik und die Diskussion über die Kontrolle der Aktivitäten transnationaler Konzerne in Entwicklungsländern', *diskurs*, vol. 3 (1980), pp. 73-96.

F. Wolter, 'Factor Proportions, Technology and West German Industry's International Trade Patterns', *Weltwirtschaftliches Archiv*, vol. 113 (1977), pp. 250-67.

8 RICH COUNTRY INTERESTS AND THIRD WORLD DEVELOPMENT: THE NETHERLANDS*

Jacob Everts

Introduction

General Position

The international position and policies of the Netherlands have been fundamentally affected by the Second World War. Before the war, the Netherlands relied on the balance of power within its European environment, expecting in this way to safeguard its integrity and promote its interests. It practiced a policy of lying low between rival forces and only occasionally ventured out to help defuse international tensions and promote humanitarian causes. The shock of its wartime experience converted the Netherlands with one stroke from political neutralism to international co-operation in the form of alliances and integration. Thus, while the basic geographic, economic and cultural conditions of the metropolitan country had in essence not changed,[1] the way in which it perceived its interests was fundamentally affected.

With the zeal of the converted, it has since joined regional and international organizations in almost every field — military, economic, political, cultural, etc. — and had consistently tried to strengthen such organizations. One analysis ranks the Netherlands second among countries in terms of the numbers of memberships of international organizations. Dutch nationals have played and are still playing an important role in the management and secretariats of these organizations, a role disproportionate to the size of the country.

The Netherlands is often compared to the Scandinavian countries with which it has indeed many political and other similarities. But, its almost complete integration into a network of alliances distinguishes the country not only from Sweden (non-NATO, non-EEC), but also from Norway (non-EEC) and even from Denmark, which though belonging to NATO and EEC will want to stay close to its Nordic partners that do not belong to those organizations. The Netherlands is in this respect more similar to its Benelux partners.

*This paper was written in January 1980.

248

In size, the Netherlands is almost a mini-state (117th among the UN members with more than one million inhabitants), but in other aspects it ranks relatively high. Its population (14 million) ranks 47th among the UN members; in total GNP it ranks 14th and in GNP *per capita* it ranks 11th (excluding oil-exporting countries). It has one of the highest literacy rates in the world and the longest life expectancies at birth, belongs to the six countries with the highest indicators of health care and among the five countries with the highest public expenditures for education. Although the Dutch continue to consider themselves a small country with little 'power' in the traditional sense, the above-mentioned factors may consciously or unconsciously support a tendency — which we shall later explore — to play a distinct role on the international scene.

For *security* the Netherlands is completely dependent upon NATO; the traditional role of the navy dating back to its seventeenth century golden age and its colonial past has gradually been reduced in comparison to land and air forces. Dutch forces are fully integrated in NATO, the main exception being the contingents made available for UN operations.

The Netherlands sees it *political* future strongly influenced by its Western European ties. With the *Benelux* treaty having been substantially overtaken in the economic field by the EEC and now more or less limited to fringe issues, relations with Belgium and Luxembourg are mainly seen from a pragmatic angle. Although a certain Benelux solidarity has developed over the years, political integration is not considered an active issue in the context of Benelux. Rather it is in the *European Communities* that the hope for political integration is vested. The European movement which, in the Netherlands, can be traced back to Coudenhove-Kalergi's Paneuropa ideals is strongly supported. At the same time there is considerable concern about the dangers of the halfway solution that the EEC represents. Smaller countries in particular may be deprived of chunks of their sovereignty without sufficient supranational authority being vested in a (reasonably) independent body. Hence the Dutch pressure for increased power for the European Commission, a substantive role for a directly elected European parliament, etc. It is not possible in the context of this review to analyze these issues more fully nor to weigh the influence exercized upon Dutch attitudes by the presence of its powerful German neighbour.

It is clear, however, that in the *economic* field many of the expectations entertained have come true: the EEC has provided a large market for Dutch industry and permitted the important service sector as well as an efficient agricultural sector to operate over a wider area.² There are, however, some doubts even in the economic field. The Dutch support for the EEC assumed that the Community would follow liberal foreign trade policies, thus continuing a pattern upon which the Dutch economy had always depended. But there are opposing forces, not only in the sector of agricultural policy which is in fact highly protective and, incidentally, quite beneficial to Dutch farmers, but also in certain sensitive industrial sectors. The Netherlands remains a strong supporter of liberal trade, which it considers to be in the long-term interests of world relations and indeed of the EEC itself. But its influence in the councils of the EEC is limited, and there is always a temptation to accept 'temporary' protectionist solutions proposed by other members if they coincide with the interests of certain local industries threatened by competition, whether from Third World or other countries.

The next sections discuss the way in which the Third World features in this post-Second World War picture of the Netherlands.

The Place of the Third World in International Relations³

No analysis of Dutch attitudes to the Third World would be truly helpful if it neglected the strong influence exercised by history. Few European countries have a history of such intensive and pervasive overseas contacts as the Netherlands have had. From the late sixteenth century onwards trade with and colonization of the countries in Asia, the Americas and parts of Africa have influenced not only the Netherlands' economy but the whole structure of its society. A large and prosperous middle class was created that still is the backbone of the country and outward-looking in its orientation. Opportunities overseas also generated a spirit of adventure that even today inspires youth to go out into the world, away from the cold and crowded homeland.

The nineteenth century witnessed an increasing concentration upon the islands that today form Indonesia, and a deeper involvement in the life of that country in its broader aspects than just the trade which had been the hallmark of two centuries of 'rule' by the United East India Company. Policies of the colonial era were embodied in the 'Culture System' (1830-70) which resulted in large transfers of tropical produce to the home country, there to be traded at high profits. It was replaced by the 'Liberal Policy' by which the forces of liberal economic policies were thought to ensure prosperity not only for the agricultural estates and other enterprises based on western finance and technology but also for the indigenous population. When the liberal policy did not produce the positive results expected and Indonesian society became impoverished it was, in its turn, replaced around 1900 by the so-called 'Ethical Policy'. The proponents of this policy sought to strengthen the innate forces and values of Indonesian society and to promote an enlightened and viable system of symbiosis which would allow both societies to prosper.[4] Each of these policies may now seem at best outdated, or even just thin cloaks for a policy of colonial exploitation and domination, and they were indeed accompanied by bloody suppression of local revolts. They are recalled here, however, in order to explain how at least in some sectors of Dutch society these alternative policies were discussed and followed with intense interest and how Dutch thinking with regard to the relations between Western society and what was then called 'the East' were strongly stimulated in the process.[5] These policies were also influenced by, and in turn had an effect upon, the work of the missionary societies which had their home base in the religious organizations of the Netherlands, both Protestant and Catholic. The Dutch colonial service, particularly under the ethical policy, also felt a responsibility that went beyond the commercial interests of the mother country.

Thus, in the shadow of commercial exploitation and political domination, trends of social and ethical awareness and scientific interest developed which today are still recognizable in Dutch attitudes to Third World problems, though sometimes in strikingly different attire. Missionary zeal in the proper sense, for instance, is still in evidence.[6] But one wonders whether the opinionated attitudes and the sometimes irksome tendencies to preach about international behaviour could not be qualified as the less attractive scions of the same missionary tradition!

The colonial involvement has also produced a vast body of academics and technicians with expert knowledge in tropical health, agriculture, water management, anthropology, linguistics, etc. Their return in the late 1940s and the 1950s from the colonies stimulated efforts to redeploy this reservoir of expertise in other tropical countries. Although their involvement was in some political circles decried as neo-colonialism they — as well as their successors graduating from institutions in the Netherlands specializing in tropical skills — have been the main basis of the initial Dutch involvement in technical assistance and commercial enterprise in the Third World. (A very special influence upon Dutch policy towards the Third World must be accorded to the presence in the Netherlands of Jan Tinbergen whose brilliance and devotion were increasingly addressed to the future of the world community and stimulated the involvement and response of a whole generation of academics and professionals.)

There are other perhaps less tangible elements affecting foreign policy with regard to the Third World that need to be mentioned. One factor seems to a certain extent to be the counterpart of the 'absorption' of the country in security, economic and political alliances described in the previous section. Even though the Dutch have adopted this historic development with conviction, they clearly do not want — in the foreseeable future — to lose their identity:

(a)   They consider themselves a country that may be small but is definitely distinct by history and character from its neighbours. They may realize the benefits derived from their unique opportunity to associate with these cultural spheres (Germanic, Anglo-Saxon and French) surrounding them at the 'crossroads of Europe'; they may speak the languages of those countries tolerably well; they may be bound to their neighbours by inseparable links of commerce and geography; they may be dependent upon their NATO partners for security. But they will not be smothered or boxed in completely. Expressed in terms of foreign policy they feel that their identity — and their negotiating power — is strengthened by a distinct and recognizable attitude in questions of world politics.

(b)   They feel that they have a special interest in and concept of world relations, and — as a relatively small nation — a special opportunity for a distinct policy by the grace of which they can reach over the borders of Western alliances towards the countries 'across the seas' without being hindered by any big power image.

(c)   They desire on that basis to be indentified as a progressive partner in the post-colonial society of nations. Whether that wish is also based on a sense of guilt over the colonial past is difficult to establish. There is a growing literature assessing the Dutch role in Indonesia and the presence of a large group of Moluccans in the country is a constant reminder of the anomalies of colonization. But public opinion polls on attitudes to the Third World do not strongly bring out such guilt feelings. Maybe they are still subconsciou.. One might suspect that the disproportionately large aid programme for Surinam[7] reflects a sense of guilt over the Dutch role in that country, which was populated by slaves and semi-forced labour. But it can also simply be qualified as a 'platinum handshake'. With regard to Indonesia, the situation is more complex: one might rather suspect a mixture of guilt and nostalgic attachment to that country and its people.

It can also be argued that the vigorous efforts of the Dutch to be involved in problems of the Third World is a form of 'sublimation' of the trauma of its separation from Indonesia in which both guilt and the fear of loss of indentity take their place. For a trauma it has been. Not perhaps because Indonesia became independent after three centuries of Dutch involvement — that had already been accepted as an inevitable, albeit gradual, tendency — but because independence came so suddenly and violently and was so complete, and because its preparation by the build-up of the necessary educational, political and organizational infrastructure had, notwithstanding the Ethical Policy, not progressed sufficiently to ensure safe passage (guilt!). The sudden separation from Indonesia was also a trauma because it brought forcefully home that the Kingdom of the Netherlands which had been the third largest colonial power, was losing almost all status (identity!) with the great world powers, who had in pre-war and wartime days been very interested in the strategic and economic importance of the Indonesian archipelago. One noteworthy instance of 'sublimation' is perhaps the role that the Netherlands has played in convening and chairing the Intergovernmental Group on Indonesia, the consortium of aid donors and Indonesia created in 1967: with one stroke the fixation on bilateral relations with Indonesia became 'sublimated' in a world wide endeavour to assist that country in adapting to its new environment and goals. For Indonesia it was clearly no problem to accept or even welcome that Dutch role: the Dutch had knowledge and interest and, being small, were not 'dangerous'.

It must be said that the posture of the Netherlands as an outward-looking and progressive partner in the society of nations has not prevented the persistence and even resurgence of some narrow and parochial elements in its foreign policy. Similarly, the Netherlands is still in the process of translating its general posture into concrete and consistent policies for certain areas (for instance, China, Latin America, the Arab world and certain parts of Africa) where it had only limited contact and experience.

The foreign policy of the Netherlands towards the Third World is primarily expressed in the worldwide forum, that is in the United Nations and its subsidiary bodies. The limited power that a country like the Netherlands can exercise is deliberately enhanced by seeking close co-operation with 'like-minded' countries of the West (Canada, the Nordic countries) and countries like Yugoslavia whose policies are considered progressive and representative of Third World wishes. The like-minded Western countries often find themselves in the role of trying to unfreeze hard line positions of the industrialized group and thus help to promote the dialogue. Also they have often undertaken 'spearhead' action, for instance by contributing to special funds and accepting debt alleviation, in order to demonstrate the viability of certain solutions or the fairness of certain Third World wishes.

It is inevitable that these tactics will sometimes raise the suspicion that the Netherlands tries to reap political benefits by supporting progressive proposals while calculating rather cynically that its vital economic interests will not be affected because other developed countries will anyhow prevent their acceptance. These matters are hard to prove. On the one hand, it is certainly true that the progressive image that the Netherlands enjoys in the developing countries enhances the country's international status in Third World countries. (It may even be helpful to some exporters and investors in doing business with these countries!) On the other hand, Dutch negotiating delegations are usually not homogeneous enough for this kind of machiavellian double play to be successful. And as far as spearhead actions are concerned they can usually not be considered as void gestures.

However that may be, it is clear that the pursuit of such strategies in world-wide forums can only have a limited impact: they have to be supplemented and balanced by consistently influencing the policies of the more powerful partners with whom the Netherlands is bound in the EEC, the OECD and elsewhere and from whom it must avoid becoming isolated. The Netherlands tries to exert this influence without losing its limited freedom of manoeuvre and while reserving for itself the right to follow its own convictions. This puts an extra stress on the negotiating capacities of its representatives who have to operate within these organizations in a constructive way, not so much because that would be more congenial to the Dutch character than obstructive tactics but because it is in the long run a more effective attitude for a small partner.

Dutch Interests and the Third World

With an outward looking posture and an economy as open as that of the Netherlands, there are naturally many fields where Dutch interests are substantially affected by relations with the Third World and where interest groups can be identified which may be in a position to influence government policies. In reviewing these fields no special attention is given to security interests because it is felt that since decolonization Dutch policies towards the Third World are no longer influenced by specific security concerns except in the broadest sense of world-wide security considerations.

Trading Interests. The free flow of goods and services is vital to the economy of the Netherlands. Although trade with developing countries is only a minor part of total Dutch trade, commercial interests are an important element in relations with the Third World.

Only a small percentage of Dutch *imports* of raw materials, semi-finished and finished products originates in developing countries (8.8 per cent in 1975 excluding petroleum and derivates).[8] For finished products the percentage was 3.5 (in comparison, OECD countries received a weighted average of 11.5 per cent of their imports of finished products from LDCs).[9]

These percentages are indeed quite low (they do, however, apply to a total import volume that is much higher than for most OECD countries; the import/GNP ratio for the Netherlands is more than 40 per cent). For petroleum and derivates the Netherlands is almost completely dependent on imports from Third World countries and even the vast reserves of natural gas are being husbanded under new policies for reduced exports and increased liquid gas imports. Reopening of the coal mines is expected to remain uneconomical for the present decade, and there are no other local raw materials.

The ratio of *exports* to GNP for the Netherlands is also one of the highest among the OECD countries (41 per cent in 1977). Again, the share of developing countries in Dutch exports is quite low (10.7 per cent in 1977 compared to a weighted average of 23.5 per cent in OECD countries).[10] Nevertheless, in view of the importance of high exports to the Dutch economy, LDC markets cannot be neglected.

Transit trade is an important part of trade. Rotterdam, the largest harbour complex in the world, serves as the predominant gateway to Europe for imports of oil, minerals, grains, etc. and exports of chemicals, piecegoods, etc. Rotterdam also houses the largest refinery complex in Europe. Returns on heavy investments in harbours, storage facilities, handling equipment and connecting inland traffic, as well as employment of management and labour in these sectors, depend entirely on continued and increasing international trade including that with Third World countries. Specially related to Third World countries is merchandise trade in tropical products; though diminished it is still important (tea, coffee, cocoa, tropical hardwoods, oils and fats, tobacco, etc.).

In the services sector, sea transport is still a Dutch speciality even though many ships are under flags of convenience. Air transport grows steadily with a world-wide clientele. Banks have traditionally had a strong foothold in Asia and good connections with Latin America and have recently expanded operations in the Middle East. Insurance companies also operate outside the Netherlands.

Only for certain service operations is there a special dependence on developing countries. This applies, for instance, to civil engineering, harbour and road construction, dredging, land reclamation, drainage and irrigation. A typical Dutch speciality finding application in Third World countries is the provision of consulting services in such fields as tropical agriculture, agriculture in general, water management and river control.

In summary, the Netherlands depends very heavily on the availability of raw materials, several of which originate in LDCs, and on the proceeds of agricultural and industrial exports and services. Although the percentage of exports and services that is related to LDCs is small the absolute amounts are sizable and for certain sectors LDC markets are vital. It is from those sectors that pressure originates for government support of exports, for instance through continued tying of bilateral development assistance.

Investments. The picture of Dutch investments in developing countries is dominated by a number of multinationals who have their headquarters (partly) in the Netherlands: Royal Dutch Shell, Unilever, Philips, Estel and AKZO are the largest, ranking 1, 4, 5, 50 and 53 among non-US industries and 3, 12, 16, 93 and 99 world-wide (1978). Their combined industrial operations as well as their markets outside the Netherlands far outweigh internal production and sales. They are, however, important local employers, and recipients of overseas remittances. Their investments are the main factor in making the Netherlands the fifth to seventh largest direct private investor in developing countries in flows during the years 1974-77 and the sixth in stock (1976).[11] Other industries, not belonging to the group of large multinationals, account for a relatively modest size of flows and stock as can be concluded from the rather low level of government investment guarantees issued to them.

Although the economic power of the multinationals is considerable, their direct influence on Dutch Third World policy is probably less important, or at least less evident, than could be expected. They have their own, and probably more effective, channels through which to foster their interests in developing countries. Also the situation in the Netherlands is such that any undue exercise of power by the business community on Dutch policies could not go unnoticed and would generate strong political reactions. It is, however, evident that in certain fields, for instance oil and gas supplies, government policies will be designed in close co-operation with the oil companies including Royal Dutch Shell. In a more general sense the interests of the country are served by an international economic and political climate that is not hostile to private investment. The government has indeed consistently supported international efforts to promote investment guarantee schemes, investment codes, etc., while at the same time co-operating in the context of the UN programme for transnational corporations in finding solutions to the requirements of a new international economic order (NIEO). The Netherlands business community also understood early that it is in their interest to participate actively in the search for policies that take due account of new trends in relations with developing countries and have, for instance, tried to work in that direction through the International Chamber of Commerce.

Trade Unions. Dutch trade unions have always maintained close international links, particularly with their sister organizations in Europe, and the denominational international trade union organizations. Their growing links with trade union movements in developing countries have resulted in an active role both in co-operation with that movement and in influencing public opinion in the Netherlands in favour of workers' rights and social reforms in developing countries. Latin America figures prominently in these links.

Dutch trade unions, which are quite powerful, have generally endorsed liberal trade policies within the context of overall Dutch economic policy, which they have helped to shape. This does not mean, however, that trade unions are not becoming concerned — as are other interest groups — about the implications of the structural changes in the world economy, as witnessed by the growing industrialization of the developing countries and the subsequent diversification of their exports. The problem, which is particularly felt in the sensitive sectors of textiles, shoes, etc., is further reviewed under 'Some Current Issues'.

Church Organizations. Churches and missionary organizations have been and are a significant source of inspiration in stimulating the awareness of underdevelopment as a problem of, mainly, moral dimensions. At the same time they have, in the particular situation in the

Netherlands, to be recognized as in 'interest' group of a special kind:

(a)   In colonial times the missionary societies were very active in Indonesia and Surinam. They are still important there but are also heavily involved in Africa and in other continents. In some countries the missionary relationship has been replaced by contacts on an equal footing between Dutch churches and the young independent churches in the Third World. The organizations concerned value these contacts and the 'signals' received through them and want them to continue.

(b)   The post-war surge towards liberalisation within the churches, while temporarily blocked in its main thrusts by conservative opposition particularly from the Catholic hierarchy in Rome,[12] encountered less opposition to the search for new international solidarity. Generally, modern theologians and laymen, engaged in reassessing their views on the vocation of the church in society, identified with reform movements, particularly those in the Third World. The progressive role of Dutch churches and churchmen in the World Council of Churches, and in the Pax Christi movement are illustrative.

The Academic Community. The large body of academic and technical knowledge about tropical issues (see earlier) has been the basis for a remarkable post-war growth of institutions specifically designed for research, training and education in development. This community of scientists and teachers can well be called an 'interest group' in the narrow sense of the word in that they not only help to keep the development issue alive but will naturally seek ways to continue and expand their activities. The government indeed supports the academic community through several channels; the 1980 development assistance budget for instance contained approximately $90 million for a variety of such purposes.

All universities have chairs in different fields relating to Third World problems. Several have more or less autonomous institutions.[13] Separate institutions for international education, not directly linked to universities are, among others: the Institute for Social Studies, the Royal Tropical Institute, the Center for the Study of Education in Changing Societies, the Bouwcentrum International Education, the International Training Center for Aerial Survey and Earth Sciences and the Institute for Hydraulic and Sanitary Engineering. A network of courses, some of them specifically designed for students from developing countries and held in English or French, cover general development problems as well as specializations (agriculture, drainage and irrigation, small-scale industrialization, industrial management, hydraulic and sanitary engineering, aerial surveying). Some institutions have twinning arrangements with sister organizations in developing nations and try to transfer their training activities to those countries. Research related to development is going on in a large number of institutions. Efforts to co-ordinate and give direction to all these activities are now underway through government sponsored advisory machinery but it is clear that the academic community will try to use these 'streamlining' efforts to increase rather than temper its involvement in development issues.

Voluntary Agencies. Some of the institutions and organizations mentioned above as well as numerous organizations not specifically linked to the business community, trade unions, churches or academic circles are to be considered as interest groups. Their role in public opinion formation and in policy formulation is discussed later. In the present context their operational activities are to be mentioned because their experience as well as their interest in continuing such operations have influenced government policies quite strongly. As such they are in fact a special form of 'interest group'. Their field activities in developing countries are subsidized by the government to the tune of approximately $150 million in 1980 (this figure covers co-financing, some special programmes and the volunteer programme, but not the academic activities in developing countries mentioned under the previous section). The level of these subsidies may seem small in the context of the total ODA and non-ODA development budget (1980, $2,000 million) but they are vital for the agencies concerned who are keenly aware of the value of their co-operation with the government.

Some Recent Developments in Dutch Policy vis-à-vis the Third World

In the context of this overview it is not possible to describe Dutch policy *vis-à-vis* the Third World comprehensively. There is, however, ample literature on this subject.[14] Some basic recent developments are indicated below under two headings: development assistance and other elements of the North-South relations respectively, but it should be understood that the two fields are in the Dutch view and in the formulation of Dutch policies closely linked. One such link is that many actions designed to improve North-South relations are financed from the development assistance budget.

Development Assistance.

(a) *Level and Quality.* The Netherlands has surpassed the international volume target of 0.7 per cent of GNP, reaching 0.82 per cent disbursements in 1978. Terms were also better than the DAC targets. Internally a target of 1.5 per cent has been accepted for the 1979-83 period which does not, however, relate to GNP but to NNI at factor costs and to the budget (commitments) rather than disbursements. Also, the internal target includes a number of non-ODA activities (approximately 15 per cent of the total) covering such items as: restructuring Dutch industry in the face of LDC exports, measures for migrant workers from LDCs, assistance to LDC repatriates, interest subsidies on development loans, infrastructure and operating costs for Dutch institutions for international education and research, personnel costs of the Ministry, and information. For 1980 the internal target of 1.5 per cent NNI comes to approximately $2,000 million. The steep and continued increase from 0.26 per cent in 1963 to the present level was possible because, as shall be explored later, public opinion was strongly interested in development assistance and all major political parties had accepted this commitment, be it with differences of view about the time-schedule in which to achieve it. Thus the commitment (1.5 per cent of NNI) is for the time being virtually immune from the danger of budget cuts to which other budget items are susceptible at times of economizing; on the other hand the room provided in the past by rising budget levels is now reduced to the rate of increase in the NNI, making it somewhat more difficult to accommodate new initiatives or meet special wishes from pressure groups. The virtual unanimity on the main issue does not prevent differences of view on such other issues as the relationship between commerce and aid, the destination and form of assistance and the question whether certain non-ODA items should be removed from − or could be brought under − the development assistance budget.

(b) *Multilateral Assistance.* The Netherlands has traditionally channelled 25 to 30 per cent of its ODA through multilateral channels (UN organs, World Bank, regional banks) because of their objectivity, expertize and administrative and management capabilities, and, particularly in respect of UN programmes, because of the influence of recipients in decision-making. Through numerous special contributions for specific multilateral programmes the Netherlands has supported innovative multilateral actions, for instance, Capital Development Fund, Center of Economic and Social Information of the UN (CESI), UN Research Institute for Social Development, ESCAP activities, UN Revolving Fund for Natural Resources Exploration, IFAD, Common Fund for commodities. Dutch interest in issues of development strategy has led to their support for the UN preparations of the Second and Third Development Decades and recently the Brandt Commission. In the non-UN sphere a recent example is the support given to the International Foundation for Development Alternatives (IFDA).

One wonders whether the use of special contributions for certain sympathetic purposes could not be viewed as a form of undue influence or even interference in the decision-making process, particularly when used in the UN. A small country like the Netherlands may escape that reproach more easily than one of the great powers. But it will still be necessary to assure that the activity has the full support of the Secretariat and at least a number of influential countries.

(c) *Bilateral Assistance.* Bilateral aid has grown faster than multilateral aid and has also acquired a stronger political dimension since the Cabinet decided in 1974 that it would be a proper vehicle to translate into practical measures the Netherlands' views on what have become the dominant aims of Dutch development co-operation, namely poverty alleviation and socio-economic restructuring. In earlier years a more arm's length policy was followed which relied mainly on the international machinery of consultative groups and consortia to bring out the recipient country's priorities and policies. That policy has gradually been replaced by a more active involvement in the judgemental process on policies and projects. Intriguing questions can be raised about the possible impact of these tendencies and of the 'two-pronged' approach developed by the government[15] upon the relations between donor and recipient and, more generally upon the whole field of structural relations beween North and South. Some of these questions will be dealt with later.

Other Elements of the North-South Dialogue. Development assistance is only one of the issues in the North-South dialogue. It may still be high on the international agenda and some elements remain the subject of lively debate in the Netherlands, but it appears that once the UN targets were achieved the main attention in the Netherlands shifted to the more structural issues in North-South relations and to the implications of the changing relationships for the country. The basic attitude of the Netherlands is one of understanding for Third World wishes and of preparedness to give meaningful content to the concept of a New International Economic Order. Proposals supported by the Netherlands — some of which have been mentioned above — relate to the design of a programme for transnational corporations, the search for an investment code, the UNCTAD programme for commodities including the Common Fund, access to markets for manufactures and the creation of LDC-oriented news services. There are, however, several factors that severely limit the freedom of action.

One is the realization that many of these subjects are coming under the growing responsibilities of the European Communities. Whereas in the past the Netherlands was reluctant to accept any EEC discipline that was not mandated by the Rome treaties, it is now recognized that many structural problems can only be usefully discussed if the EEC as a whole is prepared to face them. In these matters the cherished 'independent identity' becomes somewhat of a hollow phrase. If progress in the NIEO is to be achieved, the policy of the EEC has to become progressive. The EEC will have to develop a development policy and the Netherlands should use whatever political freedom of manoeuvre it has to promote its views on world-wide issues in that forum.

A second factor is that some elements of the NIEO will directly affect Dutch interests. This is nothing new but it is sufficient to mention such issues as Dutch shipping interests, Dutch dependence on oil imports and access to the Dutch market for manufactured products from LDCs to illustrate that the time is coming when Dutch sympathy for Third World interests will have to stand the acid test of practical application. The last example (imports of LDC manufactures) is more fully discussed in 'Some Current Issues'.

Public Opinion and Policy Formulation

Public Opinion

It can be said without exaggeration that development issues play an important role in public opinion in general and are the subject of numerous activities in a multitude of opinion-making forums. The Netherlands' situation and experience in this respect are quite unique and justify fuller description. The general origins of the Dutch interest in the world around them have been touched upon earlier. But it might be useful to explore the question of how the Dutch people themselves, that is the general public, are motivated in their attitudes to relations between the rich and the less fortunate of this world.

Investigations by the government and others[16] show that, in the view of the general public, constructive involvement in development issues is primarily justified on moral grounds, by compassion for the poor, by the Christian mandate of neighbourly love and by the unacceptability of continued misery in this world while poverty in the Netherlands itself has virtually been eliminated; in other words, on considerations that go back to the long religious and charitable traditions of the country. Considerations of self-interest of the North and Cold War motives are shown to play a secondary role. Analysis and reasoning as well as theological or philosophical justifications seem no more to be required or desired by the interviewed: we simply 'have to do it' (which mostly equals giving aid). How 'hard' these convictions are remains of course a big question. If people were asked where budget cuts are to be made development aid might well be a candidate. And when sacrifices are asked in periods of unemployment (see p. 269), the developing countries may receive less sympathy. However, opinion leaders in the public domain as well as the leaders of private groups are firmly behind a vigorous involvement in Third World issues.

Special emphasis should be laid on the role that successive governments have played in building up public support among opinion leaders and in stimulating the interest of the general public. At an early stage — in 1963 — the visibility of the commitment to development was increased by the creation of a State Secretary for Development Cooperation, and from 1965 a full Minister within the Ministry of Foreign Affairs. Interestingly, all incumbents of that post in Centre/Right Cabinets have come from the Christian Democratic parties. This does not, however, imply any less sense of a commitment in the Socialist parties; indeed, when the major Socialist party was called upon to fill the post from 1973 through 1977 that commitment was most convincingly expressed in innovative polices.[17]

Under the responsibility of the Minister for Development Cooperation, a widespread and intensive information and educational programme on concrete issues of development as well as wider policy questions was set up. The Special Information Service for Development, with a budget of approximately $5 million, finances a number of publications with a large readership.[18] It also issues documentation dossiers, popular brochures, fact sheets and press reports and sponsors films, televison and radio programmes. Mention should also be made of the publications by the National Advisory Council whose role is described later.

Responding to the 1970 UN Resolution on the Second Development Decade (paragraph 84), the Minister established the National Committee for Information and Awareness-Raising on Development Cooperation (NCO) composed of representatives of some 60 national organizations. The NCO can approve proposals for public financing of projects presented by these and other organizations already active in the field of information and awareness-raising. The experience with this programme is very interesting. It has grown rapidly: for 1979 some 90 large projects and many smaller projects in a total programme of approximately $6 million were approved covering almost anything one can think of, from the parochial to the sophisticated. The salaries for more than 250 full or part-time staff members of these organizations are included. Projects are mainly directed at group guidance: in this way information on world problems is related to the people's own problems at the local level and thereby more easily brought home and understood than through mass media approaches.

Since 1974 the mandate of the NCO has been broadened and deepened to put development in a wider context by stressing not just poverty as such but also the inequalities between countries and within countries, both poor and rich, as well as the causes of these inequalities, whether economic, political, institutional or other. The government through the NCO is thus actually supporting critical analysis and even controversial presentations by all sorts of pressure groups, refusing only to finance organizations or activities that aim at the overthrow of recognized governments or the support of internal violence in developing countries.

Private groups that have made Third World issues the main centre of their attention and try to influence public opinion are numerous and multiplying. There are now more than 500 such groups at the national, provincial or local level. They include the churches; youth groups; special centres of study and information mostly directed by young academics; some 170 'world-shops' selling goods from developing countries and using these contacts to bring the plight of the poor countries as well as the causes of inequality and exploitation to the attention of their visitors; action groups (the situation of foreign 'guest workers' in the Netherlands and elsewhere, cane sugar versus beet sugar, no coffee from Angola, the apartheid policies in South Africa, independence for Namibia); etc. Some of these groups concentrate upon the political aspects. Others are mainly supporting programmes in developing countries. Many raise private funds and some receive NCO assistance for awareness-raising projects in the Netherlands (see above) or enjoy subsidies on projects in the Third World under the co-financing programme (see p. 259). (It is not feasible in the context of this review to enter into further details on such phenomena as the discussion in the churches after Uppsala and Beirut, and the Second Vatican Concilium or the activities of the World Council of Churches and Pax Christi and the participation of Dutch citizens therein, except to note that they are significant.)

The press gives extensive coverage to problems of development, North-South issues, human rights, as well as parliamentary discussions and international conferences about these subjects. Scientific periodicals on economics, finance and foreign policy frequently contain contributions or issue special editions devoted to North-South and development questions. Universities and special academic institutions, workshops, etc. have courses and conduct research, often supported by fieldwork, and are sources of numerous books and reports.

Much of this publicity is constructively critical (unfortunately it is sometimes also rather meddlesome and pedantic). Targets include the Netherlands aid programme, the role of business, the human rights record, the attitudes of the North in UN dialogues, the adverse effects of aid on poverty groups and the linkages between the rich countries and the elites in developing countries.

Observing the present pattern of public opinion and the influence exerted by information and education of the public, it seems justified to conclude that Third World issues have now reached a high level of awareness in the Netherlands. One can say that interest in the Third World is a broadly based though perhaps not deeply rooted phenomenon of general public opinion; and that among public opinion leaders and policy-makers' concern with the Third World has become an attitudinal characteristic which will not be easily eroded by the vicissitudes of international developments although the way in which that concern translates into policy views will evolve over time. (Some recent evolutions are discussed in 'Some Current Issues'.)

Policy Formulation

Dutch cabinets are coalition cabinets in which policy formulation is a joint process. The Minister for Development Co-operation has primary responsibility for aid and has, particularly since the change of government in 1973, an increasing influence in other relations with the Third World. The exercise of this influence is facilitated by his integration into the Ministry of Foreign Affairs which provides him with a large and capable staff, gives him direct access to the embassises where development assistance co-ordinators are being stationed and protects him from the isolation experienced by some ministers for development co-operation in other countries. The fact that he does not have a Ministry of his own does not negatively affect his position within the

Cabinet. On the contrary, the post has proved attractive to some very active politicians. This naturally reflects the public interest in Third World issues but also the fact that he can exert considerable influence on Cabinet decisions regarding subjects that come under the direct responsibility of other Ministers. And he has a lot of money to spend: a potent factor in the bureaucratic in-fighting that seems common to all administrations.

Parliament devotes much attention to development issues and both Chambers have special committees. Differences in basic outlook among the larger parties are minimal – they all devote extensive paragraphs of their manifestos or programmes to Third World issues. They all support the development assistance targets and, in the typically Dutch political configuration, they each have close affinities to some 'interest groups' that are supported by funds from the development budget. Several of the research institutes attached to the major parties have come out with basic policy papers on Third World affairs. Diversities among the parliamentary groups arise mainly on political issues (Chile, Cuba, South Africa, Zimbabwe-Rhodesia) in which the Minister for Foreign Affairs will also be involved and on the relation between development assistance and commercial interests. Although parliamentary discussions are detailed and conducted with gusto,[19] there appears to be a much larger basic consensus than in many other countries. A long-standing practice of inviting parliamentarians to act as observers or even delegation members in certain UN conferences, though generating some questions of accountability, is generally considered helpful in basing the dialogue between Cabinet and Parliament on relevant international issues.

Policy formulation is supported by discussions in the National Advisory Council for Development Cooperation (NAR). The Council, created in 1964 with Jan Tinbergen as its first Chairman, now has some 70 members which include church and missionary representatives, university professors, business and trade union representatives, development workers, journalists and scientists – in fact, all the major interest groups identified earlier are represented. Through working groups, the Council prepares comprehensive and professional recommendations.[20] These recommendations as well as possible minority opinions are thoroughly discussed between the Minister and selected council members and play a useful role as inputs into policy-making by government and Parliament.

Influence on policy formulation by the large 'constituency' of groupings interested in Third World issues requires special mention. This influence is partly institutionalized by their – mostly indirect –

participation in the NAR. They also find their special fields of interest well served by the 'awareness-raising' activities of the NCO within the country and by the programme for co-financing of field activities in developing countries. But their concern extends beyond their parochial interests and expresses itself in 'actions', congresses, policy statements and critical representations that force the government to be continuously 'on its toes' and to engage in dialogues that are less institutionalized. A typical example is an open letter dated 8 November 1978 addressed to the Minister for Development Cooperation by the Workgroup Church and Development Cooperation of the Dutch Council of Churches in which his policies and intentions were strongly questioned. After a discussion with the Workgroup, the Minister defended his position in an equally strongly worded letter of 1 February 1979. Both documents were published by the Information Service. Such representations are not limited to the field of development assistance but are also directed to other elements of North-South relations. The government does not shun the wider dialogue. This is witnessed, for instance, by its support for a large seminar held in the Netherlands by the International Foundation for Development Alternatives (IFDA) in July 1979.

Finally, policy formulation is, both in timing and content, linked to the agenda of international consultations. The Dutch system of preparation, negotiation, reporting, etc., is similar to that in other countries. Some special features (contact with 'like-minded' countries, efforts to influence the policies of other developed countries through EEC and OECD/DAC, 'spearhead' function and 'starter' contributions) have been mentioned earlier. What could, however, distinguish the Netherlands from some other developed countries is that the atmosphere of the international dialogue and the issues arising at specific moments are almost instantly and strongly reflected in the national policy formulation process, due to the pervasive information network and active participation in the international dialogue by the different groups mentioned above, that are instrumental in shaping Dutch policies.

Summarizing, the Dutch scene is characterized by a strongly institutionalized form of policy formulation in which interest groups participate fully as well as by inputs through less institutionalized channels from groups and individuals concerned with Third World issues and quite vocal in expressing their views.

Some Current Issues

In this section, two subjects are discussed as an illustration of the way in which Dutch policies with regard to North-South relations have developed, and an effort is made to evaluate the positions taken by the government to meet the challenges presented in each case. In the first case the challenge has mainly been to find a solution for the conflicting interests of Dutch industry and LDC exporters. In the second case, Dutch attitudes are evaluated with regard to the probems that a poverty-oriented development policy may encounter nationally and internationally.

Structural Adjustments to Imports of Manufactures from LDCs

One of the imporant LDC demands under the NIEO is for increased access of manufactures to Northern markets. Basically the Netherlands accepts that demand. The Centre for the Promotion of Imports from Developing Countries is an offspring of this view.[21] The need for the industrialized countries to adjust their own productions accordingly is also recognized. Industrial adjustment is, of course, a continuous and general process responding to the forces of competition and the opportunities of technological innovation. The Netherlands economy has shown great adaptability to post-war challenges resulting from the OEEC/OECD liberalizations and European integration.

Low cost imports of manufactures from developing countries are a minor factor in this process of adaptation. In 1976 they represented only approximately 3.9 per cent (SITC 5-8 excl. 68) of total imports compared to an OECD total of 11.5 per cent, although their share tends to grow faster in the Netherlands than in other OECD countries (9 per cent over 1967-75 compared to an overall OECD figure of 6 per cent).

Several factors are, however, responsible for the growing concern over LDC imports, small as they are. They occur in sensitive sectors — for instance textiles, clothing and leather goods — which are labour intensive, employing vulnerable groups and operating in relatively d,pressed regions. The effects have been compounded by their occurrence in a period of relative stagflation, which seriously limits the scope for reorientation. Compensation for losses in the internal markets by increased exports by the same sectors can only be partial. A review published by OECD in 1975 details the situation in the clothing industry,[22] and data in Budget document 1980 (Ch. V, Attachment 3, p. 82) shows the dramatic loss of employment in the above sectors (from 15.9 per cent of the labour force in 1965 to 7.6 per cent in 1977).

In 1973 the Government embarked upon a programme specifically designed to facilitate structural adjustment to LDC imports.[23] The Government's general policy for industrial adaptation through sector studies and assistance by the Netherlands Restructuring Company, was supplemented by special funds which could be used to take anticipatory restructuring measures in order to make room for growing LDC imports. The funds would help to finance reorganization, new machinery, retraining, etc. The experience with the programme has however been disappointing. By the end of 1978, only some $30 million had been committed mainly in the textile and related industries with limited amounts for the wood, cocoa and telecommunications industries. The reasons for this limited and rather unbalanced record are several.

First, it has been difficult to give practical effect to the concept that the assistance should anticipate rather than deal ex post with competitive LDC imports; the difficulty of finding alternative production and employment opportunities at a time of recession compounded this situation. Secondly, competition came not only or even mainly from LDCs but from industrialized countries, including Eastern Europe. Thirdly, the need to restructure industry in the face of cheap imports was not unique to the Netherlands. A co-ordinated policy in the EEC and, if possible, the OECD would be required; otherwise, phased out Dutch production capacity might simply be replaced by production in another developed country. Joint action is, however, difficult to achieve. Fourthly, the sector expertise required for determining the developmental aspects of projects was scarce. And, finally, it was found that decision-making by the business community in the field of restructuring is generally only marginally influenced by government policies.

In the light of these difficulties the programme has clearly not found the support in industry and in the trade unions needed for its success as a vigorous, separate and forward-looking instrument of development policy. It has certainly not assuaged all concerns felt by industry and particularly the trade unions in the face of factories closing down and workers becoming unemployed. Maybe the time was not yet ripe[24] for North-South solidarity to overcome trade unions' concerns for unemployment and industry's disbelief in anticipatory judgments. However this may be, the government has apparently felt the need for a change of emphasis (Budget Message, 1980) in two directions. In the first place, support will be given to policies for industrial restructuring in the context of the EEC[25] and the OECD and to consultations and sectorwise research in UNIDO aimed at identifying opportunities for

LDC industrialization and access to DC-markets. In the second place, the size of the Dutch restructuring programme will be reduced; at the same time firms in sectors where a growth of the LDC market share is foreseen will be eligible for assistance in developing investment projects in LDCs through the Netherlands Finance Company for Developing Countries (FMO). It is clear that these policy intentions will have to be worked out in detail before their potential success can be judged.

Poverty Orientation

The emphasis on poverty alleviation in development policy — to which Robert McNamara's 1973 address to the World Bank Governors gave strong impetus — while justified and valuable, also raises issues that can become controversial. In a comprehensive memorandum of September 1976[26] the government indicated its decision to concentrate bilateral assistance on the alleviation of poverty. The consequences of this decision in two areas are reviewed hereafter as well as the refinements which the new government, while accepting the 1976 memorandum as the basis for its own programme, introduced on the occasion of the submission of the 1980 budget.[27] These two areas are: the selection of the countries upon which to concentrate bilateral assistance; and the identification of target groups.

With regard to the selection of 'concentration' countries, the 1976 memorandum added a third criterion, next to the degree of poverty of the country and the actual need for external assistance, formulated as follows: 'whether the country pursues a policy which mainly benefits the poorest. (Or, whether there is a social and political structure which offers this prospect . . .)[28] With regard to 'poverty target groups' the 1980 memorandum explains how the quality of bilateral aid can be improved and directed to those most in need of it.

Rather than review the two memoranda which go into considerable detail, a few questions will be raised to indicate some problems that may occur in the implementation of this policy.

(1) With regard to *country selection* two sets of questions arise:

(a) Is it possible to limit assistance to the countries that fulfil all three criteria, and can 'objective' criteria be developed and applied that permit clear choices?

Since the 1976 memorandum was written, it has become clear that the addition of the third criterion has not led to great changes in the existing list of concentration countries. The need for continuity in the programme proved strong. Only some countries were added on the basis of one third criterion; some were removed, but more for political reasons or because they no longer belonged to the poorest than because they did not fulfil the third criterion.[29] In retrospect a former minister remarked that there are 'in a concentration country many opportunities to honour in a differentiated way the measure to which the several criteria are fulfilled'.[30] The 1980 memorandum seems to confirm this view by assuming that the close association with concentration countries will permit the government to adapt its aid instruments to each recipient's special 'ranking' on the ladder of criteria. In fact, selection of concentration countries will probably never be an objective process: and the element of judgement by the donor will remain preponderant, including political judgement reflecting the donor's views on a country's principles and practices of self-reliance, social restructuring, growth and poverty alleviation.

(b) How will a recipient country react to the process of being subjected to this sort of judgement? And, on the other hand, what instruments has one individual donor to judge and influence a recipient's policies; in other words: how will a donor government balance the need to answer criticisms from its own Parliament, action groups, etc. with the respect due to sovereign partners who alone can weigh the competing forces determining their policy options?

Again, the 1980 memorandum shows confidence that a donor can with impunity discuss such issues with a recipient; but one wonders whether this optimism is fully justified in view of the sensitivities of recipient countries, the tendencies towards critical postures in some Dutch circles and the extreme complexities of the issues. Fortunately for the Netherlands, most of the concentration countries have consortia or consultative groups in which policies are discussed multilaterally on the basis of country expertise which far surpasses the expertise that a small donor can master, whereas one can also rely on the valuable multilateral reports of the World Bank, ILO, WHO, etc. Multilateral forums like consortia are also more appropriate to assess whether a recipient country is not only nominally professing the principles that, in the Dutch view, would qualify it for assistance but is actually taking measures towards poverty alleviation and socio-political restructuring in a dedicated, realistic and consistent manner.

Incidentally, the above questions can also be seen in a worldwide context: one wonders whether the whole complex of implementation by individual countries — both 'donors' and 'recipients' — of the UN development strategies which now escapes all but the most cursory review could not be brought into focus by a system of group-wise analysis and discussion analogous to the consortium/consultative group concept or, otherwise, on a regional basis.)

(2) With regard to the concept of 'target groups' the main questions are how to design and implement poverty-oriented projects for target groups and how, within a policy of priority for poverty alleviation, assistance can be justified that is not specially directed to such target groups.

(a) Poverty-oriented projects are complex and require larger and better trained staff[31] as well as more expertise for project preparation and implementation. Although the Netherlands has large reservoirs of expertise in relevant sectors (agriculture, water supply, tropical hygiene, etc.) the more crucial sociological aspects of addressing poverty groups cannot readily be covered by Western educated experts. The use of non-governmental intermediaries as intended by the government may help, but only partly. Evaluation of results in terms of poverty allevia-tion is equally complex; the need for such evaluation is politically more evident than under the policy of the late 1960s and early 1970s which relied mainly on the recipient's own list of priority projects and did not pretend to 'second guess' so much the recipient's policies. And the loftier the aim of poverty alleviation, the more difficult will it be to prove 'success' through evaluation and the easier it will be for critics at home to come up with stories of cases where aid has benefited the rich rather than the poor.

The 1980 memorandum sounds a note of realism in this respect: it would be an impossible demand that all advantages would accrue to the target groups, because richer groups will almost always profit from the assistance. The memorandum therefore considers a project acceptable if at least 50 per cent of its advantages benefit the target group.

(b) The complexities of projects directly benefiting target groups and the time-consuming process of detailed consultations with recipients for the preparation of these often small-scale projects will make it practically impossible to spend the high amounts in the development budget solely on such projects, even when the local curr-ency and recurring costs portions would be dramatically increased (which is however unlikely in view of the pressure exercised by export interested groups in these times of slackness at home). For these reasons, and in response to LDC wishes as well as donor interests in continuity and commercial relations, support for 'traditional' projects would have to continue. This conclusion is however opposed by those purists who, more or less dogmatically, hold that traditional assistance must be abolished (even if that would imply a sizable reduction of total

flows) because experience has, in their opinion, taught that it only aggravates inequality.[32] This criticism has been countered by the government which maintains that, in line with its 'two pronged' theory (see note 15), alleviating poverty and satisfying basic needs are only possible under conditions of sufficient growth for which 'traditional' resource transfers remain vital. How to ensure, however, that assistance not specifically directed to target groups will still be in line with the 1976 policy to make all bilateral aid poverty-oriented? The 1980 memorandum goes a step further than just asserting that assistance of this nature, while intended to strengthen the self reliance of the recipients, will be mainly given to countries with an acceptable social policy – the third criterion – and thus have a better chance to affect the poverty groups positively. It explains that in each case careful analysis and choice should ensure that even if more than half of the advantages from the assistance will benefit other than the poorest groups, these groups will in the long run not be worse off in absolute terms. It then goes into considerable detail on the elements to be taken into account.

(3) Reviewing these policy guidelines and their detailed elaboration one cannot but wonder whether the desire to respond by all means to the public concern about poverty orientation in matters of development assistance has not led to an almost unworkable pattern of cumbersome procedures and specious considerations (like, for instance, the 50 per cent criterion) and has not created a thick layer of considerations which only the highly sophisticated and initiated can penetrate. And will the results really satisfy that public concern? Or is there an inherent risk of disenchantment, precisely because the Dutch are generally too sceptical to accept success stories on their face value and too dogmatic to take the pronounced high principles of policy with a grain of salt?

One also wonders whether the confidence is justified that the intensive discussions that the government envisages with each recipient about its internal policies – and about the room these permit for pursuing the donor's aims of poverty-oriented assistance – will not lay considerable stress on donor-recipient relations. It is to be remembered that Third World countries basically resent interference in internal policies and have vented their suspicions that the poverty argument is a ploy to distract attention from the failure of at least some donors to reach the aid targets (see Ambassador Akhund's carefully worded intervention in OECD, May 1979 issue of the OECD *Observer*). Maybe a small donor like the Netherlands with an acceptable level of aid will escape such suspicion, but, on the other hand, its clout is very limited and the time and attention a recipient government can give to all sorts of intricacies advanced by a small donor are also finite.

(4) A final point can be raised about the relation between poverty-oriented policies and the proposals for a NIEO. As said before, a trend towards more attention for structural issues in North-South relations is noted in Dutch public opinion, now that the implications of the UN development strategies are better understood and, at the same time, the subject of the volume of development assistance provided by the country has lost priority interest. Will the turn to poverty-oriented development assistance also extend to the issues of structural changes in the international order in the sense that such changes should be considered acceptable only if they specifically help the poor countries and the poorest in those countries?

Basically this would seem a logical conclusion for a government which has decided that development makes little or no sense if it aggravates inequalities and leaves the poor in poverty. But it will be difficult to find proper instruments for selective action in favour of the poorest in those fields which are at the core of the NIEO discussion.[33] Commodity agreements, access to markets for manufactures and fairer tariff structures can hardly discriminate in favour of the poorer countries. Also, they will in fact often be more advantageous for the modern sector in developing countries and thus, depending on internal policies, penalize the poverty groups. Is that a reason not to pursue such measures? Only the 'purists' may draw that extreme conclusion. The Netherlands government is certainly not of that view. On the contrary, the 1980 memorandum on development co-operation[34] is, in its advocacy of structural measures to strengthen the economic self reliance of developing countries, quite open about the tensions that can arise between the two 'prongs' of its development policy: one approach in favour of increased self reliance (whether by the promotion of structural changes or by the provision of the type of assistance indicated above) and the other approach in favour of the poorest. While clearly hoping that the two approaches can often be made to run parallel ('agreements for commodities of special interest to the poorest countries'; but examples are not very convincing, and in other policy areas few opportunities are mentioned), the ultimate word is that structural measures must be judged on their own merits taking account of LDC wishes. That opens the door to an impressive list of policy declarations about structural change. Space unfortunately does not allow us to explore here the viability of all these declarations and their underlying assumptions.

(5) In summary, one may conclude that the Dutch position on 'poverty' discussed in this section reflects some of the basic attitudes and interests of the Netherlands in regard to Third World development as described in the previous sections:

(a) The pronounced commitment to the alleviation of poverty is clearly akin to the moral/humanistic justifications that the general public gives for development assistance. Although this policy orientation has perhaps sharpened the divergencies of view on development models, which the 'two-pronged' theory may not be able to paper over fully, that theory may nevertheless provide the government with a politically viable framework to continue a policy which combines a large aid effort with a programme directed at structural change.

(b) The detailed and intense search for procedures and criteria expected to guarantee that the benefits of bilateral assistance will indeed reach the poor reflects the need for the government to face close scrutiny of its actions, as well as a general Dutch tendency towards perfectionism coupled with the sophistication that a large 'aid constituency' (churches, academics, voluntary agencies) brings to bear.

(c) The fact that this assistance for the poor is being given only partly in untied form and that local currency financing is mentioned only sparsely may be linked to Dutch commercial interests.

(d) The decision to direct, in a 'two-pronged' approach, development assistance not only to poverty alleviation but also to structural change (even though structural change is mainly achieved through other measures than aid) can partly be linked to the political and commercial interest in continuous contacts with certain developing countries and to the need to use the available funds expeditiously. It is, however, also connected to the increased awareness of public opinon that 'development' is not just a poverty issue but concerns basic inequalities that have to be understood politically and approached structurally.

(e) The efforts to implement the poverty-oriented aid programme in continuous and intense discussions with the recipients may have something to do with missionary zeal, including its less attractive sides but is basically a reflection of the solidarity which the Dutch feel that, as a small nation with a special and progressive concept of world relations, they can and should exemplify.

Notes

1. The important effects of the 'loss' of Indonesia are discussed in the next section.

2. The export interests of the Netherlands are heavily concentrated upon its Community partners (70 per cent in 1978).

3. See also Joris J.C. Voorhoeve, *Peace, Profits and Principles* (Martinus Nijhoff, 1979), *passim.*

4. See for instance, on land tenure policies, Wolf Ladejinsky quoted in L. Walinsky (ed.), *Agrarian Reform as Unfinished Business*, World Bank (Oxford University Press, 1977), p. 58.

5. J.H. Boeke, *Economics and Economic Policy of Dual Societies* (New York, 1953), in which the author refers to his earlier work on 'dualistic economies' (1910) and the reconstruction of agricultural societies.

6. Some ten per cent of all Catholic missionaries are Dutch whereas only two per cent of the world's Catholics live in Holland; Protestant missionary work is continuing though less through involvement of expatriates than through support of local churches and organizations.

7. A ten-year programme of approximately $1.5 billion; budget 1979: $85 million, population approximately 400,000.

8. NAR Report No. 60, based on UN trade statistics, p. 7 and Table 3.

9. The situation with regard to the import of finished products from developing countries is further discussed under 'Some Current Issues'.

10. Data collected by the IDS at the University of Sussex.

11. OECD, *Investing in Developing Countries*, 4th revised edition (January 1979), Tables 5 and 9. See also, United Nations, 'Transnational Corporations in World Development. A Re-examination'. Document E/C10/38 dated 20 March 1978.

12. John A. Coleman, *The Evolution of Dutch Catholicism, 1958-1974* (Berkeley, 1978).

13. To name a few: Netherlands Economic Institute, Division of Balanced International Growth, Rotterdam,; Center for Development Planning, Rotterdam; Institute for the Study of Less Developed Countries, Amsterdam; Institute for Development Problems, Tilburg; Third World Center, Nijmegen; Center for World Food Studies, Amsterdam/Wageningen; International Agrarian Center, Wageningen.

14. See, for example, the Budget Messages over the period 1974-80, the memorandum on Bilateral Development Cooperation, 1976 and *Internationale Samenwerking*, all published by the Information Service for Development. See also Reports of the National Advisory Council, Netherlands submissions to the Development Assistance Committee of OECD and other literature quoted in the notes.

15. In this approach bilateral assistance can be used in two ways. On the one hand it can support a country in its efforts to develop its independence and thus reduce external inequalities. On the other hand the assistance directed to the poorer segments of the population of a given country would be designed to reduce specific internal inequalities. In this theory the two emancipation processes, the external as well as the internal one, should be promoted simultaneously: 'A two-pronged policy is needed which covers both macro economic structures and the fulfilment of basic needs . . . ' (Budget Message, 1979).

16. Netherlands Institute for Public Opinion, *Report to the National Committee for Information and Awareness-Raising on Development Cooperation* (October 1971); Netherlands Institute for Statistics, *Confidential Report on the Public Image of the Dutch Volunteer Foundation* (1976), p. 35; Government Information Service, *Reports* (1975, 1978).

17. 'Commentaries' on development policies during 1973-7 by a number of authors, including Bos, Corea, Emmery, Heldring, Tinbergen; with a postscript by Jan P. Pronk, *International Spectator* (September 1977), p. 533f.

18. A documentary magazine with up to 80 pages of articles (20,000 copies gratis), an illustrated semimonthly information periodical of some 20 pages (60,000 copies gratis) and more popular issues for high school students (30,000 bimonthly at $5 a year) and even for children aged 6-12 (500,000 copies gratis). For comparison: the largest Dutch general opinion weekly has about 150,000 subscribers; the largest economic weekly approximately 7,000.

19. In the budget discussions, 1979 the Minister had to reply to more than 200 detailed written questions.

20. Some 60 reports have been published on such diverse issues as: the aid programme, investment, trade, migrant workers, industrial restructuring, science and technology, stabilization of export earnings, indebtedness, EEC policies, acculturation, international education, the oil crisis, supranational decision-making, UNCTAD, etc.

21. The Centre for the Promotion of Imports from Developing Countries (CBI) in Rotterdam provides marketing information and assistance to LDC exporters and export organizations. The Centre acts, among other things, as a contact and display point, facilitates participation in trade fairs and organizes seminars. In 1980 about $3.5 million was made available as a government subsidy for these activities.

22. B. Evers, 'Industrial Adjustment in the Netherlands, with Special Emphasis on the Clothing Industry', *Adjustment for Trade: Studies on Industrial Adjustment Problems and Policies* (OECD, Paris), 1975.

23. Memorandum by the Ministers for Economic Affairs and for Development Cooperation, 9 December 1974 and Supplementary Memorandum, 7 November, 1975. For a detailed description, see UNCTAD, 'Adjustment Assistance Measures', (TD/B/C.2/171) (27 May 1977).

24. Louis Emmerij, 'No prophet is accepted in his own country', *Internationale Spectator* (September 1977), p. 580.

25. In a footnote on p. 43, NAR Report No. 60 ('Trade Policies and Developing Countries' of September 1978) some members (trade unionists and others) indicate the principles upon which a programme in the context of the EEC would have to be based. Among these are mentioned: internal democracy in the enterprise, mid-term planning with trade union co-operation, sharing of information and control of investments. An international reconversion fund might be created. These members also advocate that GATT should mandate compliance with ILO rules regarding safety conditions and employment (presumably in LDCs?) as well as the introduction of restructuring measures (presumably in DCs?) if employment opportunities are affected by international trade.

26. 'Memorandum on Bilateral Development Cooperation', Attachment 4 to the 1977 Budget (September 1976), published in English as *Information Brochure No. 12*.

27. 'Development Cooperation in Worldwide Economic Perspective', Information Service, Attachment 3 to the 1980 Budget (September 1979).

28. The Budget Message, 1979 reformulates and expands the selection criteria as follows: (a) the degree of poverty and the need for outside assistance; (b) the extent to which the recipient country pursues policies aimed at equitable distribution; and (c) the degree to which human rights are respected (published in English as *Information Brochure No. 15*, pp. 31-4).

29. The list of concentration countries for 1979 contains 17 countries: Bangladesh, Colombia, Cuba, Egypt, India, Indonesia, Jamaica, Kenya, North Yemen, Pakistan, Peru, Sri Lanka, Sudan, Tanzania, Tunisia, Upper Volta and

Zambia, from which Colombia, Cuba, Jamaica, Peru and Tunisia will be phased out, whereas the Sahel area will be brought into the same category as the concentration countries. Surinam and the Netherlands Antilles are in separate categories.

30. Pronk, 'Postscript' *Internationale Spectator*, p. 574.

31. Over a period of ten years the central staff of the ministry dealing with development co-operation increased by 50 per cent. It was furthermore decided recently to identify, and make provisions under the development budget for, staff in Embassies who devote more than 80 per cent of their time to development assistance programmes and projects: they will number some 70 professionals and 40 support staff.

32. There is little support for the even more dogmatic view (Wertheim and others) that aid – in any form – should be given to communist regimes only. For an interesting analysis of the 'target group' concept see L. de Jong and H.J. Tieleman, 'Dutch Support to Poor Countries and Groups; Good Intentions Don't Equal (Good) Policies', *Internationale Spectator* (1978), p. 527.

33. Some EEC measures help mainly the poorer countries (Stabex for instance) but only because most of the associated countries happen to be in that category. And Stabex, like the IMF Compensatory Financing Facility is essentially a form of development assistance, the terms of which can be adapted to the poverty (repayment capacity) of the country.

34. See note 27 and in particular the Introduction, point 3, about the two-pronged approach and Chapter IV about raw materials problems of developing countries.

9 INTERESTS OF SCANDINAVIAN COUNTRIES IN THIRD WORLD DEVELOPMENT*

Just Faaland and Ole David Koht Norbye

Background

Denmark, Norway and Sweden, which today have barely 17½ million people, are frequently referred to as the 'Scandinavian countries' as distinct from the Nordic countries which also include Finland and Iceland. Links between these countries and peoples have always been very close.

Geographically the three countries belong to the European periphery but they are nevertheless close enough to Europe's economic, political and cultural centres to be strongly influenced by mainstream developments in most fields of human activities. All three countries were neutral during the First World War, but Denmark and Norway were drawn into the Second World War through the German occupation in 1940, while Sweden remained neutral. This different experience explains in part Denmark's and Norway's decision to join NATO in 1949, while Sweden chose to remain neutral. The concern for neutrality was also behind Sweden's decision not to seek membership in the Euorpean Communities. Norway in the end remained outside the EEC for a variety of reasons which found their expression in a vote against full membership in a 1972 referendum, whereas the Danish voters having decided differently, Denmark has been an EEC member since 1973.

Endeavours to bring about closer Scandinavian co-operation have strong antecedents. Early in the post-war period the Nordic Council was established, with Finland and Iceland also as members. Close co-operation in defence policies proved impossible within this framework due to differences in the external political situation. Attempts to create a common Nordic market and a customs union failed for different reasons. *De facto*, as members of EFTA or the EEC and with trade agreements with the EEC, a common Nordic market exists for manufactured goods. In other fields of policy, social as well as cultural, there is extensive co-operation within the Nordic Council, and on a large number of foreign policy issues, not least relationships with the

279

Third World and United Nations matters, close consultations and co-operation take place between the five Nordic countries.

For 300 years up to the early part of the nineteenth century Sweden and Denmark-Norway were involved in European wars, more often than not on different sides. But with the end of the Napoleonic wars Scandinavia became a peaceful corner of Europe, albeit Denmark lost its southern provinces to Prussia half a century later. Norway gradually won its full independence through a period of union with Sweden which began with Napoleon's defeat and ended 90 years later. The long history of wars and dependence created a climate of mutual distrust and even dislike which, however, rapidly diminished against the background of common traditions and outlook.

Feudal structures were comparatively strong in Denmark and Sweden, but were never firmly established in the Norwegian 'periphery'. The languages grew somewhat more different over time, but not so different that people cannot understand each other in speech and writing. The move towards universal primary education and social services started early in all three countries, compared to most other European countries.

Strong popular movements developed rapidly in the course of the nineteenth century. Amongst these the trade unions and the socialist parties started relatively late, but became very powerful forces, and the social democratic parties have represented the strongest political movement in all three countries during the last half century. The introduction of progressive legislation started long before socialist governments took over to build comprehensive welfare state systems. The modernization of agriculture led to the establishment of strong co-operative marketing and processing organizations which have had a strong impact on social and economic developments in the three countries.

Economically, the three countries, and particularly Norway and Sweden, were relatively poor countries until the twentieth century. Poverty, shortage of agricultural land and widespread underemployment and open unemployment led to large scale emigration to overseas countries, mostly to the United States, from the first half of the last century until well into the twentieth. Mercantilist policies had encouraged the establishment of some manufacturing and mining in the seventeenth century, but industrialization and exports did not really gain ground until the 1800s. Foreign capital participated very actively in the creation of natural-resources based industries in Norway and Sweden, but enterprises owned by nationals also developed rapidly, particularly in Sweden. In Denmark, international trading enterprises made their contribution to economic development, while Norwegian entrepreneurship to a large extent went into shipping.

At the beginning of the Second World War the three countries had diversified, modern economies and their peoples had gradually climbed towards an average European level of income and standard of living. Since the war, all three countries have experienced rapid economic growth and today the Gross National Product *per capita* in Scandinavia is comparable to that of the four other richest industrialized countries (USA and Canada, Switzerland and West Germany).

In foreign transactions the three countries differ considerably. Exports of farm produce, primarily livestock products, are still an important part of Denmark's foreign earnings, and so are earnings from international trading. For Norway, fish, forest products, metals and chemical fertilizers and incomes from shipping continue to represent sizeable proportions of the total export revenue, while forest, metal and engineering products remain the cornerstones of Sweden's export trade. But in all three countries 'non-traditional' exports have increased many times, in part as a direct result of closer integration in the European and world economies through trade liberalization and memberships in EFTA and the EEC. Thus in Denmark, exports of manufactures are now higher than agricultural exports, and the predominance of semi-processed raw materials in Norway's export trade is substantially reduced.

At present the general socio-economic situation in each of the Scandinavian countries is similar albeit by no means identical. The welfare state is well established but appears to have created a backlash that has weakened the social democratic parties and led to a conservative revival. Also, there are the beginnings of a reaction (at least verbally and vocally) against the emphasis on material welfare and a search for new values and more concern for 'the quality of life'. International developments have led to a considerable slowdown of the steady economic progress to which the Scandinavians had become accustomed. Although international stagflation and the threatening energy crisis would in any case have caused difficulties, the fact that Scandinavian industrial wages are amongst the highest in the world means that industrial enterprises are particularly strongly exposed to the current economic crisis and to competition from manufacturers in countries with far lower wages. Third World competitors are increasingly regarded as a special threat to employment in Scandinavia. The established positive attitude to North-South relationships may begin to come under pressure.

In Scandinavian countries the knowledge of peoples and conditions in the Third World was neither widespread nor profound until modern mass media started to have their full impact. One reason for this is that Scandinavia did not take part in the race for colonies in the nineteenth century. (However, Denmark did keep its ancient, small possessions in Africa towards the middle of the nineteenth century, and in the Caribbean Sea until the beginning of this century; Greenland with a population of about 40,000 remains a very special case.) Contact with former colonies in the South has therefore had very little influence on knowledge and attitudes; other sources of information have been far more influential.

First, Christian missions were established in widely different parts of the world, and contacts are close between the missionaries and the voluntary associations that support their activity. The impact of mission work has been mixed. Its primary purpose is to spread the faith and thus to 'save' the people of the world. Perhaps inevitably, the missionary goal has been extended also to non-religious activities in the poor countries. This has clearly contributed to the somewhat paternalistic attitude towards the South that prevails in wide circles in Scandinavia.

Secondly, many Scandinavians have been working in far away countries, have settled there or have travelled widely as part of their work. While emigrants from Scandinavia mostly settled in the USA and in parts of the 'white' Commonwealth, quite a few ended up in more 'exotic' places and there was a feedback from these emigrants to the home countries. Businessmen established themselves in different parts of the world. The Danish East Asiatic Company is an example of large scale business involvement in the Third World. Also, all three countries, but in particular Norway, have for generations had large merchant fleets which have carried goods between all parts of the world. The sailors obtained a very superficial view of the countries they visited, mainly based on shabby and shady port districts, and their opinions of peoples and conditions were very biased. On the whole these kinds of contacts have tended to create prejudices rather than a wider understanding of the realities of the Third World.

Thirdly, as literacy has been widespread for many generations, quite a few people had learned about the South through reading; explorers like Livingstone and Stanley, and 'heroes' like General Gordon were familiar names. Unfortunately, this kind of reading tended to strengthen rather than correct the prejudices that followed from the more direct, personal involvement.

A major countervailing force springs from the general humanitarian tradition in Scandinavia and from the extension of principles of human rights and social justice to the world at large. Being outside the great power orbit, the Scandinavian 'elite' tended to be critical of the power politics of the mighty both inside Europe and in other parts of the world. Some sought information and insight beyond the observations of missionaries, businessmen, emigrants and sailors. This contributed to forming a more balanced view amongst the more educated, particularly amongst progressive and radical people who were critical also of conditions in their own countries.

Such 'elitist' opinions were conditioned by European perceptions and experiences embodied in the development of European social philosophy during the last 200 years; to a very limited extent only are they based on direct interaction with, knowledge of and respect for peoples of the Third World who in their different ways have their own traditions and values, different from those of the Scandinavian elite itself. As a result, paternalism, intolerance, impatience and even arrogance quite often surface as characteristic attributes of Scandinavians who articulate progressive ideologies with respect to developments in the Third World.

Interest in the Third World tends to be concentrated on certain countries and regions. This is reflected in the concentration of bilateral development assistance on a limited number of co-operating countries. Reasons advanced for such concentration include considerations of administrative efficiency, as well as familiarity, whether through business contacts or the missions, and general political or humanitarian interests focused on particular countries or regions. Also the use of English as an official language makes it far easier for Scandinavians to work in former British-dominated regions of the Third World. Nevertheless, Portugal's former colonies have become important areas for Scandinavian activities. The liberation of former colonies from European powers was followed with great interest and approval. The provision of assistance to the newly independent nations was, therefore, a logical consequence of the ideological support of them during their fight for independence.

To some extent different views held by Scandinavians towards peoples of the Third World tend to converge as regards practical conclusions. While many people may think of Third World people as weak, and generally unable to perform in the same manner as Scandinavians, nevertheless they feel prepared to try to help the 'underdog'. At the same time, a strong elitist view, both more sophisticated and more optimistic, seeks to articulate the scope for socio-economic development, provided some of the man-made barriers which constrain Third World development are removed.

Policy Approaches Towards the Third World

In recent years, Scandinavian governments have more readily accepted demands by developing countries for a New International Economic Order than have most of the other industrialized countries. The Danish position is to some extent influenced and constrained by membership in the European Community.

The most noticeable achievement is the success in all three countries in raising official development assistance (ODA) up to and above the long-standing UN target level of 0.7 per cent of Gross National Product: in recent years it has been reached by no other industrial nation except the Netherlands. Moreover, the Scandinavian countries have also given positive responses to other Third World claims and have at times tried, although in vain, to build bridges between inflexible positions of large industrialized OECD countries and of developing countries.

In the opinion of many analysts these positions on the part of the Scandinavian countries are better explained as an outcome of social and political forces in the three countries, than as a reflection of perceived national interests in the development of the Third World. The ideology of equality and the concern for social justice appears to be stronger in Scandinavia than in most other countries which have built welfare states.[1] The nature and strength of this ideology has, of course, developed gradually. It is linked not only to the mass mobilization of workers, but also — and earlier — to the mobilization of small farmers and peasants. In spite of the existence of a strong class of nobility in Sweden, peasants were mostly free men, and so they were in Norway, in the virtual absence of a feudal system: in these countries farmers gained and extended their political power gradually, over a long period. In Denmark, however, the structure of the society was such that the peasantry remained under control of large landowners right up to the introduction of representative democracy in the middle of the nineteenth century. Then, however, the peasants were quickly mobilized into political action.[2] In all three countries the farmers raised their economic and social status through political and other organizational action, and this was followed by the successful mobilization of the workers in trade unions and social democratic parties. Religious movements complemented in many respects the rise of the peasants and workers. In the formerly poor Scandinavian countries there was little or no opportunity for the individual to become economically and financially successful by his own energy and enterprise alone – as was considered to be the case in the United States – and the right to more equity and social justice became firmly embedded in the ideology of the growing popular movements in Scandinavia.

By the mid-1960s, after a couple of decades of rapid economic growth and building up of welfare societies that eliminated dire poverty and glaring social injustices, time seemed to be ripe for the Scandinavian peoples to take an active interest in the poor in other parts of the world. It is quite evident that the initiative and drive came from a comparatively small elite in the political parties, in a great variety of organizations and in the academic world.

Another element should be stressed. The Scandinavians have long been interested in closer international co-operation, and gave the League of Nations strong support between the wars, and the United Nations after the war. There is a clear self-interest in this attitude: small nations cannot have any influence in a world dominated by great powers, but they can make themselves felt in international organizations where they can speak, vote and act as full and equal members. To the extent that the United Nations took decisions on policies in favour of the Third World, the Scandinavians wanted to take these decisions in earnest, not merely in order to assist the developing countries, but also to build up the image, strength and authority of the United Nations.

In the post-war period the Scandinavian governments also became more active in their foreign policies than they had been before the war. There was no way back to a passive policy of neutrality after the traumatic experience of the war. The interest in making the United Nations successful as a peacekeeping organization was very strong. It quickly became accepted doctrine that unstable and unrepresentative governments in poor countries might represent a special threat to world peace. At least for the foreign policy-makers the need for economic and social development in the Third World was seen as an international concern.

These factors, including their 'elitist' origin and direction, must be taken into consideration for an understanding of the near unanimous support of developing countries, particularly for development assistance, within the leadership of political parties and popular organizations. The 'establishment' took the lead, but their initiatives have been accepted by people as is shown by most opinion polls which have been undertaken. Typically, the only major party that is against development assistance is the Danish 'progressive party' which is an anti-tax 'welfare backlash' party. For the rest, there may be disagreement between the political parties as regards some aspects of development assistance, mainly as regards choice of countries to which bilateral assistance should be given, but basically there is broad political consensus behind development co-operation policies in the three Scandinavian countries.

Attitudes to development assistance provide the most explicit illustration of the willingness of the Scandinavian peoples and governments to do something positive for the Third World. In the course of the 13-year period 1965 to 1978,[3] the percentage of GNP devoted to official development assistance was raised from 0.13 to 0.75 per cent in Denmark, from 0.16 to 0.90 per cent in Norway and from 0.19 to 0.90 per cent in Sweden. In official documents from the three countries it is stressed for example that solidarity with poor people in the Third World is a sufficient motivation for a large Swedish programme of development assistance,[4] and in the case of Norway: 'today we must first of all look at cooperation with developing countries as a question of international solidarity.'[5] In Danish documents this view is not put forward with equal strengh, but it is clearly also an essential part of Danish motivation for development assistance.[6]

Such official justification supports our contention that the main reason for the Scandinavian position on development assistance is the general acceptance of the view that the ideas of equity and social justice as applied domestically also in some measure should apply to the world as a whole. Granted, official justifications may also in some measure be just a cover for underlying vested interests. Yet, the official justification is at least evidence of what the political establishment considers to be the best argument to be given to the electorate.[7]

Other justifications are also referred to in the official documents. Self-interest is of course not absent, including reference to the fact that development of the Third World may create larger markets for exports from Scandinavian industries. In Denmark, perhaps more than in Norway and Sweden, it has been stressed during parliamentary debates that domestic industries and exporters ought to be given greater opportunities. In our evaluation such interests are a growing, but still hardly a determining factor, at least not in Norway and Sweden. The aid programmes remain untied to a large extent, so that the returns to domestic business interests from the aid programmes also remain at best indirect and uncertain.[8,9]

Norwegian and Swedish official documents repeatedly refer to the presumed positive contribution of assistance to international peace and security. The Norwegian White Paper on the subject refers to purely humanitarian reasons as a supporting argument in favour of development assistance. A Swedish official document refers to the growing interdependence in the world economy. The argument that the use of aid is a means to obtain power and influence in the world is naturally completely absent.[10]

Cultural factors probably play a minor role, although a couple of points should be mentioned. Part of Scandinavian development assistance, particularly in Norway, is channelled through non-governmental organisations, including Christian mission societies. This will certainly have some cultural impact, and is bound to strengthen local support for development aid. However, the main reason advanced for channelling aid through such organizations is that private organizations – in view of their practical experience and availability of field staff – are better able to handle certain forms of assistance. At least in Norway the belief that certain target groups can be reached more easily through private organizations has also played an important role. The other point is that the Scandinavian peoples and governments undoubtedly like to see 'like-minded' democratic societies develop in the Third World. Norwegian assistance in the 1970s to countries like Jamaica, Portugal and Turkey was undoubtedly influenced by the desire to help keep fragile democracies going.

There is an uneasy awareness in Scandinavia that development priorities in quite a few poor countries are wrong, that their planning leads to better conditions for the rich and little if any improvement for the poor, and that aid money even to poor countries makes the rich richer and the poor poorer. The ideas behind the 'basic needs' strategy have strong support in the Scandinavian countries, and there is a tendency to regard aid as a means to exercise pressure on the receiving countries to adjust their priorities and plans accordingly. So far the Scandinavian governments have largely abstained from applying such pressure. Instead they have sought to direct ODA to developing countries which explicitly aim to ensure a wide distribution of the benefits of economic growth. However, a glance at the list of recipient countries of Scandinavian ODA shows that several of these hardly can be characterized as particularly 'progressive' in their economic and social policies. This is not lost on critical observers, and criticism on this score may well increase over time. In our judgement the call for more effective basic needs policies may well become more vocal, and may influence attitudes also to the NIEO in general.

The basic premiss for Scandinavian support to the developing world, through development assistance and through a positive attitude to the demand for a NIEO, is international solidarity and social justice. But the solidarity applies to people – poor people – and not necessarily to nations even if they are poor; and social justice only concerns people, not nations. For that reason basic needs policies may have a fundamental impact on attitudes in Scandinavia. Scandinavians think of ODA in terms of a basic interest in assisting poor people, and of course also in terms of establishing a better functioning world. But they have difficulties in seeing a better functioning world emerging if poverty is not effectively eradicated within a reasonable span of time.

Opinion polls undertaken in Scandinavian countries show that there is a solid majority of the population who accept tax-financed development assistance at the level which was reached when the question was put. In general, however, only a fairly small minority wanted more development assistance. It is interesting to note, though, that at least in the case of Norway, three polls taken during a period when the assistance was increased several times (1972, 1974 and 1977), show that the number of people who thought the amount was reasonable (and also those who wanted more aid) remained practically constant. In other words, the electorate appears to accept the increases decided by politicians although there was no popular demand for them in advance.

All three Norwegian polls in the 1970s showed that about five out of six people felt it as a *duty to give assistance as long as people were suffering in developing countries*, three out of four people believed that *assistance contributes to progress even if there are many disappointing experiences*, and about three out of five people considered *development aid as an important step to prevent war*. These were the three statements out of ten that most people agreed with when asked by the pollsters. They indicate that popular support, for the moment at least, is reasonably firmly based. The support for development assistance which this indicates will hardly change overnight, and it is particularly noteworthy that disappointments do not seem to undermine the belief in the positive effects of development assistance. This is at variance with experience in several other rich countries, where frustration with unsuccessful results of development aid are advanced as major reasons for not being prepared to increase aid. However, such frustration may have been caused by unrealistic expectations, including the expectation that friends could be bought through aid. As the Scandinavian public has never been told that aid can buy political friendship, it does not have the same feeling of frustration when established aid relationships turn sour.

The NIEO contains many elements besides ODA; however, these have not been analyzed to the same extent in official documents, nor have they been subjected to public opinion research as systematically as has development assistance. Therefore, much less is known about official justifications of positions taken or the reaction of the general public to these other elements. Yet there appears to be broad understanding and acceptance in official circles for the claims of developing countries for changes in the rules governing international economic transactions.

Again, official positions in respect of NIEO are reflections of domestic experience in Scandinavia. The NIEO is seen as in many respects a somewhat curious mixture of adherence to a free trade philosophy and demands for international control of the market mechanism and even for planning internationally. In the field of manufactured goods developing countries put the emphasis on freer access to markets in rich countries; while they reserve themselves the right of protecting their own markets against foreign competition. In the field of raw materials, however, the demand is for international arrangements (the Common Fund) to control the market mechanism.

The Scandinavian countries have developed large exports of manufactured goods under reasonably free trade conditions, and have founded much of their prosperity on precisely these opportunities. They can therefore well accept in principle that it is only fair that the Third World too should be able to benefit from free trade in manufactures. As regards raw materials, the bulk of these are agricultural products, and both Norway and Sweden have interfered considerably with the free market mechanism in order to ensure stable and equitable earnings for the producers; all three countries have highly organized marketing arrangements for farm products. It is therefore in no way regarded as something strange, or contrary to prevailing domestic philosophy, to introduce more orderly marketing arrangements internationally especially for agricultural products.[11]

As regards the Third World's claim for sovereignty over its natural resources, this is well understood particularly in Norway where laws to protect national natural resources against unfettered exploitation by foreign firms were systematically introduced in the early years of this century.

Other aspects of the proposed NIEO cannot in the same way be related to domestic experiences; the conditions for technology transfer are a case in point. Others are in conflict with old perceptions, as well as with economic interests; shipping is a good example. For the Scandinavian countries the freedom of the seas has offered the opportunity for the development of merchant fleets which have had the whole world as their basis of operation, and international regulation of access to freight goods and passengers, even for the benefit of the developing countries, is in conflict with past experience; such regulation is clearly also contrary to strongly entrenched special interests.

While, therefore, Scandinavian governments do not accept the NIEO demands without some reservation and hesitation, modifications of the existing system of international trade and other transactions are seen as being needed in order to give the Third World its chance. The critical problem is what modifications to introduce. Here the logic of ideological acceptance of the principles of justice and equity sometimes runs into a head-on collision with vested interests in the Scandinavian countries.

Economic Interests in Third World Development

Natural Resources

Taken together, the three countries are well endowed with natural resources in relation to the size of their populations. This applies to agricultural land, forests, fishing grounds and mineral deposits as well as to domestic energy sources. The geographical distribution of the resources is, however, very uneven. In many instances what is lacking in one country is available in one of the neighbouring countries. However, imports into Scandinavia are necessary for a number of essential minerals, of some fuels and, of course, of tropical and semi-tropical foods and beverages. As the region is a large net exporter of several commodities such as livestock products, fish, forest products and some ores, it has common interests with other raw-material producing countries in high and stable commodity prices.

Cultivated agricultural land covers two-thirds of the area in Denmark but only two to three per cent in Norway. Productive forests vary from ten per cent of the total land area in Denmark to 60 per cent in Sweden. The annual fish catch of the Nordic countries has in recent years amounted to about one-tenth of the world total. Sweden has a large variety of mineral deposits (and there are some also in Norway), of which a few are of importance even in a world perspective; Denmark has virtually no minerals. Hydroelectric power, which is absent in Denmark, has been a dominant source of energy in Norway and Sweden. Until the recent discovery of oil in the North Sea, Scandinavia as a whole has relied heavily on imports of fossil fuels.

Traditionally, agriculture has been the most important source of livelihood in all three countries. Rapid growth in the industrial sector and improvements in productivity in farming in the course of the present century have reduced the contribution of agriculture to the national product and to employment to a few per cent. Climatic and geographical conditions make farming a high cost industry in large parts of Sweden and in virtually all of Norway. But agriculture is still essential to the pattern of rural settlement which plays a major role in Scandinavian economic planning and politics. The goal of maintaining viable rural communities, together with strategic and other non-economic considerations, is one reason why Norway and Sweden maintain a restrictive import policy towards food products in order to protect their high cost agriculture. The three Scandinavian countries taken together are net exporters of farm products, mainly because of Denmark's dominating position in this area. There are, however, great differences in the degree of self-sufficiency in the various geographical areas.

Population and Migration

If recent demographic trends continue, Scandinavia will be heading for a stationary population, in the absence of sizeable net immigration. The labour force is still growing slowly, but shorter working hours, longer holidays and earlier retirement age will certainly reduce the supply of labour, without net immigration. Given the likelihood of significant productivity increases in many economic activities, including service sectors, and with growth prospects uncertain, there is no obvious domestic economic need to favour immigration. There is free movement of labour between the Nordic countries (including Finland and Iceland), and from the other EEC countries to Denmark. As regards immigration from developing countries, Norway introduced in 1976 a temporary ban on immigration, which is still in force. At the time, the ban was justified by reference to the need to allow time to provide adequate housing and other facilities for immigrants. Under the present somewhat difficult employment conditions the ban appears likely to become more permanent than originally envisaged.

The Scandinavian populations are relatively homogeneous. At the end of 1977 the foreign population represented 1.8 per cent of the total population in both Denmark and Norway, and 5.2 per cent in

Sweden. Of this foreign population, immigrants from developing countries accounted for 30 per cent in Denmark, 18 per cent in Norway, but only nine per cent in Sweden, or around one-half per cent of the total population in each of the three countries. A very large proportion of the foreign population in Sweden was composed of Finns; Sweden also traditionally has had more Danes and Norwegians within its frontiers than there are Swedes in the two other Scandinavian countries. Again, mainly as a reflection of the large number of workers from Scandinavian neighbours, foreign workers represent a significant proportion of the labour force in Sweden (5.4 per cent in 1977, against, for example, 9.5 per cent in Germany, 7.3 per cent in France and 3 per cent in the Netherlands).

Gross immigration to Denmark from developing countries rose from 3,000 in 1966 (10 per cent of total immigration) to 5,500 in 1975 (20 per cent of total immigration). The corresponding figures for Norway were: 800 (seven per cent of total) in 1966 and 4,300 (22 per cent) in 1975; and for Sweden, 2,800 (six per cent of total) in 1966 and 5,800 (13 per cent) in 1975. In spite of immigration restrictions in Norway, immigration from developing countries still reached almost 4,000 (more than 20 per cent of total immigration) as late as in 1977. Reliable data on net migration are not available.

Scandinavian employers have tried to hire foreign workers for jobs which are difficult to fill with natives. However, thanks to strong trade union action (and in Denmark also minimum wage legislation) foreign workers are in general paid at the same rates as national workers. Sweden has perhaps gone furthest in protecting the rights of the foreigners. Thus in 1976 the rights, liberties and protection of foreign residents were included as an amendment to the Constitution, and the enfranchisement reform gave foreigners the right to vote and stand for election at the local and regional levels. Surveys of living conditions of migrants in Sweden show: 'that salaries differed very little between Swedes and foreigners, but the latter tended to have fewer reserve resources and bigger maintenance burdens. They are also more liable to be working in arduous jobs, in a difficult environment, to be on shift work, or have jobs that are below their educational standard. They are less likely to be in higher education and more likely to be in inferior housing.'[12]

In Sweden there is a 'somewhat disturbing trend towards racist attitudes (which) shows signs of developing among the native population'. This may also be true of Norway, perhaps less so of Denmark. On the whole, mass immigration to Scandinavia from distant lands of people from different cultures would probably create very considerable problems. As campaigns to collect money for suffering people in other parts of the world time and again have shown, Scandinavians stand ready to assist people with different cultures generously in their own countries, but they appear to be reluctant to have them as neighbours at home. Such reluctance notwithstanding, a significant number of political refugees from different parts of the world have been accommodated and even welcomed in Scandinavia.

Foreign Trade

The rather optimistic picture of the resource situation notwithstanding, the Scandinavian countries are not 'self-sufficient' in economic terms, as evidenced by their very extensive foreign trade. Through a high degree of specialization, partly based on available domestic raw materials and other resources, but partly on the ability of individual enterprises in goods and service producing industries to penetrate international markets, they have built up large export markets. To maintain and advance the present living standard in Scandinavian countries, a large proportion of their output − mainly processed food and industrial goods in addition to shipping services and other 'invisibles' − has to be exported in order to finance a high level of imports.

In relative terms trade with the Third World is nowadays comparatively modest, and represents merely about one-eighth of total foreign trade.[13] But it has to be remembered that as for most small countries foreign trade *per capita* is high in Scandinavia, and no less than 70 per cent of this trade is with the two free trade areas in Europe, EEC and EFTA.

Also, the trade between the Scandinavian countries, which is included under the EEC/EFTA trade, is very significant: 22 per cent of exports go to the two other Scandinavian countries and 18 per cent of imports come from these two almost domestic markets. The fact that imports from and exports to developing countries represent 'only' about 13 per cent of total exports and imports does not mean that this trade is insignificant − it represents after all between 40 and 45 per cent of all trade with countries outside the EEC/EFTA area. Moreover, in recent years the developing countries have been the fastest expanding markets for goods from the OECD countries: They contribute significantly to maintaining economic growth in the rich countries. In turn this creates better market conditions for Scandinavian goods in the OECD countries which buy more than 80 per cent of Scandinavian exports.

Exports are essential to many of the most important economic activities in Scandinavia. Most of the Norwegian merchant fleet carries freight exclusively between foreign countries, 40 per cent of the output of Swedish manufacturing industries is exported. To maintain and increase exports is therefore not only necessary in order to pay for imports, it is also crucial in order to safeguard employment and income. Imports do not only provide essential or desirable supplies of a variety of goods. They also represent an alternative source of supply, replacing domestic enterprises that have been used to supply domestic markets. The reduction and gradual abolition of protective duties has led to drastic adjustments in the industrial structure in the three countries. Firms which in earlier days could work for a cosy, relatively protected home market, have lost a large share of their local market to foreign producers. In order to survive they had to go into the export markets themselves. Many have succeeded, but a large number have failed. These changes were rather painless during the period of rapid economic expansion which allowed more firms to survive, and also provided job opportunities for the workers who became redundant in declining industries. These adjustments were almost exclusively caused by competition from imports from other industrialized countries. Only in recent years have Third World imports had a significant impact on a few industries. But unfortunately, this penetration by exporters from developing countries has occurred in a period of stagnation during which adjustments are far more difficult to undertake. This has reinforced demands for protection also in the Scandinavian countries, and often such requests concern protection against imports from developing countries, especially from the successfully industrializing countries, the NICs.

Some of the NICs have become formidable competitors in a number of industries: the very survival of established industries in several fields in Scandinavia is called in question in the face of rapidly growing capacity and productivity in the NICs. So far it is somewhat muted, but the basic question is asked whether it is really in Scandinavian interests to assist other countries in developing into powerful, modern states. The counter argument that trade has to go in both directions does not convince everybody. Some of the OPEC countries export much more than they need to pay for their imports. The most successful of the NICs in modern times hitherto, namely Japan, has become and manages to remain such a strong international competitor that it tends to run large balance-of-payments surpluses; it does not use all of its large export earnings for current imports of goods and services. If many of today's NICs were to become new Japans, already established industrialized countries would get into serious structural deficit positions. Such fears are not completely unfounded; they may also create mounting opposition in the Scandinavian countries to the NIEO, particularly to that part which deals with industrialization.

The relative share of imports from developing countries is roughly the same in Denmark, Norway and Sweden. The composition of these imports is also very similar, consisting mainly of foodstuffs, animal fodder, fuel and other raw materials including minerals: in 1976 food and raw materials accounted for 85 to 90 per cent of total imports from developing countries, half of this being crude oil and oil products.[14] Also the share of developing countries in total commodity exports from the three Scandinavian countries was roughly the same in all three countries and has not changed significantly over the last few years. The bulk of the exports consists of manufactured goods. (In the case of Denmark and Norway export of ships accounted for an important part, particularly of Norwegian exports. This type of export falls in a separate category since the transfer of ships to flags of convenience, notably in Liberia, represents mainly transactions between international shipowners.)

While in recent years Sweden has had a roughly balanced trade with developing countries, Denmark and Norway have had relatively large import surpluses (in 1976 about $450 and $300 million respectively).

The share of Scandinavian countries in direct private investments in the Third World is very small — only 1½ per cent of the OECD total in 1977 — and the bulk of it comes from Sweden, whose foreign investments are quite important in total. Twenty per cent of the employment in Swedish multinational companies are in foreign subsidiaries, and the value of the production in those subsidiaries corresponded to 40 per cent of Swedish exports. 'That puts Sweden on a level with Switzerland and Netherlands as one of the world's most multinational countries relatively speaking. Still, Swedish direct investments account for only two per cent of total foreign investment in the world as a whole, and only one per cent of foreign investments in the Third World.'[15] These investments are to a large extent explained as a means to come in behind tariff walls. Two-thirds of Swedish investments in the Third World are in three Latin American countries: Argentine, Brazil and Mexico. However, 'Investments to utilize lower production costs abroad is (*sic*) not a salient feature of Swedish foreign investments. Production abroad for re-export to Sweden is so far negligible.'[16]

In recent years one form of capital transfers to the Third World has become very important in Scandinavia, namely export credits. In 1977, almost 7½ per cent of all private export credits from OECD countries to developing countries came from Denmark, Norway and Sweden, and the year before the figure had reached 13 per cent. This may have been a temporary phenomenon, caused by the international recession. As part of the policy to maintain employment, governments quite successfully promoted exports to developing countries. This development may also be a sign of a growing interest in Scandinavia for exporting directly to the expanding markets in the Third World.

Perceptions of Interest

In all three countries there are vested interests in trade and other economic transactions with the Third World. Individuals, groups and enterprises concerned do of course use all available channels to protect their particular interests, and they undoubtedly exercise some influence on policy decisions *vis-à-vis* the Third World. As a whole, however, economic interests in the Third World are not widely felt to be particularly important. This may to some extent be due to lack of concrete information. No comprehensive study appears to have been carried out in Scandinavia which shows the number of jobs that are dependent on exports to developing countries. By contrast, people are very much aware of the number of jobs lost because of increased imports, including purchases from the Third World.

Access to raw materials is taken for granted, but there is considerable awareness of the disturbing effect of wide price fluctuations for raw materials. Opinions held with regard to private investments in factories in distant countries differ, but are predominantly hostile outside the business community. The 'radical' opinion which has vocal, possibly broad, support amongst younger people, is that foreign-owned enterprises in Third World countries are exploiters, mainly interested in using available local raw material sources and cheap − and docile − labour. Since foreign firms are assumed to use inappropriate technology and to transfer large earnings abroad, either directly or in the form of transfer prices unfavourable to host countries, these critics doubt if industrialization controlled from abroad has any development effect at all in the Third World. This view has to some extent penetrated governments as well. Opposition against private investments abroad also comes from the trade unions, which fear that such investments reduce domestic investments and job creation, and indeed tend to transfer jobs away from the domestic economy. Such fears are, of course, not uncommon in other rich countries as well.

While the perceptions of the economic pay-off from greater prosperity in the Third World may be weak in the Scandinavian populations at large, the understanding of mutual interdependence is fairly strong in the government administration and also amongst politicians. The need for a continued massive transfer of resources to the Third World is recognized in the OECD, and not least in the Scandinavian countries; the issue is how to mount and organize it. The Scandinavians have their own response to this question: if other industrialised countries raised their Official Development Assistance to the same relative levels as in Scandinavia, no less than about 20 billion additional dollars would be flowing into the developing countries annually. Such arguments are not taken seriously by the large, 'hardheaded' rich nations. Scandinavian 'do-gooders' are looked upon with a mixture of disbelief and contempt. The Scandinavian countries and the Netherlands have hitherto been willing to play their allotted part in the transfer of resources in the form of ODA, even though they are fully aware of the fact that their resource transfers are merely a drop in the bucket compared to what really is required to make the Third World fit for its own development and for their acting as an engine of growth for the rich countries. Scandinavian ideological commitment to large scale ODA and to institutional changes in the world economy as required for the establishment of a NIEO may remain strong. Yet, national economic interests may in the end change the position taken also by Scandinavian countries, which are hardheaded enough not to conduct forever a 'go it alone' policy which cannot succeed. There is therefore a clear danger that the like-minded countries at some stage will be forced into more selfish and defensive policies.

The Policy-Making Process

The gradual expansion of official development assistance in the Scandinvian countries gives some insight into the decision-making process. As far as *multilateral* development assistance is concerned, its expansion is clearly linked to decisions taken in the United Nations itself, and in member institutions of the UN family. From the very beginning the Scandinavian countries took decisions in these bodies seriously, and made their contributions as required. At an early stage voluntary contributions were modest. It was only after the total volume of ODA was stepped up that the Scandinavian countries also became major donors to some of the international programmes that are financed on a voluntary basis (in particular UNDP and UNICEF).

Policies to be followed by Scandinavian governments with respect to the United Nations and other international organizations are initially conceived in the relevant parts of the government administrations, notably in the Ministries of Foreign Affairs. But these policies are also carefully scrutinized by parliamentary committees and — depending on the nature of policies concerned — decided upon by Parliaments. Non-government organizations and amongst them the UN Association and associations or more informal groups working with other UN bodies, act as pressure groups, but their more important task is to spread information on UN and Third World matters to a larger public.

Multilateral development assistance has had a strong position in the Scandinavian countries. Many influential people for a long while believed that development assistance should generally go through multilateral channels, which were considered to be more neutral and less objectionable from the point of view of the developing countries. However, in recent years the developing countries themselves have expressed special satisfaction with Scandinavian bilateral assistance, both because of its form and terms and because it comes from countries with no recent past colonial history and with little vested interest in most developing countries. This has weakened Scandinavian hesitations as regards bilateral aid and has been replaced by a more sceptical attitude towards multilateral assistance.

Bilateral development assistance started out in Scandinavia in the 1950s, in a rather arbitrary manner, and differently in each of the three countries. In 1952 the Norwegian government established a 'fund for assistance to underdeveloped countries', and initiated a large fisheries development project in Kerala in India shortly afterwards. In Sweden a 'central committee for Swedish technical assistance to less developed countries' was established the same year. The Central Committee was a parastatal body with strong participation of various large popular associations, and it initiated a major campaign for collection of money ('Sweden helps') in 1955. Denmark established a 'government working group for technical assistance' as early as 1951, which until 1955 dealt mainly with UN matters, but thereafter had a small vote for bilateral technical assistance at its disposal. Otherwise, not much happened during the 1950s, but in the beginning of the 1960s all three countries established stronger organizations for the handling of bilateral assistance. The first joint Nordic assistance project was started in 1962.

Both Norway and Sweden now have separate administrations for bilateral assistance (NORAD and SIDA) which have a considerable degree of autonomy in day-to-day decisions. They are governed by boards which include non-government representatives, but they are under the control of the respective foreign ministries. By contrast, the Danish DANIDA is an integral part of the Ministry of Foreign Affairs.[17] This difference is in Denmark justified by the importance of development assistance as a part of Danish foreign policy, whereas in Norway and Sweden it is stressed that the development assistance administrations have wide operational tasks separate from central ministries, which should be more concerned with policy matters. However, DANIDA's situation is not as different from the others as the formal arrangements might suggest; thus, there is a considerable degree of interaction between the aid administration and the relevant ministry both in Norway and Sweden, and the central planning functions are located in the Foreign Ministries.

As the aid administrations gradually have gained experience and knowledge, the staffs of these administrations have gained a strong influence in the formulation of bilateral aid policies. But the principles and important policy questions are resolved on a broader basis. All three countries have published voluminous documents in which the various aspects of development assistance policies have been discussed in detail and broad political principles have been drawn up. In some cases broadly composed commissions have produced the reports; in others the ministry has been responsible for the report, but has drawn extensively on outside resources in preparing it.

Also the bilateral assistance programmes are subject to parliamentary approval and are discussed in considerable detail by the relevant parliamentary bodies before they come up for debate and final decision. Through the involvement of non-governmental organizations, as members of boards and committees advising the aid administrations, and as direct participants in development projects and other activities, democratic participation in the formulation of Scandinavian development assistance policies is wide. It is worth remembering that it is mostly the elected leadership that becomes fully familiar in this way with problems and policies. But many of the organizations concerned conduct information programmes for their members.

One characteristic feature of bilateral assistance is that it is to a growing extent provided on the basis of the receiving countries' programmes and priorities. This introduces a duality in the decision-making process which occasionally interferes with the donor countries' own perceptions. There is also some conflict and contrast in approach between the government auditing machinery in the donor countries, which for statutory reasons is primarily concerned with responsible and efficient use of the taxpayers' money, and the actions of the aid administrations which seek to introduce flexible procedures in order to facilitate the tasks for the often over-burdened administrations of the receiving countries.

Some brief remarks may be in order on the formulation of positions taken in international negotiations on the New International Economic Order (NIEO) as a whole or on parts thereof. The most complex part of the negotiating procedure concerns those many areas where domestic vested interests are affected. Two of the main issues in the North-South dialogue are the raw material proposals, including the Common Fund, and the target of a much larger part of the world's industrial output to be produced in the Third World. As regards the raw material programme and the Common Fund, the Scandinavian countries — and Norway in particular — had no great difficulty in agreeing to the proposals put forward by UNCTAD in Nairobi in 1976: it seemed highly unlikely that any raw material agreement would contain pricing provisions which would not be acceptable or would be more than moderately expensive for consumers. But the industrial action programme creates far greater difficulties. It is easy enough to subscribe to a paper declaring that the developing countries shall account for one-quarter of the world's industrial output in the year 2000. But if this target would require a massive increase in Third World exports to Scandinavia leading to the dismantling of several industrial branches, then the policy will hurt. Such adjustments can only be accepted when accompanied by effective policies of domestic solidarity and, particularly, full employment; the latter being a fundamental and overriding policy objective in all three Scandinavian countries. The accommodation of increased imports of competing manufactures is thus totally dependent on new employment opportunities actually being created and on effective arrangements to ensure that those who will be harmed in the process of adjustment are adequately compensated. This is not an easy task, and as some areas inevitably will be harmed more than others, it will create a massive mobilization of a variety of vested interests. Scandinavian governments have gone quite far in the North-South dialogue in accepting and supporting general formulations of 'greater market access', but when the pinch comes and the request becomes one of subscribing to hard and fast commitments of giving Third World countries full and free market access for their exports — both industrial and agricultural — then the Scandinavian governments are more reticent and constrained. At that stage objections will come from various government bodies dealing with employment, with regional issues, with restructuring of manufacturing industries, etc., and such objections will be buttressed by intervention of trade unions, associations of industries and local government.

In Scandinavia, the feeling is expressed, particularly amongst younger people, that the race for higher material well-being is becoming increasingly futile. There is a search for a new life style with less stress on the use of material goods and modern services, and more on activities which raise the quality of life. The search for new values does not merely concern the consumption patterns, but also the production side and the pattern of growth. Here the ideal presented is one of more decentralized production. However, while the search for more decentralized production and human settlement patterns may be consistent with the application of modern technology, in actual fact it tends to become a 'reactionary' movement in some respects. The advocates of a policy for new values seek to preserve existing structures − e.g. the little clothing factory in a peripheral community in the Western fjord country of Norway − and they urge reversal of past changes − e.g. the movement back to small agricultural holdings. In some ways such campaigns are self-defeating because the results would be absurd, but in other respects they can prove more viable: the claim for support of uncompetitive small enterprises in certain peripheral regions can, for example, win political support. Yet, this is precisely the kind of policies which may make the industrial progress of the Third World more difficult. Indeed, it cannot be taken for granted that the movement towards 'new values' will benefit the Third World, *inter alia*, because more austere consumption patterns also imply smaller markets for manufactured goods from developing countries.

Another point is that the search for new values may lead to more and sharper conflicts within the Scandinavian countries. The 'new values' can hardly become realities without more government intervention, including more emphasis on public services, with less for the private consumer to spend on unnecessary gadgets or on even more consumer durables. However, there is a certain drift to the right politically in Scandinavia. The tax burden has become so high, the network of welfare services so tight and the size of the government bureaucracy so large that there are definite indications of a welfare state backlash in all three countries. A reaction against taxation and against government action may, of course, also turn against development assistance and against government policies which are needed in order to implement a New International Economic Order.

Future Perspectives

The interest in Scandinavia in Third World development is at best vague and undetermined. In terms of real economic interests, they lie in international trade which allow these small countries to benefit from specialization and division of labour between countries. However, direct trade with the Third World is not essential to any of the three countries except in some few branches of economic activity. To the extent that Third World development will facilitate growth and adjustment amongst Scandinavia's main trading partners, however Scandinavian interest in growth and development of the poorer countries is very strong.

The industrial world has apparently entered a very difficult period of transition which differs significantly from the preceeding decades of rapid and cumulative economic expansion, assisted by an ample supply of essential raw materials and energy resources. At this juncture the existing economic order is being questioned also by the industrialized countries, but not for the same reasons which have led the Third World to ask for a New International Economic Order. For the Third World the objective is to get a much larger share of the benefits of growth; for the industrialized market economy countries the objective is to maintain growth and full employment, and at the same time to get rid of inflation and to adapt their economies to a situation of expensive and scarce energy and other raw materials. In the industrialized countries opinions differ widely as to how to achieve these essential goals. One influential line of thought is to seek to re-establish a more pure form of market economy, with less government intervention. Such political tendencies make themselves felt in Scandinavia as well.

The positive attitudes of the Scandinavian countries towards the demands of the Third World for a NIEO are to some considerable extent based on the experiences of the first quarter-century after the Second World War, during which the 'mixed economies' of the Scandinavian countries functioned extremely well, and at the same time encouraged the belief that a balanced dosage of market mechanism and government intervention might also give the developing countries a fairer deal in the world economy. If and when this belief is shattered, Scandinavian attitudes towards the NIEO may also change.

The situation is further complicated by the fact that adjustments to accommodate larger imports from the Third World are much more difficult to undertake in a period of slow growth and serious domestic economic problems than during the expansionary period up to 1974, the experience of which still clearly has an important impact on the thinking of Scandinavian policy-makers. Also, in these countries in the near future, perceived interests may well become more parochial and more directly linked with the defence of existing economic structures than with the advantages of a dynamic world economy in which Third World development could be an important driving force.

It should once more be stressed that Scandinavian attitudes to Third World development — and to Third World demands — to a very large extent have not been based on real or perceived economic interests, but on the hitherto generally accepted ideological commitment to justice, equity and solidarity. The extension of this commitment beyond national frontiers has found its concrete expression in the willingness to grant relatively large official development assistance on generous terms. However, ODA does not harm any particular vested interests. The issue is different for other parts of the NIEO which inevitably may hurt some groups while benefiting others. As the NIEO is not based on global and consistent sets of ideas as to how the world economy ought to be functioning, but is predominantly a package of demands which may satisfy the interests of various groups of developing countries, it is unavoidable that in rich countries also parochial interests will be strongly expressed and very influential when it comes to implementing the different parts of the package. This observation holds true for the Scandinavian countries as well as for other rich nations. How and to what extent resistance to parts of the NIEO will develop, depends to a large extent on domestic political developments. Although conservative forces in the industrialized welfare states seem to accept the need for a 'safety-net' that takes care of the losers in the free-for-all economy, these forces clearly are content to make the 'net' less safe, and will hardly be predisposed towards extending the safety-net internationally

While conservative forces want to re-establish a more liberal economy which gives market forces a more dominant role, 'ecologists' and other supporters of a new life style seek to reject some aspects of technological progress, and advocate a life style based on local and individual self-sufficiency, and on 'informal sector' economic activities. The OECD Interfutures study stressed the evident danger of internal conflicts in the industrialized countries as a result of these strongly contradictory political trends. The traditional progressive and reformist left which has dominated Scandinavian politics during the better part of this century is caught between these two new tendencies, and there are signs that the majority of young people prefers either the conservative or the ecologist approaches. There is a danger that this is in practice could weaken action to promote further justice, equity and solidarity, particularly as regards the international dimension of these ideals.

Another motivation for a positive attitude to Third World development has been the belief that economic and social development in poor countries would create more stability and lessen the danger of wars. Recent events suggest that modernization instead may tend to destabilize Third World countries, encourage religious fanaticism and introduce new dangers, not only of wars but of international economic chaos. Such events certainly have a sobering effect on those many Scandinavians who believe that the world would be a good place to live in if only other peoples would learn from the Scandinavian experience. Scandinavian support of development assistance hitherto does not seem to have been weakened by the experience of disappointing economic performance in the Third World; yet, if the belief gains ground that development efforts in fact tend to bring about political instability and chaos, then Scandinavian attitudes to development assistance may also change abruptly, and in a negative direction.

Ultimately, a sustained positive attitude of the majority of people in the Scandinavian countries towards economic and social development in the Third World may depend on the establishment of a new international order, not only an economic order, which permits a stable and secure interdependence with the Third World, within which all may benefit — not excluding the vast masses of poor people in developing countries.

Notes

*This paper was initially prepared in early 1979 and was revised at the end of that year to take account of the exchange of views which took place in a conference held in November 1979 at the Institute of Development Studies at the University of Sussex.

1. 'Along with other rich nations, they have developed a welfare society. This may be unique compared with the United States, but certainly not compared with West Germany. Rather, we think that the ideology of equality that pervades, especially in the Scandinavian countries, is unique.' *Public Opinion and Information on Third World Relations in Norway, Sweden and the Netherlands*, summary paper by K. Ringdal, International Foundation for Development Alternatives (Nyon, Switzerland, 1979).

2. Some of the ideas expressed in this paragraph are analyzed in an as yet unpublished paper by Stein Rokkan: 'The Growth and Structures of Mass Politics

in the Nordic Countries'.

3. The *OECD Observer, No. 99 (July 1979)*. For other years, data can be found in Appendix II.4.

4. Quoted in reference (3), p. 1.

5. Reference (8), p. 10.

6. Reference (7), p. 21.

7. In fact it is improbable that there are any major hidden motivations for positions taken which are not reflected in official documents: the Scandinavian democracies are both active and open. Possibly there may well be an element of vanity behind the strong ODA efforts: by climbing to the top of the 'development assistance league' Scandinavia can put itself in the limelight.Thus, in a Danish official document it is stated that assistance should be increased to help the country's international reputation (reference (7), p. 21). Nevertheless, it would hardly have been possible for any Scandinavian government to have obtained political support on a sustained basis in the electorate for large-scale development assistance if it were merely or mainly regarded as a form of international oneupmanship.

8. A study undertaken by the Swedish SIDA showed that in 1977/8 one-third of the Swedish bilateral assistance 'returned to' Sweden in the form of purchases of Swedish goods and services. The figure was somewhat higher (43 per cent) for the 'programme countries', for which one third of aid took the form of tied purchases in Sweden. (Information given in a letter from SIDA.)

9. Business interests have hardly influenced the level of ODA. Direct commercial interests in Third World countries are on the whole concentrated in some few middle-income countries which in most cases fall outside the orbit of bilateral development assistance and co-operation. Up to the time of the present international economic crisis, Scandinavian export interests were mostly directed towards the rapidly expanding European markets. In the last few years, however, Third World markets have attracted growing commercial interest. This may lead to pressures for changes in aid policies, particularly so as to facilitate Scandinavian exports, but it does not in any way explain the past willingness to raise ODA to present levels.

10. Sources:references (3), (5) and (8).

11. This argument does not, of course, apply to non-agricultural raw materials, but it is recognized that existing unstable market conditions for such raw materials bring considerable harm to many developing countries.

12. Source: 'Foreign Workers: a Current Inventory', *OECD Observer*, no. 97 (March 1979).

13. The Scandinavian countries have been trading with Third World countries for several centuries. In the seventeenth and eighteenth centuries, they established trading posts and minor colonies, and they participated in such lucrative ventures as the slave trade between Western Africa and the New World. Shipping interests also became world-wide.

14. Six exporting countries account for over 50 per cent of total commodity imports, oil not included, from all developing countries both in the case of Norway and Sweden. Norway's main trade partners were Brazil (coffee), Hong Kong (textile products), Jamaica and Surinam (aluminium oxide), Israel (oranges) and Gabon (manganese ore). The most important exporters to Sweden were India (textiles, food and ores), Brazil and Columbia (coffee), Hong Kong and South Korea (textiles) and Chile (copper). Denmark imported from a wider range of developing countries.

15. Birgitta Nygren: *Relations between Sweden and the Third World*, IFDA Dossier 10 (International Foundation for Development Alternatives, Nyon, Switzerland, August 1979).

306   *Scandinavian Countries in Third World Development*

16. Ibid.
17. Also DANIDA has a board, which – *inter alia* – permits industrial and other organizations to influence its policies.

References

1. The Nordic Council, *Yearbook of Nordic Statistics* (Stockholm, several years).
.2. Olav Stokke *Norsk utviklingsbistand* (Nordiska Afrikainstitutet, Uppsala, 1975a), p.218.
3. ———*Sveriges utvecklingsbistand och bistandspolitik* (Nordiska Afrikainstitutet, Uppsala, 1975b), p. 459.
4. Jan E. Stenersen, *Norges varebytte med utviklingsland 1972-1976*, (DERAP Publication No. 76) (Chr. Michelsens Institutt, Bergen, 1979), p. 104.
5. Sverige. Utenriksdepartementet, *Sveriges samarbete med u-länderna. Huvud-betänkande av biståndspolitiska utredning.* (Statens Offentliga Utredningar 1977:13) (Stockholm, 1977), p. 401.
6. ———Bilagor. (Statens Offentliga Utredningar 1977:14) (Stockholm, 1977), p. 137.
7. Danmark. Udenrigsministeriet, *Betaenkning om Danmarks samarbejde med udviklingslandene*, Betaenkning nr. 565 (København, 1970), p. 248.
8. St. meld. no. 94 (1974-5).*Norges økonomiske samkvem med utviklings-landene* (Oslo, 1975), p. 232.
9. Birgitta Nygren, Relations between Sweden and Third World', *IFDA Dossier, No. 10, August, 1979* (Nyon, 1979), p. 11.
10. Stein Rokkan, The Growth and Structures of Mass Politics in the Nordic Countries', unpublished draft (Bergen, 1978).
11. Statistisk Sentralbyrå;*Attitudes to Norwegian Development Assistance 1977* (Oslo, 1978), p. 51.
12. Kristen Ringdal, *Meninger om utviklingshjelp 1953-75* PRIO-publication No. 16-19 (Universitetet, Oslo, 1975), p. 217.
13. Tomas Brante, *Opinionen i-u-hjälpsfrågor* (SIDA, Stockholm, 1976), p. 54.
14. Asger Schultz, 'Befolkning fortsat bag u-landshjaelpen', *Berlingske Tidende 14/8 1978.* p. 1. (Survey carried out by Gallup Instituttet.)
15. *OECD Observer, no. 97* (Paris, March 1979).
16. *OECD Observer, no. 99* (Paris, July 1979). p. 42.
17. Hans-Henrik Holm, *Danish Development Policy: Reactive and Like-Minded* (Institute of Political Science, University of Aarhus, 1978), p. 13.
18. OECD Interfutures. *Facing the Future: Mastering the Probable and Managing the Unpredictable* (Paris, August 1979).

10 RICH COUNTRY INTERESTS AND THIRD WORLD DEVELOPMENT: FRANCE

Albert Bressand

Introduction: The Distinctiveness of France

Whether through her early diplomatic recognition of the People's Republic of China or through the catalytic role that she played in convening major North-South conferences, France seems determined to play an original role in North-South politics. This independence of approach can be seen in the speech delivered in Pnom-Penh by General de Gaulle against American intervention in Vietnam, in France's military intervention in Zaire and, following the recent coming to power of the left, in her denunciation of the 'recolonization' of the Third World.

There is hardly any subject on which French policy has not made the claim, at one time or another, to be different from that of other countries. Dispassionate examination of the record suggests that this may not always be true. The question is, therefore, to what extent French relations with the Third World are in fact qualitatively different from the relations of other Western industrial countries.

Two opposite views can be heard among French policy-makers as well as among foreign observers. According to some, France's distinctiveness is mostly one of language: 'the French don't mind what they do, provided they pronounce it correctly'. Thus the Paris CIEC conference is seen as having brought little improvement over other North-South conferences, while the proposal for a 'trialogue' between Europe, Africa and the Arab League was greeted with polite amusement as just another charming Parisian initiative. French Official Development Assistance is described as little different from the Western average, especially if one subtracts French overseas territories from the statistics, while French trade policy is denounced as slightly more protectionist than the average.

Others would argue that France does play a distinctive role in North-South relations and has maintained an unusually deep interest in the development of the Third World, even if with limited means. The fact that one-third of all technical assistants working in the Third World are French, the efforts made to preserve the role of the French language throughout the world, the role played by France in initiating the Yaounde and, later, the Lomé Conventions as well as the sponsoring, together with Saudi Arabia or Kuwait, of major conferences on international economic co-operation, are all seen as concrete illustrations of French interests in Third World issues that are both qualitatively and quantitatively original.

Which of these two views is less of a caricature of the realities which we know to be complex is in part a matter of personal judgement. Although this paper does not attempt to provide a final answer, it is nevertheless built on the working assumption that an attempt must at least be made to identify some of the possible roots of France's distinctiveness — or would-be distinctiveness — even if this requires a slight departure from the framework used in the analysis of other 'rich country' interests. Whether it is eventually judged to be original or not, French policy undoubtedly succeeds in being different enough to warrant a different type of discussion.

The Roots of French Distinctiveness: Militant Intellectuals and Indifferent Public Opinion?

The spectacular growth of the 'development' community which has accompanied and sometimes preceded that of the Third World, has generated a new international idiom, the central concepts of which are expressed in terms of GNP ratios and UN Resolution numbers.

An analysis of French interests in the Third World conducted exclusively in World Bank English would however run the risk of losing sight of some important aspects of these interests, and possibly, of the roots of French distinctiveness. One of these aspects is certainly the ambiguous, but pervasive relation which French intellectuals have entertained with important Third World issues.

Policy-makers at the highest levels cannot be unaware of the symbolism of certain Third World causes for many French intellectuals, notably on the left of the political spectrum. Official rhetoric and policies are therefore bound to be aimed not only at the Third World itself but also at the 'progressive' intelligentsia which tends to fascinate even politicians of very conservative background.

If one adds that French public opinion at large has tended to display very little interest in Third World issues as described in ECOSOC English, while the intelligentsia has often been highly suspicious of the economist's preoccupation with aid, then one may have one explanation for the original shape of French policy towards the Third World.

The importance of the Third World for French intellectuals is a rather recent phenomenon, which seems to have developed only after the Soviet Union had ceased to be the major focal point of hopes and fears of French politics. After all, French involvement in far-away continents was both late and limited in terms of human settlement. Its deepening in the late nineteenth century stemmed from a reaction to difficulties on the European scene rather than from an irresistible fascination with these continents themselves.

It is a little surprising that none of the numerous writers who wrote about French colonies acquired the same stature in French popular culture as did Rudyard Kipling in Great Britain. Somehow, the roads to Saigon and Timbuktu never were travelled in quite the same way as the road to Mandalay . . . Paul Nizan's *Aden Arabie* tells about a flight away from narrow-minded Europe much more than about a search for new cultures. And although he spent a part of his short life smuggling arms into Somalia, Arthur Rimbaud has left us with few keys to other continents. Albert Camus as well as André Malraux were fascinated with universal values rather than with foreign continents when they chose Oran or Shanghai as the background of their symbolic dramas *La Peste, l'Etranger* or *La Condition Humaine.*

The French intellectuals of the post-colonial period undoubtedly share in this long tradition of looking at events in exotic lands in the perspective of national preoccupations. But the difference is that the history of the Third World has come, in the last two decades, to play a central role in the universal history which the French intelligentsia tries to read and write. As expressed by an articulate spokesman of the French left in 1979:

La visions (que la gauche a) du Tiers Monde sert de clef de voûte à tout l'édifice de ses convictions. Quant elle parle des capacités révolutionnaires du Tiers Monde, c'est sa propre incapacité à concevoir et à préparer la Révolution qui est en question. Quand elle parle du caractère progressiste de l'Etat dans les nations décolonisées, elle cherche en fait à se persuader du rôle progressiste de l'Etat dans la transformation éventuelle de notre société, c'est à dire dans l'installation du socialisme. Quand elle parle du Tiers-Monde, elle parle d'elle-même.[1]

A detailed analysis of intellectual perceptions of the Third World since the decolonization period should at least distinguish three phases.

The first phase was one of intense emotions and deep divisions, as the decolonization issue gave rise to major tensions within and between the various political alignments. Left-wing parties were, in several instances, caught unprepared by the decolonization process and were slow to adjust to it. Albert Camus was one of several prominent writers torn between their sympathy for struggles against colonial domination and their personal ties with the land of their birth. Although these tensions can sometimes still be detected below the surface of today's controversies, they have gradually given way to much more traditional alignments along the left-right spectrum.

In what can be called the second phase, enthusiastic support of national liberation movements and of the efforts of the most progressive of the newly independent nations came to be seen as part of an overall left-wing endorsement of a new political and economic order. The Vietnam War made possible the creation of a broad front of progressive intellectuals around what they perceived as the contrast between an aggressive, exploitative, American-dominated capitalist world, and liberation forces fighting for the sort of better world for which they also were striving. Hence a widely shared fascination with Third World experiences. In the words of one of the leading intellectuals who shared in this experience:

Everything seemed possible, beginning with a return to the pure sources of the revolutionary ideal, at the wellsprings of the Third World, with a great strategic detour through countries where outcasts rose up with empty bellies, guns flowering from their hands. Thus, we invented our own Third World, with the birth of Ben Bella's Algeria and Castro's Cuba, both a substitute for and regenerator of the enfeebled proletariat. From China, Lin Piao called to us, 'Long live the victorious people's war!' While the appeal of Che Guevara to 'create one, two, three Vietnams', pierced our hearts with its certitude. Each in our own way, we set ourselves to the task, most of us intent on 'putting to the torch the heart of the imperialist octopus'; others did not hesitate in forsaking everything, led on by the dream of new International Brigades. One need only recall our passionate discussions at that time, faithfully recorded in Chris Marker's film 'Le fond de l'air est rouge' to realize that each epoch nourishes its own hopes of imaginary lands.[2]

Those were the days of the Great French Cultural Fascination with China. In the wake of the May 1968 questioning of the models and values on which French politics had been based, the Great Cultural and Proletarian Revolution was seen by many as the very symbol of a different approach to politics, social relations and international affairs. For half-a-dozen years, a two-week trip to the Great Nanking Bridge, the Loyang Number One Tractor Factory and the Red Flag People's Commune fulfilled, in Parisian society, the same function, and bestowed the same prestige, as the pilgrimage to Mecca in the Islamic world. To write on China was a sure recipe for literary success in those years, when social reformers and revolutionaries looked for inspiration and guidance to books that combined, under the pen of Antonietta Macchiochi, Bruno Bettelheim or Alain Peyrefitte[3] the moral virtues of Maoist aphorisms with the intellectual excitement of the best Isaac Asimov classics. A minority even took the Chinese experience at face value and brought it to bear on the ongoing political debates within the French left and extreme left. In spite of their small numbers — sometimes almost infinitesimal — these groups and 'groupuscules' had a far-reaching and lasting influence on French politics. It is astonishing to see, in retrospect, how much of the May 1968 rhetoric and outlook had been announced in Jean-Luc Godard's film *La Chinoise*. Domestic issues, such as the economic and political role of migrant workers from developing countries, or that of the relationship beteween intellectuals and the working class, were seen in a different light. As quotations from Chairman Mao and Che Guevara became part of the French way of life, it became common to borrow concepts and lessons from Third World experiences — from the Maoist emphasis on self-reliance to the legitimacy of the urban guerrilla in the social struggle. In the numerous Internationals of the extreme left, the borderline between domestic and world causes almost vanished during those few intense years when a whole generation discovered politics through the Europe-wide 'Vietnam Committees' and the Boulevard Saint-Michel seemed to lead to the sierras of Latin America.

By the late 1970s, this intellectual climate had obviously changed. Fascination with the Chinese, or for that matter Cuban or Tanzanian, experiences gave way, first to puzzlement, then to disillusionment.

A rampant disillusion had been gradually developing as a result of the failure of various Third World revolutions to gain popular support or, when they succeeded, to bring about the economic and political progress on which French intellectuals had pinned their hopes. Aside from outright failures, the endless contradictions and verbalism in which many Third World experiences (notably those that came under the banner of African socialism) seemed to be trapped finally had to be acknowledged by the French and European left.

It is painfully ironic to remember that, in his seminal book, written in 1976, Gérard Chaliand, who was among the first to give an articulate and systematic expression to the French left's disillusionment with its former Third World enthusiasm,[4] took comfort in the only exception he saw to this painful pattern, namely that of the Chinese and Indochinese social revolutions and anti-imperialist wars. In fact, in no other region has the sense of betrayal been more obvious for Western sympathizers. The invasion of Cambodia following years of massive repression under the Pol Pot regime, the queues of angry Chinese emigrants at the 'Friendship Door' between Vietnam and China were hard to swallow. Even more disturbing, because of its theoretical repercussions, has been the domestic evolution of China itself, in which almost everything that has aroused enthusiasm among the left in the West for the last ten years is now fiercely rejected, apparently with the backing of the masses and grass roots organizations that had been widely represented as the supporters and beneficiaries of the Great Proletarian Cultural Revolution. Hence there has arisen a pervading sense of frustration expressed with vehemence in a new wave of books about China such as Jacques and Claudie Broyelle's *Second Return from China.*[5]

The new attitude of French intellectuals towards Third World revolution was highlighted by the controversies which developed in the summer of 1978 when the weekly *le Nouvel Observateur* ran a column on 'Le Tiers-Monde et la gauche'.

The former editor of a famous Maoist newspaper went as far as to write:

> We should no longer be asked to swallow the obscene falsehoods of those in whom we 'believed' during the Vietnam War, or of the 'just struggles' of the Polisario Front or of the MPLA of Agostinho Neto — barely sustained, as everyone knows, by their Algerian and Cuban friends. No one need replay for us the worn-out scenario about guilt; they should accept, without heaping invective on us, our need to declare our disgust before every form of tyranny, whatever its source. Finally, let no one charge us with being agents of American imperialism, under the pretext that Jimmy Carter aspires, like us, to campaign for the rights of man.[6]

By contrast with the interest displayed in Third World causes by the intellectual and political community, French public opinion is considered by most observers to have displayed very little interest in Third

World issues once the turmoil of decolonization was over.

Even indifference, however, cannot be taken for granted. A fairly articulate anti-foreign-aid mood was clearly perceptible in the early 1960s, so the name of a well-known journalist is still widely associated with 'cartierisme', a mood that denounced French aid as benefiting only a narrow African elite. Although 'cartierisme' does not seem to have left a deep mark on public opinion, its resurgence at times of domestic economic difficulties remains a potential danger. On the other hand, emotional campaigns on dramatic development issues, notably hunger in India and Laos, have met, from time to time, with very noticeable success. The publicly orchestrated campaign in favour of starving Biafra was so successful that, in 1979, Biafra was still one of the very few Third World 'countries' which the man in the street was able to name! A much more important factor to challenge public indifference is of course the energy crisis and the increasing role played by OPEC countries in the daily life of millions of French men and women. It is worth noticing in this respect that a narrow majority (52 per cent) of French public opinion finds it very understandable that oil-producing countries increase their prices 'as a reaction to worldwide inflation', while a large majority considers oil conservation (70 per cent), dialogue (70 per cent) and even decreases in gasoline taxes (80 per cent) rather than military intervention as the appropriate response.

Not only has the energy crisis *not* aroused widespread hostility towards OPEC countries, but a majority of French respondents to a 1979 poll sponsored by 'Frères des Hommes'[7] (71 per cent including 68 per cent among workers) are in favour of Third World industrialization. There is even a majority of 57 per cent against 25 per cent in favour of lowering tariffs on Third World products. Yet this sympathetic understanding of the objectives of Third World nations does not stop 40 per cent of the respondents feeling that jobs in France are threatened when they learn that a French company is investing in a developing country. The Third World is widely believed to have an important impact on French economic life, but in a way which remains closely associated with oil price increases rather than with a global perception of interdependence. There are in fact almost twice as many respondents (62 per cent) who think that Third World policies have a very important or fairly important impact on French inflation as those who say the same thing of Third World impact on French unemployment (45 per cent, of which 19 per cent think it 'very important').

The Policy Formulation Process

Policy formulation in France appears therefore to be a little constrained by direct public opinion pressures but more influenced, over the long run, by deeper ideological controversies.

As a result, the government and bureaucracy have usually enjoyed substantial freedom except on a few issues of a political rather than economic nature (such as the Vietnam War, migrant workers, Indochinese refugees), which acquire enough salience for pressures from intellectual circles to be taken into account. Even in these cases, the government remains free to choose to stick to its own line of conduct, as President Giscard d'Estaing did when he refused to increase aid to the 'boat-people' to the level called for by a committee which included some of the most prominent French intellectuals from Raymond Aron to Jean-Paul Sartre.

French political parties are aware of the relative indifference of public opinion and tend to be also more influenced by ideological controversies within the intelligentsia. Meeting the UN target of 0.7 per cent of GNP has always been an official objective, although the new socialist government is the first to have put real emphasis on it and to have decided to exclude aid to overseas territories from ODA statistics. No real lobby either for or against foreign aid is therefore able to play political football with bilateral or multilateral appropriation bills as Congress does in the United States.

The President and the Foreign Minister are firmly in charge of the 'high politics' of North-South diplomacy, while three major bureaucratic entities conduct between themselves the 'low politics' of day-to-day bilateral and development co-operation relations. The Ministry of Foreign Affairs, now the Ministry of External Relations, has a broad field of competence which includes however financial relations as well as development co-operation with French-speaking black Africa. Now reorganized among geographical lines, it conducts day-to-day relations with foreign countries and most international institutions. The obligation of all other ministries to use its channels (which does not mean to act under its control) has recently been reinforced as a decree has named the ambassadors the 'sole representatives of the whole French government'. Its 'Direction Générale des Relations Culturelles, Scientifiques et Techniques', has responsibility over cultural relations with and technical assistance to all countries except French-speaking black Africa, although a major reform is being considered at present.

A separate ministry (Ministère de la Coopération & du Développement) has responsibility over development co-operation with a group of countries which used to consist of the former French colonies in black Africa but now also includes the former Portuguese and Belgian African countries as well as Mauritius and the Seychelles. The relation of this ministry with the Quai d'Orsay have varied from a gradual integration in the late 1960s when it became the 'secrétariat d'Etat a la Coopéra-tion' (1964) and even a 'secrétariat d'Etat', with no reference to co-operation in its title (1968), to full independence again in the 1970s. Since May 1981, a new move towards co-operation rather than integra-tion has been made and the Ministry is now headed by a 'ministre délégué auprès du Ministre des Relations Extérieures' who continues to enjoy a very large freedom of action but is formally attached to the Foreign Minister. Strong demands on the part of French-speaking African nations for a specific channel of communication with the French leadership are quoted as the major reason why co-operation with these countries cannot be administered through ordinary procedures and in-stitutions.

In addition to its own budget to cover its operating costs, the Ministry of Cooperation has a quasi-majority in the governing body of the Fond d'Aide et de Cooperation, which is responsible for funding technical assistance and development projects in the countries with which the ministry is concerned. This governmning body has full authority over project choice and disbursements within an annual appropriation, a very unusual degree of freedom in the French adminis-tration.

Separate from the Ministère de la Coopération but working in close contact with it in the same limited number of countries (North Africa, as well as overseas territories and departments, being however added to French-speaking black Africa), the Caisse Centrale de Coopération Economique (CCCE) acts as a development bank for soft as well as hard loans. Its expertise in the identification and analysis of develop-ment projects explains the importance of the role that it plays.

As in any country, the Treasury, itself a part of the Ministère de l'Economie, insists on having a say on all North-South policy issues with financial implications. A bone of contention between the Treasury and the Quai d'Orsay is the fact that the former acts as the sole repre-sentative of the whole French government in the international financial institutions (IMF, IBRD and regional banks). All monetary and inter-national financial issues are therefore handled by the Treasury which plays a major role in preparing French participation in the OECD Development Assistance Committee, commodity agreements and

Common Fund negotiations, etc. Soft and hard loans from the Treasury ('prêts du Trésor') are also a major tool of bilateral diplomacy in all countries except those in which the Ministère de la Coopération is active. The growing privatization of Third World finance is, however, gradually eroding the political importance of these loans in the case of the more advanced LDCs.

Co-ordination between all ministries concerned with development co-operation, including technical ministries has been provided by numerous interministerial meetings which are generally chaired by the Treasury or the Ministry of Foreign Affairs. The preparation of UNCTAD, the Third World Development Decade Strategy and the 'global negotiations' have recently generated an impressive number of such meetings. For matters involving negotiations with the other members of the EEC, co-ordination is also provided by the Secrétariat Général du Comité Interministeriel (SCGI) which provides for a unified French position under the Prime Minister's authority. At the highest level, ministerial meetings ('Conseil sur l'aide') are held under the President's chairmanship to re-examine the guiding principles of French development co-operation policy.

The Guiding Principles of French Relations with the Third World

Politics is Not a Dirty Word

Until 1981, the main difference between French policy towards the Third World and that of other European countries was probably that France gave a much greater relative weight to the political and security dimensions, and did so explicitly. Although the socialist government is determined to reassess these aspect of French policy too, French attitudes are likely to remain markedly distinct.

In Europe, only a few countries such as Sweden, and more recently, Spain, are comparable to France in the importance that they seem to attach to relations with the Third World in their overall international relations. But Swedish interest in the Third World seems to be based, at least as it is described, on moral rather than political considerations, while the Spanish or Greek attitude (not to mention the short-lived burst of militant 'Third Worldism' in post-Caetano Portugal) can largely be accounted for by the economic development levels of countries that were themselves considered as developing only a few years ago.

The French attitude was, and is, likely to remain distinct, since it explicitly conceives of relations with the Third World as a way to influence international affairs.

It would of course be exaggerated to describe this attitude in terms of a search for what the Chinese used to call the alliance of the 'Second World' (the non-superpower developed countries) with the Third World against the superpowers. But an emphasis on political relations with the Third World did play an important role in the Gaullist search for an alternative to the alignment policies of traditional East-West diplomacy. A progressive attitude towards the the Third World was described as an essential element of the balancing role which France aspired to play between East and West. An emphasis on development co-operation was thus an integral element of a global posture that included withdrawal from NATO, attempts to break up the rigid Cold War alignments by pioneering the concept and policies of 'détente', and refusal of European integration inasmuch as it was identified with integration into an Atlantic Zone.

This positive attitude towards relations with independent-minded developing nations was in part a way to overcome the temptation of reacting to the decolonization process through either confrontation or isolationism. General de Gaulle's policy was indeed to turn what could have been perceived as the decline of French influence into the first step of a new missionary role for France in a world breaking away from both colonialism and Cold War hegemony.

There were limits, however, to the extent to which relations with the Third World could really be instrumental in changing the whole fabric of world politics. Implementation problems have rendered this policy more difficult to carry out in day-to-day business than brilliant successes on a few highly visible issues could have led to expect. One must contrast, for example, the extraordinary impact of the speech which General de Gaulle delivered in Pnom-Penh against American intervention in Vietnam with the difficulty of following up at the economic and industrial levels, his spectacular Latin American trip, during which he had tried to open a new field for French political and economic diplomacy. As the General would have said 'L'intendance ne suivait pas'. In the 1970s the gradual, albeit imperfect, codification of US-Soviet relations, as well as more nuanced American policies towards the Third World in the Carter period, certainly reduced the possibility of any single European country playing an independent balancing role. By contrast, the Reagan policy, and notably its sharp budgetary reductions of multilateral funding, will make room again for a French policy which is more clearly distinct.

Implementation difficulties are now more clearly realized than at the

time of the euphoria generated by the rapid and successful decolonization in black Africa. But France has never really given away the objective of playing a pioneering role in North-South diplomacy.

However, this determination to look at developing countries as political actors within an increasingly multipolar world did not mean that
France endorsed Southern views, notably as to the best approach to the
dialogue that was gradually taking shape after the Seventh Special
Session of the United Nations General Assembly. From a political
point of view, it seemed to French policy-makers that meaningful
results could only be achieved if a small but influential group of countries with sufficient political weight were to negotiate a realistic give-
and-take. Hence the co-sponsoring by France and Saudi Arabia of a
24-member Conference on International Economic Cooperation which
met in Paris from 1975 to 1977.

Of course, it is easy to argue with hindsight that the Paris Conference did not bring about any final solution, and totally failed to grasp
the energy issue. Its format did not bring as much improvement over
the traditional UN forums as had been expected, be it only because
each of the selected few countries participating in the Conference felt
compelled to keep in constant consultation with the other members of
the 'coalition' to which it belonged. Nevertheless, the Paris Conference
was a turning point in North-South relations. It contributed to keeping
in check the dynamic of conflicts which had developed, and in addition
to modest steps on the debt and commodity issues brought about a
significant improvement in the climate of relations between North and
South.

Since then, France has continued to search for appropriate forums
in which to achieve the political breakthrough that neither conventional
UN diplomacy nor a purely economic approach to North-South relations seem able to provide. Under President Giscard d'Estaing, the
emphasis was put on a 'trialogue' to bring together European, African
and Arab League countries around an agenda for co-operation that
emphasized political and security issues,a project which did not fail to
arouse opposition from countries like Libya as well as suspicion from
oil-rich countries.

No Insecurity in Talking About Security

The French acceptance of the political dimension of North-South
relations is even more noticeable as France is one of the very few
nations which has accepted dealing explicitly, almost as a matter of
routine, with the security implications of these relations. In this, it

conforms more closely to the American approach, in which national security has been, since the Point Four Programme, one of the major justifications of foreign aid than to the standard European approach in which security is almost a dirty word.

At the present time, France is in the unique position of still maintaining bilateral security assistance agreements (accords de défense) with seven African countries (Central African Republic, Comoros, Djibouti, Gabon, Ivory Coast, Senegal and Togo). These countries are thus entitled to 'call upon French military forces to defend themselves'. In addition, military technical assistance agreements (accords d'assistance militaire technique) are in force with seven African countries including the three former Belgian colonies.

The importance of this network has however been reduced as six defence agreements have been terminated and as most military facilities have been closed, most recently in Chad; only Dakar and Djibouti are left as significant French manned military bases. Under all existing agreements, French military personnel in Africa, in 1980, amounted to about 10,000, of which 4,500 were garrisoned in Djibouti, a newly independent country confronted with a volatile environment. The overall French military presence in the region is larger than this, since some naval forces are maintained in the Indian Ocean and about 4,000 more troops are stationed in the French Department of Réunion, and, under an evolving legal framework, in the island of Mayotte.

French strategic interests in Africa have of course always been linked with French material supplies. France depends indeed on Africa for about 44 per cent of her non-fuel material raw imports against 34 per cent only in the case of Europe as a whole. But broader geo-strategic considerations are at stake, at least from the French point of view. Instabilities in Africa, and the build up of Soviet influence which they consider possible even in the absence of any Soviet master plan, were seen in Paris during the 1970s as a potential threat of major importance for the security of the Mediterranean area. The new socialist government is bound to reassess the importance of these considerations in the light of its objective to do away with all policies considered as neo-colonial either in the economic or security realm.

The most spectacular illustrations of security considerations have of course been direct military interventions. Whereas the intervention in Shaba was very successful in military terms and fairly successful in political terms leading to reconciliation between Zaire and Angola, a return of refugees, and the creation of a small African security force, French interventions in Chad have taken place in a much more complex political context and have not been able to prevent, after the with-drawal of French forces, an eventual victory of Libyan-supported factions in 1981. Although it must be acknowledged that the presence of French troops was supported, though not always in public, by a large number of Chadian factions and African nations, it is obvious that there are limits to the capacity of military 'stabilization'. In the longer run, a global political and economic solution is needed.

Development Co-operation

Development co-operation is often put forward by French policy-makers as a subject to which France devotes more attention and re-sources than other industrial nations. This view seems to be widely shared by public opinion as illustrated by the answers given to the 1979 poll already quoted:

Question: Do you personally think that France, in its effort to aid developing countries, does proportionately more, less or as much as:

Answers:	Great Britain	Germany	Netherlands
does more	43	33	30
does less	7	11	8
does as much	20	19	15
no comment	30	37	47
Total	100	100	100

Yet development co-operation is both more and less important for France than for other nations. It is more important in that relations with the Third World are seen in the perspective of broader political and security concerns while resources devoted to 'co-operation' have been, and still remain, relatively important, notably in terms of human resources. But it is less important in that it arouses relatively little public interest, is only one element of a larger number of ties with the Third World, and was until recently receiving at best a stagnating share of national resources.

In terms of GNP shares, the French development co-operation effort is not exceptional and now lags behind that of several European countries.

The objective set forth in the Gorce report to maintain the high levels of transfers (two per cent of GNP) experienced in the last years of the colonial period was obviously over ambitious. Even the objective of meeting the 0.70 per cent UN target, although it has repeatedly been reaffirmed, seems difficult to reach and has not been translated into any specific timetable.

As submitted until now to the OECD Development Assistance Committee (DAC), ODA figures include concessional transfers towards French overseas territories and departments. This might be understandable in the case of the 'Territoires d'Outre Mer' (TOM) which are bound to become independent at some future time under the French Constitution: the development impact of the aid provided to Djibouti until 1977 was not different from what it is now that Djibouti is independent. But a number of observers (including, in France, the now ruling, Socialist Party) claim that this is not legitimate in the case of the 'Départements d'Outre Mer' (DOM) which are considered as an integral part of France and which received in 1977 4,622 million francs ($982 million) as against 929 million francs ($197 million) for the TOMS. As a matter of fact, transfers to both TOM and DOM are not included in ODA figures as submitted to the French Parliament. As of July 1981, it seems that M. Jean-Pierre Cot, the socialist Minister for Cooperation, is prepared to inaugurate a much more frank and sincere acknowledgement of the French ODA performance net of DOM/TOM and to announce a 0.33 per cent figure for 1980. This would be the more remarkable as the government is preparing a plan to meet (gradually) the 0.7 per cent target.

Concessional flows of private origin (80 million francs i.e. $17 million in 1977) are extremely weak when compared to those of America (which are roughly equivalent to American bilateral ODA) and Germany. This is accounted for by the absence of any large private foundations comparable to those in America and by the lesser role of the churches. These factors themselves are reinforced by the absence of public subsidies to existing private foundations and churches, a notable difference from the American and Northern European cases.

In contrast, *commercial bank loans* have increased very rapidly over the last couple of years (by 83 per cent in 1978) as French banks moved swiftly to fill the gap left by American banks in 'high risk' countries such as Brazil. This increase has been such as to generate a widespread feeling that it must now give way to stabilization of country exposures by banks and be tightly linked to French exports as opposed to balance of payments financing.

French development co-operation policy is noticeable for the emphasis which it puts on bilateral relations. This characteristic, often criticized by foreign observers, is understandable in the light of three factors.

Table 10.1: French Development Co-operation Effort: Total Transfers to Developing Countries and ODA (as per cent of GNP)

	1970	1971	1972	1973	1974	1975	1976	1977	1978	1979	1980
Total transfers	1.24	1.00	1.06	1.10	1.22	1.16	1.53	1.37	1.67	1.52	1.77
of which ODA	0.66	0.66	0.67	0.58	0.59	0.62	0.62	0.60	0.57	0.59	0.62

Source: DAC.

Table 10.2: French Net Transfers to Developing Countries by Origin (per cent of total)

	1970	1974	1975	1976	1977	1978
ODA	52.9	48.0	53.1	40.4	43.5	34.1
Other public transfers	1.5	5.7	8.4	4.8	3.0	5.8
Concessionary private transfers	0.3	0.4	0.3	0.3	0.3	0.3
Other private transfers	45.2	45.9	38.2	54.5	53.2	59.8
Total	100	100	100	100	100	100

Source: Constructed from French memoranda to DAC.

(1)   the explicit recognition of the political dimensions of North-South relations;

(2)   the absence of French influence over multinational institutions comparable to that which has been traditionally exercised by the Anglo-Saxons. France has therefore found herself ill-equipped to pursue, on the American model, national goals through multinational means; and

(3)   the existence of an impressive network of French development-oriented institutions, notably in Africa, of sufficient importance to provide France with the means to participate directly in development projects without the help of the multilateral framework which other European nations find it often more efficient to rely upon.

As a result, French multilateral aid, although it has recently increased faster than bilateral aid, still accounted for only 17.3 per cent of total French ODA in 1980

More than half of French multilateral aid is chanelled through the European Community. France, however, has clearly given priority to increasing her bilateral aid to Africa rather than to an extension in real terms of the volume of the European Development Fund in the second Lomé Convention. In contrast, the UN institutions are clearly not at the centre of French attention as they receive only seven per cent of French multilateral aid, i.e. one per cent of total French ODA, although France's contribution to UNDP has doubled over the last two years.

French Economic Interests in the Third World

Trade with the Third World had been steadily declining as a share of total French trade as decolonization and European integration went on. This trend was of course abruptly reversed as OPEC countries saw their purchasing power quadruple.

Table 10.3: French Bilateral and Multilateral ODA (millions)

	1975				1976				1977				1978			
	Francs	$	%	%GNP	Francs	$	%	%GNP	Francs	$	%	%GNP	Francs	$	%	% GNP
Total French ODA	8,972	2,093	100	0.62	10,255	2,146	100	0.62	11,140	2,267	100	0.60	12,208	2,705	100	0.57
of which: bilateral	7,667	1,789	86	0.53	8,822	1,846	86	0.53	9,420	1,917	84.5	0.51	10,608	2,350	86.9	0.49
multilateral	1,305	304	14	0.09	1,433	300	14	0.09	1,720	350	15.5	0.09	1,600	355	13.1	0.08

Source: DAC

Table 10.4: French Contributions to Multilateral Institutions ($ million)

	1975	1976	1977
EEC (EDF and EIB)	142	164	152
EEC (food aid)	51	29	42
World Bank group	83	78	99
Regional Banks	7	6	35
United Nations (of which UNDP)	21	23	22
	(11)	(10)	(10)
Total	304	300	350

Source: DAC.

French direct investments in the Third World, which reached 2,519 million francs ($ 513 million) in 1977 in gross figures and 1,298 million francs ($ 264 million) in net figures, represented 30 per cent of total French investments abroad. The corresponding figure in the case of Germany was 16 per cent.

Debt rescheduling is accepted by France as one of the contingencies of North-South relations, provided that it takes place within the well established framework of the 'Club of Paris'. Net expenditures on that account totalled $30 million in 1978 against $17 million in 1976.

The French attitude has been relatively more forthcoming on another important issue of the CIEC agenda, namely *commodity price stabilization*. Efforts made within the EEC (Stabex) to stabilize export earnings *a posteriori* are not considered by France as a substitute for more ambitious efforts at stabilizing prices *a priori*. Unlike Germany, France is therefore not in favour of a world-wide extension of the Stabex approach. Price stabilization within international commodity agreements arouses less ideological opposition in a country where it is widely considered that world commodity markets are characterized by too many oligopolistic or oligopsonistic practices for their fluctuations to be accepted as the pure expression of perfect competition.

However important these various economic aspects of North-South relations have been for France, *energy* is now the one single issue to which she gives priority. A prominent trade partner of this group of countries, France gives a special recognition to the difficulties of the oil-importing LDCs. A French memorandum was one of the impulses which led the World Bank to set up a $1.2 billion loan programme in the energy sector. Like its predecessor, the socialist government is strongly in favour of the World Bank 'energy affiliate' and is trying to

Table 10.5: Share of Third World Countries in French Trade (per cent)

	1968		1973		1976		1977		1978	
	imports	exports	imports	exports	imports	exports	imports	exports	imports	exports
non-oil LDCs			10.0	13.0	9.0	14.5	10.3	15.1	10.0	17.9
oil-exporting LDCs			9.7	4.7	17.2	8.2	16.2	8.5	14.5	8.2
Total Third World	23.0	22.8	19.7	17.7	26.2	22.7	26.5	23.6	24.5	26.1
Total in $ million	14,022	12,906	37,727	36,659	64,391	57,162	70,497	64,997	81,794	78,915

talk the Reagan Administration into a more positive attitude. A discussion of a 'Marshall plan for energy development' has been initiated, including within the administration, by the recent proposals of Maurice Lauré, the President of the Société Générale.

Conclusion and Issues for the Future

An analysis of French objectives and performance in relations with the Third World can therefore contribute, at least in the view of the author, to explaining the paradox of France's actual or would-be distinctiveness.

It is clear that, when analyzed in World Bank English, French policies are only marginally different, in either their strengths or their weaknesses, from those of other countries. As the point is made below even when it comes to geographical emphasis, French trade policy is no longer characterized by the 'chasses gardées' mentality of the colonial period. The French Franc zone is no longer a special and major trading partner. Whatever yardstick is chosen to measure it (i.e. including or excluding some or all overseas provinces), the French aid effort is at most slightly above OECD averages and at best ten per cent short of the internationally agreed target of 0.7 per cent of GNP, neither a disreputable nor an exceptional achievement. French positions on the standard NIEO issues, as expressed in UN Resolutions, have been on the whole marginally more forthcoming than those of other major Western countries, even if on some particular issues, other countries take a more 'progressive' position when they have the will and the financial means to do so, as was the case for Germany on the debt cancellation issues.

French distinctiveness lies elsewhere, and can only be understood if one broadens the analytical framework. It is to be found in the deeper emotional reactions, which Third World causes have evoked, under varying forms, among the French intelligentsia and political class. It is to be found in the more explicit recognition of the political and security dimensions of North-South relations. And it is to be found also in the way in which the 'standard' development co-operation and economic relations are managed (notably in terms of bilateral/multilateral and geographical emphasis) to take into account this broader context as well as the increasingly crucial issues related to the dialogue on energy.

Is this overall policy posture likely to be adapted to the needs of the 1980s? Contrary to the reluctance with which many specialists in the pure science of economics tend to view political factors, the present author believes that this association is likely to be more and more called for by the international environment. To view countries such as Saudi Arabia, Brazil, Mexico, Algeria, not to mention China or Cuba, only as economic actors or even more narrowly, only as outlets for manufactured goods, is to ignore the nature of international relations. The special circumstances which prevailed after the Second World War and the fact that some of the most successful 'developing nations' of the time (Japan and, later, Korea) had little political room for manoeuvre have made it possible for economists to take the political and security framework for granted and therefore to think in terms of what appeared as 'depoliticized' economic relations. But in an increasingly multipolar world, a country like France needs to perceive developing countries as political actors as well and to accept the consequences of that perception. Mexican or Brazilian trade barriers, the new role of investment as a precondition or even substitute for direct exports, are political as well as economic facts understandable only as the expression of global national development objectives.

It so happens that the French attitude towards the developing world, although it evolved in part as a way to cope with the decolonization problem and in the context of East-West rather than North-South diplomacy is able to encompass a global approach more easily than purely economic approaches.

This is certainly not to say that, in its concrete expression, this approach is necessarily well adapted to the present context. On the contrary, French policies have tended to display rigidities which suggest that a regular process of reassessment will be needed.

Among the numerous issues which would have to be addressed, three seem to be of paramount importance:

(1) the human aspects of relations, both in terms of the presence of French expatriates in the Third World and of the presence of migrant workers in France;

(2) the geographical emphasis of the various aspects of French policy; and

(3) the concrete translation into practical policies of the slogans of industrial restructuring ('redéploiement industriel') and 'organized trade expansion' which so far have provided little more than a conceptual framework for the French search of a new role in the world economic order.

(Not addressed here because it would deserve a separate essay in a global European perspective, European co-operation must have a major impact on French policy formulation, notably on the last two of these issues.)

(a) The human aspects of French relations with the Third World should be seen as a two-way relationship. Whereas in the 1960s several million migrant workers had been needed to fill the gap between French growth and French human resources, it is now French expatriates working in developing countries, on short and medium term assignments, who are likely to be the new expression of economic interdependence. The massive presence of French 'coopérants' in African countries will, at the same time, have to continue its evolution from direct involvement in the economic and cultural life of these countries towards a contribution to training local managers to do the job and set up self-sustaining technical progress.

Although there are about 1.5 million French people living in foreign countries, including 400,000 whom French consulates are aware of as living permanently or temporarily in the Third World, French companies find it extremely difficult to recruit enough personnel to develop their presence overseas. The reluctance to expatriate oneself seems decidedly greater in France than in other Western countries. Hence the very high (and even, in the light of growing Indian and Korean competition, extravagant) price tag of French expertise. The creation, within the Foreign Ministry of a 'Direction des Français de l'Etranger' illustrated the growing realization of the importance of this problem. But much more would be needed as part of a global employment policy. One should note in particular that while there are more than 40,000 French people living in Ivory Coast, there are only 24,000 in the whole of Asia and 47,000 in Latin America.

At the same time the presence in France of 1.8 million migrant workers (two-thirds of whom come from the Third World) and of a total migrant population of 4 million has become a domestic political issue. The new socialist government will have to find a way to remain faithful to its commitment to put an end to the policies of the previous government (which combined financial incentives for departing migrants with a heavy-handed policy on illegal immigration) while pursuing its goal of reducing domestic unemployment.

(b) The geographical emphasis of relations with the Third World will also present French decision-makers with difficult choices. Many foreign observers have described these relations as organized around

three circles:

(1)   the inner circle of black African countries which participate in the annual 'Conference Franco-Africaine', recently set up as a small-scale replica of Commonwealth meetings, and which receive the bulk of the development co-operation efforts;

(2)   a second circle consisting of the other African countries as well as Caribbean, Pacific and Mediterranean countries to which the EEC Lomé Convention and 'global Mediterranean policy' address themselves; and

(3)   a third circle defined negatively as the 'non-associate' LDCs which have no preferential agreement links to France either directly or through the EEC.

This view is of course not deprived of factual bases and can even be considered as a rough approximation of the institutional setting for the French *development co-operation* policy. Similarly after more than one century of colonial involvement, French *political relations* with the Third World cannot be but influenced by historical factors. Yet it would be a mistake to extrapolate to the *economic* level this political fact-of-life and to conclude hastily that French economic relations with the Third World are organized around the preservation of protected markets ('chasses gardées'). This would ignore a major reorientation which has brought the share of the French Franc Zone in total French exports from about one-third per cent in the early 1960s to five per cent in 1978. Similarly the importance of the Zone in terms of French currency holdings has almost vanished although the Zone continues to represent an element of stability and solvency for the African member countries. An economic explanation of French security concerns in Africa would likewise overlook the relative independence of political and economic factors in French policy. France had indeed very little economic interest to protect in Shaba where its investments are 40 times smaller than those of Belgium and ten times smaller than those of America. Even its imports of cobalt come from Morocco and not Zaire.

Nevertheless, a clear weakness is the insufficiency of the French presence in the more advanced countries. Steps have been taken to correct this situation such as the funding of 300 fellowships a year for students of a dozen rapidly industrializing countries, the signing of a significant oil deal with Mexico and numerous presidential and ministerial official trips to such countries. Yet American financial flows towards the seven most advanced LDCs were 35 times higher in 1975 than similar flows of French origin while they were 12 times lower in the case of French-speaking Africa. Germany, with financial flows to the seven most advanced LDCs six times higher than France, has also clearly taken a lead of major economic significance. Obviously, France cannot allow, without risk, its 'portfolio' of interests in the Third World to remain so much out of balance with the intrinsic importance of the countries considered.

(c) The third major issue which France has to address in her relations with the Third World is that of the *economic consequences on French industry* of the emerging new international division of labour. Not that trade with developing countries is the most important source of difficulties for French industry: technological change and competition from OECD countries are on the contrary considered by French experts as having a much stronger impact. But competition from low wage countries does represent a highly visible threat for certain industrial branches and, more importantly for a number of poorer regions (ten departments out of 92 according to a recent study) in which these branches had been the keystone of regional development policies during the 1960s. Moreover, in spite of findings to the contrary by the group of experts which worked (under the Chairmanship of Yves Berthelot) on the subject, 44 per cent of French public opinion does consider (according to a September 1979 poll) this competition to be one of the major reasons for present unemployment levels.

Objective and subjective reasons therefore explain why the French government, even at the time when the emphasis was put on adjusting to free market forces, has been more sensitive to the need to keep the pace of the adjustment process within socially and politically acceptable limits. Hence its emphasis on the need to 'organize' the expansion of trade, a concern to which the new government will probably give a more systematic expression.

Understandable as it can be in the French context, this policy does however raise considerable implementation problems. The translation into German and English of the slogan 'libéralisme organisé'' under which it has (imprudently) first been presented has an Orwellian 'double-think' flavour which has aroused little sympathy. Aside from the Multi-fibre Agreement, few concrete expressions of this policy have justified so far the political cost of a conceptual attitude which other Western countries have often quietly put in practice while reasserting very loudly their commitment to liberalism.

On this issue as on many other ones, France is therefore confronted with the difficult search for a synthesis between the distinctiveness that results from the French way of looking at the world and the need to take increasingly into account the common constraints of interdependence.

Notes

1. 'La Gauche et le Tiers Monde', *Le Nouvel Observateur*, 22 July 1978.

2. Jean-Pierre Le Dantec, 'Une Barberie peut en cacher une autre', *Le Nouvel Observateur*, 22 July 1978.

3. Antonietta Macchiochi, *De la Chine* (Editions du Seuil, Paris, 1971); Bruno Bettelheim, *Révolution culturelle et organization industrielle en Chine* (Maspéro, Paris, 1975); Alain Peyrefitte, *Quand la Chine s'éveillera . . . le monde tremblera* (Fayard, Paris, 1973).

4. Gérard Chaliand, *Mythes révolutionnaires du Tiers-Monde* (Editions du Seuil, Paris, 1976).

5. Jacques and Claudie Broyelle, *Deuxième retour de Chine* (Editions du Seuil, Paris, 1977).

6. Le Dantec, 'Une Barberie peut en cacher une autre'.

7. Freres des Hommes 'Les Français ont-ils peur du Tiers-Monde?', May 1979.

STATISTICAL APPENDIX

Dudley Seers and Elizabeth Housden

Preface: Conceptual and Practical Problems of Research on North-South Issues

These tables provide the statistical background to the book. They fall into two groups. The first show the characteristics of the 'rich' countries – their population, income, dependence on trade (in general and on food and energy) and their rates of inflation, etc. The second covers their transactions (in aid, trade and investment) with 'poor' countries.

Be prudent when drawing conclusions from them. In the first place, the very publication of large international tables, using several digits, imparts to many statistics an aura of respectability that is ill-deserved. Estimates of the size of population in a country of the Middle East, say (in Table I.1), do not cease to be guesses because they are printed alongside similar data for countries where the registration of births, deaths and migration is comprehensive.[1] Statistics on trends in the national income in countries like Greece are the product largely of hypotheses, even though they appear in the same tables as estimates derived mainly from administrative records or comprehensive statistical surveys for each sector.

We should not lose sight, either, of the fact that transformations to permit international comparability involve choices which are highly arbitrary. Several of the tables that follow include trade converted into US dollars (e.g. Table I.2) – which at once raises the question of the appropriateness of the exchange rate. This is – in essence – an international price index, averaging the great range of price relatives for particular sales in the same time period. If one could believe in the assumptions of perfect competition, the working of product and factor markets would produce 'equilibrium' prices that would indeed be meaningful. But in the real world, of course, many transactions are at managed prices, and the exchange rate itself is managed by governments in ways that reflect the requirements of wage policy, *inter alia*. (Perhaps one should strictly say the *array* of exchange rates is managed, because wherever exchange controls exist – the normal case –there is more than one rate.) Further problems in recent years have been introduced by the instability of the international *numeraire*, the US dollar itself.

The reduction of GDP data to a common currency introduces complicated statistical gymnastics. The statement that the *per capita* income of (say) Saudi Arabia was $526 (in 1967), Table I.1, appears to mean that this would have been the income in the United States that would have bought the same goods and services. Recent research has brought out the significance of the 'non-tradeables' (on the price of which rent has a strong influence, both directly and indirectly). Indeed, to allow for this factor alone requires the average *per capita* dollar income of large, primarily rural, countries to be adjusted substantially.[2] On top of this, the national income of such countries excludes a large range of 'informal' activities in all sectors (agriculture, manufacturing, construction and services) that escape the statistician's net — or are even in principle excluded (e.g. food processing, tailoring, nursing) because, in contrast to the United States, they are normally carried out within the household.

Many conceptual problems are hidden behind seemingly neutral titles like Gross Domestic Product. This widely used aggregate (enshrined in the UN 'System of National Accounts', or SNA) includes some imputable incomes (e.g. the rentable values of owner-occupied houses), but excludes others (e.g. the value of housework). Interpreting income averages needs care where there is heavy concentration of income, and economic growth may be very remotely related to changes in welfare, if the increment in income goes mostly to the top 15 or 20 per cent.

Estimating changes at constant prices, even when working in the currency of the country concerned, raises further difficulties. What does one mean, for example, by the government services at constant prices? And how are we to interpret its usual implicit measure, the volume of employment with no allowance for changes in productivity? One would never guess even the existence of these problems from reading the great majority of national income analyses, which treat such highly artificial statistics as if they were 'facts'.

There are severe practical problems here too. A constant price series is a way of answering a hypothetical question — what, for example, would the value of output or exports be if the prices of year A were applied to the relevant quantities in year B? Apart from all the technical snags arising out of changes in specifications of products (e.g. motor cars), there are additional difficulties when data are simply not available and one series has to 'carry' the weight of others believed to move in parallel. In many cases, a series is used as a proxy for something quite different. For example, GDP in constant prices may have been obtained by using a consumer price series to deflate components such as capital investment. Series with different base years often have to be linked together (as in Table I.3) producing a curious hybrid not really, even in principle, in the prices of any particular year.

The complexity and artificiality of the questions answered by estimates in prices that are *both* constant *and* international are naturally much greater, and so is the statistical ingenuity required to answer them. When we look at a series of, say, *Swedish* arms exports in constant *US* dollars (Table II.2), we are looking at a very sophisticated construct, which must have involved many major assumptions and posed many technical choices. Indeed a series in constant Swedish kroner (or French francs), or one with a different weighting base, might show rather different trends and fluctuations, although it would still measure changes in 'volume' (a word that conceals all the conceptual issues, and greatly oversimplifies the task of interpretation and analysis).

Still, when we analyse the relations between the North and the South, the crucial issues are not technical or even conceptual. The second group of tables covers some important links. However, the network of ways in which events and policies in the North affect development in the South is too complex to be fully captured in any set of statistical tables. Some of the most important merchandise transactions, such as sales of narcotics are too secretive to be documented. Bribes to secure contracts are not likely to appear in the balance of payments, even among 'invisible' transactions. Even returns on more visible trade depend on declarations on customs invoices: in the case of intra-corporation transactions, these reflect in fact where it is most convenient for income to be taxed (the well-known practice of 'transfer pricing'). Moreover, what appears as exports of some 'Southern' country to, say, the United States, may really be in large part the exports of affiliates of US corporations, and much of their value may accrue not to the country concerned but to the parent corporation in remittances for profits, patent rights, materials and equipment, etc.[3]

Moreover, some of the main influences on the South are qualitative and could not be covered by statistics, however comprehensive. It is impossible to measure the implications of the support given by one government to another in the proceedings of the United Nations, or the impact of joint military manoeuvres or of overseas education or of the foreign television programmes — let alone that of espionage or political intervention. Yet these influences can, especially taken together (and in a close bilateral relationship they are usually all to be found, indeed linked together by strong but unseen bonds) be far more important in shaping the patterns of development than the associated economic links, which are, at least in principle, mostly quantifiable.

Mostly but not entirely, thus as Helleiner says: 'One must not be seduced by the more readily direct investment data into believing that they tell one about the *total* role of transnational corporations':[4] he points to transfers of technology, management, etc. which are part of the 'package' offered by the TNCs.

It is very tempting to forget all this and concentrate analysis on those transactions for which statistics *can* be found. Social scientists, especially economists, naturally tend to play down the importance of variables that do not fit into their numerical models: their professional education makes it hard for them to handle qualitative factors. Politicians, too, usually prefer that official records exclude aspects incompatible with the rather sanitized view of the world assumed in public discussion, particularly at United Nations meetings: it may be inconvenient for some delegations that UNCTAD discusses, say, transactions of the TNCs — but to document links like economic espionage or corruption would be far more embarrassing.

Finally, the classifications, e.g. of countries, may not correspond to what one needs for the purpose in hand. The United Nations uses a 'Standard Country Code',[5] basically geographical. It would require much retabulation, if it were feasible at all without access to the computer tapes, to construct series for 'OPEC countries' or 'oil exporters', which would be more useful for many international analyses, so one may have to use 'Middle East' instead (as in Table II.1).

The other readily available basis for country classification is political — into countries called 'developed', 'developing' and 'centrally planned'. This classification is much less significant than it was a couple of decades ago, when criteria of income, economic structure, social development, etc. would all lead to roughly the same groupings. It now seems somewhat odd to see Portugal classed as a 'developed' economy, when Mexico and Venezuela are still merely 'developing'. It is true that such labels are adjusted from time to time. In the 1950s, Japan was classed as a 'less developed country', the less euphemistic title then used for developing countries. But there are always long delays in reclassification. Besides, there is no longer a clear 'no man's land' between rich countries and poor. It is increasingly obvious that for many purposes we should look at the world of today as a continuum of countries, instead of as two (or three) discrete groups.

Yet the possibilities of analysis are not quite as limited as they used to be. More data are available now in terms of both range and detail than in the past, especially on international trade, thanks primarily to the work of the United Nations Statistical Office, the main source used here. Even as recently as the 1960s, a statistical appendix on this scale would have been unthinkable. What are published are also more comparable and more up to date. It is convenient that a lot of figures are published for the output, trade, etc. of different countries in constant US dollars, and they are not meaningless. The use of different assumptions or different *numeraires* might well show broadly similar trends. Analysis on the world scale and international comparisons are greatly facilitated. But tables should be labelled, like many medicines, 'handle with care' (and 'keep out of the reach of young persons').

Notes

1. The 1977 population of Saudi Arabia used to be estimated in United Nations publications at 9.52 million. This has been adjusted to 7.6 million, for the same year!

2. *International Comparisons of Real Product and Purchasing Power* (International Comparison Project, Phase II), p. 14. Even for Italy and the United Kingdom, estimates based on 'purchasing power' produces much higher figures in US dollars than if the official exchange rate is used (except perhaps for an unusual period like the last half of 1980).

3. For 1966-75, 32 per cent of total merchandise imports from developing countries consisted of sales of *majority*-owned affiliates of US corporations. (Gerald Helleiner, *Inter-firm Trade and the Developing Countries*. Macmillan, 1981, p. 19.) This figure excludes affiliates with lower US participation and looser licensing arrangements, etc. Similar data are not available for other developed countries, but would also show substantial fractions.

4. Ibid.

5. Series M. no. 49 (United Nations, 1970).

TABLES CONCERNING RICH COUNTRIES

Table I.1: Population and Gross Domestic Product, 1962-1979

		A Population[1] (millions)	B GDP[2] US $ bn	GDP Per Capita US $ (in current prices)
USA	1962	186.7	564	3,020
	1967	198.8	804	4,046
	1972	208.9	1,176	5,631
	1977	216.9	1,889	8,731
	1978	218.1	2,112	9,687
	1979	220.1	2,350	10,667
Canada[3]	1962	18.6	40	2,167
	1967	20.4	62	3,013
	1972	21.8	106	4,839
	1977	23.3	200	8,573
	1978	23.5	205	8,735
	1979	23.7	227	9,586
Japan	1962	94.9	59	625
	1967	100.8	121	1,214
	1972	107.2	294	2,750
	1977	113.9	694	6,094
	1978	114.9	974	8,476
	1979	115.9	1,000	8,627
Australia	1962	10.7	17	1,674
	1967	11.8	27	2,276
	1972	13.2	50	3,847
	1977	14.1	100	7,132
	1978	14.3	116	8,126
	1979	14.4	na	na
United Kingdom	1962	53.3	80	1,498
	1967	54.8	108	1,970
	1972	55.8	156	2,798
	1977	55.9	247	4,430
	1978	55.9	310	5,545
	1979	55.9	402	7,192
France	1962	47.0	74	1,592
	1967	49.6	116	2,346
	1972	51.7	194	3,751
	1977	53.1	382	7,191
	1978	53.3	472	8,851
	1979	53.5	574	10,720

338

Table I.1: (continued)

		A Population [1] (millions)	B GDP [2] US $ bn	GDP Per Capita US $
			(in current prices)	
Germany	1962	54.8	90	1,647
	1967	59.9	124	2,075
	1972	61.7	262	4,244
	1977	61.4	516	8,396
	1978	61.3	639	10,419
	1979	61.3	761	12,419
Netherlands [3]	1962	11.8	13	1,124
	1967	12.6	23	1,805
	1972	13.3	46	3,427
	1977	13.9	107	7,721
	1978	13.9	131	9,303
	1979	14.0	149	10,624
Greece	1962	8.5	4	501
	1967	8.7	7	799
	1972	8.9	12	1,405
	1977	9.3	26	2,822
	1978	9.4	32	3,375
	1979	9.4	38	4,093
Denmark [3]	1962	4.7	7	1,572
	1967	4.8	12	2,507
	1972	5.0	21	4,160
	1977	5.1	46	9,109
	1978	5.1	56	10,958
	1979	5.1	66	12,925
Norway [3]	1962	3.6	5	1,496
	1967	3.8	9	2,257
	1972	3.9	15	3,796
	1977	4.0	36	8,853
	1978	4.1	40	9,847
	1979	4.1	47	11,486
Sweden [3]	1962	7.6	16	2,163
	1967	7.9	25	3,225
	1972	8.1	42	5,157
	1977	8.3	79	9,490
	1978	8.3	87	10,543
	1979	8.3	106	12,831
USSR	1962	221.7	183*	825
	1967	236.0	251*	1,063
	1972	247.5	378*	1,527
	1977	258.9	563*	2,176
	1978	261.2	645*	2,471
	1979	263.4	674*	2,559

Table I.1: (continued)

		A Population [1] (millions)	B GDP [2] US $ bn	GDP Per Capita US $
			(in current prices)	
Eastern Europe [4]	1962	62.3	na	na
	1967	64.8	40*	623
	1972	66.6	66*	997
	1977	69.2	163*	2,350
	1978	69.6	146*	2,092
	1979	70.1	150*	2,133
Saudi Arabia	1962	5.0^x	2	400
	1967	5.7^x	3	526
	1972	6.6^x	7	1,065
	1977	7.6^x	63	8,319
	1978	7.9^x	na	na
Kuwait	1962	[0.4]^x	2	4,571
	1967	[0.6]^x	2	4,362
	1972	0.8^x	55	5,760
	1977	1.1	13	11,884
	1978	1.2	na	na
OECD^C	1962	638.0	1,084	1,699
	1967	690.2	1,739	2,519
	1972	729.3	2,683	3,679
	1977	759.2	4,965	6,540
	1978	764.5	5,954	7,788
	1979	769.8	6,806	8,841
EEC^C	1977	268.5	1,634	6,085
	1978	269.1	2,019	7,502
	1979	269.9	2,441	9,044

Notes: 1. So far as possible population statistics are *de facto* — those reported
as *de jure* are identified as such.
2. GDP data vary between 'former' and 'present' *System of National
Accounts.*
1962 GDP converted from local currency using exchange rates given
in 1969 *Statistical Yearbook*.
1967-78 data given in dollars in source, except for USSR and East
Europe data which are also converted from local currency.
1979 GDP has been derived from *per capita* GDP figures in the
Monthly Bulletin and should therefore be considered provisional.
3. *De jure* population.
4. Czechoslovakia, Bulgaria, Hungary, Poland.

*   Net Material Product.
x   UN estimate.
[ ]   Estimates considered by UN to be of questionable reliability.
na not available.

Sources: A: UN *Demographic Yearbook* 1970, 1976; 1979 *Historical Edition*;
UN *Monthly Bulletin of Statistics*, June 1979, June 1981.
B UN, *National Accounts Yearbook*, 1971, 1975, 1976, 1979; UN,
Statistical Yearbook 1977, 1979; UN, *Monthly Bulletin of Statistics*,
June, July 1981.
C: OECD, *Main Economic Indicators* 1960-75 (*Historical*), August
1969, January 1974, December 1978, July 1981.

Table I.2: Average Annual Growth Rates, 1962-1977

	A Population %			B GDP (in volume terms)[1] %			GDP Per Capita (in volume terms)[1] %		
	1962-1967	1967-1972	1972-1977	1962-1967	1967-1972	1972-1977	1962-1967	1967-1972	1972-1977
USA	1.3	1.0	0.8	5.0	2.7	2.2	3.7	1.6	1.5
Canada	1.9	1.4	1.3	6.1	5.0	3.8	4.1	3.5	2.5
Japan	1.2	1.2	1.2	9.9	10.1	3.9	8.8	8.8	2.6 [2]
Australia	2.0	2.0	1.3	5.0	5.4	3.7 [2]	3.0	3.4	2.3 [2]
United Kingdom	0.6	0.4	0.03	3.3	2.3	1.5	2.7	2.0	1.5
France	1.1	0.8	0.5	5.5	6.0	3.1	4.4	5.1	2.5
Germany	1.8	0.6	-0.1	4.1	5.5	1.9	2.9	4.5	2.0
Netherlands	1.3	1.1	0.9	5.3	5.7	2.9	4.0	4.5	2.1
Greece	0.5	0.5	0.9	7.9	8.1	3.6	7.3	7.6	2.7
Denmark	0.4	0.8	0.4	4.6	4.6	2.3	3.7	4.0	1.9
Norway	1.1	0.4	0.5	5.1	4.5	4.8	4.3	3.7	4.2
Sweden	0.8	0.5	0.5	4.4	3.5	1.5	3.5	2.8	1.2
USSR[3]	1.3	1.0	0.9	8.0	6.6	5.8 [2]	6.3	5.6	4.8 [2]
Eastern Europe[4]	0.8	0.6	0.7	na	na	na	na	na	na
Saudi Arabia	2.7	3.0	2.9	na	10.9	8.5	na	7.8	5.3
Kuwait	10.3	8.3	6.6	na	na	na	na	na	na
OECD	1.6	1.1	0.8	na	na	na	na	na	na
EEC	na	na	na	4.4	4.9	2.3	3.4	4.3	2.0

Notes: 1. The methods used to obtain estimates of GDP at constant prices and the years to which these prices relate vary between countries. For further details refer to source.

2. 1972-6.

3. Data refer to net material product and *per capita* net material product.

4. *Czechoslovakia, Bulgaria, Hungary, Poland.*

na not available

Sources: A: Derived from Table I.1, see sources.
B: UN, *National Accounts Yearbook*, 1976, Tables 4A, 4B, 1979, Tables 6A, 6B.

Table I.3: Trade: Imports and Exports, 1962-1979

		A		% of GDP[1]	
		Imports CIF	Exports FOB		
		(in bn US$)		Imports	Exports
USA[2]	1962	16.2	21.4	2.9	3.8
	1967	26.8	31.5	3.3	3.9
	1972	55.6	49.8	4.7	4.2
	1977	147.9	120.1	7.9	6.4
	1978	182.2	142.5	8.6	6.7
	1979	217.5	176.8	9.3	7.5
Canada[2]	1962	5.8	5.9	14.5	14.8
	1967	10.3	10.6	16.6	17.1
	1972	18.9	20.2	17.8	19.0
	1977	39.5	41.3	19.8	20.7
	1978	41.7	44.1	20.3	21.5
	1979	52.6	55.1	23.2	24.3
Japan	1962	5.6	4.9	9.5	8.3
	1967	11.7	10.4	9.7	8.6
	1972	23.5	28.6	8.0	9.7
	1977	70.6	80.5	10.2	11.6
	1978	78.7	97.5	8.1	10.0
	1979	110.1	103.0	11.0	10.3
Australia[2]	1962	1.9	2.4	11.1	14.1
	1967	3.5	3.4	13.0	12.6
	1972	4.6	6.3	9.2	12.6
	1977	12.2	13.1	12.2	13.1
	1978	14.0	14.2	12.1	12.2
	1979	16.4	18.5	na	na
United Kingdom	1962	12.5	11.1	15.6	13.9
	1967	17.7	14.4	16.4	13.3
	1972	27.9	24.3	17.9	15.6
	1977	63.6	57.5	25.7	23.3
	1978	78.4	71.5	25.3	23.1
	1979	102.6	90.5	25.5	22.5
France[3]	1962	7.5	7.4	10.1	10.0
	1967	12.4	11.4	10.6	9.8
	1972	26.7	25.8	13.8	13.3
	1977	70.3	63.4	18.4	16.6
	1978	81.9	76.5	17.4	16.2
	1979	106.7	97.9	18.6	17.1
Germany F.R[3]	1962	12.3	13.3	13.7	14.8
	1967	17.4	21.7	14.0	17.5
	1972	39.8	46.2	15.2	17.6
	1977	100.7	117.9	19.5	22.8
	1978	120.7	142.1	18.9	22.2
	1979	157.7	171.4	20.7	22.5
Netherlands[3]	1962	5.3	4.6	40.8	35.4
	1967	8.3	7.3	36.1	31.7
	1972	17.2	17.4	37.4	37.8
	1977	45.5	43.6	42.9	41.1
	1978	53.0	50.1	40.5	38.2
	1979	67.3	63.7	45.2	42.8

Table 1.3: (Continued)

		A Imports CIF (in bn US$)	Exports FOB	% of GDP[1] Imports	Exports
Greece[3]	1962	0.7	0.3	17.5	7.5
	1967	1.2	0.5	17.1	7.1
	1972	2.3	0.9	19.2	7.5
	1977	6.9	2.8	26.2	10.5
	1978	7.7	3.4	24.2	10.7
	1979	9.6	3.9	25.3	10.3
Denmark	1962	2.1	1.7	30.0	24.2
	1967	3.1	2.5	25.8	20.8
	1972	5.0	4.3	23.8	20.5
	1977	13.2	9.9	28.5	21.4
	1978	14.8	11.7	26.4	20.9
	1979	18.4	14.3	27.9	21.7
Norway	1962	1.6	1.0	32.0	20.0
	1967	2.7	1.7	30.0	18.9
	1972	4.4	3.3	29.3	22.0
	1977	12.9	8.7	35.9	24.4
	1978	11.4	10.0	28.6	25.1
	1979	13.7	13.5	29.1	28.7
Sweden	1962	3.1	2.9	19.3	18.1
	1967	4.7	4.5	18.8	18.0
	1972	8.1	8.7	19.3	20.7
	1977	20.1	19.1	26.1	24.3
	1978	20.5	21.8	23.5	24.9
	1979	28.6	27.5	26.9	25.9
USSR[2]	1962	6.5	7.0	3.5	3.8
	1967	8.5	9.7	3.4	3.9
	1972	16.0	15.4	4.2	4.1
	1977	40.8	45.2	7.2	8.0
	1978	50.1	52.2	6.8	8.0
	1979	na	na		
Eastern Europe[2,4]	1962	5.9	5.7	4.0	3.8
	1967	8.7	8.6	4.2	4.1
	1972	15.7	15.8	4.5	4.5
	1977	38.7	34.8	na	na
	1978	44.3	39.8	na	na
	1979	na	na	na	na
Saudi Arabia[3]	1962	0.3	0.9	15.0	45.0
	1967	0.5	1.7	16.7	56.7
	1972	1.1	5.5	15.7	78.6
	1977	14.3	43.5	22.5	68.5
	1978	20.2	40.7	na	na
Kuwait[3]	1962	0.3	0.02	15.0	1.0
	1967	0.6	0.04	30.0	2.0
	1972	0.8	3.1	16.0	62.0
	1977	4.8	9.8	36.1	72.6
	1978	4.6	10.4	na	na

Table 1.3: (Continued)

		A Imports CIF (in bn US$)	Exports FOB	% of GDP[1] Imports	Exports
OECD[B]	1962	119.2	122.6	10.9	11.3
	1967	147.7	141.6	8.5	8.1
	1972	297.9	290.1	11.1	10.8
	1977	767.6	714.9	15.5	14.4
	1978	897.3	858.4	15.1	14.4
	1979	1,150.4	1,051.5	16.9	15.4
EEC[B]	1977	385.5	379.2	23.6	23.2
	1978	459.3	459.3	22.7	22.7
	1979	598.8	574.1	24.5	23.5

Notes: Data from UN, *Yearbook*, 1963 have been converted from local currencies using the conversion factors supplied.
1. 1979 '% of GDP' figures are provisional – see notes Table I.1.
2. Imports fob.
3. Special system of trade.
4. Czechoslovakia, Bulgaria, Hungary, Poland.
For further details of trade systems see source A, 1976.
Sources: A. UN, *Yearbook of International Trade Statistics*, 1963, 1965, 1970/1, 1976, 1979.
B: OECD, *Trade By Commodities, Series B*, 1969, 1972, 1977, 1979.

Table I.4: Volume Indices of Exports and Imports, 1962-1980 (1970 = 100)

Exports[1]

	1962	1967	1972	1977	1978	1979	1980
USA	60	81	108	147	165	184	196
Canada	44	73	115	138	152	155	153
Japan	28	73	115	199	201	199	233
Australia	50	74	119	136	134	147	na
United Kingdom	67	78	111	152	160	163	167
France	47	67	124	166	177	194	198
Germany	44	71	115	161	164	176	183
Netherlands	43	65	121	157	161	175	175
Greece	44	78	130	217	254	270	na
Denmark[3]	57	80	114	133	142	157	164
Norway[3]	na	76	115	145	180	191	203
Sweden	53	75	113	135	140	154	na
USSR[4]	54	85	106	166	173	na	na
Bulgaria[4]	40	84	120	209	230	na	na
Czechoslovakia[4]	66	85	117	158	170	na	na
GDR[4]	57	84	123	169	182	na	na
Hungary[4]	52	81	128	190	193	na	na
Poland[4]	50	85	123	189	199	na	na
Saudi Arabia[5]	na	75	171	267	239	274	294
Kuwait[5]	na	na	114	62	68	74	55
OECD[6]	51	74	116	156	165	175	na
EEC[6]	52	74	116	157	164	174	na

Notes: 1. Volume of exports − (line 72, IFS) (source A).
2. Volume of imports − (line 73, IFS) (source A).
3. including ships (which are otherwise excluded from this table).
4. source B.
5. crude petroleum exports (line 72aa, IFS).
6. source C.
na not available.
A change in the base year from 1970 to 1975 in all sources has necessitated the linking of two series.

Sources: A: *International Financial Statistics,* vol. 22, Nov. 1969; vol 28, Feb. 1975; vol. 32, Mar. 1979; vol. 34, May 1981.
B: UN, *Yearbook of International Trade Statistics,* Special Table G, 1976, 1977, 1979.
C: *National Accounts of OECD Countries,* vol. 1, 1976; vol. 1, 1981.

			Imports[2]				
1962	1967	1972	1977	1978	1979	1980	
49	75	123	151	166	166	154	USA
51	85	129	168	175	194	183	Canada
33	65	113	138	201	223	210	Japan
53	79	90	131	128	139	na	Australia
66	85	116	137	145	160	153	United Kingdom
43	67	123	164	173	193	205	France
46	63	122	158	167	182		Germany
45	67	111	133	141	150	147	Netherlands
45	77	123	158	162	179	na	Greece
54	75	100	123	128	136	123	Denmark[3]
na	73	101	149	131	138	153	Norway[3]
54	74	101	134	123	142	na	Sweden
66	87	124	189	217	na	na	USSR[4]
50	97	128	202	216	na	na	Bulgaria[4]
60	87	110	152	158	na	na	Czechoslovakia[4]
46	71	110	164	164	na	na	GDR[4]
53	74	111	160	180	na	na	Hungary[4]
55	82	139	224	228	na	na	Poland[4]
na	na	na	na	na	na	na	Saudi Arabia[5]
na	na	na	na	na	na	na	Kuwait[5]
51	74	116	145	152	165	na	OECD[6]
52	72	117	146	153	168	na	EEC[6]

Table I.5: Dependence: Net Imports of Food and Energy, 1962-1979

| | | Food (SITC 0) | | Energy (SITC 3) | |
		Net imports US $ bn	% of GDP[1]	Net imports US $ bn	% of GDP[1]
USA[2]	1962	0.07	0.01	1.02	0.18
	1967	−0.06	−0.01	1.15	0.14
	1972	0.61	0.05	3.12	0.26
	1977	−2.24	−0.11	40.00	2.13
	1978	−4.16	−0.20	40.74	1.93
	1979	−6.34	−0.27	58.01	2.47
Canada[2]	1962	−0.46	−1.15	0.13	0.33
	1967	−0.60	−0.97	0.11	0.18
	1972	−0.79	−0.75	−0.65	−0.61
	1977	−1.08	−0.54	−1.25	−0.63
	1978	−1.23	−0.60	−1.05	−0.51
	1979	−1.63	−0.72	−2.40	−1.06
Japan	1962	0.37	0.63	1.02	1.72
	1967	1.37	1.13	2.21	1.82
	1972	2.78	0.95	5.72	1.95
	1977	8.82	1.27	30.99	4.47
	1978	9.84	1.01	31.09	3.19
	1979	12.61	1.26	44.99	4.50
Australia[2]	1962	−0.99	−5.82	0.18	1.05
	1967	−1.20	−4.48	0.14	0.54
	1972	−2.00	−4.01	−3.67	−7.37
	1977	−3.43	−3.42	−0.55	−0.55
	1978	−3.41	−2.95	−0.74	−0.64
	1979	−5.35	na	−0.51	na
United Kingdom	1962	3.73	4.68	1.09	1.36
	1967	3.97	3.66	1.66	1.53
	1972	4.39	2.81	2.51	1.61
	1977	6.92	2.84	5.51	2.20
	1978	6.72	2.17	4.68	1.51
	1979	8.38	2.08	3.04	0.76
France [3]	1962	0.36	0.48	0.88	1.18
	1967	0.27	0.23	1.45	1.25
	1972	−0.75	−0.39	2.95	1.52
	1977	1.06	0.28	13.20	3.46
	1978	0.49	0.10	13.89	2.95
	1979	−0.77	−0.13	19.46	3.39
Germany FR[3]	1962	2.54	2.81	0.32	0.35
	1967	2.78	2.24	1.01	0.81
	1972	4.61	1.76	2.46	0.94
	1977	8.47	1.64	14.11	2.73
	1978	9.43	1.48	15.03	2.35
	1979	9.87	1.30	25.27	3.32

Table I.5: (Continued)

Netherlands[3]	1962	−0.45	−3.46	0.15	1.15
	1967	−0.61	−2.65	0.29	1.26
	1972	−1.51	−3.28	0.19	0.41
	1977	−2.72	−2.57	0.45	0.42
	1978	−3.37	−2.58	0.23	0.18
	1979	−3.76	−2.52	1.39	0.93
Greece[3]	1962	0.01	0.33	0.05	1.18
	1967	0.04	0.51	0.09	1.28
	1972	0.00	0.02	0.00	0.00
	1977	−0.17	−0.64	0.91	3.50
	1978	−0.14	−0.46	1.11	3.50
	1979	−0.02	−0.05	1.58	4.16
Denmark	1962	−0.59	−8.01	0.05	3.32
	1967	−0.75	−6.19	0.30	2.47
	1972	−0.87	−4.21	0.46	2.21
	1977	−1.78	−3.87	1.91	4.15
	1978	−2.48	−4.44	2.01	3.59
	1979	−2.85	−4.32	3.05	4.62
Norway	1962	0.00	0.06	0.12	2.14
	1967	−0.04	−0.50	0.18	2.11
	1972	−0.11	−0.75	0.22	1.48
	1977	−0.16	−0.45	−0.21	−0.58
	1978	−0.09	−0.23	−0.71	−1.76
	1979	−0.15	−0.32	−2.80	−5.96
Sweden	1962	0.23	1.42	0.41	0.48
	1967	0.35	1.37	0.49	1.93
	1972	0.46	1.09	0.75	1.80
	1977	1.14	1.46	3.16	4.05
	1978	1.17	1.34	2.92	3.35
	1979	1.32	1.25	5.41	5.10
USSR[2]	1962	−0.11	−0.06	−0.96	−0.52
	1967	0.47	0.19	−1.37	−0.55
	1972	0.79	0.20	−2.24	−0.59
	1975	6.12	1.26	−8.99	−1.85
Eastern Europe[2,4,5]	1962	na	na	na	na
	1967	0.00	0.00	0.14	0.66
	1972	−0.05	−0.14	0.54	1.57
	1977	0.28	0.39	1.82	2.56
	1978	0.16	0.23	2.49	3.57
Saudi Arabia[3]	1962	na	na	na	na
	1967	0.16	5.34	−2.01	−67.04
	1972	0.25	3.57	−5.38	−79.00
	1977	1.28	2.02	−43.23	−68.11
	1978	1.94	na	−40.25	na
Kuwait[3]	1962	na	na		
	1967	0.08	3.13	−2.85	−59.87
	1972	0.12	2.50	−8.39	−74.25
	1977	0.46	3.42	−8.58	−63.91
	1978	0.54	na	−9.54	na

Table I.5: (Continued)

OECD[B]	1967	8.15	0.46	11.50	0.66
	1972	9.68	0.38	23.39	0.87
	1977	20.29	0.41	134.10	2.70
	1978	18.27	0.31	136.74	2.29
	1979	17.09	0.25	195.80	2.28
EEC[B]	1977	16.25	0.99	49.06	3.00
	1978	16.03	0.79	50.72	2.51
	1979	16.68	0.68	72.08	2.95

Notes: Unless otherwise specified, imports are cif and exports fob under a 'general' system of trade.
Data from UN, *Yearbooks* 1963 and 1969 have been converted from local currencies using the conversion factors supplied.
1. 1979 '% of GDP' figures are provisional – see notes, Table I.1.
2. Imports fob.
3. Special system of trade.
4. Czechoslovakia and Hungary only.
5. 1967, figures are not SITC: they refer to 'foodstuffs' and 'minerals, fuels and metals'.
  – (minus) net exports.
na   not available.
Sources: A: UN, *Yearbook of International Trade Statistics*, 1963, 1969, 1972/3, 1979.
   B: OECD, *Trade by Commodities*, Series B. 1969, 1972, 1976, 1979.

Table I.6: Consumer Prices, 1962-1980 (1970 = 100)

	1962[1]	1967	1972	1977	1978	1979	1980
USA	78	86	108	156	168[2]	187	213
Canada	78	89	108	165	180	197	216
Japan	na	84	111	204	211	219	238
Australia	80	91	112	208	224	244	267
United Kingdom	73	85	117	249	270	306	364
France	73	85[2]	112	183	200	221	249
Germany[3]	81	93	111	146	150	156	165
Netherlands	70	88	116	176	183	191	202
Greece	83	95	107	227	255	304	383
Denmark	65	84	113	189	208	228	254
Norway	70	85	114	178	193	202	222
Sweden	72	89	114	180	198	212	238
USSR[4]	101	100	100	100	101	102	na
Bulgaria	95	97	100	102	103	108	na
Czechoslovakia	98	93	100	103	105	109	112
GDR[3]	101	100	99	96	96	na	na
Hungary[5]	99	98	105	125	131	142	157
Poland	91	96	100	124	134	144	na
Kuwait	na	na	100[6]	154	166	175	na

Notes: 1. 1962 figures from ILO 1972 have been converted from base 1963 to base 1970.
2. Series linked to former series.
3. Includes relevant data relating to Berlin.
4. Includes Byelorussian SSR and Ukranian SSR.
5. 1962 and 1967, Budapest only.
6. Base year.
na Not available.
Statistics are not uniformly representative of changes in price levels, and vary in reliability — for further discussion and references see sources.
Sources: ILO *Yearbook of Labour Statistics*, 1972, 1977, 1978, and 1980.

Table II.1: Trade Relations with the Third World, 1967-1979 (in $ billions)

	A DEVELOPING COUNTRIES[1]				A MIDDLE EAST[2]			
	Imports from cif	Exports to fob	% total imports	% total exports	Imports from cif	Exports to fob	% total imports	% total exports
USA[3]								
1967	7.7	9.5	28.7	30.1	0.31	0.73	1.2	2.3
1972	14.2	14.0	25.6	28.1	0.64	1.67	1.2	3.4
1977	66.9	42.2	45.3	35.1	12.4	9.0	8.4	7.5
1978	75.6	51.2	41.5	35.9	12.3	10.9	6.8	6.1
1979	98.0	61.1	45.1	34.6	15.7	9.7	7.2	6.7
Canada[3]								
1967	0.89	0.75	8.5	7.1	0.07	0.02	0.7	0.2
1972	1.6	1.3	8.6	6.4	0.18	0.08	1.0	0.4
1977	4.9	3.4	12.5	8.4	1.3	0.49	3.4	1.2
1978	4.8	4.0	11.6	9.0	1.3	0.52	3.0	1.2
1979	5.8	4.8	11.1	8.6	1.5	0.54	2.9	1.0
Japan								
1967	4.5	4.6	38.9	43.7	1.5	0.33	12.8	3.2
1972	9.8	10.9	41.8	38.2	3.4	1.0	14.4	3.6
1977	39.8	37.3	56.4	46.4	20.2	8.2	28.6	10.2
1978	42.2	44.8	53.6	46.0	20.5	9.8	26.0	10.1
1979	62.0	46.4	56.3	45.1	28.9	9.6	26.3	9.3
Australia[3]								
1967	0.53	0.80	15.3	23.7	0.18	0.94	5.1	2.8
1972	0.59	1.3	12.9	20.9	0.16	0.13	3.4	2.0
1977	2.6	3.1	21.5	23.8	0.90	0.58	7.5	4.4
1978	2.9	3.8	20.7	26.5	0.95	0.61	6.8	4.3
1979	3.7	5.1	22.3	27.7	1.2	0.85	7.3	4.6

Table II.1 (continued)

United Kingdom	1967	4.4	3.2	24.8	22.6	1.0	0.58	5.6	4.1
	1972	5.6	5.0	20.0	20.5	1.6	1.1	6.0	4.4
	1977	13.4	14.5	24.8	22.6	5.7	5.2	9.0	9.1
	1978	14.5	18.4	18.5	25.7	5.8	6.4	7.5	8.9
	1979	17.7	19.2	17.3	21.2	6.4	6.2	6.2	6.9
France[4]	1967	3.2	2.6	26.0	22.7	0.71	0.22	5.7	1.9
	1972	5.4	4.5	20.0	17.6	1.8	9.5	6.8	4.8
	1977	18.7	15.5	26.6	24.4	9.5	3.0	13.5	5.0
	1978	19.2	17.6	23.4	23.0	9.6	3.8	11.8	4.7
	1979	26.0	22.0	24.4	22.5	13.0	4.6	12.2	4.7
Germany[4]	1967	3.5	3.0	19.9	13.7	0.70	0.65	4.1	3.0
	1972	6.1	5.3	15.5	11.4	1.3	1.1	3.3	2.5
	1977	20.7	20.7	20.6	17.6	5.7	7.8	5.6	6.7
	1978	21.7	23.9	18.0	16.8	5.5	8.8	4.6	6.2
	1979	29.6	24.5	18.8	14.3	7.5	7.6	4.8	4.4
Netherlands[4]	1967	1.4	0.78	16.2	10.6	0.42	0.13	5.1	1.8
	1972	3.2	1.6	18.5	9.2	1.6	0.29	9.1	1.7
	1977	10.7	4.7	23.5	10.8	5.3	1.4	11.7	3.1
	1978	10.7	5.5	20.2	10.9	4.7	1.8	8.9	3.6
	1979	14.3	6.5	21.2	10.2	6.1	2.0	9.1	3.1
Greece[4]	1967	0.14	0.04	12.2	8.1	0.05	0.02	4.3	3.1
	1972	0.26	0.09	11.2	10.6	0.14	0.04	5.8	5.2
	1977	1.2	0.71	17.1	25.6	0.65	0.38	9.4	13.8
	1978	1.4	0.83	18.2	24.6	0.77	0.46	10.1	13.7
	1979	2.3	1.0	24.0	26.8	1.1	0.59	11.9	15.3
Denmark	1967	0.35	0.22	11.1	8.8	0.11	0.05	3.6	1.9
	1972	0.52	0.40	10.3	9.4	0.22	0.07	4.3	1.7
	1977	1.6	1.3	11.8	13.2	0.47	0.35	3.6	3.5
	1978	1.4	1.4	9.5	12.0	0.37	0.44	2.5	3.7
	1979	1.9	1.6	10.6	11.1	0.51	0.50	2.8	3.5

Table II.1: (Continued)

		DEVELOPING COUNTRIES[1]				MIDDLE EAST[2]			
		Imports from cif	Exports to fob	% total imports	% total exports	Imports from cif	Exports to fob	% total imports	% total exports
Norway	1967	0.22	0.20	8.0	11.2	0.03	0.02	1.0	1.2
	1972	0.38	0.33	8.6	10.1	0.11	0.04	2.6	1.3
	1977	1.3	1.2	10.3	13.8	0.47	0.11	3.7	1.2
	1978	1.2	1.2	10.6	11.5	0.42	0.13	3.7	1.3
	1979	1.3	1.4	9.2	10.5	0.33	0.15	2.4	1.1
Sweden	1967	0.52	0.41	11.1	9.0	0.11	0.06	2.4	1.3
	1972	0.78	0.83	9.7	9.5	0.15	0.12	1.8	1.4
	1977	2.7	2.5	13.4	13.2	0.98	0.79	4.9	4.2
	1978	2.6	3.1	12.7	14.0	1.1	0.87	5.1	4.0
	1979	3.8	3.6	13.1	12.9	1.2	1.2	4.3	4.3
USSR[3]	1967	1.1	1.4	13.0	14.6	0.08	0.16	1.0	1.6
	1972	1.8	2.1	11.6	13.7	0.36	0.49	2.2	3.2
	1977	6.5	5.6	15.8	12.3	1.1	1.4	2.6	3.0
	1978	7.3	7.1	14.5	13.5	1.2	2.2	2.3	4.1
	1979	na	na	na	na	na	na	na	na
Eastern Europe[3,5]	1967	0.68	0.76	7.1	6.3	0.09	0.18	0.94	1.5
	1972	1.1	1.3	5.0	6.0	0.16	0.37	0.74	1.7
	1977	2.5	3.0	6.5	8.5	0.44	1.1	1.1	3.2
	1978	2.7	3.5	6.0	8.8	0.69	1.4	1.5	3.4
	1979	na	na	na	na	na	na	na	na
Saudi Arabia[4]	1967	0.15	0.32	30.5	19.1	0.06	0.13	12.6	7.5
	1972	0.36	1.2	31.9	21.1	0.24	0.30	21.0	5.3
	1977	3.3	10.4	23.1	23.9	2.0	1.6	14.2	3.6
	1978	2.8	9.1	13.7	22.3	0.80	1.4	3.9	3.5
	1979	na	na	na	na	na	na	na	na

Kuwait[4]	1967	0.09	0.03	15.5	73.4	0.05	0.03	8.8	62.1
	1972	0.18	0.69	22.8	22.5	0.07	0.10	8.3	3.2
	1977	1.0	3.5	20.9	36.2	0.15	0.89	3.0	9.1
	1978	0.88	3.6	19.1	34.5	0.22	0.87	4.7	8.3
	1979	na	na	na	na	na	na	na	na
OECD[6],[B]	1967	32.8	29.6	22.2	20.9	6.6	3.4	4.5	2.4
	1972	59.6	53.8	20.0	18.5	14.9	7.4	5.0	2.6
	1977	224.0	174.6	29.2	24.4	119.9	65.9	15.6	9.2
	1978	242.9	215.9	27.1	25.2	120.2	77.0	13.4	9.0
	1979	324.8	247.8	28.2	23.6	166.4	76.0	14.5	7.2
EEC[B]	1977	88.6	75.2	23.0	19.8	48.4	33.8	12.5	8.9
	1978	94.8	93.9	20.6	20.4	48.3	39.3	10.5	8.6
	1979	125.6	106.4	21.0	18.5	65.6	38.5	10.9	6.7

Notes: 1. Refers to 'Developing Market Economies' as laid down in the UN, *Standard Country Code* (Statistical Papers Series M, no. 49, Annex II). Does not include Yugoslavia.
2. UN *Standard Country Code*, as above.
3. Imports fob.
4. Special System of Trade.
5. Czechoslovakia, Bulgaria, Hungary, Poland. GDR is included in the data for 1967 and 1972 only.
6. OECD 'Developing Countries' includes Yugoslavia.
na not available.

Sources: A: UN, *Yearbook of International Trade Statistics* 1970/1, 1976, 1977, 1979.
B: OECD, *Trade by Commodities*, Series B, 1969, 1972, 1977, 1979.

Table II.2: Exports of Major Weapons to the Third World, by Supplier, 1962-1980[1] (in $ million at constant 1975 prices)

	1962	1967	1972	1977	1978	1979	1980
USA[2]	368	481	1,166	4,826	5,244	2,063	3,013
USSR[2]	1,029	1,545	1,225	2,156	3,682	3,678	3,006
United Kingdom	124	203	369	536	488	413	311
France[2]	121	68	351	1,282	1,236	1,000	1,235
Germany	2	4	37	60	87	286	210
Netherlands	3	–	27	72	64	167	162
Canada[2]	3	11	39	29	117	28	–
Eastern Europe	17	13	14	18	23	62	50
Sweden	*	–	5	5	5	51	79
Japan[2]	24	30	–	–	14	21	–
Other industrial Western Countries	3	79	65	515	669	490	489
Others	10	32	176	200	536	434	390
Total A[3]: Eastern Europe and USSR	1,046	1,558	1,239	2,174	3,705	3,740	3,056
Total B[3]: Countries named except Eastern Europe and USSR	645	797	1,994	6,810	7,255	4,029	5,010
Total C[3]: A + B + Other Industrial Western Countries + Others	1,703	2,465	3,473	9,699	12,165	8,693	8,945

Notes:
1. Countries are listed in order of average values 1970-8.
   'Major weapons' covers aircraft, missiles, ships and armoured vehicles. Values include licences sold to the Third World for production of major weapons.
2. Includes sales to Vietnam.
3. Items may not total, due to rounding.
   -- Nil.
   * <0.5 million dollars.
   Refer to source for 'Third World' coverage.
Sources: Stockholm International Peace Research Institute (SIPRI), *Yearbook*, 1978, 1981.

Table II.3: Net Flow of Private Capital to Developing Countries and Multilateral Agencies, 1962-1979 ($ million)

	1962	as % of GNP	1967	as % of GNP	1972	as % of GNP	1977	as % of GNP	1978	as % of GNP	1979	as % of GNP
USA	819	0.14	2,090	0.26	4,029	0.35	6,999	0.37	9,218	0.43	13,037	0.55
Canada	55	0.14	59	0.10	409	0.39	1,060	0.54	773	0.38	1,205	0.54
Japan	118	0.20	214	0.18	1,258	0.43	2,488	0.36	6,336	0.65	4,708	0.47
Australia	–	–	26	0.10	146	0.33	200	0.21	78	0.07	231	0.19
United Kingdom	323	0.41	326	0.29	861	0.57	5,830	2.38	8,376	2.69	9,018	2.28
France	418	0.56	499	0.43	736	0.38	2,787	0.73	4,761	1.00	5,077	0.89
Germany	143	0.16	599	0.48	757	0.29	4,307	0.84	4,992	0.78	3,827	0.50
Netherlands	49	0.37	115	0.49	338	0.74	1,172	1.11	1,599	1.23	543	0.36
Denmark	7	0.10	– 3.2	–0.03	22	0.10	101	0.23	206	0.40	167	0.28
Norway	*	*	15	0.17	– 9.1	–0.06	249	0.70	276	0.70	313	0.69
Sweden	19	0.12	61	0.25	74	0.18	774	0.99	535	0.61	323	0.32

Notes: * incomplete.
Private capital flows here include:
  (i) direct investment;
  (ii) bilateral and multilateral portfolio investment;
  (iii) private export credits;
    and for 1972 data onwards
  (iv) grants by private voluntary agencies.
GNP is at market prices.
For further definitions and breakdowns refer to sources cited.
Sources: OECD, *Development Co-operation Review*, 1973, 1978, 1980.

Table II.4: Net Flow of Official Development Assistance to Developing Countries and Multilateral Agencies, 1962-1979 ($ million)

	1962	as % of GNP	1967	as % of GNP	1972	as % of GNP	1977	as % of GNP	1978	as % of GNP	1979	as % of GNP
USA	3,182	0.56	3,472	0.43	3,349	0.29	4,682	0.25	5,664	0.27	4,684	0.20
Canada	35	0.09	198	0.32	492	0.47	991	0.50	1,060	0.52	1,026	0.46
Japan	85	0.14	379	0.31	611	0.21	1,424	0.21	2,215	0.23	2,637	0.26
Australia	74	0.43	157	0.60	272	0.61	400	0.42	588	0.55	620	0.52
United Kingdom	421	0.52	485	0.44	609	0.40	1,103	0.45	1,460	0.47	2,067	0.52
France	945	1.27	826	0.71	1,321	0.67	2,267	0.60	2,705	0.57	3,370	0.59
Germany	405	0.45	509	0.41	808	0.31	1,717	0.33	2,347	0.37	3,350	0.44
Netherlands	65	0.49	114	0.49	307	0.67	908	0.86	1,073	0.82	1,404	0.93
Denmark	8	0.10	26	0.21	96	0.45	258	0.60	388	0.75	448	0.75
Norway	7	0.14	15	0.17	63	0.41	295	0.83	355	0.90	429	0.93
Sweden	19	0.12	60	0.25	198	0.48	779	0.99	783	0.90	956	0.94

Note: GNP is at market prices.
Sources: OECD, *Development Co-operation Review*, 1973, 1978, 1980.

Table II.5: Loans and Grants by Multilateral Agencies: Gross Disbursements, 1962-1979 ($ million)

			Loans			
	1962	1967	1972	1977	1978	1979p
IBRD	409	561	1,192	2,540	2,976	3,893
IDA	25	368	299	1,158	1,038	1,303
IFC	18	26	70	174	169	244
IDB	37	183	456	944	993	1,074
African Dev. Bank	–	– 38	12	73	93	165
Asian Dev. Bank	–	–30	57	364	461	485
Caribbean Dev. Bank	–	–	–	23	20	32
African Dev. Fund	–	–	–	26	44	na[2]
EEC/EDF	–	1	10	na	na	na
EEC/EIB	–	39	(32)	152	190	616
IMF Trust Fund	–	–	–	175	878	680[1]
BADEA	–	–	–	8	55	na
AFESD	–	–	–	86	220	na
Is.DB	–	–	–	15	117	na
GODE	–	–	–	950	645	na
OAPEC, SPACC	–	–	–	–	–	na
SAAFA	–	–	–	13	–	na
OSF	–	–	–	162	83	na
Other OPEC	–	–	–	(250)	(335)	na
Total Loans	489	1,178	2,128	7,113	8,317	(9,128)
Middle East Loans	–	–	–	1,484	1,455	271[1]
			Grants			
EEC/EDF	54	104	222	473[3]	729[3]	848
UN	182	270	602	1,404	1,711	(2,000)
IDB	–	–	–	–	14	–
Other	–	–	–	21	6	(22)
Total Grants	236	374	824	1,898	2,460	(2,870)
Total Loans and Grants	725	1,552	2,952	9,011	10,777	(11,998)

Notes: 1. Net figure.
      2. Included with African Development Bank.
      3. Including STABEX.

Abbreviations:
BADEA	–	Arab Bank for Economic Development in Africa
AFESD	–	Arab Fund for Economic and Social Development
Is.DB	–	Islamic Development Bank
GODE	–	Gulf Organisation for Development in Egypt
OAPEC	–	Special Account of the Arab OPEC Countries
SAAFA	–	Special Arab Aid Fund for Africa
OSF	–	OPEC Special Fund
p	–	preliminary
( )	–	Secretariat estimate in whole or in part
–	–	nil or negligible
na	–	not available

Sources: OECD, *Development Assistance Review*, 1968.
        OECD, *Development Co-operation Review*, 1974, 1978, 1979, 1980.

Table II.6: Total Debt and Total Annual Debt Service of Developing Countries by Source of Lending, 1962-1980 ($ billion)

Source of Lending	1962 A	1962 B	1967 A	1967 B	1972 A	1972 B	1977 A	1977 B	1978 A	1978 B	1979[p] A	1979[p] B	1980[e] A	1980[e] B
1. DAC countries and capital markets	18.6	2.7	38.6	5.3	77.1	11.6	202.4	35.5	261.4	49.9	298.6	62.7	342.0	76.1
ODA	7.0	0.5	15.9	1.0	26.0	1.6	41.4	2.0	49.0	2.3	49.5	2.4	52.0	2.6
Total export credits	8.1	1.8	15.7	3.0	29.0	6.4	65.8	16.8	84.7	21.0	100.5	26.6	120.0	32.0
Capital markets[1]	3.5	0.4	7.0	1.3	22.1	3.6	95.2	16.7	127.7	26.6	148.6	33.7	170.0	41.5
2. International organizations	3.3	0.3	5.8	0.6	12.0	1.1	33.5	2.6	40.2	3.2	48.0	3.8	56.0	4.5
3. Centrally planned economies	2.0	0.1	3.7	0.3	7.3	0.6	12.5	1.2	13.6	1.4	16.0	1.8	18.2	2.3
4. OPEC countries	–	–	–	–	0.6	–	10.8	0.7	13.2	0.9	15.3	1.6	18.5	2.2
5. Other LDCs	0.1	–	0.3	–	1.2	0.2	3.3	0.5	4.1	0.7	5.1	1.0	6.3	1.3
6. Unspecified and adjustments	–	–	–	–	–	–	2.4	0.7	4.1	0.8	5.0	1.1	5.0	1.5
Total	24.0	3.1	48.4	6.2	98.2	13.5	264.9	41.2	336.6	56.9	388.0	72.0	446.0	87.9
% increase over previous year	15	7	15	13	13	24	22	27	27	38	15	27	15	22

Notes: 1. Bank loans (other than export credits) including loans through offshore centres; bonds; and other private lending.
p – preliminary.
e – estimate.

Source: A (Total debt disbursed); B (Total annual debt service): OECD, *Development Co-operation Review*, 1977, 1980.

Table II.7: Total Debt (Disbursed) by Group of Developing Countries, 1967-1980 (US$ billion)

	1967		1972		1977		1978		1979[p]		1980[e]	
	Debt	As % of total	Debt	As % of total	Debt	As % of total	Debt	As % of total	Debt	As % of total	Debt	As % of total
Non-oil LDCs	41	86	82	84	218	82	272	81	314	81	360	81
OPEC countries	7	14	16	16	47	18	65	19	74	19	86	19
Total LDCs	48	100	98	100	265	100	337	100	388	100	446	100

Source: OECD, *Development Co-operation Review*, 1977-1980.

Table II.8 Total Annual Debt Service Expressed as Per Cent of Exports (US$ billion)

GROUP	1967		1972		1977		1978		1979[p]		1980[e]	
	Debt service	% of exports	Debt service	% of exports	Debt service	% of exports	Debt service	% of exports	Debt service	% of exports	Debt service	% of exports
Non-oil LDCs	5.8	21.4	11.1	23.7	31.4	23.0	43.9	28.1	55.0	28.6	65.9	na
OPEC countries	0.4	3.2	2.4	8.9	9.8	6.5	13.0	8.9	17.0	8.2	22.0	na
Total LDCs	6.2	15.6	13.5	18.2	41.2	14.3	56.9	18.9	72.0	18.0	87.9	na

Notes: p – preliminary.
      e – estimates.
      na – not available.

Sources: OECD *Development Co-operation Review*, 1977, 1980;
        United Nations, *Yearbook of International Trade Statistics*, 1976, 1979 (Special Table A).

Table II.9: Direct Investment Flows from DAC Countries[1] to Developing Countries[2] 1965-1979 (US$ million)

	Annual Average		1975	1976	1977	1978	1979
	1965-1967	1970-1972					
USA	1,147	1,770	7,241	3,119	4,866	5,619	7,986
United Kingdom	204	322	797	986	1,223	1,173	1,506
Germany FR	147	426	816	765	846	1,025	818
Japan	80	229	223	1,084	724	1,318	691
France	339	212	274	246	265	413	681
Italy	59	206	150	213	162	71	455
Switzerland	46	65	208	226	211	174	416
Belgium	47	44	69	236	70	138	254
Canada	34	105	300	430	390	452	175
Netherlands	90	212	229	245	486	444	167
Sweden	27	40	82	125	126	115	127
Australia	23	85	48	75	84	68	113
Other countries[3]	4	30	58	108	46	143	102
Total	2,245	3,745	10,495	7,858	9,499	11,153	13,491

Notes: 1. Countries listed in descending order of % share in total flows, 1979.
2. Includes flows to Cyprus, Gibraltar, Greece, Malta, Portugal, Spain, Turkey, Yugoslavia.
3. Austria, Denmark, Norway, and New Zealand, Finland after 1972.

Sources: UN, *Transnational Corporations in World Development*, 1978.
OECD, *Development Co-operation*, 1980.

NOTES ON CONTRIBUTORS

Albert Bressand is at the Institut Français des Relations Internationales.

Vince Cable is a Senior Research Officer at the Overseas Development Institute, London.

Robert Cassen is Professorial Fellow in Economics at the Institute of Development Studies, Brighton, Sussex.

Ronald Dore is at the Technical Change Centre, London.

Jacob Everts has worked for the United Nations and the Joint Ministerial Committee of the World Bank and the Fund ('Development Committee') and has been a consultant for UNCTAD and other development agencies. He now lives in Wassenaar, the Netherlands.

Just Faaland is Director of the Christian Michelsen Institute, Bergen, Norway.

Stuart Harris is Professor of Resource Economics and Head of Resources Programme at the Centre for Resource and Environmental Studies, Australian National University, Canberra.

Elizabeth Housden is an Economic Assistant with the Agricultural Engineers Association, London.

Richard Jolly is Deputy-Executive Director of Unicef in New York.

John Mathieson is Senior Fellow at the Overseas Development Council, Washington, DC.

Manfred Nitsch is Professor of the Political Economy of Latin America at the Institute of Latin American Studies, Free University of Berlin.

Ole David Koht Norbye is a Research Fellow at the Christian Michelsen Institute, Bergen, Norway.

John Sewell is President of the Overseas Development Council, Washington, DC, and directs its research programme.

Dudley Seers is a Professorial Fellow at the Institute of Development Studies, Brighton, Sussex.

Bernard Wood is the founding Director of the North-South Institute, an Independent non-profit-making and non-partisan institute for research and information on international development. He also serves in a senior consultative capacity in Canada and internationally.

Robert Wood is former Director of the Overseas Development Institute, London.

INDEX